2275C: Maintaining a Microsoft® Windows Server™ 2003 Environment

Information in this document, including URL and other Internet Web site references, is subject to change without notice. Unless otherwise noted, the example companies, organizations, products, domain names, e-mail addresses, logos, people, places, and events depicted herein are fictitious, and no association with any real company, organization, product, domain name, e-mail address, logo, person, place or event is intended or should be inferred. Complying with all applicable copyright laws is the responsibility of the user. Without limiting the rights under copyright, no part of this document may be reproduced, stored in or introduced into a retrieval system, or transmitted in any form or by any means (electronic, mechanical, photocopying, recording, or otherwise), or for any purpose, without the express written permission of Microsoft Corporation.

The names of manufacturers, products, or URLs are provided for informational purposes only and Microsoft makes no representations and warranties, either expressed, implied, or statutory, regarding these manufacturers or the use of the products with any Microsoft technologies. The inclusion of a manufacturer or product does not imply endorsement of Microsoft of the manufacturer or product. Links are provided to third party sites. Such sites are not under the control of Microsoft and Microsoft is not responsible for the contents of any linked site or any link contained in a linked site, or any changes or updates to such sites. Microsoft is not responsible for webcasting or any other form of transmission received from any linked site. Microsoft is providing these links to you only as a convenience, and the inclusion of any link does not imply endorsement of Microsoft of the site or the products contained therein.

Microsoft may have patents, patent applications, trademarks, copyrights, or other intellectual property rights covering subject matter in this document. Except as expressly provided in any written license agreement from Microsoft, the furnishing of this document does not give you any license to these patents, trademarks, copyrights, or other intellectual property.

© 2005 Microsoft Corporation. All rights reserved.

Microsoft, Active Directory, ActiveX, Authenticode, BizTalk, IntelliMirror, MSDN, PowerPoint, Windows, Windows Media, Windows NT, and Windows Server are either registered trademarks or trademarks of Microsoft Corporation in the United States and/or other countries.

All other trademarks are property of their respective owners.

1 2 3 4 5 6 7 8 9   QWE   9 8 7 6 5

Course Number: 2275C
Part Number: 46512
Released: 08/2005

END-USER LICENSE AGREEMENT FOR OFFICIAL MICROSOFT LEARNING PRODUCTS - STUDENT EDITION

PLEASE READ THIS END-USER LICENSE AGREEMENT ("EULA") CAREFULLY. BY USING THE MATERIALS AND/OR USING OR INSTALLING THE SOFTWARE THAT ACCOMPANIES THIS EULA (COLLECTIVELY, THE "LICENSED CONTENT"), YOU AGREE TO THE TERMS OF THIS EULA. IF YOU DO NOT AGREE, DO NOT USE THE LICENSED CONTENT.

1. **GENERAL.** This EULA is a legal agreement between you (either an individual or a single entity) and Microsoft Corporation ("Microsoft"). This EULA governs the Licensed Content, which includes computer software (including online and electronic documentation), training materials, and any other associated media and printed materials. This EULA applies to updates, supplements, add-on components, and Internet-based services components of the Licensed Content that Microsoft may provide or make available to you unless Microsoft provides other terms with the update, supplement, add-on component, or Internet-based services component. Microsoft reserves the right to discontinue any Internet-based services provided to you or made available to you through the use of the Licensed Content. This EULA also governs any product support services relating to the Licensed Content except as may be included in another agreement between you and Microsoft. An amendment or addendum to this EULA may accompany the Licensed Content.

2. **GENERAL GRANT OF LICENSE.** Microsoft grants you the following rights, conditioned on your compliance with all the terms and conditions of this EULA. Microsoft grants you a limited, non-exclusive, royalty-free license to install and use the Licensed Content solely in conjunction with your participation as a student in an Authorized Training Session (as defined below). You may install and use one copy of the software on a single computer, device, workstation, terminal, or other digital electronic or analog device ("Device"). You may make a second copy of the software and install it on a portable Device for the exclusive use of the person who is the primary user of the first copy of the software. A license for the software may not be shared for use by multiple end users. An "Authorized Training Session" means a training session conducted at a Microsoft Certified Technical Education Center, an IT Academy, via a Microsoft Certified Partner, or such other entity as Microsoft may designate from time to time in writing, by a Microsoft Certified Trainer (for more information on these entities, please visit www.microsoft.com). WITHOUT LIMITING THE FOREGOING, COPYING OR REPRODUCTION OF THE LICENSED CONTENT TO ANY SERVER OR LOCATION FOR FURTHER REPRODUCTION OR REDISTRIBUTION IS EXPRESSLY PROHIBITED.

3. **DESCRIPTION OF OTHER RIGHTS AND LICENSE LIMITATIONS**

    3.1 *Use of Documentation and Printed Training Materials.*

    3.1.1 The documents and related graphics included in the Licensed Content may include technical inaccuracies or typographical errors. Changes are periodically made to the content. Microsoft may make improvements and/or changes in any of the components of the Licensed Content at any time without notice. The names of companies, products, people, characters and/or data mentioned in the Licensed Content may be fictitious and are in no way intended to represent any real individual, company, product or event, unless otherwise noted.

    3.1.2 Microsoft grants you the right to reproduce portions of documents (such as student workbooks, white papers, press releases, datasheets and FAQs) (the "Documents") provided with the Licensed Content. You may not print any book (either electronic or print version) in its entirety. If you choose to reproduce Documents, you agree that: (a) use of such printed Documents will be solely in conjunction with your personal training use; (b) the Documents will not republished or posted on any network computer or broadcast in any media; (c) any reproduction will include either the Document's original copyright notice or a copyright notice to Microsoft's benefit substantially in the format provided below; and (d) to comply with all terms and conditions of this EULA. In addition, no modifications may made to any Document.

    Form of Notice:

    Copyright undefined.

    © 2005. Reprinted with permission by Microsoft Corporation. All rights reserved.

    Microsoft and Windows are either registered trademarks or trademarks of Microsoft Corporation in the US and/or other countries. Other product and company names mentioned herein may be the trademarks of their respective owners.

    3.2 *Use of Media Elements.* The Licensed Content may include certain photographs, clip art, animations, sounds, music, and video clips (together "Media Elements"). You may not modify these Media Elements.

    3.3 *Use of Sample Code.* In the event that the Licensed Content include sample source code ("Sample Code"), Microsoft grants you a limited, non-exclusive, royalty-free license to use, copy and modify the Sample Code; if you elect to exercise the foregoing rights, you agree to comply with all other terms and conditions of this EULA, including without limitation Sections 3.4, 3.5, and 6.

    3.4 *Permitted Modifications.* In the event that you exercise any rights provided under this EULA to create modifications of the Licensed Content, you agree that any such modifications: (a) will not be used for providing training where a fee is charged in public or private classes; (b) indemnify, hold harmless, and defend Microsoft from and against any claims or lawsuits, including attorneys' fees, which arise from or result from your use of any modified version of the Licensed Content; and (c) not to transfer or assign any rights to any modified version of the Licensed Content to any third party without the express written permission of Microsoft.

3.5   *Reproduction/Redistribution Licensed Content.* Except as expressly provided in this EULA, you may not reproduce or distribute the Licensed Content or any portion thereof (including any permitted modifications) to any third parties without the express written permission of Microsoft.

4.   **RESERVATION OF RIGHTS AND OWNERSHIP.** Microsoft reserves all rights not expressly granted to you in this EULA. The Licensed Content is protected by copyright and other intellectual property laws and treaties. Microsoft or its suppliers own the title, copyright, and other intellectual property rights in the Licensed Content. You may not remove or obscure any copyright, trademark or patent notices that appear on the Licensed Content, or any components thereof, as delivered to you. **The Licensed Content is licensed, not sold.**

5.   **LIMITATIONS ON REVERSE ENGINEERING, DECOMPILATION, AND DISASSEMBLY.** You may not reverse engineer, decompile, or disassemble the Software or Media Elements, except and only to the extent that such activity is expressly permitted by applicable law notwithstanding this limitation.

6.   **LIMITATIONS ON SALE, RENTAL, ETC. AND CERTAIN ASSIGNMENTS.** You may not provide commercial hosting services with, sell, rent, lease, lend, sublicense, or assign copies of the Licensed Content, or any portion thereof (including any permitted modifications thereof) on a stand-alone basis or as part of any collection, product or service.

7.   **CONSENT TO USE OF DATA.** You agree that Microsoft and its affiliates may collect and use technical information gathered as part of the product support services provided to you, if any, related to the Licensed Content. Microsoft may use this information solely to improve our products or to provide customized services or technologies to you and will not disclose this information in a form that personally identifies you.

8.   **LINKS TO THIRD PARTY SITES.** You may link to third party sites through the use of the Licensed Content. The third party sites are not under the control of Microsoft, and Microsoft is not responsible for the contents of any third party sites, any links contained in third party sites, or any changes or updates to third party sites. Microsoft is not responsible for webcasting or any other form of transmission received from any third party sites. Microsoft is providing these links to third party sites to you only as a convenience, and the inclusion of any link does not imply an endorsement by Microsoft of the third party site.

9.   **ADDITIONAL LICENSED CONTENT/SERVICES.** This EULA applies to updates, supplements, add-on components, or Internet-based services components, of the Licensed Content that Microsoft may provide to you or make available to you after the date you obtain your initial copy of the Licensed Content, unless we provide other terms along with the update, supplement, add-on component, or Internet-based services component. Microsoft reserves the right to discontinue any Internet-based services provided to you or made available to you through the use of the Licensed Content.

10.   **U.S. GOVERNMENT LICENSE RIGHTS.** All software provided to the U.S. Government pursuant to solicitations issued on or after December 1, 1995 is provided with the commercial license rights and restrictions described elsewhere herein. All software provided to the U.S. Government pursuant to solicitations issued prior to December 1, 1995 is provided with "Restricted Rights" as provided for in FAR, 48 CFR 52.227-14 (JUNE 1987) or DFAR, 48 CFR 252.227-7013 (OCT 1988), as applicable.

11.   **EXPORT RESTRICTIONS.** You acknowledge that the Licensed Content is subject to U.S. export jurisdiction. You agree to comply with all applicable international and national laws that apply to the Licensed Content, including the U.S. Export Administration Regulations, as well as end-user, end-use, and destination restrictions issued by U.S. and other governments. For additional information see <http://www.microsoft.com/exporting/>.

12.   **TRANSFER.** The initial user of the Licensed Content may make a one-time permanent transfer of this EULA and Licensed Content to another end user, provided the initial user retains no copies of the Licensed Content. The transfer may not be an indirect transfer, such as a consignment. Prior to the transfer, the end user receiving the Licensed Content must agree to all the EULA terms.

13.   **"NOT FOR RESALE" LICENSED CONTENT.** Licensed Content identified as "Not For Resale" or "NFR," may not be sold or otherwise transferred for value, or used for any purpose other than demonstration, test or evaluation.

14.   **TERMINATION.** Without prejudice to any other rights, Microsoft may terminate this EULA if you fail to comply with the terms and conditions of this EULA. In such event, you must destroy all copies of the Licensed Content and all of its component parts.

15.   <u>**DISCLAIMER OF WARRANTIES.**</u> TO THE MAXIMUM EXTENT PERMITTED BY APPLICABLE LAW, MICROSOFT AND ITS SUPPLIERS PROVIDE THE LICENSED CONTENT AND SUPPORT SERVICES (IF ANY) *AS IS AND WITH ALL FAULTS,* AND MICROSOFT AND ITS SUPPLIERS HEREBY DISCLAIM ALL OTHER WARRANTIES AND CONDITIONS, WHETHER EXPRESS, IMPLIED OR STATUTORY, INCLUDING, BUT NOT LIMITED TO, ANY (IF ANY) IMPLIED WARRANTIES, DUTIES OR CONDITIONS OF MERCHANTABILITY, OF FITNESS FOR A PARTICULAR PURPOSE, OF RELIABILITY OR AVAILABILITY, OF ACCURACY OR COMPLETENESS OF RESPONSES, OF RESULTS, OF WORKMANLIKE EFFORT, OF LACK OF VIRUSES, AND OF LACK OF NEGLIGENCE, ALL WITH REGARD TO THE LICENSED CONTENT, AND THE PROVISION OF OR FAILURE TO PROVIDE SUPPORT OR OTHER SERVICES, INFORMATION, SOFTWARE, AND RELATED CONTENT THROUGH THE LICENSED CONTENT, OR OTHERWISE ARISING OUT OF THE USE OF THE LICENSED CONTENT. ALSO, THERE IS NO WARRANTY OR CONDITION OF TITLE, QUIET ENJOYMENT, QUIET POSSESSION, CORRESPONDENCE TO DESCRIPTION OR NON-INFRINGEMENT WITH REGARD TO THE LICENSED CONTENT. THE ENTIRE RISK AS TO THE QUALITY, OR ARISING OUT OF THE USE OR PERFORMANCE OF THE LICENSED CONTENT, AND ANY SUPPORT SERVICES, REMAINS WITH YOU.

16.   <u>**EXCLUSION OF INCIDENTAL, CONSEQUENTIAL AND CERTAIN OTHER DAMAGES.**</u> TO THE MAXIMUM EXTENT PERMITTED BY APPLICABLE LAW, IN NO EVENT SHALL MICROSOFT OR ITS SUPPLIERS BE LIABLE FOR ANY SPECIAL, INCIDENTAL, PUNITIVE, INDIRECT, OR CONSEQUENTIAL DAMAGES WHATSOEVER (INCLUDING, BUT NOT

LIMITED TO, DAMAGES FOR LOSS OF PROFITS OR CONFIDENTIAL OR OTHER INFORMATION, FOR BUSINESS INTERRUPTION, FOR PERSONAL INJURY, FOR LOSS OF PRIVACY, FOR FAILURE TO MEET ANY DUTY INCLUDING OF GOOD FAITH OR OF REASONABLE CARE, FOR NEGLIGENCE, AND FOR ANY OTHER PECUNIARY OR OTHER LOSS WHATSOEVER) ARISING OUT OF OR IN ANY WAY RELATED TO THE USE OF OR INABILITY TO USE THE LICENSED CONTENT, THE PROVISION OF OR FAILURE TO PROVIDE SUPPORT OR OTHER SERVICES, INFORMATION, SOFTWARE, AND RELATED CONTENT THROUGH THE LICENSED CONTENT, OR OTHERWISE ARISING OUT OF THE USE OF THE LICENSED CONTENT, OR OTHERWISE UNDER OR IN CONNECTION WITH ANY PROVISION OF THIS EULA, EVEN IN THE EVENT OF THE FAULT, TORT (INCLUDING NEGLIGENCE), MISREPRESENTATION, STRICT LIABILITY, BREACH OF CONTRACT OR BREACH OF WARRANTY OF MICROSOFT OR ANY SUPPLIER, AND EVEN IF MICROSOFT OR ANY SUPPLIER HAS BEEN ADVISED OF THE POSSIBILITY OF SUCH DAMAGES. BECAUSE SOME STATES/JURISDICTIONS DO NOT ALLOW THE EXCLUSION OR LIMITATION OF LIABILITY FOR CONSEQUENTIAL OR INCIDENTAL DAMAGES, THE ABOVE LIMITATION MAY NOT APPLY TO YOU.

17. **LIMITATION OF LIABILITY AND REMEDIES.** NOTWITHSTANDING ANY DAMAGES THAT YOU MIGHT INCUR FOR ANY REASON WHATSOEVER (INCLUDING, WITHOUT LIMITATION, ALL DAMAGES REFERENCED HEREIN AND ALL DIRECT OR GENERAL DAMAGES IN CONTRACT OR ANYTHING ELSE), THE ENTIRE LIABILITY OF MICROSOFT AND ANY OF ITS SUPPLIERS UNDER ANY PROVISION OF THIS EULA AND YOUR EXCLUSIVE REMEDY HEREUNDER SHALL BE LIMITED TO THE GREATER OF THE ACTUAL DAMAGES YOU INCUR IN REASONABLE RELIANCE ON THE LICENSED CONTENT UP TO THE AMOUNT ACTUALLY PAID BY YOU FOR THE LICENSED CONTENT OR US$5.00. THE FOREGOING LIMITATIONS, EXCLUSIONS AND DISCLAIMERS SHALL APPLY TO THE MAXIMUM EXTENT PERMITTED BY APPLICABLE LAW, EVEN IF ANY REMEDY FAILS ITS ESSENTIAL PURPOSE.

18. **APPLICABLE LAW.** If you acquired this Licensed Content in the United States, this EULA is governed by the laws of the State of Washington. If you acquired this Licensed Content in Canada, unless expressly prohibited by local law, this EULA is governed by the laws in force in the Province of Ontario, Canada; and, in respect of any dispute which may arise hereunder, you consent to the jurisdiction of the federal and provincial courts sitting in Toronto, Ontario. If you acquired this Licensed Content in the European Union, Iceland, Norway, or Switzerland, then local law applies. If you acquired this Licensed Content in any other country, then local law may apply.

19. **ENTIRE AGREEMENT; SEVERABILITY.** This EULA (including any addendum or amendment to this EULA which is included with the Licensed Content) are the entire agreement between you and Microsoft relating to the Licensed Content and the support services (if any) and they supersede all prior or contemporaneous oral or written communications, proposals and representations with respect to the Licensed Content or any other subject matter covered by this EULA. To the extent the terms of any Microsoft policies or programs for support services conflict with the terms of this EULA, the terms of this EULA shall control. If any provision of this EULA is held to be void, invalid, unenforceable or illegal, the other provisions shall continue in full force and effect.

Should you have any questions concerning this EULA, or if you desire to contact Microsoft for any reason, please use the address information enclosed in this Licensed Content to contact the Microsoft subsidiary serving your country or visit Microsoft on the World Wide Web at http://www.microsoft.com.

Si vous avez acquis votre Contenu Sous Licence Microsoft au CANADA :

DÉNI DE GARANTIES. Dans la mesure maximale permise par les lois applicables, le Contenu Sous Licence et les services de soutien technique (le cas échéant) sont fournis *TELS QUELS ET AVEC TOUS LES DÉFAUTS* par Microsoft et ses fournisseurs, lesquels par les présentes dénient toutes autres garanties et conditions expresses, implicites ou en vertu de la loi, notamment, mais sans limitation, (le cas échéant) les garanties, devoirs ou conditions implicites de qualité marchande, d'adaptation à une fin usage particulière, de fiabilité ou de disponibilité, d'exactitude ou d'exhaustivité des réponses, des résultats, des efforts déployés selon les règles de l'art, d'absence de virus et d'absence de négligence, le tout à l'égard du Contenu Sous Licence et de la prestation des services de soutien technique ou de l'omission de la 'une telle prestation des services de soutien technique ou à l'égard de la fourniture ou de l'omission de la fourniture de tous autres services, renseignements, Contenus Sous Licence, et contenu qui s'y rapporte grâce au Contenu Sous Licence ou provenant autrement de l'utilisation du Contenu Sous Licence. PAR AILLEURS, IL N'Y A AUCUNE GARANTIE OU CONDITION QUANT AU TITRE DE PROPRIÉTÉ, À LA JOUISSANCE OU LA POSSESSION PAISIBLE, À LA CONCORDANCE À UNE DESCRIPTION NI QUANT À UNE ABSENCE DE CONTREFAÇON CONCERNANT LE CONTENU SOUS LICENCE.

EXCLUSION DES DOMMAGES ACCESSOIRES, INDIRECTS ET DE CERTAINS AUTRES DOMMAGES. DANS LA MESURE MAXIMALE PERMISE PAR LES LOIS APPLICABLES, EN AUCUN CAS MICROSOFT OU SES FOURNISSEURS NE SERONT RESPONSABLES DES DOMMAGES SPÉCIAUX, CONSÉCUTIFS, ACCESSOIRES OU INDIRECTS DE QUELQUE NATURE QUE CE SOIT (NOTAMMENT, LES DOMMAGES À L'ÉGARD DU MANQUE À GAGNER OU DE LA DIVULGATION DE RENSEIGNEMENTS CONFIDENTIELS OU AUTRES, DE LA PERTE D'EXPLOITATION, DE BLESSURES CORPORELLES, DE LA VIOLATION DE LA VIE PRIVÉE, DE L'OMISSION DE REMPLIR TOUT DEVOIR, Y COMPRIS D'AGIR DE BONNE FOI OU D'EXERCER UN SOIN RAISONNABLE, DE LA NÉGLIGENCE ET DE TOUTE AUTRE PERTE PÉCUNIAIRE OU AUTRE PERTE

DE QUELQUE NATURE QUE CE SOIT) SE RAPPORTANT DE QUELQUE MANIÈRE QUE CE SOIT À L'UTILISATION DU CONTENU SOUS LICENCE OU À L'INCAPACITÉ DE S'EN SERVIR, À LA PRESTATION OU À L'OMISSION DE LA 'UNE TELLE PRESTATION DE SERVICES DE SOUTIEN TECHNIQUE OU À LA FOURNITURE OU À L'OMISSION DE LA FOURNITURE DE TOUS AUTRES SERVICES, RENSEIGNEMENTS, CONTENUS SOUS LICENCE, ET CONTENU QUI S'Y RAPPORTE GRÂCE AU CONTENU SOUS LICENCE OU PROVENANT AUTREMENT DE L'UTILISATION DU CONTENU SOUS LICENCE OU AUTREMENT AUX TERMES DE TOUTE DISPOSITION DE LA U PRÉSENTE CONVENTION EULA OU RELATIVEMENT À UNE TELLE DISPOSITION, MÊME EN CAS DE FAUTE, DE DÉLIT CIVIL (Y COMPRIS LA NÉGLIGENCE), DE RESPONSABILITÉ STRICTE, DE VIOLATION DE CONTRAT OU DE VIOLATION DE GARANTIE DE MICROSOFT OU DE TOUT FOURNISSEUR ET MÊME SI MICROSOFT OU TOUT FOURNISSEUR A ÉTÉ AVISÉ DE LA POSSIBILITÉ DE TELS DOMMAGES.

LIMITATION DE RESPONSABILITÉ ET RECOURS. MALGRÉ LES DOMMAGES QUE VOUS PUISSIEZ SUBIR POUR QUELQUE MOTIF QUE CE SOIT (NOTAMMENT, MAIS SANS LIMITATION, TOUS LES DOMMAGES SUSMENTIONNÉS ET TOUS LES DOMMAGES DIRECTS OU GÉNÉRAUX OU AUTRES), LA SEULE RESPONSABILITÉ 'OBLIGATION INTÉGRALE DE MICROSOFT ET DE L'UN OU L'AUTRE DE SES FOURNISSEURS AUX TERMES DE TOUTE DISPOSITION DEU LA PRÉSENTE CONVENTION EULA ET VOTRE RECOURS EXCLUSIF À L'ÉGARD DE TOUT CE QUI PRÉCÈDE SE LIMITE AU PLUS ÉLEVÉ ENTRE LES MONTANTS SUIVANTS : LE MONTANT QUE VOUS AVEZ RÉELLEMENT PAYÉ POUR LE CONTENU SOUS LICENCE OU 5,00 $US. LES LIMITES, EXCLUSIONS ET DÉNIS QUI PRÉCÈDENT (Y COMPRIS LES CLAUSES CI-DESSUS), S'APPLIQUENT DANS LA MESURE MAXIMALE PERMISE PAR LES LOIS APPLICABLES, MÊME SI TOUT RECOURS N'ATTEINT PAS SON BUT ESSENTIEL.

À moins que cela ne soit prohibé par le droit local applicable, la présente Convention est régie par les lois de la province d'Ontario, Canada. Vous consentez Chacune des parties à la présente reconnaît irrévocablement à la compétence des tribunaux fédéraux et provinciaux siégeant à Toronto, dans de la province d'Ontario et consent à instituer tout litige qui pourrait découler de la présente auprès des tribunaux situés dans le district judiciaire de York, province d'Ontario.

Au cas où vous auriez des questions concernant cette licence ou que vous désiriez vous mettre en rapport avec Microsoft pour quelque raison que ce soit, veuillez utiliser l'information contenue dans le Contenu Sous Licence pour contacter la filiale de succursale Microsoft desservant votre pays, dont l'adresse est fournie dans ce produit, ou visitez écrivez à : Microsoft sur le World Wide Web à http://www.microsoft.com

Contents

Introduction
Course Materials 2
Prerequisites 3
Course Outline 4
Setup 7
Demonstration: Using Microsoft Virtual PC 8
Microsoft Learning 9
Microsoft Certified Professional Program 12
Multimedia: Job Roles in Today's Information Systems Environment 15
Facilities 16

Module 1: Preparing to Administer a Server
Overview 1
Lesson: Introduction to Administering a Server 2
Lesson: Configuring Remote Desktop to Administer a Server 12
Lesson: Managing Remote Desktop Connections 26
Lab: Preparing to Administer a Server 34

Module 2: Preparing to Monitor Server Performance
Overview 1
Lesson: Introduction to Monitoring Server Performance 2
Lesson: Performing Real-Time and Logged Monitoring 7
Lesson: Configuring and Managing Counter Logs 16
Lesson: Configuring Alerts 24
Lab: Preparing to Monitor Server Performance 35

Module 3: Monitoring Server Performance
Overview 1
Multimedia: The Primary Server Subsystems 2
Lesson: Monitoring Server Memory 3
Lesson: Monitoring Processor Usage 10
Lesson: Monitoring Disks 16
Lesson: Monitoring Network Usage 23
Lesson: Monitoring Best Practices 30
Lab: Monitoring Server Performance 41

Module 4: Maintaining Device Drivers
Overview 1
Lesson: Configuring Device Driver Signing Options 2
Lesson: Using Device Driver Rollback 15

Module 5: Managing Disks
Overview 1
Lesson: Preparing Disks 2
Lesson: Managing Disk Properties 13
Lesson: Managing Mounted Drives 20
Lesson: Converting Disks 24
Lesson: Creating Volumes 31
Lesson: Creating Fault-Tolerant Volumes 38
Lesson: Importing a Foreign Disk 49
Lab: Managing Disks 52

Module 6: Managing Data Storage
Overview 1
Lesson: Managing File Compression 2
Lesson: Configuring File Encryption 13
Lesson: Configuring EFS Recovery Agents 26
Lesson: Implementing Disk Quotas 32
Lab: Managing Data Storage 38

Module 7: Managing Disaster Recovery
Overview 1
Lesson: Preparing for Disaster Recovery 2
Lesson: Backing Up Data 7
Lesson: Scheduling Backup Jobs 25
Lesson: Restoring Data 32
Lesson: Configuring Shadow Copies 37
Lesson: Recovering from Server Failure 50
Lab: Managing Disaster Recovery 64
Course Evaluation 69

Module 8: Software Maintenance Using Windows Server Update Services
Overview 1
Lesson: Introduction to Windows Server Update Services 2
Lesson: Installing and Configuring Windows Server Update Services 11
Lesson: Managing Windows Server Update Services 20
Lab: Maintaining Software by Using Windows Server Update Services 33

Module 9: Securing Windows Server 2003
Overview 1
Lesson: Introduction to Securing Servers 2
Lesson: Implementing Core Server Security 10
Lesson: Hardening Servers 25
Lesson: Microsoft Baseline Security Analyzer 38
Lab: Securing Windows Server 2003 49
Course Evaluation 53

Index

About This Course

This section provides you with a brief description of the course, audience, suggested prerequisites, and course objectives.

Description

This three-day, instructor-led course provides students with the knowledge and skills that they need to effectively maintain server resources, monitor server performance, and safeguard data on a computer running one of the operating systems in the Microsoft® Windows Server™ 2003 family.

Audience

This course is intended for individuals who are employed as, or are seeking employment as, systems administrators or systems engineers.

Student prerequisites

This course requires that students have completed Course 2274: *Managing a Microsoft Windows Server 2003 Environment* or that they have equivalent knowledge and skills.

Course objectives

After completing this course, the student will be able to:

- Prepare to administer server resources.
- Configure a server to monitor system performance.
- Monitor system performance.
- Manage device drivers by configuring device driver signing and restoring a device driver.
- Manage hard disks.
- Manage data storage.
- Manage disaster recovery.
- Maintain software by using Microsoft Software Update Services.
- Maintain Windows Server 2003 security.

Student Materials Compact Disc Contents

The Student Materials compact disc contains the following files and folders:

- *Autorun.inf*. When the compact disc is inserted into the compact disc drive, this file opens StartCD.exe.
- *Default.htm*. This file opens the Student Materials Web page. It provides you with resources pertaining to this course, including additional reading, review and lab answers, lab files, multimedia presentations, and course-related Web sites.
- *Readme.txt*. This file explains how to install the software for viewing the Student Materials compact disc and its contents and how to open the Student Materials Web page.
- *StartCD.exe*. When the compact disc is inserted into the compact disc drive, or when you double-click the StartCD.exe file, this file opens the compact disc and allows you to browse the Trainer Materials DVD.
- *StartCD.ini*. This file contains instructions to launch StartCD.exe.
- *Addread*. This folder contains additional reading pertaining to this course.
- *Appendix*. This folder contains appendix files for this course.
- *Flash*. This folder contains the installer for the Macromedia Flash browser plug-in.
- *Fonts*. This folder contains fonts that might be required to view the Microsoft Office Word documents that are included with this course.
- *Media*. This folder contains files that are used in multimedia presentations for this course.
- *Mplayer*. This folder contains the setup file to install Microsoft Windows Media® Player.
- *Webfiles*. This folder contains the files that are required to view the course Web page. To open the Web page, open Windows Explorer, and in the root directory of the compact disc, double-click **StartCD.exe**.
- *Wordview*. This folder contains the Word Viewer that is used to view any Word document (.doc) files that are included on the compact disc.

Document Conventions

The following conventions are used in course materials to distinguish elements of the text.

Convention	Use
Bold	Represents commands, command options, and syntax that must be typed exactly as shown. It also indicates commands on menus and buttons, dialog box titles and options, and icon and menu names.
Italic	In syntax statements or descriptive text, indicates argument names or placeholders for variable information. Italic is also used for introducing new terms, for book titles, and for emphasis in the text.
Title Capitals	Indicate domain names, user names, computer names, directory names, and folder and file names, except when specifically referring to case-sensitive names. Unless otherwise indicated, you can use lowercase letters when you type a directory name or file name in a dialog box or at a command prompt.
ALL CAPITALS	Indicate the names of keys, key sequences, and key combinations—for example, ALT+SPACEBAR.
`monospace`	Represents code samples or examples of screen text.
[ ]	In syntax statements, enclose optional items. For example, [*filename*] in command syntax indicates that you can choose to type a file name with the command. Type only the information within the brackets, not the brackets themselves.
{ }	In syntax statements, enclose required items. Type only the information within the braces, not the braces themselves.
|	In syntax statements, separates an either/or choice.
▶	Indicates a procedure with sequential steps.
...	In syntax statements, specifies that the preceding item may be repeated.
. . .	Represents an omitted portion of a code sample.

Introduction

Contents

Introduction	1
Course Materials	2
Prerequisites	3
Course Outline	4
Setup	7
Demonstration: Using Microsoft Virtual PC	8
Microsoft Learning	9
Microsoft Certified Professional Program	12
Multimedia: Job Roles in Today's Information Systems Environment	15
Facilities	16

Information in this document, including URL and other Internet Web site references, is subject to change without notice. Unless otherwise noted, the example companies, organizations, products, domain names, e-mail addresses, logos, people, places, and events depicted herein are fictitious, and no association with any real company, organization, product, domain name, e-mail address, logo, person, place or event is Intended or should be inferred. Complying with all applicable copyright laws is the responsibility of the user. Without limiting the rights under copyright, no part of this document may be reproduced, stored in or introduced into a retrieval system, or transmitted in any form or by any means (electronic, mechanical, photocopying, recording, or otherwise), or for any purpose, without the express written permission of Microsoft Corporation.

The names of manufacturers, products, or URLs are provided for informational purposes only and Microsoft makes no representations and warranties, either expressed, implied, or statutory, regarding these manufacturers or the use of the products with any Microsoft technologies. The inclusion of a manufacturer or product does not imply endorsement of Microsoft of the manufacturer or product. Links are provided to third party sites. Such sites are not under the control of Microsoft and Microsoft is not responsible for the contents of any linked site or any link contained in a linked site, or any changes or updates to such sites. Microsoft is not responsible for webcasting or any other form of transmission received from any linked site. Microsoft is providing these links to you only as a convenience, and the inclusion of any link does not imply endorsement of Microsoft of the site or the products contained therein.

Microsoft may have patents, patent applications, trademarks, copyrights, or other intellectual property rights covering subject matter in this document. Except as expressly provided in any written license agreement from Microsoft, the furnishing of this document does not give you any license to these patents, trademarks, copyrights, or other intellectual property.

© 2005 Microsoft Corporation. All rights reserved.

Microsoft, Active Directory, ActiveX, Authenticode, BizTalk, IntelliMirror, MSDN, PowerPoint, Windows, Windows Media, Windows NT, and Windows Server are either registered trademarks or trademarks of Microsoft Corporation in the United States and/or other countries.

All other trademarks are property of their respective owners.

Introduction

- Name
- Company affiliation
- Title/function
- Job responsibility
- Systems administration experience
- Windows Server operating systems experience
- Expectations for the course

Course Materials

> - Name card
> - Student workbook
> - Student Materials compact disc
> - Course evaluation
> - Assessments

The following materials are included with your kit:

- *Name card*. Write your name on both sides of the name card.
- *Student workbook*. The student workbook contains the material covered in class, in addition to the hands-on lab exercises.
- *Student Materials compact disc*. The Student Materials compact disc contains Web page that provides you with links to resources pertaining to this course, including additional readings, review and lab answers, lab files, multimedia presentations, and course-related Web sites.

    Note To open the Web page, insert the Student Materials compact disc into the CD-ROM drive, and then in the root directory of the compact disc, double-click **StartCD.exe**.

- *Assessments*. There are assessments for each lesson, located on the Student Materials compact disc. You can use them as pre-assessments to identify areas of difficulty, or you can use them as post-assessments to validate learning.
- *Course evaluation*. Near the end of the course, you will have the opportunity to complete an online evaluation to provide feedback on the course, training facility, and instructor.

    To provide additional comments or feedback on the course, send e-mail to support@mscourseware.com. To inquire about the Microsoft Certified Professional program, send e-mail to mcphelp@microsoft.com.

Prerequisites

- Course 2274: *Managing a Microsoft Windows Server 2003 Environment* or equivalent knowledge and skills
- A+ certification or equivalent knowledge and skills
- Network+ certification or equivalent knowledge and skills

This course requires that you meet the following prerequisites:

- Course 2274: *Managing a Microsoft® Windows Server™ 2003 Environment* or equivalent skills and knowledge
- To successfully complete Course 2275, you should be able to:
  - Describe the Windows Server 2003 family and the basics of a Windows Server 2003 network environment.
  - Create and modify a user account, a computer account, a group, and an organizational unit (OU).
  - Identify the tools that are used to perform various administrative tasks.
  - Describe permissions and how they enable resource access.
  - Describe the purpose and function of Group Policy in the Windows Server 2003 environment.
  - Explain the purpose and function of auditing accounts and resources.

Course Outline

- Module 1: Preparing to Administer a Server
- Module 2: Preparing to Monitor Server Performance
- Module 3: Monitoring Server Performance
- Module 4: Maintaining Device Drivers
- Module 5: Managing Disks

Module 1, "Preparing to Administer a Server," describes the role of a systems administrator in performing server administration locally and remotely; which tools to use; and which permissions are required to administer a server. It also discusses how to administer remote connections and why that is an important aspect of system administration. This module is the foundation for the rest of the course. After completing this module, you will be able to administer a server to manage all the systems administrator tasks that are discussed in the rest of the course.

Module 2, "Preparing to Monitor Server Performance," is the first of two modules that discuss the concept of performance monitoring, performance objects, and counters, and it explains how to create a baseline to compare server performance. After completing this module, you will be able to create a performance baseline.

Module 3, "Monitoring Server Performance," discusses collecting performance data by monitoring the four primary server subsystems and their effect on server performance. It also covers how to use the Performance console and Task Manager in Windows Server 2003 to identify system bottlenecks. After completing this module, you will be able to monitor server performance.

Module 4, "Maintaining Device Drivers," provides information about device drivers and how they are used with the Windows Server 2003 operating system. This module covers in detail the configuration of device drivers and describes how to use device drivers to prevent startup and stop problems. After completing this module, you will be able to maintain device drivers.

Module 5, "Managing Disks," discusses partitions, describes how to create and use partitions, explains the differences between basic and dynamic disks, and explains how to use each disk type. This module explains how to use Disk Management and a new command line tool, DiskPart, to manage your disks. This module also covers in detail how to manage volumes. After completing this module, you will be able to manage disks.

Course Outline *(continued)*

- Module 6: Managing Data Storage
- Module 7: Managing Disaster Recovery
- Module 8: Software Maintenance Using Windows Server Update Services
- Module 9: Securing Windows Server 2003

Module 6, "Managing Data Storage," discusses file and folder compression and how to use it to manage data stored on your network storage devices. This module also covers Encrypted File System (EFS), a method that helps secure files and folders against intruders to your systems. It also describes disk quotas and explains how a systems administrator uses disk quotas After completing this module, you will be able to manage data storage.

Module 7, "Managing Disaster Recovery," provides information about disaster recovery methods. This module explains how to use tools to back up and restore data that is critical to your systems and describes the tools that you can use to start a server if it cannot be started normally. After completing this module, you will be able to manage disaster recovery.

Module 8, "Software Maintenance Using Windows Server Update Services," explains what Windows Server Update Services (WSUS) is, how it works, and how it can help keep networks up-to-date with the latest service packs available from Microsoft. After completing this module, you will be able to use WSUS to maintain software.

Module 9, "Securing Windows Server 2003," provides an overview of securing servers, including implementing core server security, hardening servers for various roles, and using Security Configuration Wizard (SCW) and Microsoft Baseline Security Analyzer (MBSA).

Appendix A, "Administering Microsoft Windows Server 2003 by Using Scripts," provides information about using scripts to perform the administration tasks taught in this course.

Appendix B, "Partition Styles," provides information about the way that information about the partition is stored.

Appendix C, "Foreign Disks Volume Status in Disk Management," describes the types of status that an administrator can encounter when working with foreign disks.

Appendix D, "Which Recovery Tool Do I Use?" is a job aid that describes which disaster recovery tools to use in a disaster.

Setup

- The virtual environment is configured as one Windows Server 2003 domain: Contoso.msft
- DEN-DC1 is the domain controller
- DEN-SRV1 and Den-SRV2 are member servers
- DEN-CL1 is a workstation running Windows XP Professional, Service Pack 2
- Server computers are running Windows Server 2003, Enterprise Edition, Service Pack 1

Course files

There are files associated with the labs in this course. The lab files are located in the folder C:\Program Files\Microsoft Learning\2275\Labfiles\LabXX on the student virtual machine.

Classroom setup

Each student machine has Microsoft Windows XP Professional installed and is running Microsoft Virtual PC 2004.

The name of the domain is contoso.msft. The domain is named after Contoso, Ltd., a fictitious company that has offices worldwide.

The domain controller is named DEN-DC1, and there are two member servers, DEN-SRV1 and DEN-SRV2. All three computers are running Windows Server 2003 Enterprise Edition with Service Pack 1 (SP1). The workstation computer is named DEN-CL1 and is running Windows XP Professional with Service Pack 2 (SP2).

The domain has been populated with users, groups, and computer accounts for each administrator to manage.

Demonstration: Using Microsoft Virtual PC

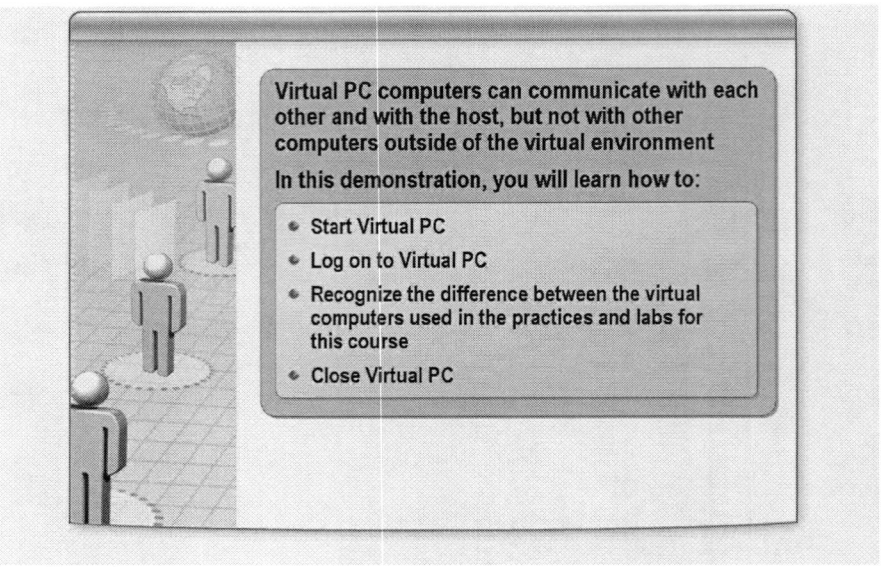

In this demonstration, your instructor will help familiarize you with the Virtual PC environment in which you will work to complete the practices and labs in this course. You will learn:

- How to open Virtual PC.
- How to start Virtual PC.
- How to log on to Virtual PC.
- How to switch between full screen and window modes.
- How to tell the difference between the virtual machines that are used in the practices for this course.
- That the virtual machines can communicate with each other and with the host, but they cannot communicate with other computers that are outside of the virtual environment. (For example, no Internet access is available from the virtual environment.)
- How to close Virtual PC.

Keyboard shortcuts

While working in the Virtual PC environment, you might find it helpful to use keyboard shortcuts. All Virtual PC shortcuts include a key that is referred to as the HOST key or the RIGHT-ALT key. By default, the HOST key is the ALT key on the right side of your keyboard. Some useful shortcuts include:

- ALT+DELETE to log on to the Virtual PC
- ALT+ENTER to switch between full screen mode and window modes
- ALT+RIGHT ARROW to display the next Virtual PC

For more information about Virtual PC, see Virtual PC Help.

Microsoft Learning

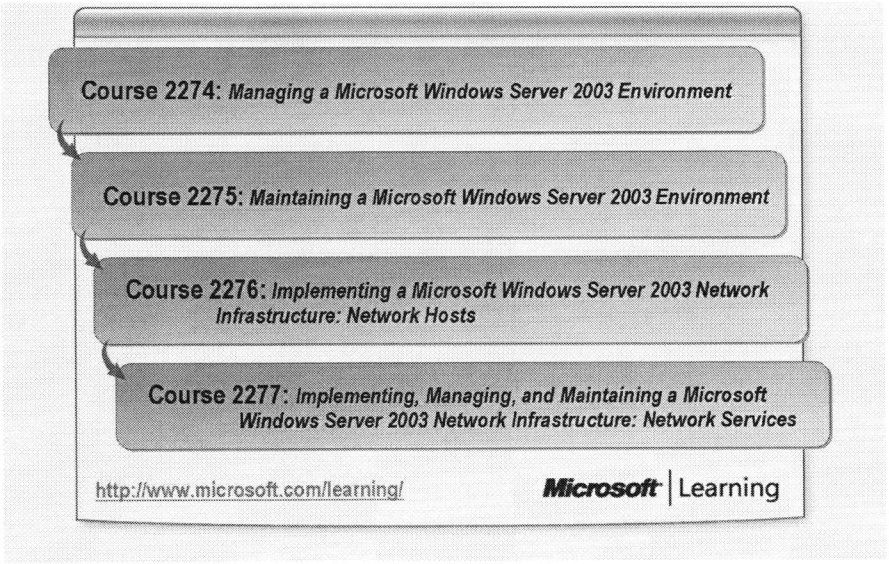

Microsoft Learning develops Official Microsoft Learning Products for computer professionals who design, develop, support, implement, or manage solutions by using Microsoft products and technologies. These learning products provide comprehensive, skills-based training in instructor-led and online formats.

Additional recommended learning products

Each learning product relates in some way to other learning products. A related product might be a prerequisite; a follow-up course, clinic, or workshop in a recommended series, or a learning product that offers additional training.

It is recommended that you take the following courses in this order:

- Course 2274: *Managing a Microsoft Windows Server 2003 Environment*
- Course 2275: *Maintaining a Microsoft Windows Server 2003 Environment*
- Course 2276: *Implementing a Microsoft Windows Server 2003 Network Infrastructure: Network Hosts*
- Course 2277: *Implementing, Managing, and Maintaining a Microsoft Windows Server 2003 Network Infrastructure: Network Services*
- Course 2278: *Planning and Maintaining a Microsoft Windows Server 2003 Network Infrastructure*
- Course 2279: *Planning, Implementing, and Maintaining a Microsoft Windows Server 2003 Active Directory Infrastructure*

Other related learning products might become available in the future, so for up-to-date information about recommended learning products, visit the Microsoft Learning Web site.

Microsoft Learning information

For more information, visit the Microsoft Learning Web site at http://www.microsoft.com/learning/.

Microsoft Learning Product Types

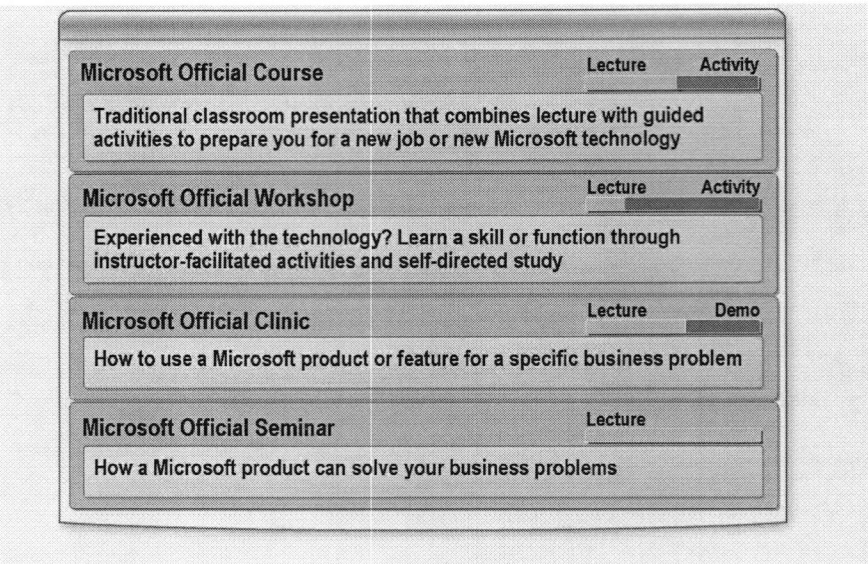

Microsoft Learning offers four types of instructor-led products type. Each is specific to a particular audience type and level of experience. The different product types also tend to suit different learning styles. These types are as follows:

- Microsoft Official Courses are for information technology (IT) professionals and developers who are new to a particular product or technology and for experienced individuals who prefer to learn in a traditional classroom format. Courses provide a relevant and guided learning experience that combines lecture and practice to deliver thorough coverage of a Microsoft product or technology. Courses are designed to address the needs of learners engaged in planning, design, implementation, management, and support phases of the technology adoption lifecycle. They provide detailed information by focusing on concepts and principles, reference content, and in-depth hands-on lab activities to ensure knowledge transfer. Typically, the content of a course is broad, addressing a wide range of tasks necessary for the job role.

- Microsoft Official Workshops are for knowledgeable IT professionals and developers who learn best by doing and exploring. Workshops provide a hands-on learning experience in which participants use Microsoft products in a safe and collaborative environment based on real-world scenarios. Workshops are the learning products where students learn by doing through scenario and through troubleshooting hands-on labs, targeted reviews, information resources, and best practices, with instructor facilitation.

- Microsoft Official Clinics are for IT professionals, developers and technical decision makers. Clinics offer a detailed "how to" presentation that describes the features and functionality of an existing or new Microsoft product or technology, and that showcases product demonstrations and solutions. Clinics focus on how specific features will solve business problems.

- Microsoft Official Seminars are for business decision makers. Through featured business scenarios, case studies, and success stories, seminars provide a dynamic presentation of early and relevant information on Microsoft products and technology solutions that enable decision makers to make critical business decisions. Microsoft Official Seminars are concise, engaging, direct-from-the-source learning products that show how emerging Microsoft products and technologies help our customers serve their customers.

Microsoft Certified Professional Program

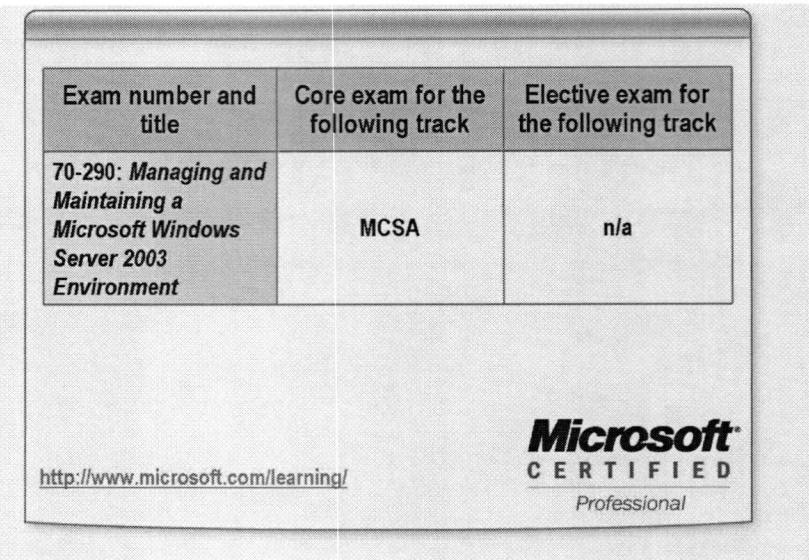

Microsoft Learning offers a variety of certification credentials for developers and IT professionals. The Microsoft Certified Professional (MCP) program is the leading certification program for validating your experience and skills, keeping you competitive in today's changing business environment.

Related certification exams

This course, in combination with Course 2275: *Maintaining a Microsoft Windows Server 2003 Environment*, helps students to prepare for Exam 70-290: *Managing and Maintaining a Microsoft Windows Server 2003 Environment*. To prepare for the exam, you should complete both courses.

Exam 70-290 is a core exam for the Microsoft Certified Systems Administrator certification.

MCP certifications

The MCP program includes the following certifications:

- MCDST on Windows XP

  The Microsoft Certified Desktop Support Technician (MCDST) certification is designed for professionals who successfully support and educate end users and troubleshoot operating system and application issues on desktop computers running the Windows operating system.

- MCSA on Windows Server 2003

  The Microsoft Certified Systems Administrator (MCSA) certification is designed for professionals who implement, manage, and troubleshoot existing network and system environments based on the Windows Server 2003 platform. Implementation responsibilities include installing and configuring parts of systems. Management responsibilities include administering and supporting systems.

- MCSE on Windows Server 2003

    The Microsoft Certified Systems Engineer (MCSE) credential is the premier certification for professionals who analyze business requirements and design and implement infrastructure for business solutions based on the Windows Server 2003 platform. Implementation responsibilities include installing, configuring, and troubleshooting network systems.

- MCAD

    The Microsoft Certified Application Developer (MCAD) for Microsoft .NET credential is appropriate for professionals who use Microsoft technologies to develop and maintain department-level applications, components, Web or desktop clients, or back-end data services, or who work in teams developing enterprise applications. The credential covers job tasks ranging from developing to deploying and maintaining these solutions.

- MCSD

    The Microsoft Certified Solution Developer (MCSD) credential is the premier certification for professionals who design and develop leading-edge business solutions with Microsoft development tools, technologies, platforms, and the Microsoft Windows DNA architecture. The types of applications MCSDs can develop include desktop applications and multi-user, Web-based, N-tier, and transaction-based applications. The credential covers job tasks ranging from analyzing business requirements to maintaining solutions.

- MCDBA on Microsoft SQL Server™ 2000

    The Microsoft Certified Database Administrator (MCDBA) credential is the premier certification for professionals who implement and administer SQL Server databases. The certification is appropriate for individuals who derive physical database designs, develop logical data models, create physical databases, use Transact-SQL to create data services, manage and maintain databases, configure and manage security, monitor and optimize databases, and install and configure SQL Server.

- MCP

    The Microsoft Certified Professional (MCP) credential is for individuals who have the skills to successfully implement a Microsoft product or technology as part of a business solution in an organization. Hands-on experience with the product is necessary to successfully achieve certification.

- MCT

    Microsoft Certified Trainers (MCTs) demonstrate the instructional and technical skills that qualify them to deliver Official Microsoft Learning Products through a Microsoft Certified Partner for Learning Solutions.

Certification requirements

Requirements differ for each certification category and are specific to the products and job functions addressed by the certification. To become a Microsoft Certified Professional, you must pass rigorous certification exams that provide a valid and reliable measure of technical proficiency and expertise.

For More Information See the Microsoft Learning Web site at http://www.microsoft.com/learning/.

You can also send e-mail to mcphelp@microsoft.com if you have specific certification questions.

Acquiring the skills tested by an MCP exam

Official Microsoft Learning Products can help you develop the skills that you need to do your job. They also complement the experience that you gain while working with Microsoft products and technologies. However, no one-to-one correlation exists between Official Microsoft Learning Products and MCP exams. Microsoft does not expect or intend for the courses to be the sole preparation method for passing MCP exams. Practical product knowledge and experience is also necessary to pass MCP exams.

To help prepare for MCP exams, use the preparation guides are available for each exam. Each Exam Preparation Guide contains exam-specific information such as a list of topics on which you will be tested. These guides are available on the Microsoft Learning Web site at http://www.microsoft.com/learning/.

Multimedia: Job Roles in Today's Information Systems Environment

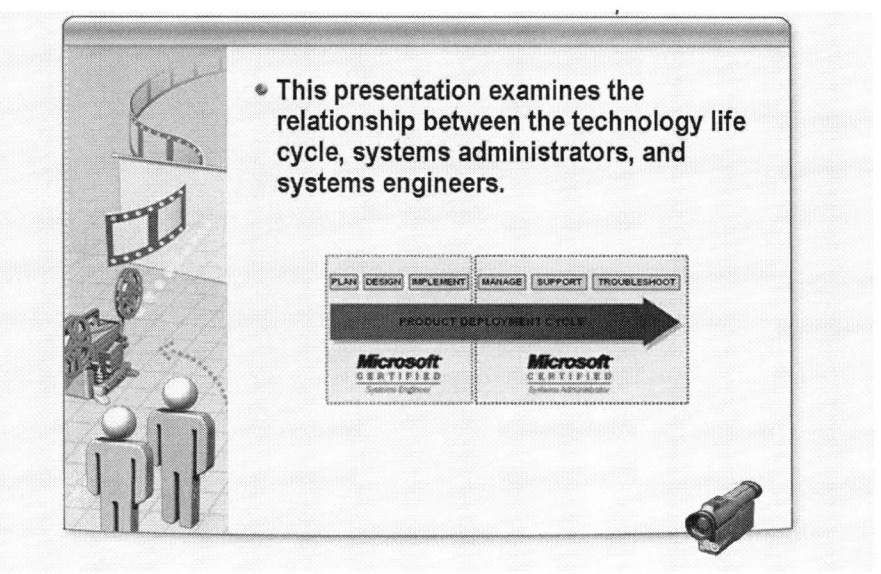

File location

To view the *Job Roles in Today's Information Systems Environment* presentation, open the Web page on the Student Materials compact disc, click **Multimedia**, and then click the title of the presentation. Do not open this presentation unless your instructor tells you to do so.

Facilities

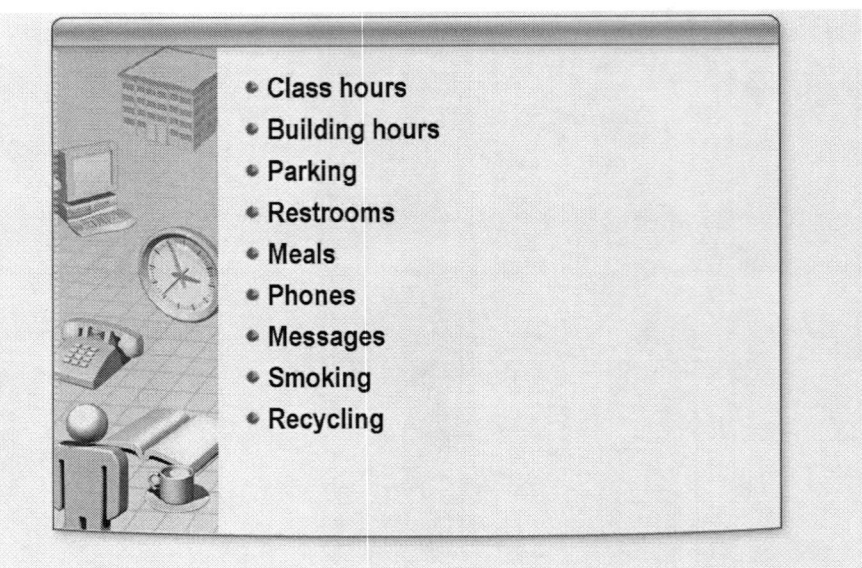

Module 1: Preparing to Administer a Server

Contents

Overview	1
Lesson: Introduction to Administering a Server	2
Lesson: Configuring Remote Desktop to Administer a Server	12
Lesson: Managing Remote Desktop Connections	26
Lab: Preparing to Administer a Server	34

Information in this document, including URL and other Internet Web site references, is subject to change without notice. Unless otherwise noted, the example companies, organizations, products, domain names, e-mail addresses, logos, people, places, and events depicted herein are fictitious, and no association with any real company, organization, product, domain name, e-mail address, logo, person, place or event is intended or should be inferred. Complying with all applicable copyright laws is the responsibility of the user. Without limiting the rights under copyright, no part of this document may be reproduced, stored in or introduced into a retrieval system, or transmitted in any form or by any means (electronic, mechanical, photocopying, recording, or otherwise), or for any purpose, without the express written permission of Microsoft Corporation.

The names of manufacturers, products, or URLs are provided for informational purposes only and Microsoft makes no representations and warranties, either expressed, implied, or statutory, regarding these manufacturers or the use of the products with any Microsoft technologies. The inclusion of a manufacturer or product does not imply endorsement of Microsoft of the manufacturer or product. Links are provided to third party sites. Such sites are not under the control of Microsoft and Microsoft is not responsible for the contents of any linked site or any link contained in a linked site, or any changes or updates to such sites. Microsoft is not responsible for webcasting or any other form of transmission received from any linked site. Microsoft is providing these links to you only as a convenience, and the inclusion of any link does not imply endorsement of Microsoft of the site or the products contained therein.

Microsoft may have patents, patent applications, trademarks, copyrights, or other intellectual property rights covering subject matter in this document. Except as expressly provided in any written license agreement from Microsoft, the furnishing of this document does not give you any license to these patents, trademarks, copyrights, or other intellectual property.

© 2005 Microsoft Corporation. All rights reserved.

Microsoft, Active Directory, ActiveX, Authenticode, BizTalk, IntelliMirror, MSDN, PowerPoint, Windows, Windows Media, Windows NT, and Windows Server are either registered trademarks or trademarks of Microsoft Corporation in the United States and/or other countries.

All other trademarks are property of their respective owners.

Overview

- Introduction to Administering a Server
- Configuring Remote Desktop to Administer a Server
- Managing Remote Desktop Connections

Introduction

A major responsibility of a systems administrator is to administer the servers in an organization. Because most systems administrators are not located in the same room as the servers they manage, it is important to understand how to manage servers remotely, as well as from the server console.

This module describes how to use Microsoft® Windows Server™ 2003 to administer servers, what tools to use, and what permissions are required to administer a server. It also discusses how to administer remote connections and why that is an important aspect of system administration.

Objectives

After completing this module, you will be able to:

- Explain the tasks, tools, and rights that are required to administer a server.
- Configure Remote Desktop for Administration and client preferences.
- Manage remote desktop connections.

Lesson: Introduction to Administering a Server

- Group Memberships Used to Administer a Server
- What Is the Run as Feature?
- What Is Computer Management?
- Role of MMC in Remote Administration
- Practice: Introduction to Administering a Server

Introduction

This lesson introduces the tasks, tools, and rights that are required to administer a server. This information is the foundation that you need to perform your job as a systems administrator. This lesson describes the proper use and function of the server administration tools and explains the concepts of remote and local server administration.

Lesson objectives

After completing this lesson, you will be able to:

- Describe the group memberships that are used to administer a server.
- Describe the purpose and function of the **Run as** feature.
- Describe the role of the Computer Management tool in remote administration.
- Describe the role of the Microsoft Management Console (MMC) in remote administration.
- Configure MMC to manage a server remotely.

Group Memberships Used to Administer a Server

Built-in domain local group	Description
Administrators	• Performs all administrative tasks on clients and servers
Backup Operators	• Backs up, restores servers by using Backup
Account Operators	• Creates, deletes, modifies user accounts and groups
Server Operators	• Shares disk resources, backs up and restores files
Print Operators	• Sets up, manages network printers

Introduction

To administer a server, you need appropriate permissions. You will need to understand these permissions to assign them appropriately and to perform your own administrative duties. The easiest way to assign administrative permissions is through domain local groups.

Built-in domain local groups

In a domain, built-in groups are created in the Active Directory® directory service. These groups have preset permissions that limit group member access to system tasks. These groups cannot be deleted.

The following list describes the most commonly used built-in domain local groups and their predetermined level of permissions.

- *Administrators*. Members of the Administrators domain local group can perform all functions that the operating system supports. Administrators can assign themselves any user rights that they do not have by default. The membership of the Administrators domain local group should be restricted to only users who require full system access and are highly trusted. Log on as an administrator only when necessary.

  Be cautious when adding other users to the Administrators group. For example, if a help desk technician is responsible for the printers in your organization, add the technician to the Print Operators group instead of the Administrators group.

- *Backup Operators*. Members of the Backup Operators domain local group can back up and restore files by using the Backup tool.

- *Account Operators.* Members of the Account Operators domain local group can manage user accounts, groups, computer accounts, and InetOrgPerson accounts. The exception is that only a member of the Administrators domain local group can modify the Administrators domain local group or any operator domain local group.
- *Server Operators.* Members of the Server Operators domain local group can share disk resources, log on to a server interactively, create and delete network shares, start and stop services, format the hard disk of the server, and shut down the computer. They can also back up and restore files by using the Backup tool.
- *Print Operators.* Member of the Print Operators domain local group can set up local and network printers to ensure that users can easily connect to and use printer resources.

Note The Administrators, Server Operators, and Backup Operators groups can also be found on member servers and stand-alone servers as built-in local groups.

Domain local groups can protect resources

Using a variety of built-in domain local groups and their associated permission levels can protect resources from security breaches. A systems administrator should always be assigned to the most restricted group that provides the appropriate rights and the permissions that are necessary to accomplish the task. For example, a systems administrator who manages only printers and backup server data should be a member of the printer operators group and should have authority to back up server data.

Domain local group permissions

Members of the built-in domain local groups are assigned permissions to perform system tasks, such as backing up files, restoring files, and changing the system time. You can use these groups for administering resources, such as file systems or printers that are located on any computer in the domain where common access permissions are required.

When you run your computer as a member of the Administrators domain local group, the system is vulnerable to Trojan horse attacks and other security risks. The simple act of visiting an Internet site or opening an e-mail attachment can lead to system damage, because an unfamiliar Internet site or e-mail attachment may contain Trojan horse code that can be downloaded to the system and executed.

Note In a domain environment, members of the Domain Admins global group are automatically added to the Administrators domain local group and to the Administrators local group on each computer. All other built-in groups do not have any members by default.

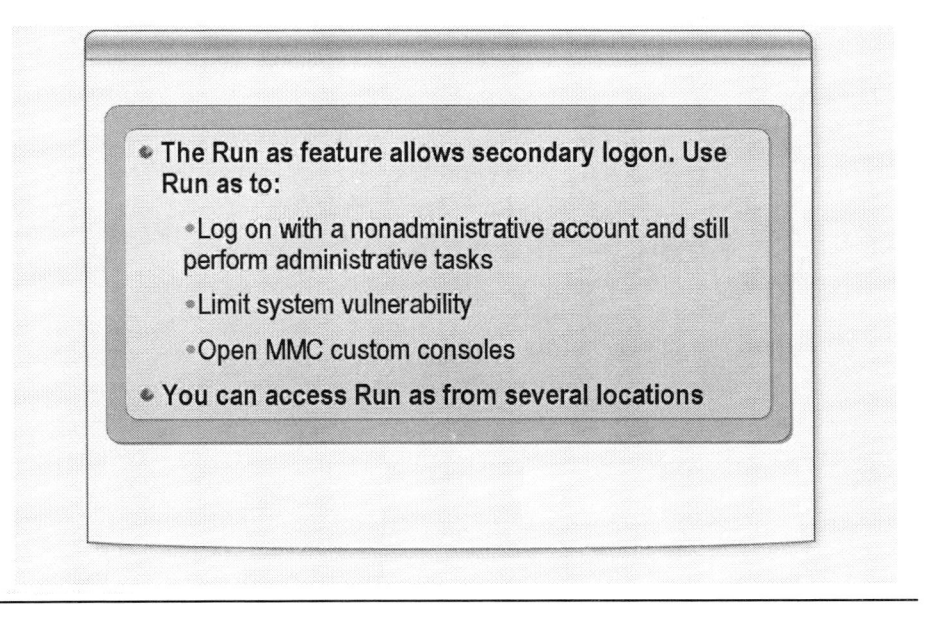

What Is the Run as Feature?

> - The Run as feature allows secondary logon. Use Run as to:
>   - Log on with a nonadministrative account and still perform administrative tasks
>   - Limit system vulnerability
>   - Open MMC custom consoles
> - You can access Run as from several locations

Introduction

By using the **Run as** feature, also known as a secondary logon, administrators can log on with a nonadministrative account and still perform administrative tasks. Each time an administrative task is performed, the required administrative tool is run using the credentials of a user account with administrative permissions.

Requires two user accounts

To use **Run as** to perform administrative tasks requires two user accounts: a regular account with basic privileges and an administrative account. Each administrator should use an exclusive administrative account.

Login with your non-administrative account and use the **runas** command for system administration tasks. This practice preserves network security, limiting system exposure while you perform nonadministrative tasks. Some items, such as Windows Explorer, the Printers folder, and desktop items, are launched indirectly by Windows. These items cannot be started with **Run as**.

For tasks that cannot be performed by using the **runas** command, such as upgrading the operating system or configuring system parameters, log off your user account and then log on with your administrator account.

Use Run as to open MMC-created custom consoles

To administer local or remote computers, you can use the **Run as** command to open custom consoles you have created in the Microsoft Management Console (MMC). Using the **Run as** command offers you access to the services and administrative tools that are included in the console, while providing you with the appropriate permissions on the system for the components that are administered by the console.

Any user can use Run as

Although the **Run as** command is primarily intended for systems administrators, any user with multiple accounts can use **Run as** to start programs under different account contexts without logging off.

Three ways to use Run as

There are three ways to use the **Run as** command:

- You can right-click a program located on the **Start** menu, and then click **Run as**.
- You can right-click a program in Windows Explorer, and then click **Run as**.
- You can also use the **runas** command from a command prompt. This method is typically used for scripting administrative tasks or to start a command shell in the local administrative context. To use **Run as** from a command prompt, type **runas /user:***domain_name\user_name program_name*

For example, to run the Computer Management tool from the command line as an administrator, open a command prompt and then type **runas /user:contoso\admininistrator "mmc %windir%\system32 \compmgmt.msc"**

Set up runas shortcuts

You can also set up **runas** shortcuts to the services and administrative tools that you use most often, including Performance, Computer Management, Device Manager, and Disk Manager.

See the following table for commands.

Tool	Command line
Computer Management	runas /user:contoso\administrator "mmc %windir%\system32\ compmgmt.msc"
Device Manager	runas /user:contoso\administrator "mmc %windir%\system32\ devmgmt.msc"
Disk Manager	runas /user:contoso\administrator "mmc %windir%\system32\ diskmgmt.msc"
Active Directory	runas /user:contoso\administrator "mmc %windir%\system32\dsa.msc"
MMC	runas /user:contoso\administrator mmc
Command Prompt	runas /user:contoso\administrator cmd
Performance Monitor	runas /user:Contoso\administrator "mmc %windir%\system32\perfmon.msc"

Note Windows Server 2003 SP1 includes a new version of the Administration Tools. These tools can be installed on computers running Windows Server 2003 and Windows XP. Previous versions of the Administration Tools must be uninstalled before installing the SP1 version.

What Is Computer Management?

Tool	Description
System tools	• Monitor system events • Create and manage shared resources • View a list of connected users • View device configurations
Storage tools	• Set properties for storage devices • Update disk information
Services and applications tools	• Manage applications and services • Start and stop system services

A collection of administrative tools
Use to manage remote and local computers

Definition

Computer Management is a collection of administrative tools that you can use to administer a local computer or remote computers.

Use Computer Management to manage computers

You can use Computer Management to:

- Monitor system events, such as logon times and application errors.
- Create and manage shared resources.
- View the list of users who are connected to a local or remote computer.
- Start and stop system services, such as Task Scheduler and Indexing Service.
- Set properties for storage devices.
- View device configurations and add new device drivers.
- Manage applications and services.

Computer Management console

The Computer Management console organizes the administrative tools into the following three categories:

- System Tools
- Storage
- Services and Applications

The following sections describe the tools in these categories and explain how to use them to perform administrative tasks.

System Tools

These System Tools manage system events and system performance:

- *Event Viewer*. Use Event Viewer to manage and view events that are recorded in the application, security, and system logs. You can monitor the logs to track security events and to identify possible software, hardware, and system problems.

- *Shared Folders*. Use Shared Folders to view connections and resources that are in use on the computer. You can create, view, and manage shared resources; view open files and sessions; and close files and disconnect sessions.

- *Local Users and Groups*. Use Local Users and Groups to create and manage your local user accounts and groups.

- *Performance Logs and Alerts*. Use Performance Logs and Alerts to monitor and collect data about your computer's performance.

- *Device Manager*. Use Device Manager to view the hardware devices that are installed in your computer, update device drivers, modify hardware settings, and troubleshoot device conflicts.

Storage

You use the tools in Storage to manage the properties of storage devices.

- *Removable Storage.* Use Removable Storage to track your removable storage media and to manage the libraries or data-storage systems that contain them.

- *Disk Defragmenter*. Use Disk Defragmenter to analyze and defragment volumes on your hard disks.

- *Disk Management.* Use Disk Management to perform disk-related tasks, such as converting disks or creating and formatting volumes. Disk Management helps you manage your hard disks and the partitions or volumes they contain.

Services and Applications

The tools in Services and Applications help you manage services and applications on the specified computer.

- *Services*. Use Services to manage services on local and remote computers. You can start, stop, pause, resume, or disable a service. For example, you can use Services to stop a service on a remote computer.

- *WMI Control*. Use WMI Control to configure and manage the Windows Management Service.

- *Indexing Service*. Use Indexing Service to manage the Indexing service and to create and configure additional catalogs to store index information.

Role of MMC in Remote Administration

- **Microsoft Management Console**
  - Provides an interface to snap-ins that manage hardware, software, and network services
- **Use MMC in remote administration to:**
  - Perform tasks that are frequently accomplished on remote computers
  - Manage similar tasks on many remote computers

Introduction

Microsoft Management Console (MMC) provides an interface that you can use to create, save, and open administrative tools, called snap-ins, that manage the hardware, software, and network components of Windows Server 2003. When you open an administrative tool in MMC, you can specify whether to apply the tool on the local computer or on a remote computer.

Use MMC for remote and local administration

To perform similar tasks on many servers, use MMC snap-ins. Most of the administrative tools that are provided with Windows Server 2003 family operating systems are MMC snap-ins that you can use to administer remote servers as well as your local computer.

Advantages of MMC snap-ins

The advantages of using MMC snap-ins are that you can:

- Create a console that contains the tools you use for the tasks you perform most often. For example, you use Computer Management to administer a remote server.

- Set the focus for a tool to any of the servers that you administer, and switch between servers and tools within a single MMC console. For example, you can use the Computer Management snap-in to view the performance of multiple remote servers.

Note If Windows Firewall is enabled on a remote server, port 445 must be opened to allow the administrative tools to work as expected for remote computer administration.

Practice: Introduction to Administering a Server

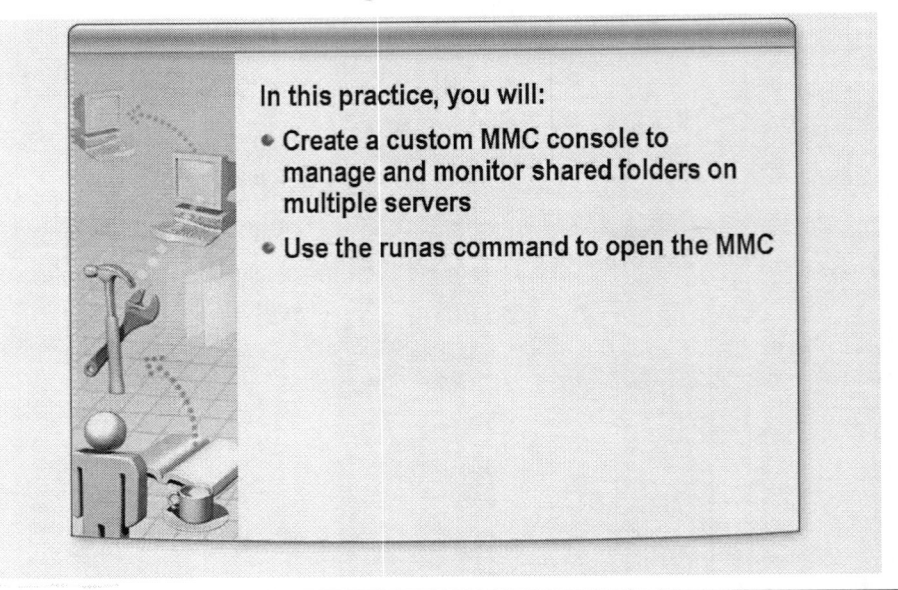

Objective

In this practice, you will:

- Create a custom MMC console to manage and monitor shared folders on multiple servers.
- Use the **runas** command to open the MMC.

Instructions

Ensure that the DEN-DC1 and DEN-CL1 virtual machines are running.

Practice

▶ **Create a custom MMC console to manage and monitor shared folders on multiple servers**

1. Start the DEN-DC1 virtual machine. (Wait for the machine to be fully started before proceeding to step 2.)
2. Start the DEN-CL1 virtual machine.
3. With the active window being DEN-CL1 virtual machine, press <RIGHT> ALT+DELETE.
4. Log on to the domain as Paul West.
    a. In the **Log on to Windows** box, in the **User name** text box, type **Paul**.
    b. In the **Password** box, type **Pa$$w0rd**. (The 0 is a zero.)
    c. In the **Log on to** box, ensure that **Contoso** is displayed and then click **OK**.
5. On the **Start** menu, click **Run**.
6. In the **Run** dialog box, type **mmc** and then click **OK**.
7. In the **Console1** window, click the **File** menu and then click **Add/Remove Snap-in**.
8. In the **Add/Remove Snap-in** dialog box, click **Add**.
9. In the **Add Standalone Snap-in** dialog box, double-click the items to add as follows.

10. Add a Computer Management snap-in for the local machine.
    a. In the **Computer Management** dialog box, ensure that **Local computer** is selected.
    b. Click **Finish**.
11. Add a **Computer Management** snap-in for DEN-DC1.
    a. In the **Computer Management** dialog box select **Another computer** and type **DEN-DC1**.
    b. Click **Finish**.
12. In the **Add Standalone Snap-in** dialog box, click **Close**.
13. In the **Add/Remove Snap-in** dialog box, click **OK**.
14. In the Computer Management (Local) tree, expand **System Tools**, expand **Shared Folders**, and then click **Shares**. Notice that you are unable to view the shares.
15. In the Computer Management (DEN-DC1) tree, expand **System Tools**, expand **Shared Folders**, and then click **Shares**. Notice that you are unable to view the shares.
16. Save the console on the desktop as **MMC1**.
    a. Click the **File** menu and then click **Save As**.
    b. Click **Desktop**.
    c. In the **File name** box, type **MMC1**, and then click **Save**.
17. Close **MMC1**.

Practice

▶ **Use the runas command to open the MMC**

1. Right-click **MMC1** and then click **Run as**.
2. Click the option button next to **The following user** and, in the **User name** box, type **Contoso\Administrator** and, in the **Password box**, type **Pa$$w0rd**, and then click **OK**.
3. Verify that you can monitor shares on DEN-CL1 and DEN-DC1.
4. Close all open windows and log off of DEN-CL1.

Important Do not shut down the virtual machines.

Lesson: Configuring Remote Desktop to Administer a Server

- What Is Remote Desktop for Administration?
- Why Use Remote Desktop for Administration?
- What Are the Requirements for Remote Desktop Service?
- What Are Client Preferences for Remote Desktop Connection?
- Remote Desktop Connection vs. Remote Desktops
- Guidelines for Using Remote Administration Tools
- Practice: Configuring Remote Desktop to Administer a Server

Introduction

This lesson explains how to configure Remote Desktop for Administration and how to configure the client to allow access to the servers by using Remote Desktop for Administration. This lesson also describes how to establish the connection between the administrator's computer and the server.

Lesson objectives

After completing this lesson, you will be able to:

- Describe Remote Desktop for Administration and explain how it works.
- List the uses for Remote Desktop for Administration.
- List the requirements for Remote Desktop Service.
- Explain client preferences for Remote Desktop.
- Explain the differences between Remote Desktops and Remote Desktop Connections.
- Apply guidelines for using Remote Administration tools.
- Enable and use Remote Desktop.

What Is Remote Desktop for Administration?

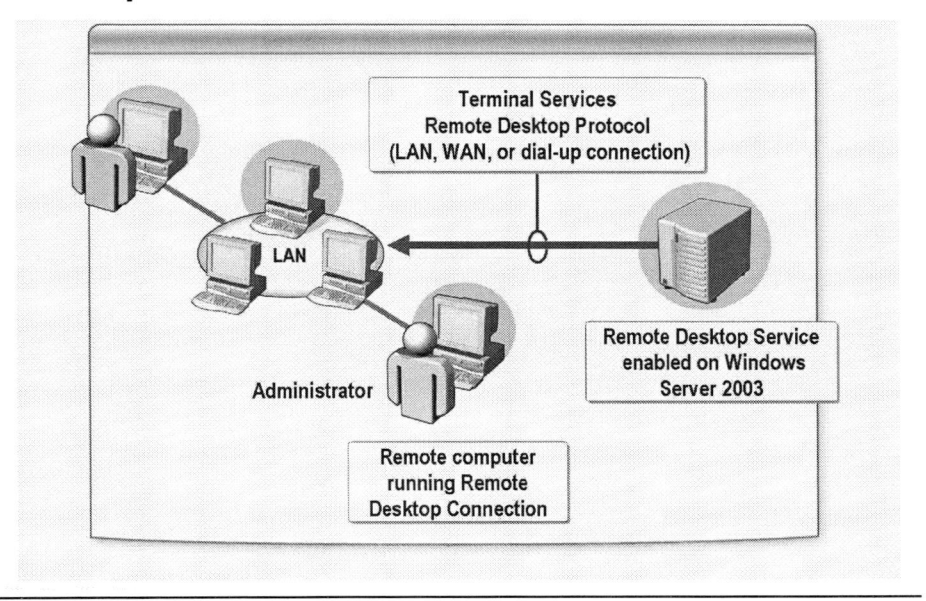

Introduction

By using Remote Desktop for Administration, you can manage one or more remote computers from a single location. In a large organization, you can use remote administration to centrally manage many computers that are located in other buildings or even in other cities. In a small organization, you can use remote administration to manage a single server that is located in an adjacent office.

Remote access to servers

Remote Desktop for Administration provides access to a server from a computer at another location by using Remote Desktop Protocol (RDP). RDP transmits the user interface to the client session, and it also transmits the keyboard and mouse clicks from the client to the server.

You can create up to two simultaneous remote connections. Each session to which you log on is independent of other client sessions and the server console session. When you use Remote Desktop for Administration to log on to the remote server, it is as if you are logged on to the server locally.

Remote Desktop Connection and Remote Desktops snap-in

Remote Desktop for Administration provides two tools that you can use to administer a remote server: Remote Desktop Connection and the Remote Desktops snap-in.

Each instance of the Remote Desktop Connection tool creates its own window and allows you to administer one remote server per window.

The Remote Desktops snap-in is useful for administrators who remotely administer multiple servers or for administrators who must connect to the console session remotely. The Remote Desktops snap-in displays a split window with a console tree on the left and remote connection information in the details pane on the right.

Remote Desktops allows no more than two desktop connections to the server at one time.

Note To allow more than two Remote Desktop connections, you must install Terminal Services. For more information about Terminal Services, see the white paper, *Technical Overview of Terminal Services*, under **Additional Reading** on the Student Materials compact disc.

Remote Desktop Service   Remote Desktop Service provides server access. It is installed with Windows Server 2003 and must be enabled before you can configure Remote Desktop Administration.

Note If Windows Firewall is enabled on the remote server, port 3389 must be open for Remote Desktop clients to be able to connect to the server.

Why Use Remote Desktop for Administration?

> - Provide remote access to most configuration settings
> - Diagnose a problem and test multiple solutions quickly
> - Allow access to servers from anywhere in the world
> - Perform time-consuming batch administrative jobs, such as tape backups
> - Upgrade server applications and operating systems remotely

Introduction

Remote Desktop for Administration is a convenient and efficient service that can greatly reduce the overhead that is associated with remote administration. For example, Remote Desktop for Administration allows multiple systems administrators to manage remote servers.

Remote sessions

Remote Desktop for Administration allows you either to start a new remote session on a server or to remotely take over the console session on a server. However, there can be only one console session running on a server at one time. If you log on to the console remotely while another administrator is logged on to the console session, the first administrator is locked out.

Note System messages that are sent to the console are displayed at the console session and not at the other remote sessions.

Run earlier versions of Windows

By using Remote Desktop Connection, systems administrators can also fully manage computers that are running Windows Server 2003 family operating systems from computers that are running earlier versions of Windows.

Access to configuration settings

Remote Desktop for Administration is useful because it provides remote access to most configuration settings, including Control Panel, which usually cannot be configured remotely.

By using a Remote Desktop session, you can access MMC, Active Directory, Microsoft Systems Management Server, network configuration tools, and most other administrative tools.

Multiple uses

Using Remote Desktop for Administration can help you diagnose a problem and test multiple solutions quickly.

You can access the servers from anywhere in the world by using a wide-area network (WAN), a virtual private network (VPN), or a dial-up connection. When you run a time-consuming batch administrative job, such as a tape backup, you can start the job, disconnect from the corporate network, and later reconnect to check progress.

You can use Remote Desktop for Administration to upgrade server applications remotely and to perform tasks that are not usually possible unless you are working at the console.

Administrative tasks are quicker and more intuitive than using command-line utilities, although it is still possible to open a command prompt.

What Are the Requirements for Remote Desktop Service?

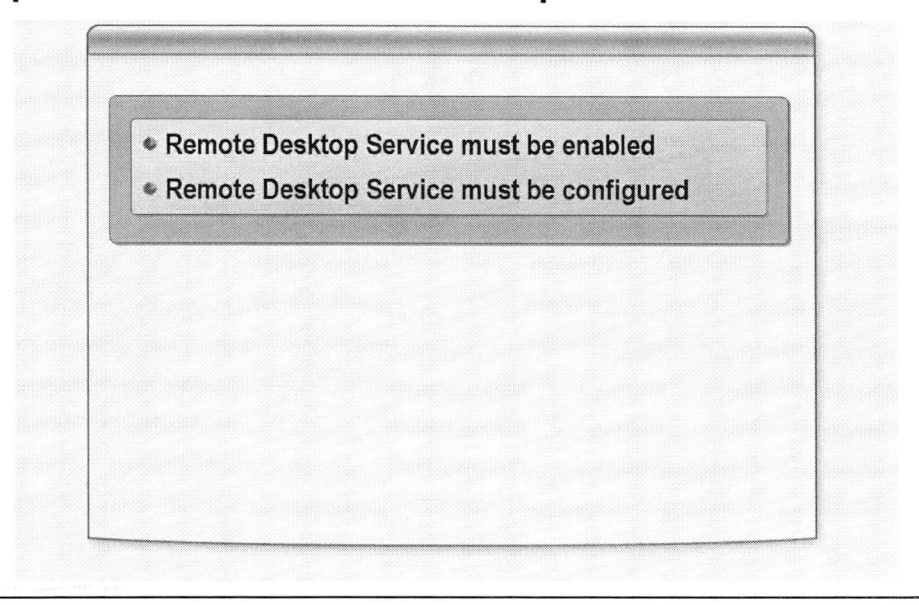

```
• Remote Desktop Service must be enabled
• Remote Desktop Service must be configured
```

Introduction

Clients running Remote Desktop Connection or Remote Desktops connect to the Remote Desktop Service on the remote server. Understanding how to enable and configure Remote Desktop Service is essential for remote administration.

Remote Desktop Service configuration

Remote Desktop Service must be enabled locally on the remote server by a systems administrator who is working at the console. The systems administrator must have the appropriate permissions to administer the computer. By default, members of the local Administrators group have remote connection privileges to the remote server.

The built-in domain local group Remote Desktop Users is assigned the right to log on to servers in the domain remotely through Remote Desktop. By default, this group has no members. If any user that is not a member of the Administrators group needs to use Remote Desktop for Administration then add them to this group.

Remote Desktop Service is enabled on the **Remote** tab of System Properties by selecting the **Allow users to connect remotely to this computer** check box.

What Are Client Preferences for Remote Desktop Connection?

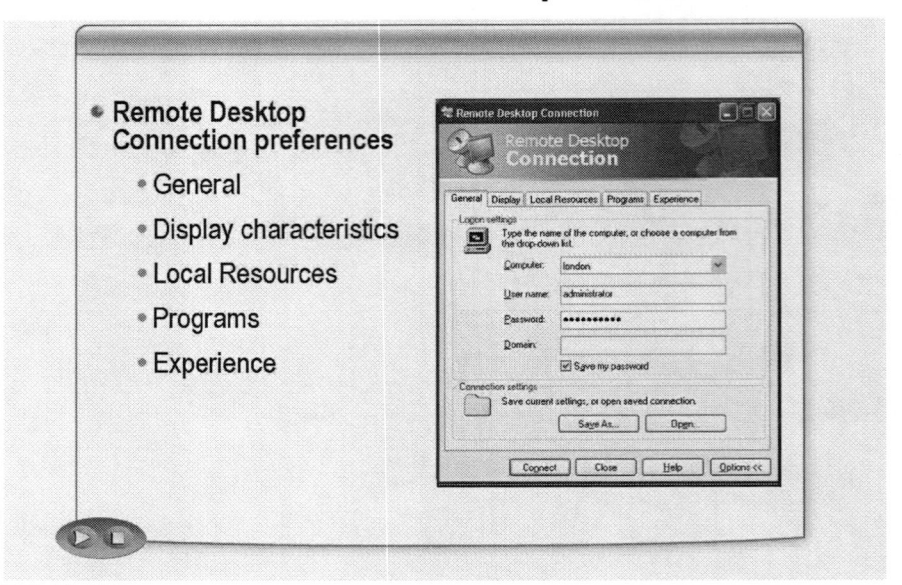

- **Remote Desktop Connection preferences**
  - General
  - Display characteristics
  - Local Resources
  - Programs
  - Experience

Introduction

To configure your remote desktop connection, you must set up client preferences. To do this, use the Remote Desktop Connection interface to configure the information about the connection and the client computer.

General

Use the **General** tab to provide information that is required for automatic logon to the remote server. This information includes the name of the server, the user name and password, and the domain name. If you save your password and connection settings, on later visits you can save time by opening a saved connection.

Display

Use the **Display** tab to change the screen size and color settings of the remote desktop and to hide or display the connection bar in full-screen mode.

Local Resources

Use the **Local Resources** tab to allow or restrict remote desktop access to the disk drives, serial ports, printers, sound, or Windows key combinations on your local computer. Allowing access from the remote desktop is called *resource redirection*. When you allow the remote desktop to have access to these resources, the remote desktop can use the resources for the duration of the session.

If you choose to make your local disk drive available to the remote desktop, easy access to files to or from the remote is the benefit. Conversely, the remote desktop has access to the contents of your local disk drive. If this access is not appropriate, you can clear the **Disk drives** check box to keep your local disk drive from being redirected to the remote desktop.

Programs

Use the **Programs** tab to specify that a program starts upon connection to the remote server.

Experience   Use the **Experience** tab to improve the performance of your remote server connection by allowing certain characteristics of the remote Windows session, such as the Desktop background, to appear as if they are enabled on the remote computer. You can also improve the performance of your connection by selecting a faster connection speed. The default connection speed, 56 kilobits per second (Kbps), offers good performance for most networks. Use the faster speed settings to enable richer graphical features, such as desktop wallpaper or menu sliding and fading.

Remote Desktop Connection vs. Remote Desktops

Service	Functions
Remote Desktop Connection	• Connects to one server per instance • Displays connections full screen or in a window • Opens a remote server session by default
Remote Desktops	• Connects to multiple servers simultaneously • Displays connections in the MMC console • Opens a console session by default

Introduction

Windows Server 2003 comes with two clients that allow administrators to connect to the remote desktop:

- Remote Desktop Connection
- Remote Desktops snap-in

Remote Desktop Connection

Using Remote Desktop Connection, you can connect to one server. You can run multiple copies of Remote Desktop Connection to connect to multiple servers, but you must switch between Remote Desktop Connection sessions to manage each server. Each connection can be displayed full screen or in a window.

When you connect to a server using Remote Desktop Connection, you will open a remote session by default.

Remote Desktops snap-in

You can use the Remote Desktops snap-in to connect to multiple servers simultaneously. Each connection is displayed in an MMC console. The console tree displays the name of the server and the details pane displays the remote session.

When you connect to a server by using Remote Desktops, the console session opens by default.

Use the command line tool

You can also connect to the console session on a remote server by using the **Run** command and the **mstsc** command-line tool with the **/console** option. Command-line options for **mstsc** can be included as part of the target in a shortcut.

For example, you can use the command **Mstsc /console /v:DEN-DC1 /w:800 /h:600** to open a remote console connection to DEN-DC1 using a window size of 800 by 600.

See the following table for common **mstsc** command-line options.

Switch	Description
ConnectionFile	**Specifies the name of an .rdp file for the connection.**
/v:*server*	**Specifies the remote computer to which you want to connect.**
/console	**Connects to the console session of the specified Windows Server 2003 server.**
/f	**Starts Remote Desktop connection in full-screen mode.**
/w:*width* /h:*height*	**Specifies the dimensions of the Remote Desktop Screen.**
/?	**Displays help for mstsc.**

Guidelines for Using Remote Administration Tools

Tool	Use to:
Computer Management	Manage and monitor server: • Events • Shared folders • Data storage • Start and stop services
Remote Desktop for Administration	Perform any administrative task that is possible at the server console

Introduction

Windows Server 2003 operating systems provide several tools that support remote location server management. These tools expand your flexibility because you can work as though you are physically present at each server in your organization. By understanding the functions of each tool, you can choose the most appropriate one for your remote administration tasks.

Computer Management tool tasks

The tasks that you can perform by using the Computer Management tool in remote administration are described in the following table.

Application	Task
Server configuration	Manage and monitor shared folders
Accounts	Modify users and groups
Network connectivity	Monitor events
	Manage and monitor performance logs and alerts
	Start and stop services
Data storage	Manage data storage

Important With the Computer Management MMC, you do not need to be a local administrator on the server you are administering. You only need to have permissions to perform the specific tasks that you need to perform. To use Remote Desktop for Administration, you must have access to connect to the remote desktop on each server. By default, only members of the Administrators group and the Remote Desktop Users groups have the required permissions.

Remote Desktop for Administration tasks

The following table describes the use of each Remote Desktop for Administration tool.

Application	Task
Software applications	Install software applications
Server configuration	Defragment a disk
	Domain controller promotion/demotion
	Modify Microsoft .NET Framework configuration
	Modify folder options
Device drivers	Modify device drivers
Update software	Install service packs
	Install hotfixes
	Update system management properties
Desktop options	Modify date and time
	Modify display settings
	Modify fonts
	Modify regional and language settings
	Modify Distributed File System (DFS) services
Hardware configurations	Modify keyboard options
	Modify mouse options
	Modify modem options
	Modify power options
	Modify printer options
	Add and remove printers
Network connectivity	Modify Internet options
	Modify network connection configuration
	Monitor network connections
	Modify accessibility options
	Modify Internet Information Services (IIS) settings
Schedule tasks	Modify scheduled tasks
Accounts	Modify system options
	Modify user and group accounts
Licensing and certificate	Modify licensing
	Modify certificates
Remote services	Modify Component Services
	Modify Data Sources Open Database Connectivity (ODBC)
	Configure and enable Routing and Remote Access
	Modify Terminal Services
Data storage	Manage data storage

Practice: Configuring Remote Desktop to Administer a Server

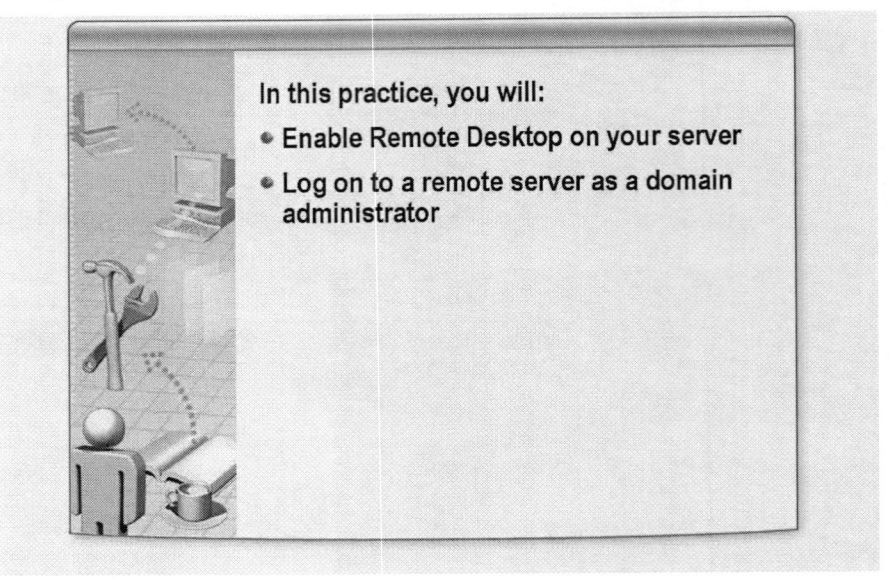

Objective

In this practice, you will:

- Enable Remote Desktop on your server.
- Log on to a remote server as a domain administrator.

Instructions

Ensure that the DEN-DC1 and DEN-CL1 virtual machines are running.

Practice

▶ **Enable Remote Desktop on your server**

1. Make sure that the DEN-DC1 virtual machine is the active Window. Press <RIGHT>ALT+DELETE.
2. Log on to the domain as **Administrator** with the password of **Pa$$w0rd**.
3. Click **Start**, right-click **My Computer**, and then click **Properties**.
4. On the **Remote** tab, in the **Remote Desktop** box, select the **Enable Remote Desktop on this compuer** check box. Click **OK** at the Remote Sessions dialog box.
5. Click **OK** to close all dialog boxes.

Practice

▶ **Log on to a remote server as a domain administrator**

1. Make sure that the DEN-CL1 virtual machine is the active window.
2. Log on as **Paul** with a password of **Pa$$w0rd**.
3. Click the **Start** menu, point to **All Programs**, point to **Accessories**, point to **Communications**, and then click **Remote Desktop Connection**.

   Alternately, you can open a command prompt and use the **mstsc** command to connect to DEN-DC1:

   mstsc /v:DEN-DC1 /f

4. Connect to the DEN-DC1 computer using the following parameters:

User name	Administrator
Password	Pa$$w0rd
Domain	Contoso

5. Verify that DEN-DC1 appears at the top of the screen.
6. Log off the remote computer.
7. Close all windows and log off of DEN-CL1 and DEN-DC1.

Important Do not shut down the virtual machines.

Lesson: Managing Remote Desktop Connections

- What Are Timeout Settings for Remote Desktop Connections?
- What Is Terminal Services Manager?
- Best Practices for Remote Administration
- Practice: Managing Remote Desktop Connections

Introduction

As a systems administrator, you must monitor users, sessions, and applications on the remote server and perform various tasks to manage the server connection. In this lesson, you will learn the importance of managing Remote Desktop Connection and learn how to terminate sessions that are no longer in use.

Lesson objectives

After completing this lesson, you will be able to:

- Explain timeout settings in Terminal Services Configuration.
- Explain Terminal Services Manager and when it is used.
- Describe best practices for remote administration.
- Manage and monitor remote desktop connections.

What Are Timeout Settings for Remote Desktop Connections?

- Remote connections consume valuable server resources
- Use timeout settings to preserve server resources

Timeout Settings	Description
End a disconnected session	Forces a user to log off after disconnecting
Active session limit	Disconnects the user after the time limit is exceeded
Idle session limit	Disconnects the user after the amount of idle time is exceeded

Introduction

Each Remote Desktop connection consumes valuable server resources. To ensure that resources are properly used, administrators should configure timeout settings for Remote Desktop connections.

Establish timeout sessions

You must establish timeout sessions for these connections because as long as a session is active, it continues to consume valuable server resources. When a session is disconnected but not logged off, that session is using one of two available connections to the server.

Log off a session

Logging off from a session ends the session that is running on the server. Any applications that are running in the session are closed, and unsaved data is lost.

Disconnect a session

After you establish a connection with a remote server, the connection remains open until you log off. When you disconnect from a session, the session continues to run on the server. The user can log on to the server and resume the session. The session remains open until the user logs off, until an administrator closes it, or until the timeout setting is reached.

Timeout options

Use Terminal Services Configuration to set the appropriate timeouts. The following timeout options are available when viewing the **Sessions** tab in the properties of **RDP-Tcp**:

- *End a disconnected session.* Allows you to set the maximum amount of time that a disconnected session remains open on a server.
- *Active session limit.* Allows you to set the maximum amount of time that a user's session can remain active on the server.
- *Idle session limit.* Allows you to set the length of time that a session can be idle before it is logged off.

By default the timeout options are configured per user in the Properties of each user. To override the user settings and use server based timeout options select the **Override user settings** check box. Group Policy can also be used to configure the timeout options for users or servers.

What Is Terminal Services Manager?

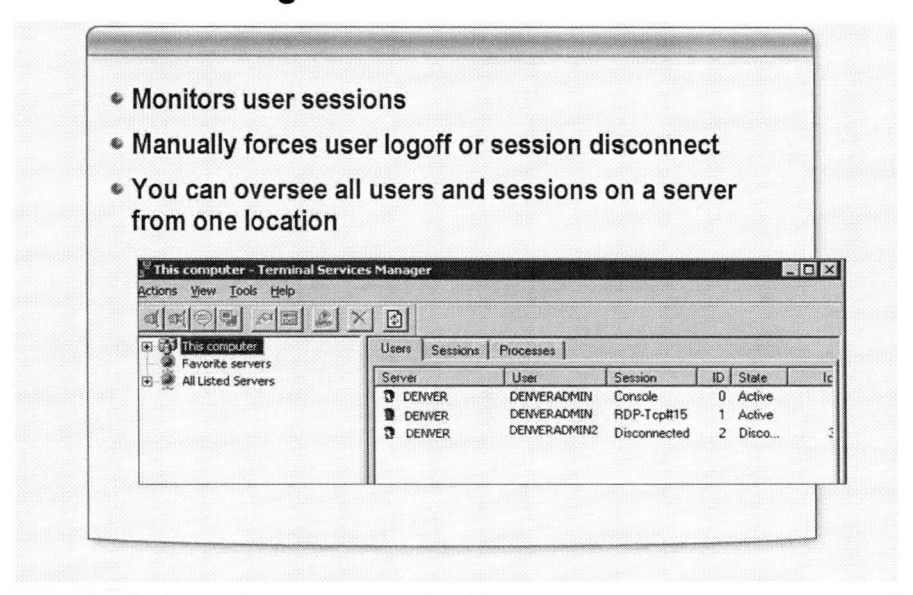

- Monitors user sessions
- Manually forces user logoff or session disconnect
- You can oversee all users and sessions on a server from one location

Introduction

You can use Terminal Services Manager to view information about Remote Desktop sessions on your server. Use this tool to monitor users and sessions on each server and to manage disconnected sessions from the remote server.

Obtain administrative information

Use Terminal Services Manager to obtain administrative information about the established Remote Desktop sessions. You can oversee all users and sessions on a terminal server from one location.

Monitor disconnected sessions

Using Terminal Services Manager, you can view the disconnected sessions on the server. Disconnected sessions display the word "Disconnected" under the Session and the State columns.

Important A disconnected session must be logged off in order to terminate it. It is important to log off all sessions when they are no longer in use, so that the limited number of remote connections can be used most efficiently.

Log off disconnected sessions

The **Log Off** command enables you to log off a user from a session on the server. Be aware that logging off a user without warning can result in loss of data at the user's session. When you log off a user, all processes end, and the session is deleted from the server.

Best Practices for Remote Administration

- Coordinate remote administration tasks with other administrators
- Use Terminal Services for application sharing
- Configure the Remote Desktop session to disconnect when connection is broken
- Configure disconnect and reset timeouts
- Avoid tasks that require reboots
- Avoid relying on server console messages

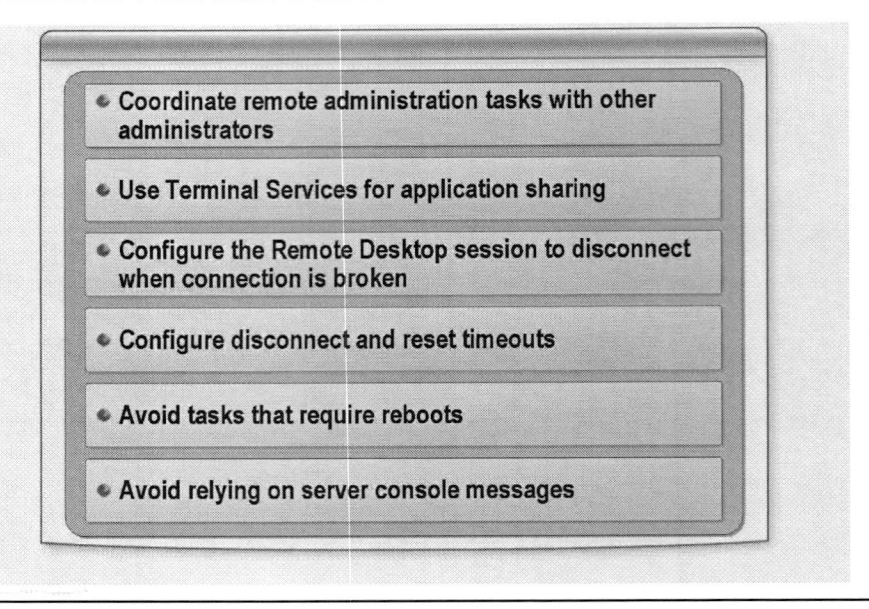

Introduction

Use the following best practices for Remote Administration.

Coordinate remote administration tasks with other administrators

The Remote Desktop feature of Windows Server 2003 is not meant to provide a managed multi-user experience. Using the two remote connections plus the console can implement a collaborative operation, but it is not designed to support general access by multiple simultaneous administrators. In particular, ensure that administrators do not run potentially destructive applications at the same time. For example, two administrators trying to reconfigure the disk subsystem can undermine each other's work, or even worse, destroy data. Use the Terminal Services Manager tool or the query user command line utility to check for the presence of other administrators.

Use Terminal Services for application sharing

Many general office applications require special installation, install scripts, or environment management to perform well in a remote session. Terminal Services provides these when you install Terminal Server, but they are not available for Remote Desktop for Administration. For general desktop and application remote access requirements, use a dedicated server with Terminal Server installed.

Configure the Remote Desktop session to disconnect when connection is broken

This is the default setting, and is especially important if you perform system updates over unreliable network connections. If a session is interrupted due to a network problem, the session goes into a disconnected state and continues executing the processes that were running before the interruption occurred. If the session is configured to reset when the connection breaks, all processes running in that session will stop, this is similar to stopping an application by using End Task.

Configure disconnect and reset timeouts

Because it is not possible to have more than two remote sessions, remote administrators might be locked out of a server if two remote sessions (using different user accounts) are in either an active or disconnected state. When configuring disconnect timeouts, it is critical that sessions that are disconnected do not get reset prematurely. If disconnected sessions are reset too quickly then minor network interruptions may stop lengthy tasks that are in progress, such as disk defragmentation or batch scripts.

Avoid tasks that require reboots	Some tasks, for example system upgrades and domain controller promotion, require reboots at their completion. These tasks work correctly from within a Remote Desktop session, but you should be aware that something as simple as a floppy disk in the drive or a bad boot sector on the disk could prevent the server from restarting. Therefore, it is advisable not to remotely reboot mission-critical servers unless you have the ability to physically intervene at the server if a problem occurs.
Avoid relying on server console messages	It is not possible to see server console messages when logging on using Terminal Services unless you are connected to the console session. Therefore, it is good practice to check the Server event logs, rather than rely on a system pop-up.

Practice: Managing Remote Desktop Connections

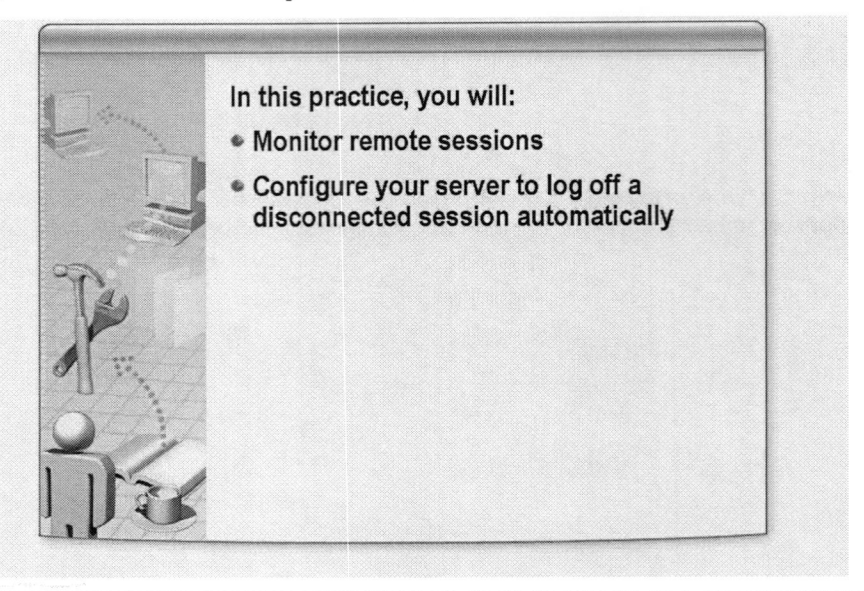

Objective

In this practice, you will:

- Monitor remote sessions.
- Configure your server to log off a disconnected session automatically.

Instructions

Ensure that the DEN-DC1 and DEN-CL1 virtual machines are running.

Practice

▶ **Monitor remote sessions**

1. On DEN-CL1, log on as **Paul** with a password of **Pa$$w0rd**.
2. On the **Start** menu, point to **All Programs**, point to **Accessories**, point to **Communications**, and then click **Remote Desktop Connection**.
3. Connect to the DEN-DC1 computer using the following parameters:

User name	Administrator
Password	Pa$$w0rd
Domain	Contoso

4. Verify that DEN-DC1 appears at the top of the screen.
5. Close the Remote Desktop window without logging off. Click **OK** in the **Disconnect Windows session** dialog box.
6. Switch to the DEN-DC1 virtual machine.
7. Log on as **Administrator** with a password of **Pa$$w0rd**.
8. Click **Start**, point to **Administrative Tools**, and then click **Terminal Services Manager**.
9. If a **Terminal Services Manager** message box appears, click **In the future, do not show this message**, and then click **OK**.
10. Right-click the disconnected session, and then click **Log Off**. Click **OK**.
11. Close Terminal Services Manager.

▶ **Configure your server to log off a disconnected session automatically**

1. Click **Start**, point to **Administrative Tools** and then click **Terminal Services Configuration**.
2. Right-click **RDP-Tcp** and then click **Properties**.
3. On the **Sessions** tab, click the **Override user settngs** check box, next to **End a disconnected session**, select **1 minute**, and then click **OK**.
4. Close Terminal Services Configuration.
5. Switch to the DEN-CL1 virtual machine.
6. On the **Start** menu, point to **All Programs**, point to **Accessories**, point to **Communications**, and then click **Remote Desktop Connection**.
7. Connect to the DEN-DC1 computer using the following parameters:

User name	Administrator
Password	Pa$$w0rd
Domain	Contoso

8. Verify that DEN-DC1 appears at the top of the screen.
9. Close the Remote Desktop window without logging off. Click **OK** in the **Disconnect Windows session** dialog box.
10. Switch to the DEN-DC1 virtual machine.
11. Click **Start**, point to **Administrative Tools**, and then click **Terminal Services Manager**.
12. View the disconnected session until it is removed in one minute.
13. Close Terminal Services Manager.
14. Log off of DEN-DC1 and DEN-CL1.

▶ **To prepare for the next lab**

- Start the DEN-SRV1 virtual machine.

Important Do not shut down the virtual machines.

Lab: Preparing to Administer a Server

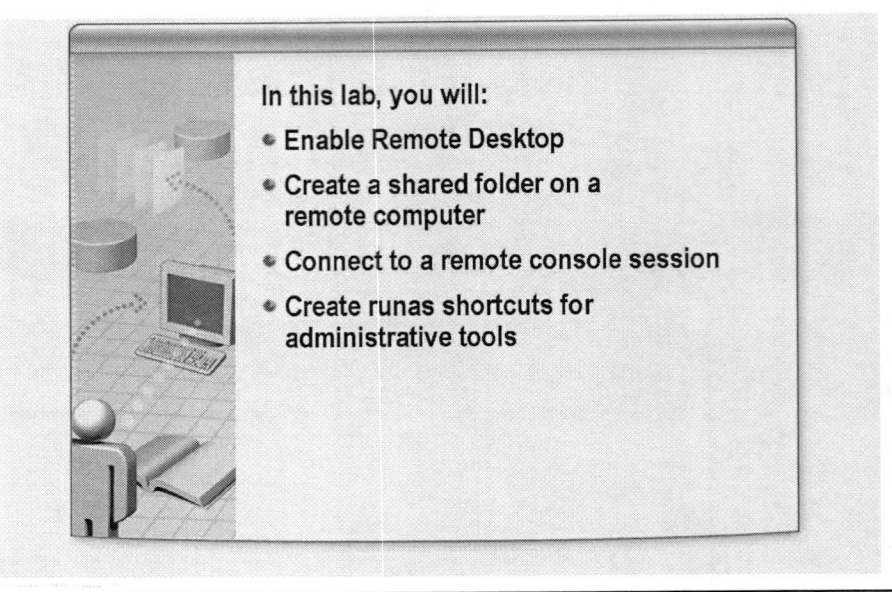

Objectives

After completing this lab, you will be able to:

- Enable remote desktop.
- Create a shared folder on a remote computer.
- Connect to a remote console session.
- Create **runas** shortcuts for administrative tools.

Instructions

Ensure that the DEN-DC1, DEN-SRV1 and DEN-CL1 virtual machines are running.

Scenario

You are a systems administrator for Contoso, Ltd. You want to configure a remote console session so that you can use your workstation to view the consoles of both DEN-DC1 and DEN-SRV1. You will also configure shortcuts for Administrative tools that run as Domain Administrator on DEN-SRV1.

Estimated time to complete this lab: 30 minutes

Exercise 1
Enabling Remote Desktop

You will enable Remote Desktop on DEN-SRV1 for remote administration.

Tasks	Specific instructions
1. Log on to DEN-SRV1 as domain Administrator.	▪ On DEN-SRV1, press<RIGHT>ALT+DELETE and log on as **Administrator** with a password of **Pa$$w0rd**.
2. Enable Remote Desktop.	a. Click **Start**, right-click **My Computer** and then click **Properties**. b. Click the Remote tab and then check the **Enable Remote Desktop on this computer** check box.

Exercise 2
Creating a Shared Folder on a Remote Computer

In this exercise, you will create a shared folder on a remote computer by using Computer Management and Remote Desktop Connection.

Tasks	Specific instructions
1. Log on to DEN-CL1 as Paul.	■ Press <RIGHT>ALT+DELETE and log on as **Paul** with a password of **Pa$$w0rd**.
2. Create a shared folder on DEN-DC1 using MMC1.	a. Use **Run as** to start MMC1 as Contoso\Administrator. b. Under Computer Management (DEN-DC1), click **Shares**. c. Create and share C:\DATA1. d. Configure Administrators to have full access and other users to have read-only access.
3. Create a shared folder on DEN-DC1 using Remote Desktop Connection.	a. Open Remote Desktop Connection and connect to DEN-DC1 as administrator. b. Open Computer Management on the remote computer. c. Create and share C:\DATA2. d. Configure Administrators to have full access and other users to have read-only access.
4. Log off from the remote connection.	■ Log off from the remote connection.

Exercise 3
Connecting to a Remote Console Session

In this exercise, you will connect to a remote console session by using Remote Desktop Connection.

Tasks	Specific instructions
1. Open Task Manager on DEN-SRV1.	a. Switch to DEN-SRV1. b. Right-click the task bar and then click **Task Manager**.
2. Use Remote Desktop Connection on DEN-CL1 to view the console on the DEN-SRV1 computer.	a. Switch to DEN-CL1. b. Run **MSTSC.exe** with the **/console** switch. c. Log on to the DEN-SRV1 console as **Administrator** with the password of **Pa$$w0rd**.
❓ What happens to the DEN-SRV1 virtual machine while you are viewing the console session from DEN-CL1?	
3. Close Task Manager through Remote Desktop Connection.	a. In the DEN-SRV1 remote window, close **Task Manager**. b. Log off of the remote DEN-SRV1 session. c. Close all windows on DEN-CL1 and then log off.

Exercise 4
Creating runas Shortcuts to Administration Tools

In this exercise, you will create shortcuts to commonly used administrative tools.

Tasks	Specific instructions
1. On DEN-SRV1, create a shortcut to Computer Management.	a. Log on to DEN-SRV1 as **Administrator** with the password of **Pa$$w0rd**. b. On the desktop create a shortcut to Computer Management using the following: **runas/user:contoso\administrator "mmc %windir%\system32\compmgmt.msc"**
2. Create a shortcut to Active Directory Users and Computers.	▪ On the desktop create a shortcut to Active Directory Users and Computers using the following: **runas/user:contoso\administrator "mmc %windir%\system32\dsa.msc"**
3. Test each shortcut.	▪ ITest each shortcut and verify that the correct tool appears.
4. Complete the lab exercise.	a. Close all programs and shut down all computers. Do not save changes. b. To prepare for the next module, start the DEN-DC1 and DEN-SRV1 virtual computers.

Module 2: Preparing to Monitor Server Performance

Contents

Overview	1
Lesson: Introduction to Monitoring Server Performance	2
Lesson: Performing Real-Time and Logged Monitoring	7
Lesson: Configuring and Managing Counter Logs	16
Lesson: Configuring Alerts	24
Lab: Preparing to Monitor Server Performance	35

Information in this document, including URL and other Internet Web site references, is subject to change without notice. Unless otherwise noted, the example companies, organizations, products, domain names, e-mail addresses, logos, people, places, and events depicted herein are fictitious, and no association with any real company, organization, product, domain name, e-mail address, logo, person, place or event is intended or should be inferred. Complying with all applicable copyright laws is the responsibility of the user. Without limiting the rights under copyright, no part of this document may be reproduced, stored in or introduced into a retrieval system, or transmitted in any form or by any means (electronic, mechanical, photocopying, recording, or otherwise), or for any purpose, without the express written permission of Microsoft Corporation.

The names of manufacturers, products, or URLs are provided for informational purposes only and Microsoft makes no representations and warranties, either expressed, implied, or statutory, regarding these manufacturers or the use of the products with any Microsoft technologies. The inclusion of a manufacturer or product does not imply endorsement of Microsoft of the manufacturer or product. Links are provided to third party sites. Such sites are not under the control of Microsoft and Microsoft is not responsible for the contents of any linked site or any link contained in a linked site, or any changes or updates to such sites. Microsoft is not responsible for webcasting or any other form of transmission received from any linked site. Microsoft is providing these links to you only as a convenience, and the inclusion of any link does not imply endorsement of Microsoft of the site or the products contained therein.

Microsoft may have patents, patent applications, trademarks, copyrights, or other intellectual property rights covering subject matter in this document. Except as expressly provided in any written license agreement from Microsoft, the furnishing of this document does not give you any license to these patents, trademarks, copyrights, or other intellectual property.

© 2005 Microsoft Corporation. All rights reserved.

Microsoft, Active Directory, ActiveX, Authenticode, BizTalk, IntelliMirror, MSDN, PowerPoint, Windows, Windows Media, Windows NT, and Windows Server are either registered trademarks or trademarks of Microsoft Corporation in the United States and/or other countries.

All other trademarks are property of their respective owners.

Overview

- Introduction to Monitoring Server Performance
- Performing Real-Time and Logged Monitoring
- Configuring and Managing Counter Logs
- Configuring Alerts

Introduction

Monitoring server performance is an important part of maintaining and administering an operating system. Routine performance monitoring ensures that you have up-to-date information on computer operation. Performance monitoring also provides data that you can use to predict growth and assess how proposed system configuration changes will affect system operation.

Objectives

After completing this module, you will be able to:

- Establish a performance baseline.
- Perform real-time and logged monitoring.
- Configure and manage counter logs.
- Configure alerts.

Lesson: Introduction to Monitoring Server Performance

- **Why Monitor Performance?**
- **Multimedia: Creating a Performance Baseline**
- **Guidelines for Establishing a Baseline**

Introduction

This lesson explains the concept of performance monitoring, a baseline, performance objects, and counters. It also describes how to establish a performance baseline.

Lesson objectives

After completing this lesson, you will be able to:

- Explain why administrators monitor performance.
- Explain what a baseline is and when to create one.
- Explain the guidelines for establishing a baseline.

Why Monitor Performance?

> - By monitoring performance, you obtain data that you can use to:
>   - Understand workload and its effect on system resources
>   - Identify resource-use trends
>   - Test proposed configuration changes
>   - Diagnose and optimize the system
> - Uncover bottlenecks

Introduction

Monitoring performance is a necessary part of preventive maintenance for your server. By routinely monitoring the performance of your server over periods ranging from days to weeks to months, you can establish a baseline for server performance. This information will provide comparative data that will support system analysis and problem solving.

Why monitor performance?

You use performance data to:

- Understand your workload characteristics and their corresponding effect on your system's resources.
- Observe changes and trends in workload characteristics and resource usage so you can plan for future upgrades.
- Monitor the effects of changes or other performance tuning efforts.
- Diagnose problems.
- Identify components or processes to be optimized optimization.

Analysis of performance data and bottlenecks

Analysis of performance data can reveal problems, such as excessive demand on certain resources that results in bottlenecks. A bottleneck exists when the performance of a resource adversely affects the performance of the whole system. Demand on the single resource may become excessive enough to cause a bottleneck of the four subsystems: memory, processor, disk, and network.

Some of the reasons that bottlenecks occur are:

- Subsystems are insufficient, so additional or upgraded components are required. For example, insufficient memory is a common cause of bottleneck.
- Subsystems are not sharing workloads evenly and need to be balanced. For example, an older network card that is installed on a new server may cause a bottleneck.
- A subsystem is malfunctioning and needs to be replaced. For example, abnormally low throughput on a network card may indicate that it is failing.
- A program is monopolizing a particular resource. For example, a program that was written by a consultant may not be sharing memory correctly.
- A subsystem is incorrectly configured. For example, an older multispeed network card may be configured for 10 megabits per second (Mbps) when it should be set to 100 Mbps.

Multimedia: Creating a Performance Baseline

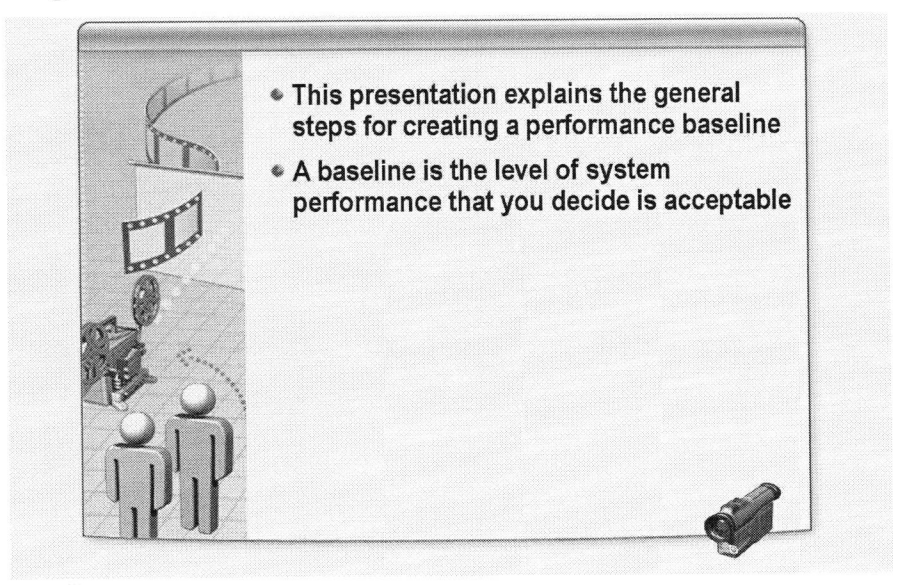

File location

To view the *Creating a Performance Baseline* presentation, open the Web page on the Student Materials compact disc, click **Multimedia**, and then click the title of the presentation.

Objectives

After completing this presentation you will be able to:

- Explain the purpose of a baseline.
- Describe how to use the Performance console.

Key points

Key points from the presentation are summarized in the following list:

- Baseline

    Take samples of counter values every 30 to 45 minutes for a week, during peak, low, and normal operations.

- General steps for creating a baseline

    a. Identify resources

    b. Capture data

    c. Store data

- Four major system resources for performance baselines
    - Memory
    - Processor
    - Physical disk
    - Network
- Performance object

    A performance object is the data generated by a system component or resource. Each performance object provides counters, which represent data about specific aspects of system performance. Performance objects can have multiple instances.

Guidelines for Establishing a Baseline

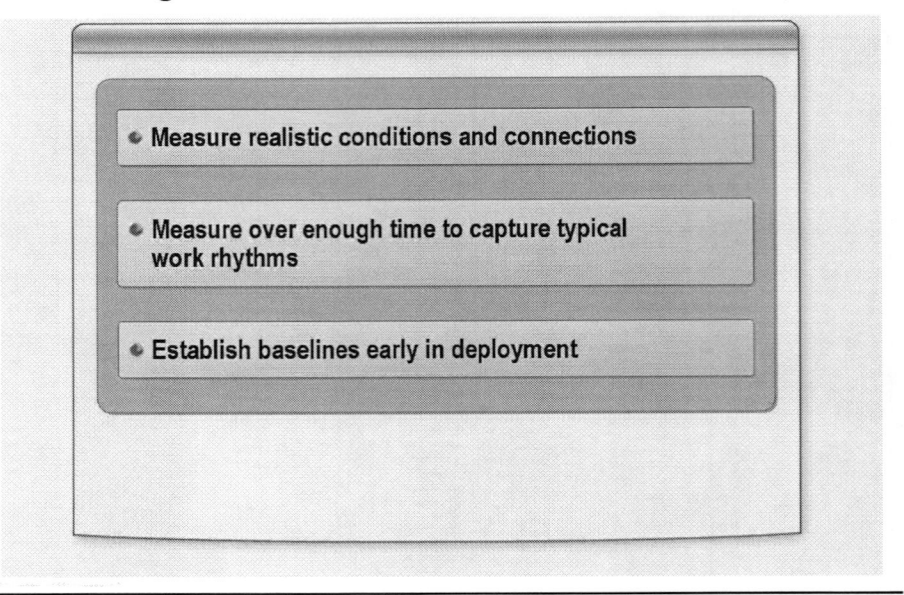

- Measure realistic conditions and connections
- Measure over enough time to capture typical work rhythms
- Establish baselines early in deployment

Introduction

You derive a baseline measurement from a collection of data over an extended period, during varying but typical workloads and network connections. The baseline is a measure of specified resource behavior during normal activity.

Factors to consider when determining a baseline

You should consider the following factors when determining a baseline:

- When you determine your baseline, it is important to know the type and timing of system load. This helps you associate kinds of load with resource usage and to determine whether the level of performance during those intervals is reasonable. Collect this performance data over an extended period of low, average, and peak usage, to understand acceptable system performance. This determination is your baseline.

  Observing performance over time you might see a pattern of performance showing the normal impact of simultaneous logon or logoff (at shift change) or the predictable slowdown during system backup. From observed performance and an understanding of cause and effect, you can determine acceptable performance.

- Baselines established early in the deployment phase support deployment problem solving.

Employing a baseline

You should consider the following factors when employing a baseline:

- Establishing a baseline early helps you to quickly identify and resolve system bottlenecks.
- Use your baseline to watch for long-term changes in usage patterns that require increased capacity.

Lesson: Performing Real-Time and Logged Monitoring

- What Is Real-Time and Logged Monitoring?
- What Is Task Manager?
- What Is the Performance Console?
- Why Monitor Servers Remotely?
- Practice: Performing Real-Time Monitoring

Introduction

The primary monitoring tools in Microsoft Windows Server 2003 are the Performance console and Task Manager.

This lesson describes how to perform monitoring by using Performance and Task Manager.

Lesson objectives

After completing this lesson, you will be able to:

- Explain real-time monitoring and logged monitoring.
- Describe Task Manager.
- Describe the Performance console.
- Explain the reasons for monitoring remote servers from a workstation.
- Monitor real-time performance.

What Is Real-Time and Logged Monitoring?

Real-Time Monitoring
- Monitors the system
- Processes and updates data from the operating system
- Documents the state of memory, processor, storage and network

Logged Monitoring
- Collects and stores data for a span of time
- Detects bottlenecks and records system changes
- Performed in Performance Logs and Alerts

Introduction

Administrators can use logged monitoring to monitor servers on a continuous basis. By configuring logged monitoring, you can establish a performance baseline and use trend analysis to identify server problems. For example, if users complain that an application server is gradually slowing down, you can check that server's log files to support problem analysis.

Administrators must also investigate specific problematic events. By enabling real-time monitoring, administrators can track events for analysis. For example, if a help-desk technician tells you that the printers attached to the print server are printing intermittently, a real-time monitor, such as Task Manager or System Monitor, will greatly aid investigation.

Real-time monitoring

With real-time monitoring, System Monitor processes and updates data counters as soon as the data is received from the operating system. You use real-time monitoring to establish the current state of the four subsystems: memory, processor, disk, and network. For example, if users complain about the slow response time of a client/server application in a situation that caused no previous problems, you can use System Monitor to diagnose the problem.

Logged monitoring

Logged monitoring involves collecting and storing data over time. Use the data to establish a baseline, detect bottlenecks, and recognize gradual system changes Use the Performance Logs and Alerts tool for logged monitoring.

Example of logged monitoring

For example, when your organization acquires a new server, to understand its capabilities, you can configure several counters to track memory usage, CPU usage, disk usage, and network usage. You can use the data that you collect to determine the normal range of counter values for your environment.

You can also set up logs to monitor events over time. This way, you can determine whether events such as backup, domain replication, or evenings and weekend remote connections contribute to server bottlenecks.

What Is Task Manager?

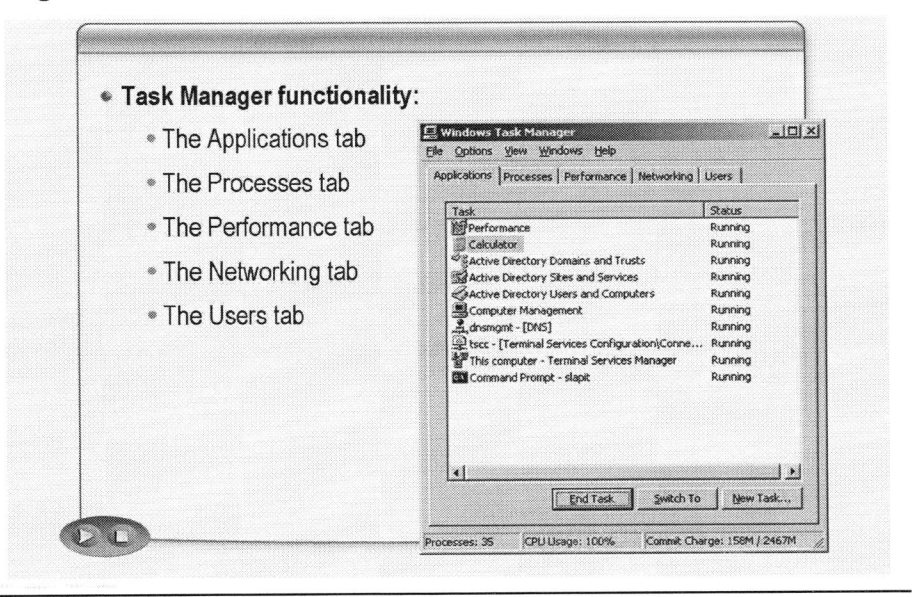

- **Task Manager functionality:**
  - The Applications tab
  - The Processes tab
  - The Performance tab
  - The Networking tab
  - The Users tab

Introduction

Task Manager provides an overview of system activity and performance. It provides information about programs and processes that are running on your computer. It also displays the most commonly used performance measures for processes. You can use Task Manager to perform real-time monitoring.

Task Manager function

Use Task Manager to monitor key performance indicators:

- View open programs status and end programs that are not responding.
- Assess the activity of running processes with up to 15 parameters and view graphs and data about CPU and memory usage.
- View network status when network card is installed.
- See connected users, see what files they are working, and send messages to users.

Task Manager has five tabs:

Applications tab

The **Applications** tab displays the status of open programs. On this tab, you can end, switch to, or start a program.

Processes tab

The **Processes** tab displays information about active processes. For example, you can display information about CPU and memory usage, page faults, handle count, and other parameters.

Performance tab

The **Performance** tab displays a dynamic overview of your computer's performance, including:

- Graphs of CPU and memory usage.
- The number of handles, threads, and processes running on your computer.
- The amount, in kilobytes, of physical, kernel, and commit memory. Physical memory is total memory, kernel memory is the memory that the system kernel and device drivers use, and commit memory is the amount of memory that is allocated to programs and the operating system.

Networking tab

The **Networking** tab displays a graphic representation of network performance. It provides a simple, qualitative indication of the network (or networks) status. The **Networking** tab displays only if a network card is installed.

On this tab, you can view the quality and availability of your network connections.

Users tab

The **Users** tab displays the names of users who have a local or remote session running on the computer. **Client Name** specifies the name of the client computer that the session is started from if it is remote. **Session** is either a console or the name of an RDP session that can be managed in the Terminal Services Manager snap-in.

What Is the Performance Console?

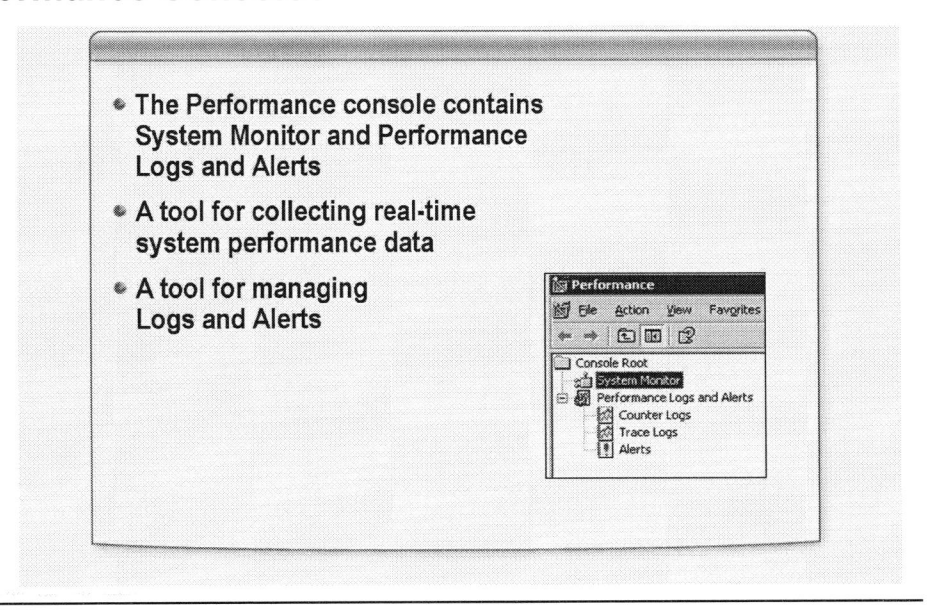

- The Performance console contains System Monitor and Performance Logs and Alerts
- A tool for collecting real-time system performance data
- A tool for managing Logs and Alerts

Introduction

Windows Server 2003 provides the following tools as part of the Performance console for monitoring resource usage on your computer:

- System Monitor
- Performance Logs and Alerts

System Monitor capabilities

With System Monitor, you can collect and view system services hardware resources and the activity data.

With System Monitor you can collect and view the real-time performance data of local or remote computers.

To setup data collection, specify performance objects, performance counters, and performance object instances.

- A *performance object* is a collection of counters associated with a monitored resource or service.
- A *performance counter* is a data item that is associated with a performance object. For selected counters, System Monitor displays a value representing a specific aspect of performance that corresponds to a performance object.
- *Performance object instances* are multiples of the same object type. For example, if a system has multiple processors, the **Processor** object type has multiple instances.

View logged counter data

You can view logged counter data with System Monitor. You can also export logged data to spreadsheet or database for analysis and report generation.

Using System Monitor, you can create graphs, histograms, and reports of the performance counter data. The graph view (default) offers the widest choice of settings.

View	Description
Graph	Supports real-time analysis of system processes
	Employs a time line to display counter data
Histogram	Supports processor bottleneck detection
	Employs a bar chart to display one value per counter instance
Report	Supports counter numerical value monitoring
	Employs a table to display one value per counter instance

Performance Logs and Alerts capabilities

Performance Logs and Alerts support both local and remote computers. Use logging for detailed analysis and record-keeping. Retaining and analyzing log data that is collected over time can be helpful for capacity and upgrade planning.

Collect performance data

With Performance Logs and Alerts, you can collect performance data by using two types of logs: counter logs and trace logs. You can also set an alert on a counter that sends a message, runs a program, or starts a log when the counter's value exceeds or falls below a specified setting.

Define settings

Use Performance Logs and Alerts to define settings for counter logs, trace logs, and alerts. The details pane of the console window shows counter logs and alerts that you have created. You can define multiple counter logs or alerts to run simultaneously. Each counter log or alert represents a saved configuration that you define.

If you configure the log for automatic starting and stopping, a single log can generate many individual log data files. For example, if you generate a log file for each day's activity, one file closes at 11:59 P.M., and a file to record the next day's activity opens immediately after.

Other functions

Data that Performance Logs and Alerts collect can be viewed during collection as well as after collection. Collection occurs regardless of whether any user is logged on to the computer that is being monitored.

You can define start and stop times, file names, file sizes, and other parameters for automatic log generation. You can manage multiple logging sessions from a single console window.

Why Monitor Servers Remotely?

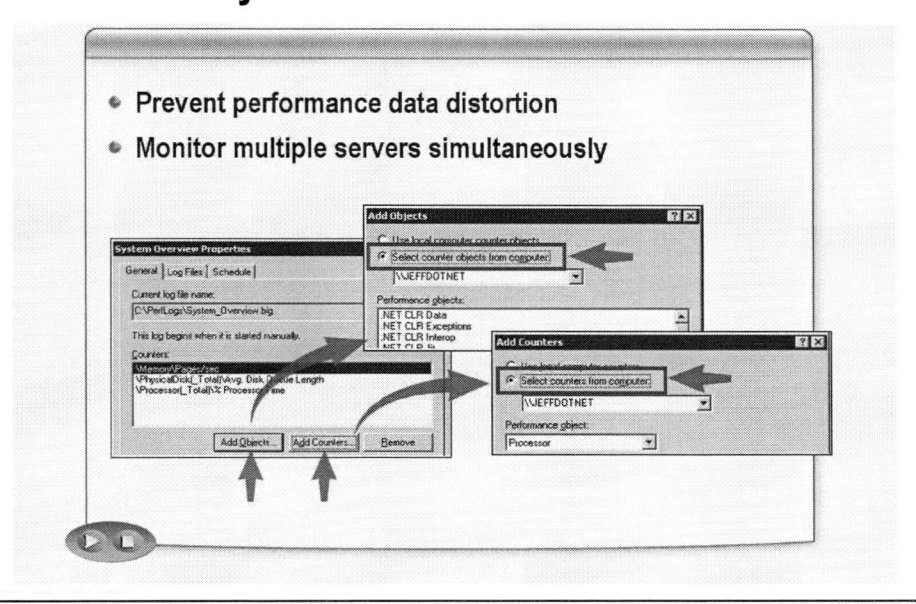

- Prevent performance data distortion
- Monitor multiple servers simultaneously

Why monitor a remote server from a workstation?

The additional load that Task Manager and Performance put on the server can cause misrepresentation of the data that you are collecting. By monitoring the server from a remote location, you reduce the likelihood of this misrepresentation occurring.

Also, administrators are often responsible for many servers making it impractical to monitor each individually.

Options in the Performance console for monitoring a remote server

The Performance console provides the following options that you can use to monitor a remote server:

- You can add objects or counters to a remote server. On the **General** tab, click **Add Objects** or **Add Counters**.
- You can log objects or counters from a computer regardless of where the service is run. Click **Select counter objects from computer** or **Select counters from computer**. Specify the name of the computer that you want to monitor, such as \\MyLogServer.

Counter availability

The counters for monitoring specific applications such as Exchange 2003 or SQL Server™ 2005 are installed on the server with the application. To use application specific counters when monitoring from a workstation, you must specifically install the counters on the workstation. Typically, counters are installed with application management and client tools.

Important If you plan to monitor remote computers, you must have been delegated the appropriate authority to gain access to them.

Practice: Performing Real-Time Monitoring

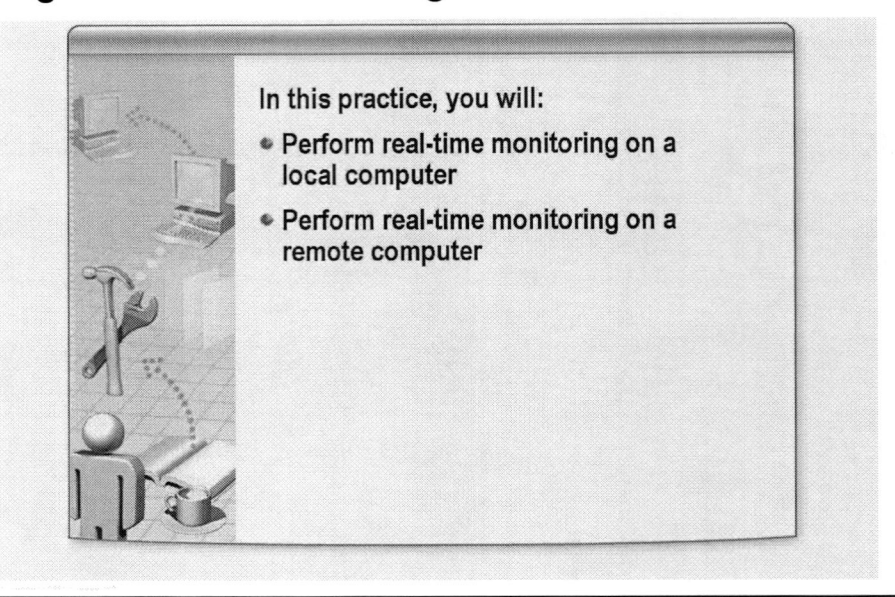

Objective

In this practice, you will:

- Perform real-time monitoring on a local computer.
- Perform real-time monitoring on a remote computer.

Instructions

Ensure that the DEN-DC1 and DEN-SRV1 virtual machines are running.

Practice

▶ **Perform real-time monitoring on a local computer**

1. On the DEN-DC1 virtual machine, log on as **Administrator** with a password of **Pa$$w0rd**.
2. Press <RIGHT>ALT+DELETE, and then click **Task Manager**.
3. Click the **Applications** tab. Notice that no applications are running.
4. Click **New Task**, and, in the **Open** box, type **calc** and then click **OK**. Notice that Calculator is now listed as an application.
5. Click the **Processes** tab and find calc.exe in the **Image Name** column. Notice the percentage of CPU utilization and memory usage.
6. Right-click **calc.exe** and then click **End Process**.
7. Click **Yes** to confirm ending the calc.exe process.
8. Click the **Performance** tab and view the level of CPU utilization and memory usage.
9. Close Task Manager.

▶ **Perform real-time monitoring on a remote computer**

1. On the DEN-DC1 virtual machine, click **Start**, point to **Administrative Tools**, and then click **Performance**. Notice that, by default, three counters are being monitored on the local computer: Memory:Pages/sec, PhysicalDisk:Avg. Disk Queue Length, and Processor:% Processor Time.

2. Click the graph and then press **CTRL+E** to create a new counter set (clear the existing counters).

3. Right-click the graph and then click **Add Counters**.

4. In the **Select counters from computer** box, type **\\DEN-SRV1**.

5. In the **Performance object** box, click **Processor**.

6. Click the **Select counters from list**, click **% Processor Time**, and then click **Add**.

7. In the **Performance object** box, click **Memory**.

8. Click the **Select counters from list**, click **Available MBytes**, and then click **Add**.

9. Click **Close**. Notice that the graph for both objects is fairly level, % Processor Time may show some small spikes in utilization.

10. On the DEN-SRV1 virtual machine, log in as **Administrator** with a password of **Pa$$w0rd**.

11. On the DEN-DC1 virtual machine, look at the changes in the graph. The % Processor Time spiked sharply and Available Mbytes has fallen as part of the logon process.

12. Close **Performance**.

Important Do not shut down the virtual machines.

Lesson: Configuring and Managing Counter Logs

- What Is a Counter Log?
- Counter Log File Formats
- Why Schedule Counter Logs?
- Practice: Configuring and Managing Counter Logs

Introduction

Use counter logs to gather data about various aspects of performance objects. For example, for the **Memory** object, counter logs gather data about available memory, cache memory, and virtual memory. Counter logs are built into the operating system and continually capture data.

Lesson objectives

After completing this lesson, you will be able to:

- Define counter, counter log, and counter log data.
- Explain the counter log file formats.
- Explain the reasons for scheduling a counter log.
- Configure and manage counter logs.

What Is a Counter Log?

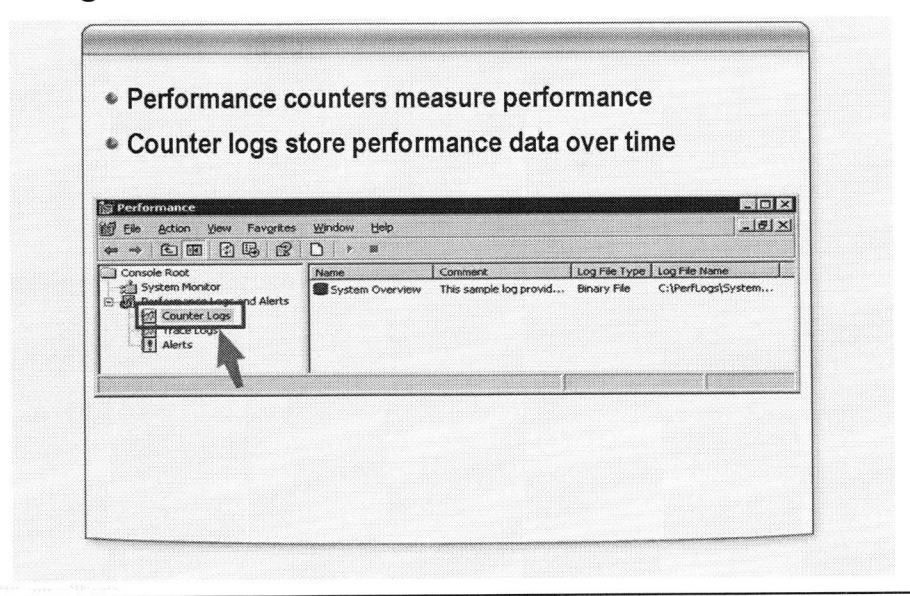

- Performance counters measure performance
- Counter logs store performance data over time

Introduction	Windows Server 2003 collects data about system resources, such as disks, memory, processors, and network components. This data is described as a performance object and is typically named for the component that generates the data. For example, the **Processor** object is a collection of performance data about the processors on your system.
Performance counter	A variety of performance objects are built into the operating system. Each performance object provides performance counters that represent data about specific aspects of a system or service. Counters are used to measure various aspects of performance. For example, the Pages/sec counter provided by the **Memory** object tracks the rate of memory paging.
Counter logs	Counter logs are counters that specify what data is stored in the log file. You use counter logs to select counters to collect performance data. You can use the Performance Logs and Alerts to create counter logs. In the interface, you select counter logs by using the **Counter Logs** option. The right pane of the Performance console window shows counter logs that you have created. You can define multiple counter logs to run simultaneously. Each counter log is a saved configuration that you define.

Counter log information in the Performance console

The following table describes the information about the counter logs that is provided by the columns in the right pane of the Performance console.

Column	Description
Name	The name of the counter log. It describes the type of data you are collecting or the condition you are monitoring.
Comment	Any descriptive information about the counter log.
Log File Type	The log file format that you define. For counter logs, this format can be binary, binary circular, text file (comma delimited), text file (tab delimited), or SQL.
Log File Name	The path and base file name that you defined for the files that are generated by this counter log. The base file name is used for automatically naming new files.

Counter log data

Counter log data is the information that you collect automatically from local or remote computers by configuring Performance Logs and Alerts.

Counter log data:

- Can be viewed by using System Monitor.
- Can be exported to spreadsheet programs or databases for analysis and generating reports.
- Is used to compare the values against the counter thresholds to verify that resource usage or other system activity is within acceptable limits.

Counter Log File Formats

Log File Format	Description	When to use
Text File (Comma delimited)	Comma-delimited log file (.csv)	Export to spreadsheet
Text File (Tab delimited)	Tab-delimited log file (.tsv)	Export to spreadsheet
Binary File	Sequential, binary-format log file (.blg)	Record intermittent data instances
Binary Circular File	Circular, binary-format log file (.blg)	Record continuously to same log file
SQL Database	Name SQL database and log set	Collect enterprise level performance data

The following table describes the log file formats that you can use to set file parameters for a counter log.

Log file format	Description	When to use
Text File (Comma delimited)	Defines a comma-delimited log file, with a .csv file extension.	Use this format, for example, to export the log data into a spreadsheet program.
Text File (Tab delimited)	Defines a tab-delimited log file, with a .tsv file extension.	Use this format, for example, to export the log data into a spreadsheet program.
Binary File	Defines a sequential, binary-format log file, with a .blg file extension. Only binary file formats can accommodate instances that are not persistent throughout the duration of the log.	Use this file format to record data instances that are intermittent—that is, stopping and resuming after the log begins to run. Use the **tracerpt** command-line tool to convert binary files into a comma-delimited log file.

(*continued*)

Log file format	Description	When to use
Binary Circular File	Defines a circular, binary-format log file, with a .blg file extension.	Use this file format to record data continuously to the same log file, overwriting previous records with new data when the file reaches its maximum size. Use the **tracerpt** command-line tool to convert binary files into a comma-delimited log file.
SQL Database	Defines the name of an existing SQL database and log set within the database where the performance data will be read or written.	Use this file format to collect performance data at an enterprise level rather than on a per-computer basis.

Use the text file format or the binary file format if you must export the data to a spreadsheet program later. The binary file format is more compact than the text file format, but you must convert it to the text file format before you export it to a spreadsheet. Use the **tracerpt** command-line tool to convert binary files into a comma-delimited log file. For example, type **tracerpt logfile.blg –o logfile.csv**.

Note Additional information about the **tracerpt** command-line tool can be found on the Tracerpt page of the Microsoft Windows XP Professional Product Documentation Web site.

Why Schedule Counter Logs?

> **Schedule counter logs to:**
> - Create a performance baseline
> - Determine the effect of replication between domain controllers
> - Identify bottlenecks resulting from morning login or evening remote access
> - Monitor evening backups for bottleneck
> - Scan for bottleneck related system slowdowns

Introduction

Imagine the cost of devoting staff to 24-hour system monitoring. Thankfully, this necessary task can be automated. You can schedule counter logs to create a performance baseline, look for bottlenecks, monitor system events, and collect information about how system events affect the server.

Why schedule counter logs?

You can schedule counter logs to:

- Create a performance baseline.
- Determine the effect on the overall system when replication occurs between domain controllers.
- Determine whether a bottleneck occurs when users log on in the morning.
- Determine whether a bottleneck occurs when users connect remotely in the evening.
- Determine whether Backup causes a bottleneck when it runs in the evening.
- Determine whether a bottleneck occurs during certain times of the day when users complain that the network slows down.

Practice: Configuring and Managing Counter Logs

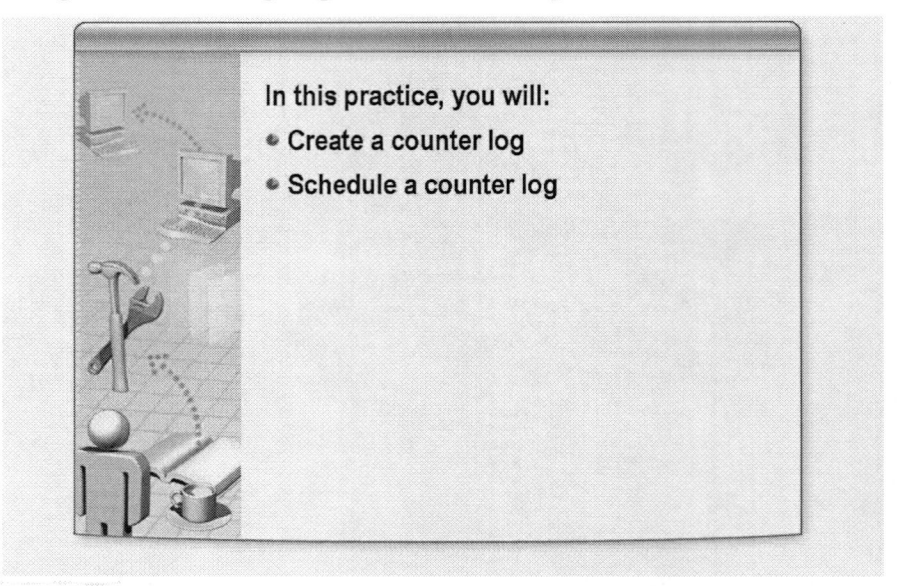

Objective

In this practice, you will:

- Create a counter log.
- Schedule a counter log.

Instructions

Ensure that the DEN-DC1 virtual machine is running.

Practice

▶ **Create a counter log**

1. On the DEN-DC1 virtual machine, click **Start**, point to **Administrative Tools**, and then click **Performance**.
2. Expand **Performance Logs and Alerts** and click **Counter Logs**.
3. Right-click **Counter Logs** and click **New Log Settings**.
4. In the **Name** box, type **PracticeLog** and then click **OK**. Notice that the default location of the log is C:\PerfLogs.
5. Click **Add Counters**.
6. In the **Select counters from computer** box, type \\DEN-DC1.
7. In the **Performance object** box, click **Processor**.
8. Click **Select counters from** list, click **% Processor Time**, and then click **Add**.
9. Click **Close**.
10. In the **Interval** box, type **1**.
11. Click the **Log Files** tab.
12. In the **Log file type** box, click **Text File (Comma delimited)**, and then click **OK**.
13. Click **Yes** to create the C:\PerfLogs folder. Notice that PracticeLog has a green icon to indicate it is running.

14. After about one minute, right-click **PracticeLog** and then click **Stop**.
15. To view the contents of the counter log, open the file C:\perflogs\PracticeLog_000001 in Notepad. Notice that the log file has a header row that describes the contents of the file.
16. Close Notepad.

▶ **Schedule a counter log**
1. In **Performance**, right-click **PracticeLog** and then click **Properties**.
2. Click the **Schedule** tab.
3. In the **Stop log** area, click **After**, and set time to 1 minute.
4. In the **Start log** area, click **At**, and set the time to be 2 minutes from now.
5. Click **OK**.
6. Wait two minutes and notice that the icon beside PracticeLog turns green to indicate that it is active.
7. Wait one minute and notice that the icon beside PracticeLog turns red to indicate that it has stopped.
8. Close **Performance**.

Important Do not shut down the virtual machines.

Lesson: Configuring Alerts

- What Is an Alert?
- Limitations of Alerts
- What Is Event Viewer?
- What Is EventCombMT?
- Practice: Configuring and Viewing Alerts

Introduction

Because administrators cannot constantly monitor all servers in the environment, administrators use alerts keep abreast of system performance that exceeds a set range. Performance Logs and Alerts are also used to collect hardware resource and system performance data.

Lesson objectives

After completing this lesson, you will be able to:

- Explain an alert.
- Explain limitations of alerts.
- Explain what Event Viewer is.
- Explain what EventCombMT is.
- Configure and view alerts.

What Is an Alert?

> - A feature that detects out of range values
> - A counter setting called a threshold
> - A mechanism that:
>   - Log events
>   - May send a message
>   - May start a counter log
>   - May initiate a program
> - A measure based on baselines

Definition

An *alert* is a feature that detects when a predefined counter value exceeds or falls below a specified setting. The specified setting on the counter is called the *alert threshold*. An action to notify administrators or fix the problem is initiated when an alert is triggered.

Why use alerts?

By using the alert feature, you can define a counter value that triggers actions, such as sending a network message, running a program, or starting a log.

Alerts are useful if you are not actively monitoring a particular counter threshold value but want to be notified when it exceeds or falls below a specified setting so that you can investigate and determine the cause of the change. For example, you can set an alert to notify you when the number of failed logon attempts exceeds a specified number.

You may want to set alerts based on established performance baseline values for your system.

Functions of an alert

You can set an alert on a counter to perform the following functions:

- Make an entry in the application event log.

  For example, enable this option if you want a record of all the events that cause an alert.

- Start a log when the selected counter's value exceeds or falls below the alert threshold.

  For example, a burdened processor indicates a bottleneck, you set an alert to take affect when usage exceeds 85 percent.

- Send a message.

  For example, in the previous bullet, an alert takes effect at 85 percent processor usage, sending the administrator a report.

- Run a program.

    Enable this option if you want a program to run when an event occurs. For example, you may want to trigger database compaction when disk space is getting low.

Note To send a message, the Messenger service must be running. This service is disabled by default in Windows Server 2003.

Limitations of Alerts

- Permissions constrain alert creation
- Dependent services constrain alert actions
  - Example: Messenger service
- Faulty remote connections impair the reliability of alerts

Introduction

Alerts are useful because they are an active way to monitor what is happening on a server, but users need to be aware of their limitations.

Limitations of alerts

Alerts are also subject to limitations some important limitations:

- Security permissions

    Some users are unable to configure alerts. Creating an alert requires administrative permissions on the computer being monitored. When alerts are being configured by someone not logged in with an administrative account, alerts have an option to configure an account with administrative permissions in the **Run As** box.

- Dependent services

    The triggering of alerts is managed by the Performance Logs and Alerts Service, and this service has no dependencies. However the actions specified for an alert may have dependencies.

    For example, if you configure an alert to send a network message to the Administrator, this action is dependent upon the Messenger service. It must be running on the monitored server and on the administrator workstation to enable the message transmission.

- Network communication for remote monitoring

    We noted in an earlier module the benefits of remote performance monitoring, however, this strategy is limited by the quality of the network connection. If there are network communication problems then alerts may not be triggered by the remote server. In addition, if you are monitoring network performance and generating statistics, any connection problem that impedes transmission of data will affect the accuracy of recorded data.

What Is Event Viewer?

- A tool for viewing and configuring event logs
- A way to view the application log
- A collection of log files with a 16 MB default size
- Filter events based on type, source, computer, and time

What is Event Viewer?

With Event Viewer, you can monitor events recorded in event logs. Typically a computer stores events the Application, Security, and System logs. Additional event logs may be created, depending on the computer's role and the installed applications. For example, when you install the DNS service on a computer running Windows Server 2003, a DNS Server log is also created on the server.

Application log

The Application log contains events written by alerts that have been triggered by applications or services running on the computer. Using Event Viewer, you can:

- Configure log settings
- Filter events

Log settings

In the properties of the Application log, the **General** tab allows you to determine log-size limits, action when limits are reached, and clear the log.

The maximum size of the Application log should be high enough to assure important events are not missed. If the Application log size is too small, then a problem occurring on the weekend might fill the entire log and push out the original entries that may provide clues to the cause of the problem. The default application log size of 16 megabytes (MB) is sufficient for most situations.

You configure how events will be logged in the Application log when it has reached its maximum size. You can configure the application log to overwrite events, to only overwrite events older than seven days, or to never overwrite events. If a log is full and overwriting is constrained, no new events can be captured.

Filter events

An Application log may contain thousands of events. Filtering the Application log makes it easier to find relevant information, including alerts. You can configure Application log filtering based on:

- Event type
- Event source
- Computer
- Time

What Is EventCombMT?

> - A utility for parsing event logs on multiple servers
> - Searching can be based on:
>   - Event ID
>   - Event type
>   - Source
>   - Log
> - Finds alerts on many servers quickly

What is EventCombMT? EventCombMT is a multithreaded tool that parses event logs from many servers at the same time, spawning a separate thread of execution for each server that is defined in the search criteria.

Note EventCombMT is included with the Windows Server 2003 Resource Kit. The Resource Kit tools can be downloaded from the Microsoft Download Center Web site.

Search capabilities EventCombMT allows you to:

- Define either a single Event ID, or multiple Event IDs to search for.

  You can include a single event ID, or multiple event IDs separated by spaces.

- Define a range of Event IDs to search for.

  The endpoints are inclusive. For example, if you want to search for all events between and including Event ID 528 and Event ID 540, you would define the range as 528 > ID < 540. This feature is useful because most applications that write to the event log use a sequential range of events. This means you can easily get a list of all events generated by a particular application.

- Limit the search to specific event logs.

  You can choose to search the system, application, and security logs. If executed locally at a domain controller, you can also choose to search FRS, DNS and Active Directory® directory service logs.

- Limit the search to specific event message types.

  You can choose to limit the search to error, informational, warning, success audit, failure audit, or success events.

EventCombMT and alerts

An alert writes events to the local Application log. In a multiple-server scenario, it is tedious to check the Application log on each server daily. You can use EventCombMT to simultaneously search many servers for alerts.

Practice: Configuring and Viewing Alerts

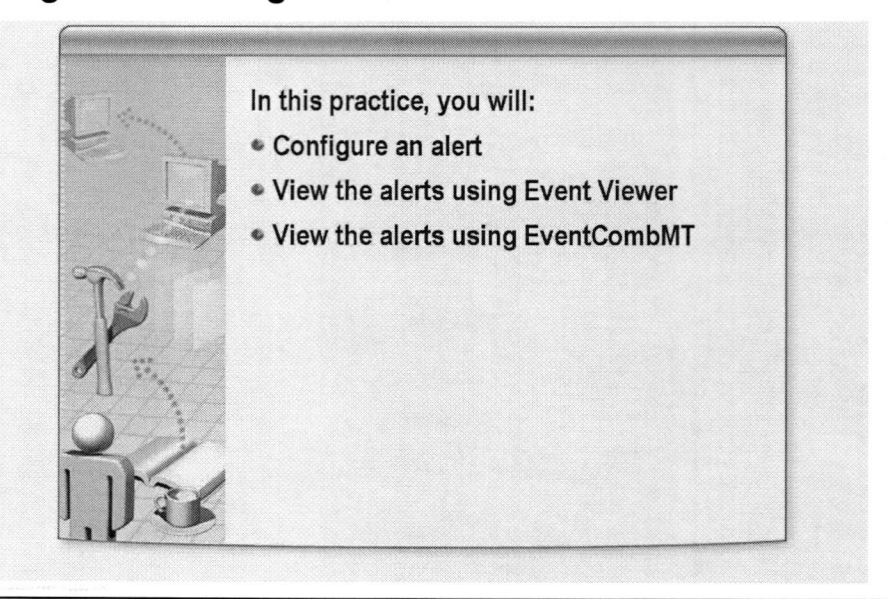

Objective

In this practice, you will:

- Configure an alert.
- View the alerts using Event Viewer.
- View the alerts using EventCombMT.

Instructions

Ensure that the DEN-DC1 and DEN-SRV1 virtual machines are running.

Practice

▶ **Configure an alert**

1. On the DEN-DC1 virtual machine, click **Start**, point to **Administrative Tools**, and then click **Performance**.
2. Expand **Performance Logs and Alerts** and then click **Alerts**.
3. Right-click **Alerts** and then click **New Alert Settings**.
4. In the **Name** box, type **PracticeCPUAlert**, and then click **OK**.
5. Click **Add**.
6. In the **Select counters from computer** box, type **\\DEN-DC1**.
7. In the **Performance object** box, click **Processor**.
8. Click the **Select counters from** list, click **% Processor Time**, and then click **Add**.
9. Click **Close**.
10. In the **Limit** box, type **80**.
11. Click the **Action** tab. Notice that writing an alert to the Application log is selected by default.
12. Click the **General** tab.
13. Click **Add**.
14. In the **Select counters from computer** box, type **\\DEN-SRV1**.

15. In the **Performance object** box, click **Processor**.
16. Click the **Select counters from** list, click **% Processor Time**, and then click **Add**.
17. Click **Close**.
18. In the **Limit** box, type **80**.
19. In the **Run As** box, type **Administrator** and then click **Set Password**.
20. Enter **Pa$$w0rd** in both the **Password** and **Confirm Password** fields and then click **OK**.
21. Click the **Action** tab. Notice that writing an alert to the Application log is selected by default.
22. Click **OK**.
23. Close **Performance**.
24. Press <RIGHT>ALT+DELTE, and then click **Task Manager**.
25. Click the **Performance** tab.
26. Click **Start**, click **Run**, type **D:\2275\Practices\Mod02 \CPULoop.bat**, and then click **OK**. Notice that the CPU Usage rises above 80 percent.
27. After approximately one minute, close the cmd window.
28. Close **Task Manager**.

▶ **View the alerts using Event Viewer**

1. On the DEN-DC1 virtual machine, click **Start**, point to **Administrative Tools**, and then click **Event Viewer**.
2. In the left pane, click **Application**.
3. There are several **Information** events with a source of SysmonLog. Double-click one of them.
4. Read the description portion of the event. It indicates that the \\DEN-DC1\Processor(_Total)\%Processor Time counter was over 80 percent.
5. Click **Cancel** and then close Event Viewer.

▶ **View the alerts using EventCombMT**

1. On the DEN-SRV1 virtual machine, click **Start**, click **Run**, type **\\DEN-DC1\D$\2275\Practices\Mod02\cpuloop.bat**, and then click **OK**. Click **Run** at the security warning.
2. After approximately one minute, close the cmd window.
3. On DEN-DC1, click **Start**, click **Run** and then, in the **Run** dialog box, type **D:\2275\Practices\Mod02\eventcombMT.exe**. Click **OK**.
4. Click **OK** to close the **Simple Instructions** dialog box.
5. Ensure that **contoso.msft** is listed in the **Domain** box.
6. Right-click the text box below **Select To Search/Right Click to Add**. A context menu appears.
7. Click **Get DCs in Domain**. DEN-DC1 appears in the list.
8. In the **Choose Log Files to search** section, clear the **System** check box and select **Application**.

9. Select the **Error, Informational,** and **Warning Event Types** check boxes.
10. In the box before > **ID** <, type **2031**. In the box after > **ID** <, type **2037**.
11. Ensure that **ALL SOURCES** is displayed.
12. Click **DEN-DC1** and then click **Search**.
13. Double-click **EventCombMT.txt** and maximize Notepad. Notice that the file includes event information for DEN-DC1.
14. Close Notepad.
15. Double-click **DEN-DC1-Application_LOG.txt** to view the events recorded.
16. Close Notepad and Windows Explorer.
17. In the EventCombMT utility, click the **Searches** menu, and then click **Save This Search**.
18. Type **CPU Usage**, and then click **OK**.

▶ **To prepare for the next module**
1. Close all programs and shut down all computers. Do not save changes.
2. To prepare for the next module, start the DEN-DC1 virtual computer.

Lab: Preparing to Monitor Server Performance

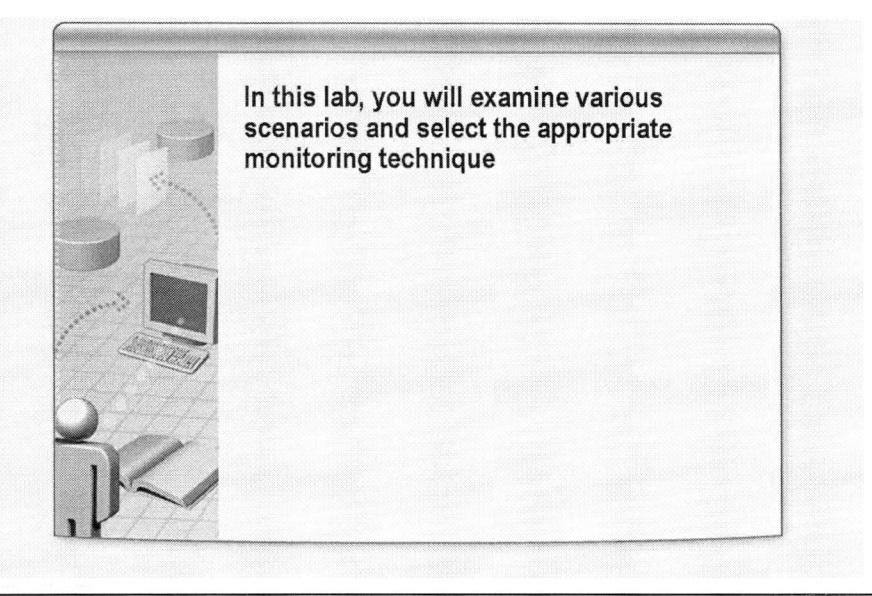

Objectives

After completing this lab, you will be able to:

- Examine various scenarios and select the appropriate monitoring technique.

Prerequisites

None.

Estimated time to complete this lab: 20 minutes

Exercise 1
Selecting the Appropriate Monitoring Technique

In this exercise, you will select the appropriate monitoring technique based on the following scenarios. R=Real Time, L=Logging, A=Alerts. If more than one technique will work, put your selections in order of preference.

Scenario	Monitoring technique(s)
1. Determine when the hard disk is running out of free space.	
2. Provide management with information that can be used for budgeting purposes.	
3. Determine the number of users that a specific server configuration should support.	
4. Analyze a trend.	
5. Monitor multiple servers.	
6. Determine when to increase capacity.	
7. Find intermittent performance problems.	
8. Investigate why a computer application is slow or inefficient.	
9. Determine when to add additional system resources.	
10. Determine when to upgrade the system.	
11. Determine how a server should be used.	
12. Determine expected response times for specific numbers of users and system use.	
13. Analyze data to find and resolve abnormalities in the system use.	
14. Monitor use over time.	
15. Determine a preventive maintenance schedule for your servers.	
16. Create a baseline for a server.	
17. Monitor the effects of replication.	
18. Troubleshoot a server.	
19. Plan for growth.	
20. Find a slow memory leak.	

(*continued*)

Scenario	Monitoring technique(s)
21. Find a fast memory leak.	
22. Monitor intermittent disk thrashing.	
23. Monitor continuous disk thrashing	
24. Monitor a remote computer.	
25. Respond to user complaints that a server seems to be running slowly.	
26. Monitor a computer 24 hours a day, seven days a week.	

THIS PAGE INTENTIONALLY LEFT BLANK

Module 3: Monitoring Server Performance

Contents

Overview	1
Multimedia: The Primary Server Subsystems	2
Lesson: Monitoring Server Memory	3
Lesson: Monitoring Processor Usage	10
Lesson: Monitoring Disks	16
Lesson: Monitoring Network Usage	23
Lesson: Monitoring Best Practices	30
Lab: Monitoring Server Performance	41

Information in this document, including URL and other Internet Web site references, is subject to change without notice. Unless otherwise noted, the example companies, organizations, products, domain names, e-mail addresses, logos, people, places, and events depicted herein are fictitious, and no association with any real company, organization, product, domain name, e-mail address, logo, person, place or event is intended or should be inferred. Complying with all applicable copyright laws is the responsibility of the user. Without limiting the rights under copyright, no part of this document may be reproduced, stored in or introduced into a retrieval system, or transmitted in any form or by any means (electronic, mechanical, photocopying, recording, or otherwise), or for any purpose, without the express written permission of Microsoft Corporation.

The names of manufacturers, products, or URLs are provided for informational purposes only and Microsoft makes no representations and warranties, either expressed, implied, or statutory, regarding these manufacturers or the use of the products with any Microsoft technologies. The inclusion of a manufacturer or product does not imply endorsement of Microsoft of the manufacturer or product. Links are provided to third party sites. Such sites are not under the control of Microsoft and Microsoft is not responsible for the contents of any linked site or any link contained in a linked site, or any changes or updates to such sites. Microsoft is not responsible for webcasting or any other form of transmission received from any linked site. Microsoft is providing these links to you only as a convenience, and the inclusion of any link does not imply endorsement of Microsoft of the site or the products contained therein.

Microsoft may have patents, patent applications, trademarks, copyrights, or other intellectual property rights covering subject matter in this document. Except as expressly provided in any written license agreement from Microsoft, the furnishing of this document does not give you any license to these patents, trademarks, copyrights, or other intellectual property.

© 2005 Microsoft Corporation. All rights reserved.

Microsoft, Active Directory, ActiveX, Authenticode, BizTalk, IntelliMirror, MSDN, PowerPoint, Windows, Windows Media, Windows NT, and Windows Server are either registered trademarks or trademarks of Microsoft Corporation in the United States and/or other countries.

All other trademarks are property of their respective owners.

Overview

- **Multimedia: The Primary Server Subsystems**
- **Monitoring Server Memory**
- **Monitoring Processor Usage**
- **Monitoring Disks**
- **Monitoring Network Usage**
- **Monitoring Best Practices**

Introduction

Today's business environment demands that systems administrators ensure that their servers are efficient and reliable. To optimize your server's performance, you must collect performance data that helps you to identify system bottlenecks.

This module covers how to collect performance data by monitoring primary server subsystems. It also covers how to identify system bottlenecks by using the Performance console and Task Manager in Microsoft® Windows Server™ 2003.

Objectives

After completing this module, you will be able to:

- Explain how the four primary server subsystems affect server performance.
- Monitor server memory.
- Monitor processor usage.
- Monitor disks.
- Monitor network usage.
- Use best practices for monitoring server performance.

Multimedia: The Primary Server Subsystems

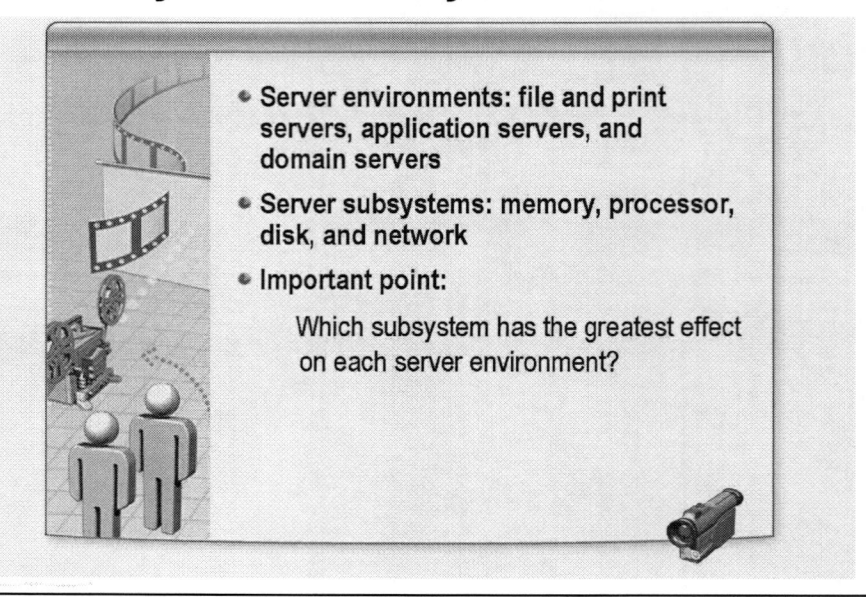

File location

To view the presentation *The Primary Server Subsystems,* open the Web page on the Student Materials compact disc, click **Multimedia**, and then click the title of the presentation. Do not open this presentation unless the instructor tells you to do so.

Objective

After completing this lesson, you will be able to describe the effect of each primary subsystem on server performance.

Server subsystems

The four primary subsystems are:

- Memory

    Server memory is the subsystem that is most important to general server performance. If the server does not have enough random access memory (RAM) to hold the data that it needs, it must temporarily store the data on the disk. Disk access is much slower than RAM, so storing data on the disk can significantly degrade server performance.

- Processor

    The most important aspect of processor performance is its level of usage. When an application or other software uses more than its share of the processor's cycles, all the other software that is running operates much more slowly.

- Disk

    The access speed of the physical disk drive can greatly affect the speed at which applications operate and data is loaded. Also, the disk storage space must be sufficient for you to install applications, store data, and have enough space for the paging file.

- Network

    The performance of your network is affected by the speed of both the hardware in your network infrastructure and the software that is running on your servers and clients.

Lesson: Monitoring Server Memory

- Why Monitor Server Memory?
- Identify and Resolve Memory Bottlenecks
- Practice: Monitoring Server Memory

Introduction

Memory significantly affects server performance. Low memory conditions can slow the operation of applications and services on your server and can also affect the performance of other resources on your server. Therefore, monitoring and analyzing memory usage is one of the first steps to take when you assess the performance of your server.

Lesson objectives

After completing this lesson, you will be able to:

- Explain the purpose of monitoring server memory.
- Identify and resolve memory bottlenecks.
- Monitor memory by using server monitoring tools.

Why Monitor Server Memory?

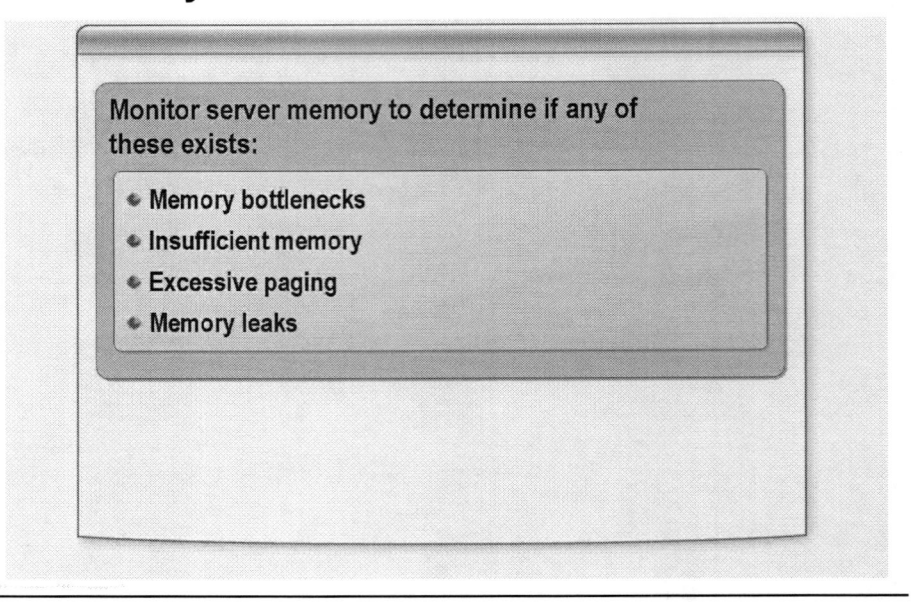

> Monitor server memory to determine if any of these exists:
> - Memory bottlenecks
> - Insufficient memory
> - Excessive paging
> - Memory leaks

Introduction

Lack of memory is the most common cause of serious performance problems in computer systems. Even if you suspect other problems, check memory counters to rule out a memory shortage.

Conditions to look for

Monitor server memory to assess the amount of available memory and the level of paging, and to observe the effects of a memory shortage. Monitoring server memory can help you determine whether any of the following conditions exists:

- Memory bottleneck

    Low memory conditions can slow the operation of applications and services on your server and can impact the performance of other resources on your server. For example, when your server is low on memory, paging can be prolonged, resulting in more work for your disks. Because it involves reading and writing to disk, this paging activity may compete with other disk transactions, thereby intensifying a disk bottleneck.

    In turn, all this work by the disk can mean that the processor is used less or is doing unnecessary work, such as processing numerous interrupts due to repeated page faults. *Page faults* occur when the server cannot locate requested code or data in the physical memory that is available to the requesting process. As a result, applications and services become less responsive. Therefore, it is important to monitor memory regularly to detect memory bottlenecks.

- Insufficient memory

    Insufficient memory is the reason for the symptoms we encounter with low memory, and excessive paging. By monitoring server memory, you can use the baseline established to predict when you will need additional memory, and avoid some of these problems.

- Excessive paging

    The indication of memory shortage is frequent paging. *Paging* is the process of moving fixed-size blocks of code and data from RAM to disk by using units called *pages* to free memory for other uses.

    Although some paging is acceptable, because it enables you to use more memory than actually exists, constant paging slows server performance. Reducing paging significantly improves server responsiveness.

- Memory leak

    A memory leak occurs when applications allocate memory for use but do not free allocated memory when finished. As a result, available memory is used up over time, often causing the server to stop functioning properly.

Identify and Resolve Memory Bottlenecks

Memory counter	Acceptable average range	Desired value	Action
Pages/sec	Below 5	Low	Find the process that is causing paging Add RAM
Available Bytes	Minimum of 5% of total memory	High	Find the process that is using RAM Add RAM
Committed Bytes	Less than physical RAM	Low	Find the process that is using RAM Add RAM
Pool Nonpaged Bytes	Remain steady, no increase	Not applicable	Check for memory leak in application

Introduction

It is very important to understand how memory bottlenecks are resolved because they are so common. Adding additional memory is the most effective way to improve server performance.

Paged and nonpaged RAM

In Windows Server 2003, RAM is divided into two categories: paged and nonpaged. Paged RAM is virtual memory. Windows Server 2003 gives each application a private memory range called a *virtual memory space* and by mapping that virtual memory to physical memory. To each application the virtual memory space appears to be the full memory range of the computer.

Nonpaged RAM cannot use virtual memory. Data that is placed into nonpaged RAM must remain in memory and cannot be written to or retrieved from disk. For example, data structures that are used by interrupt routines or those that prevent multiprocessor conflicts within the operating system use nonpaged RAM.

Virtual memory system

The virtual memory system in Windows Server 2003 combines physical memory, the file system cache, and disk into an information storage and retrieval system. The system stores program code and data on disk until it is needed, and then moves it into physical memory. Code and data that are no longer in active use are written to disk. However, when a computer does not have enough memory, code and data must be written to and retrieved from the disk more frequently—a slow, resource-intensive process that can become a system bottleneck.

Hard-page faults

The best indicator of a memory bottleneck is a sustained, high rate of hard-page faults. *Hard-page faults* occur when the data that a program requires is not found in its working set (the physical memory visible to the program) or elsewhere in physical memory, and must be retrieved from disk. Sustained hard-page fault rates—over five per second—indicate a memory bottleneck.

Counters used to determine whether memory is a bottleneck

Use the following Performance memory counters to determine whether memory is causing a bottleneck in the system.

The following list includes two types of counters. The first type of counter is a rate counter, such as Pages/sec and Page Faults/sec. A rate counter samples an increasing count of events over time. To display the rate of activity, the rate counter divides the cache in count values by the change in time. Therefore, to obtain an accurate result, you must monitor rate counters over time—typically for 30 to 60 seconds.

The second type of counter is an instantaneous counter, such as Available Bytes and Committed Bytes. Instantaneous counters display the most recent measurement.

- *Pages/sec*. Number of requested pages that were not immediately available in RAM, and thus were accessed from the disk or were written to the disk to make room in RAM for other pages. Generally, if the value of this counter exceeds five for extended periods, memory may be a bottleneck in the system. Also, if multiple pagefiles are in use and spread across multiple physical disks then the impact of paging is reduced and the pages/sec may exceed five without affecting performance.

- *Available Bytes*. Amount of available physical memory. Available Bytes is normally low, because Windows Disk Cache Manager uses extra memory for caching and then returns memory when requests for memory occur. However, if Available Bytes is consistently below 5 percent of the total memory on a server, it is an indication that excessive paging is occurring.

- *Committed Bytes*. Amount of virtual memory that is committed to either physical RAM for storage or to pagefile space. If the amount of committed bytes is larger than the amount of physical memory, more RAM may be required.

- *Pool Nonpaged Bytes*. Amount of RAM in the nonpaged pool system memory area where space is acquired by operating system components as they accomplish their tasks. If the Pool Nonpaged Bytes value shows a steady increase without a corresponding increase in activity on the server, it may indicate that a process with a memory leak is running, and you should monitor it closely.

In Task Manager, to determine whether memory is causing a bottleneck in the system, use the PF Usage memory counter. This counter displays the amount of paging used by the system. A steady increase may indicate that a running process has a memory leak.

Actions to resolve memory bottleneck

If you determined that the memory is a system bottleneck, you can perform the following actions to improve performance:

- In systems with a high number of page faults, add additional memory to reduce the number of page faults.

- In systems with a high number of page faults, move some processes to a different server to reduce load.

- If a memory leak is suspected in a process, identify the process and resolve the leak. A memory leak is resolved by fixing the offending process. For prepackaged software memory leaks are often fixed in service packs. For customized and internally developed software you much contact the developers to fix the problem.

Practice: Monitoring Server Memory

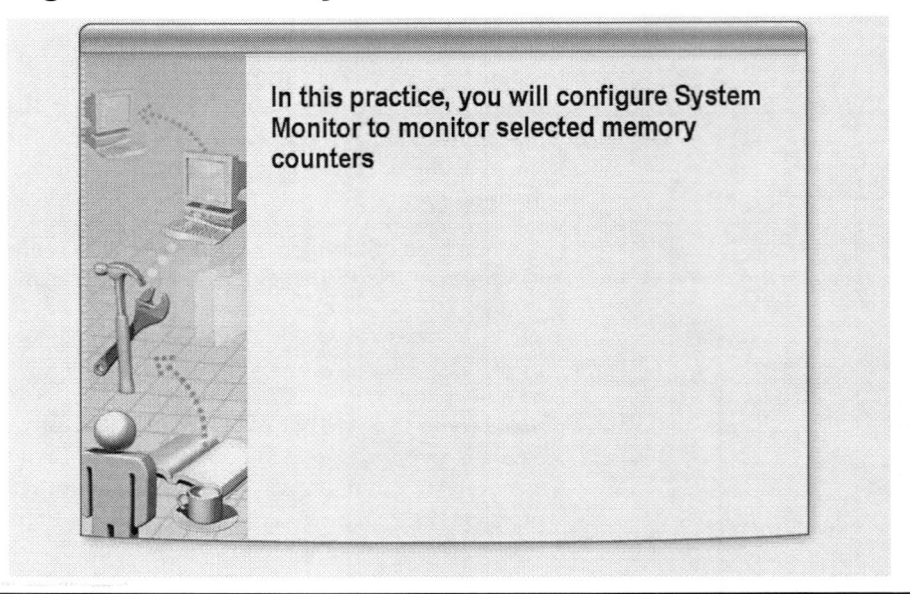

Objective

In this practice, you will:

- Configure System Monitor to monitor selected memory counters.

Instructions

Ensure that the DEN-DC1 virtual machine is running.

Practice

▶ **Configure System Monitor to monitor selected memory counters**

1. Log on as **Administrator** with a password of **Pa$$w0rd**.
2. Click **Start**, point to **Administrative Tools**, and then click **Performance**.
3. Click the graph and press CTRL+E to clear the existing counters.
4. In System Monitor, add the following memory counters: **Memory\Available MBytes**, **Memory\Committed Bytes**, **Memory\Pool Nonpaged bytes**, and **Memory\Pages/sec**.
5. Right-click the graph and then click **Properties**.
6. Click the **General** tab, and, in the **Sample automatically every** box, type **5**, and then click **OK**.
7. To allow time for the averaging mechanism of the counters to stabilize, wait for 15 seconds before proceeding.

   Switch to the report view (press CTRL+R), and then fill in the following information as your baseline:

   a. Available MBytes _____

   b. Committed Bytes _____

   c. Pool Nonpaged Bytes _____

   d. Pages/sec _____

8. Start Task Manager, click the **Performance** tab, and then record the PF Usage value:

   PF Usage _____

9. Open the D:\2275\Practices\Mod03 folder, start **leakyapp.exe**, and then click **Start Leaking**.

    Wait for a minimum of 15 seconds before proceeding to allow the averaging mechanism of the counters to stabilize.

10. Fill in the current information for the following counters:

    a. Available MBytes _____

    b. Committed Bytes _____

    c. Pool Nonpaged Bytes _____

    d. Pages/sec _____

11. Start Task Manager, click the **Performance** tab, and then record the PF Usage value:

    PF Usage _____

12. Compare the information from before starting leakyapp.exe to the information after starting leakyapp.exe. Notice that the Available Mbytes counter is dropping at the same rate that the Committed Bytes counter is rising. If you leave leakyapp.exe open too long, you may receive a warning about virtual memory running low or your system may crash.

13. Switch to **My Leaky App**, click **Stop Leaking**, and then click **Exit**.

    Wait for a minimum of two minutes before proceeding to allow the averaging mechanism of the counters to stabilize.

14. Fill in the current information:

    a. Available MBytes _____

    b. Committed Bytes _____

    c. Pool Nonpaged Bytes _____

    d. Pages/sec _____

15. Start Task Manager and record the PF Usage:

    PF Usage _____

16. Verify that your counters are back to their baseline levels.

17. Close all windows.

Important Do not shut down the virtual machines.

Lesson: Monitoring Processor Usage

- What Is Processor Usage?
- Identify and Resolve Processor Bottlenecks
- Practice: Monitoring Processor Usage

Introduction

After memory consumption, processor activity is the most important data to monitor on your server. To determine whether a busy processor is efficiently handling all the work on your computer or whether it is overwhelmed, you must examine the processor usage.

Lesson objectives

After completing this lesson, you will be able to:

- Explain processor usage.
- Identify and resolve processor bottlenecks.
- Monitor processor usage by using server monitoring tools.

What Is Processor Usage?

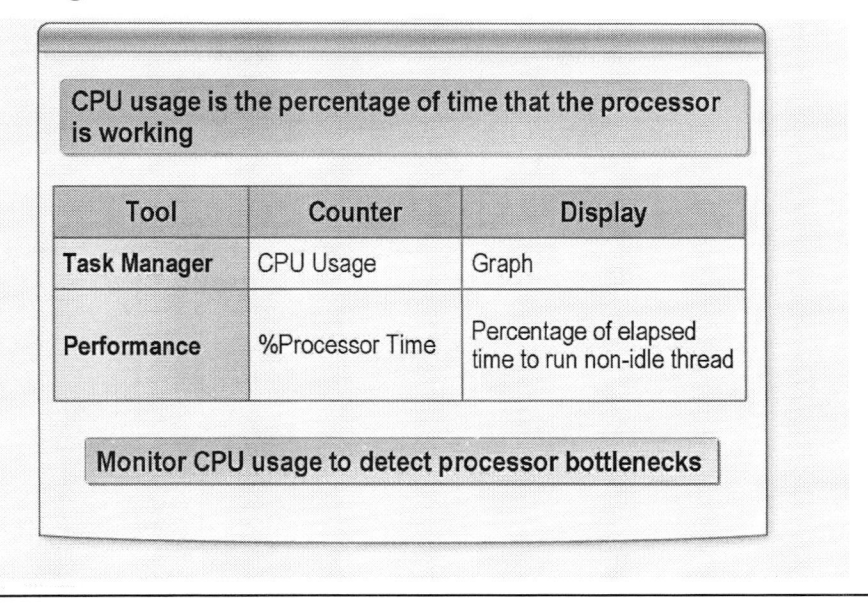

Tool	Counter	Display
Task Manager	CPU Usage	Graph
Performance	%Processor Time	Percentage of elapsed time to run non-idle thread

CPU usage is the percentage of time that the processor is working

Monitor CPU usage to detect processor bottlenecks

Definition

Processor usage, also called *CPU usage*, is the percentage of time that the processor is working. You must monitor processor usage to detect processor bottlenecks.

In Windows Server 2003, you can use Task Manager and Performance to monitor processor activity and usage. The counter that defines processor usage in each of these tools is:

- CPU Usage in Task Manager.
- % Processor Time in Performance.

CPU Usage

In Task Manager, CPU Usage displays a graph indicating the percentage of time the processor is working. This counter is a primary indicator of processor activity. View this graph to see how much processing time you are using. If your computer seems to be running slowly, this graph may display a high percentage.

% Processor Time

In Performance, % Processor Time is the percentage of elapsed time that the processor spends to execute a non-idle thread. Each processor has an idle thread that consumes cycles when no other threads are ready to run.

This counter is the primary indicator of processor activity. It displays the average percentage of busy time observed during the sample interval. It calculates this value by monitoring the time that the idle process is active and subtracting that value from 100 percent.

It is important to monitor this counter on symmetric multiprocessing (SMP) systems just as it is on single-processor systems. SMP enables any one of the multiple processors in a computer to run any operating system or application thread simultaneously with other processors in the system. Observe processor usage patterns for individual processors and for all processors over an extended period. Also, consider the number of threads in the system's processor queue to determine whether high processor usage is limiting the system's ability to accomplish work.

Identify and Resolve Processor Bottlenecks

Processor counter	Acceptable average range	Desired value	Action
% Processor Time	Less than 85%	Low	Find process using excessive processor time Upgrade or add another processor
System: Processor Queue Length	Less than 2	Low	Upgrade or add additional processor
Server Work Queues: Queue Length	Less than four	Low	Find process using excessive processor time Upgrade or add another processor
Interrupts/sec	Depends on processor	Low	Find controller card generating interrupts

Introduction

Almost every activity that occurs on a server involves the processor. The processor on an application server is generally busier than the processor on a file and print server. As a result, the level of processor activity, and what is considered normal, is different between the two types of servers.

Two of the most common causes of processor bottlenecks are CPU-bound applications and drivers, and excessive interrupts that are generated by inadequate disk or network subsystem components.

Identify a bottleneck

Monitor processor counters to help determine whether the processor is causing a bottleneck:

- *% Processor Time*. Measures the amount of time that the processor is busy. When processor usage consistently runs over 85 percent, the processor is a system bottleneck. Analyze processor usage by monitoring individual processes to determine what is causing the processor activity.

- *System: Processor Queue Length*. Number of requests in the queue for the processor. It indicates the number of threads that are ready to be executed and are waiting for processor time. Generally, a processor queue length that is consistently less than two is acceptable. To determine the cause of the congestion, you must further analyze the individual processes that are making requests on the processor.

- *Server Work Queues: Queue Length*. Number of requests in the queue for the selected processor. A consistent queue of over four indicates processor congestion.

- *Interrupts/sec*. Number of interrupts that the processor is servicing from applications or from hardware devices. Windows Server 2003 can handle thousands of interrupts per second. A dramatic increase in this counter value without a corresponding increase in system activity indicates a hardware problem. The problem could be a device that is unable to keep up with the rest of the system, like a disk controller or network interface card (NIC).

For example, if a conflict occurs between a hard disk controller and a network adapter card, monitor the disk controller and network adapter card. Determine whether excessive requests are being generated by monitoring the queue lengths for the physical disk and network interface. Generally, if the queue length is greater than two requests, check for slow disk drives or network adapters that could be causing the queue length backlog.

Actions to resolve processor bottleneck

If you determined that the processor is a system bottleneck, you can perform the following actions to improve performance:

- Add a faster processor if the system is a file and print server.
- Add multiple processors for application servers, especially if the application is multithreaded.
- Offload processing to another system on the network, such as users, applications, or services.
- Upgrade your network card, disk adapter card, or controller cards. In general, 32-bit intelligent adapters are recommended. Intelligent adapters provide better overall system performance because they allow interrupts to be processed on the adapter itself, thereby relieving the processor of this work.

Practice: Monitoring Processor Usage

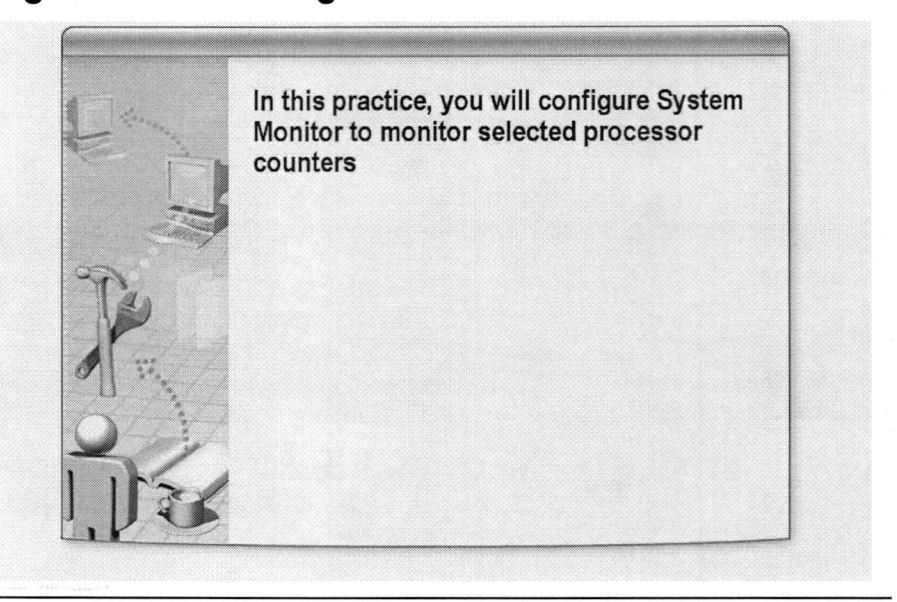

Objective

In this practice, you will:

- Configure System Monitor to monitor selected processor counters.

Instructions

Ensure that the DEN-DC1 virtual machine is running.

Practice

▶ **Configure System Monitor to monitor selected processor counters**

1. On DEN-DC1, click **Start**, point to **Administrative Tools**, and then click **Performance**.
2. Click the graph and press CTRL+E to clear the existing counters.
3. Click **System Monitor**, and then add the **Processor\% Processor Time** counter and the **System\Processor Queue Length** counter.
4. Record the information for the following counters:

    a. Processor\% Processor Time _____

    b. System\Processor Queue Length _____

5. Open D:\2275\Practices\Mod03, and then start the **cpustres.exe** application.
6. Set the **Activity** level for Thread 1 to **Maximum**.
7. Record the information for the following counters:

    a. Processor\% Processor Time _____

    b. System\Processor Queue Length _____

8. Is the **cpustres.exe** command causing a bottleneck? How can you tell?

   _____

   _____

9. Close all windows.

Important Do not shut down the virtual machines.

Lesson: Monitoring Disks

- Why Monitor Disks?
- Identify and Resolve Disk Bottlenecks
- Practice: Monitoring Disks

Introduction

The disk subsystem handles the storage and movement of programs and data on your server, giving it a powerful influence on the overall responsiveness of your server. The Performance console provides disk-specific counters that enable you to measure disk activity and throughput.

Lesson objectives

After completing this lesson, you will be able to:

- Explain the purpose of monitoring disks.
- Identify and resolve disk bottlenecks.
- Monitor disks by using System Monitor.

Why Monitor Disks?

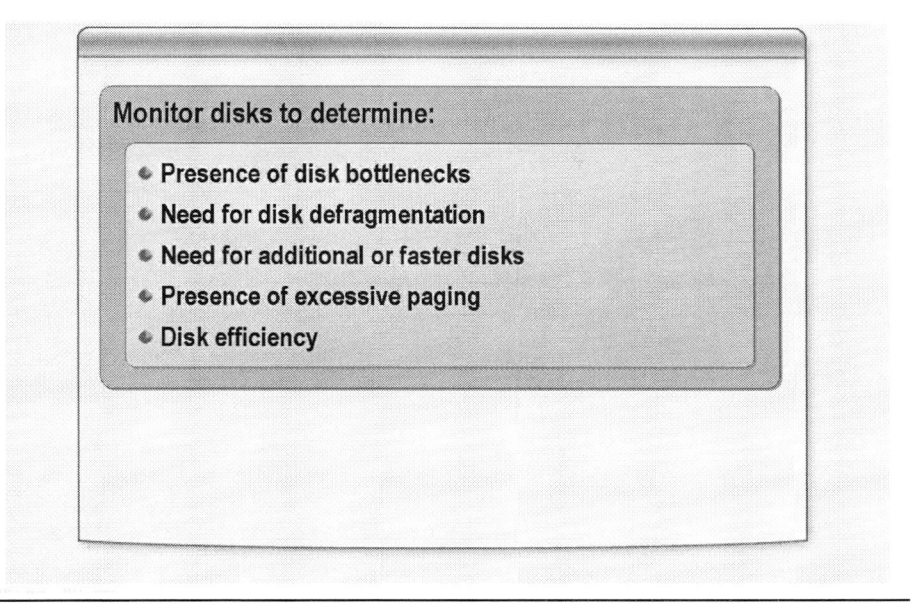

> **Monitor disks to determine:**
> - Presence of disk bottlenecks
> - Need for disk defragmentation
> - Need for additional or faster disks
> - Presence of excessive paging
> - Disk efficiency

Introduction

Monitor disks to keep your systems working efficiently. You can also use the data that you collect when you monitor disks to plan for future hardware and software upgrades.

Disk bottlenecks

The existence of a disk bottleneck is indicated by the presence of all of the following conditions:

- Sustained rate of disk activity well above your baseline
- Persistent disk queues that are longer than two per disk
- Absence of a significant amount of paging

Without this combination of factors, it is unlikely that a disk bottleneck exists.

Monitoring disk efficiency

Consider disk capacity and disk throughput when evaluating your starting configuration. Use the bus, controller, cabling, and disk technologies that produce the best throughput that is practical and affordable. Most computers perform adequately with moderately priced disk components. However, if you want to obtain the best performance, you may want to evaluate the latest disk components that are available.

If your configuration contains various types of disks, controllers, and buses, the differences in their designs can affect throughput rates. You might want to test throughput by using these various disk systems to determine whether some components produce less favorable results overall or only for certain types of activity, and then replace those components as needed.

Also, certain kinds of volume-set configurations can offer performance benefits. For example, striped volumes can provide better performance because they increase throughput by enabling multiple disks to service sequential or clustered input/output (I/O) requests. A *striped volume* is a volume whose data is interleaved across two or more physical disks. The data on this type of volume is allocated alternately and evenly to each of the physical disks. A striped volume cannot be mirrored or extended.

> **Note** For more information about striped volumes, see Module 5, "Managing Disks," in Course 2275, *Maintaining a Microsoft Windows Server 2003 Environment*.

System Monitor supports monitoring volume sets with the same performance objects and counters that are provided for individual disks. Notice that hardware-based Redundant Array of Independent Disks (RAID) devices report all activity to a single physical disk and do not show distribution of disk operations among the individual disks in the array. RAID is a category of disk drives that combine two or more drives into one volume for fault tolerance and performance.

Be aware of the seek time, rotational speed, access time, and data transfer rate of your disks by consulting manufacturer documentation. Also consider the bandwidth of cabling and controllers. The slowest component determines the maximum possible throughput, so be sure to monitor each component.

To compare the performance of different disks, monitor the same counters and activity on the disks. If you find differences in performance, you might want to distribute workload to the disk that performs better, or replace slower performing components.

Identify and Resolve Disk Bottlenecks

Physical disk counter	Acceptable average range	Desired value	Action
% Disk Time	Under 90%	Low	Monitor to see if paging is occurring Upgrade disk subsystem
Current Disk Queue Length	0–3	Low	Upgrade disk subsystem
Avg. Disk Bytes/Transfer	Baseline or higher	High	Upgrade disk subsystem
Disk Bytes/sec	Baseline or higher	High	Upgrade disk subsystem

Introduction

Disks store programs and the data that programs process. While waiting for a computer to respond, it is frequently the disk that is the bottleneck. In this case, the disk subsystem can be the most important aspect of I/O performance. However, problems can be hidden by other factors, such as the lack of memory.

Performance disk counters are available with both the **LogicalDisk** and **PhysicalDisk** performance objects. **LogicalDisk** monitors logical partitions of physical drives. It is useful to determine which partition is causing the disk activity, which may indicate the application or service that is generating the requests. **PhysicalDisk** monitors individual hard disk drives and is useful for monitoring disk drives as a whole.

Important Both **LogicalDisk** and **PhysicalDisk** objects are automatically enabled on demand. Therefore, you do not have to enable them manually with the **diskperf –y** command.

Counters used to determine whether the disk is a bottleneck

When analyzing disk subsystem performance and capacity, monitor the following Performance disk subsystem counters for bottlenecks:

- *% Disk Time*. Indicates the amount of time that the disk drive is busy servicing read and write requests. If this is consistently close to 100 percent, the disk is being used very heavily. Monitoring individual processes helps determine which process or processes are making the majority of the disk requests.

- *Current Disk Queue Length*. Indicates the number of pending disk I/O requests for the disk drive. This value should be less than or equal to the number of spindles, plus 2. For a single hard drive, the value should be 3 or less.

- *Avg. Disk Bytes/Transfer*. The average number of bytes transferred to or from the disk during write or read operations. The larger the transfer size, the more efficient the system is running.

- *Disk Bytes/sec.* This is the rate at which bytes are transferred to or from the disk during write or read operations. The higher the average, the more efficient the system is running.
- *LogicalDisk\% Free Space.* This is the amount of disk space available.

Actions to resolve disk bottleneck

If you determine that the disk subsystem is a system bottleneck, a number of solutions are possible, including the following:

- Defragment the disk by using Disk Defragmenter.
- Rule out a memory shortage. When memory is scarce, the Virtual Memory Manager writes more pages to disk, resulting in increased disk activity. Before you add hardware, make sure that memory shortage is not the source of the problem because low memory is a common cause of bottlenecks.
- Add a faster controller, such as Ultra320 Small Computer System Interface (SCSI), or an on-board caching controller.
- Optimize data location on disks by moving high usage files to their own disks. For example, moving the Windows Server 2003 paging file or database transaction logs to their own disk or mirrored set.
- Add more disk drives in a RAID environment. This solution spreads the data across multiple physical disks and improves performance, especially during read operations.
- Offload processing to another system on the network, such as users, applications, or services.
- Implement high performance external storage such as a Storage Area Network (SAN). A SAN typically has higher performance than an internal disk.

Practice: Monitoring Disks

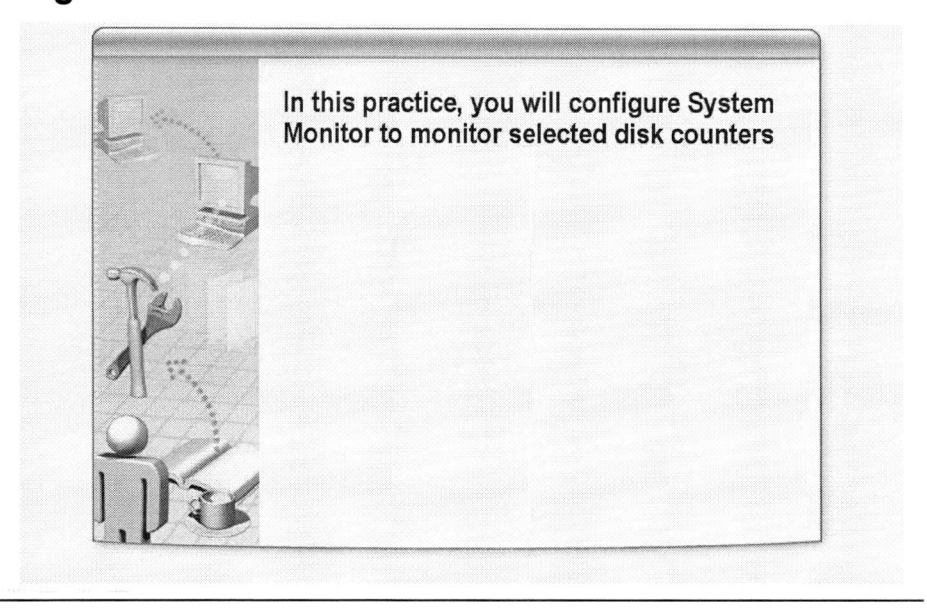

> In this practice, you will configure System Monitor to monitor selected disk counters

Objective

In this practice, you will:

- Configure System Monitor to monitor selected disk counters.

Instructions

Ensure that the DEN-DC1 virtual machine is running.

Practice

▶ **Configure System Monitor to monitor selected disk counters**

1. On DEN-DC1, click **Start**, and click **Help and Support**. Record how long it takes to start **Help and Support**.

   _____

2. Close Help and Support Center.
3. Click **Start**, point to **Administrative Tools**, and then click **Performance**.
4. Click the graph and press CTRL+E to clear the existing counters.
5. Click **System Monitor**, and then add the following counters:
   a. Memory\Pages/sec
   b. PhysicalDisk\% Disk Time
   c. PhysicalDisk\Current Disk Queue Length
   d. Processor\% Processor Time
6. Record the information for the following counters:
   a. Memory\Pages/sec _____
   b. PhysicalDisk\%Disk Time _____
   c. PhysicalDisk\Current Disk Queue Length _____
   d. Processor\% Processor Time _____

7. Open D:\2275\Practices\Mod03 and start the **disk.bat** application.

8. Switch to report view, and then record the information for the following counters:

   a. Memory\Pages/sec _____

   b. PhysicalDisk\%Disk Time _____

   c. PhysicalDisk\Current Disk Queue Length _____

   d. Processor\% Processor Time _____

9. On the **Start** menu, click **Help and Support** and record how long it takes to start Help.

   _____

10. Is **disk.bat** causing a disk bottleneck? How can you tell?

    _____

    _____

11. Close all windows.

▶ **To prepare for the next practice**
- Start the DEN-SRV1 virtual machine.

Important Do not shut down the virtual machines.

Lesson: Monitoring Network Usage

- What Is Network Usage?
- Identify and Resolve Network Bottlenecks
- Practice: Monitoring Network Usage

Introduction

Communication across a network is increasingly important in any work environment. Similar to the processor or disks on your system, the behavior of the network affects the operation of your system. Optimize your system's performance by regularly monitoring network usage, such as network traffic and resource usage.

Lesson objectives

After completing this lesson, you will be able to:

- Explain network usage.
- Identify and resolve network bottlenecks.
- Monitor network usage by using server monitoring tools.

What Is Network Usage?

> - Percentage of network bandwidth in use on the segment being monitored
> - Network bottlenecks affect user experience
> - Typical causes of network bottlenecks are:
>   - Overloaded server
>   - Overloaded network
>   - Loss of network integrity

Definition

Network usage is the percentage of network bandwidth that is in use on the segment that is being monitored.

Network bandwidth

Network bandwidth is measured in several different ways:

- The rate at which bytes are transferred to and from the server.
- The rate at which data packages are sent by the server. Data packages include frames, packets, segments, and datagrams.
- The rate at which files are sent and received by the server.

Effective network bandwidth varies widely depending upon the transmission capacity of the link, the server configuration, and the server workload.

Why monitor network usage?

You monitor network usage to detect network bottlenecks. Network bottlenecks directly affect the experience of the user at the client workstation and the entire network. A network bottleneck limits the number of clients that can simultaneously access your server.

Typical causes for network bottlenecks are:

- An overloaded server. If a server is performing many roles on the network then the combined network traffic generated by these roles may be too much for the network. For example, a file server will generate a large amount of network traffic. If a file server also hosts a busy computer running Microsoft SQL Server™, the overall network traffic generated may be more than the network card or network capacity.
- An overloaded network. The overall network traffic on the network may be too high for its configuration. For example, many busy servers attached to the same switch may overload the switch backplane. Or, the combined traffic of all the requests between clients and servers may overwhelm the network backbone.

- Loss of network integrity. If the network is not reliable then it will act as a bottleneck. For example, lost packets due to faulty switch ports can significantly slow down network communication as computers wait for the timeout period for missing packets to expire before the packets are resent.

Identify and Resolve Network Bottlenecks

Network interface counter	Acceptable average range	Desire high or low value	Action
Network Utilization (in Task Manager)	Generally lower than 30%	Low	Upgrade network adapter or physical network
Network Interface: Bytes Sent/sec	Baseline or higher	High	Upgrade network adapter or physical network
Network Interface: Bytes Total/sec	Baseline or higher	High	Perform further analysis to determine cause of problem. Upgrade or add another adapter.
Server: Bytes Received/Sec	Less than 50% of the capacity of the bandwidth of the network card	NA	Upgrade network adapter or physical network

Introduction

Network bottlenecks are difficult to monitor because most networks are complex. Also, many elements can affect the performance of the network. You can monitor various objects and counters on the network, such as server, redirector, network segment, and protocols. Determining which ones to monitor depends upon the environment.

Counters used to determine whether the network is a bottleneck

Use the following commonly monitored counters to form an overall picture of how the network is being used and to help uncover network bottlenecks:

- *Task Manager: % Network utilization.* The percentage of the network bandwidth in use for the local network segment. You can use this counter to monitor the effect of various network operations on the network, such as user logon validation and domain account synchronization.

- *Network Interface: Bytes Sent/sec.* The number of bytes that are sent by using this network adapter card.

- *Network Interface: Bytes Total/sec.* The number of bytes that are sent and received by using this network adapter card. Use this counter to determine how the network adapter is performing. The Bytes Total/sec counter should report high values, to indicate a large number of successful transmissions.

- *Server: Bytes Received/sec.* Compare the bytes received per second counter to the total bandwidth of your network adapter card to determine whether your network connection is creating a bottleneck. To allow room for spikes in traffic, you should usually use no more than 50 percent of capacity. If this number is very close to the capacity of the connection, and processor and memory use are moderate, the connection might be causing a problem.

Actions to resolve a network bottleneck

By viewing the preceding counters, you can view the amount of activity on the server for logon requests and data access. If you determine that the network subsystem is causing a bottleneck, you can perform various actions to alleviate the bottleneck. These actions include the following:

- Add servers to the network, thereby distributing the processing load.

- Verify that network cards have properly autonegotiated the network speed and duplex. Manually set the port speed and duplex on both the server network card and switch port if necessary.

- Use dual network cards with load balancing to increase the network capacity of a single server. This solution also provides fault tolerance for the network cards in the server.

- Implement a fully switched network. Using switches instead of hubs eliminates most packet collisions on Ethernet networks and significantly increases the overall throughput on the network. Higher quality switches have a faster backplane for greater capacity.

- Check and improve the physical components, such as routers, switches, and cabling. Update these components to increase overall network speed. For example, raise the speed on the network backbone to 1 gigabit per second (Gbps).

- Divide your network into multiple subnets or segments, attaching the server to each segment with a separate adapter. This method reduces congestion at the server by spreading server requests.

- Divide your network traffic into appropriate segments. For example, configure your network so that systems that are shared by the same group of people are on the same subnet. This reduces traffic on the network backbone.

- Unbind network adapters that are used infrequently.

- For best performance, use adapters with the highest bandwidth that is available. Note, however, that increasing bandwidth increases the number of transmissions and in turn creates more work for your system. For example, the system must generate more interrupts. Remove unused network adapters to reduce overhead.

- Use offline folders to work on network applications without being connected to a network. Offline folders make use of client-side caching, thereby reducing network traffic.

Practice: Monitoring Network Usage

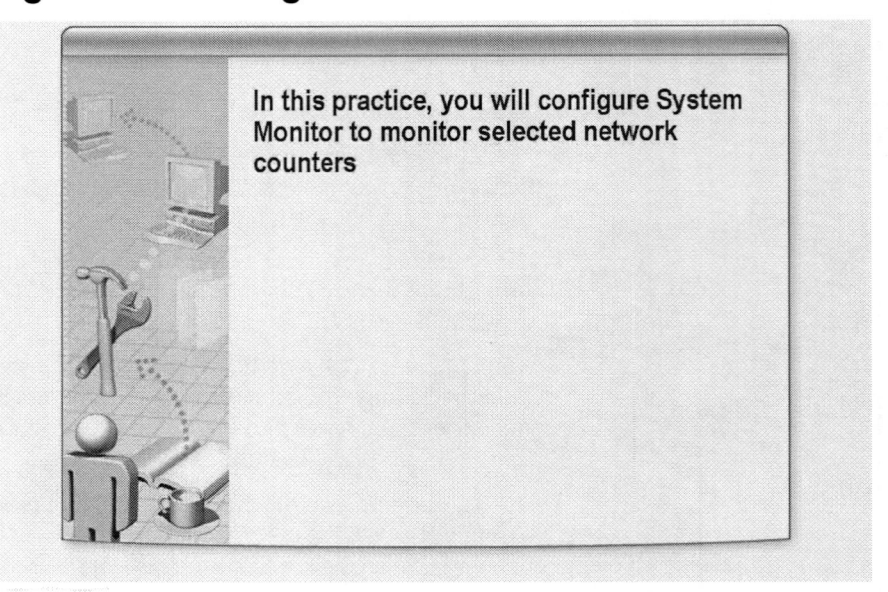

Objective

In this practice, you will:

- Configure System Monitor to monitor selected network counters.

Instructions

Ensure that the DEN-DC1 and DEN-SRV1 virtual machines are running.

Practice

▶ **Configure System Monitor to monitor selected network counters**

1. Start the DEN-SRV1 virtual machine.
2. Log on to DEN-SRV1 as **Administrator** with the password of **Pa$$w0rd**.
3. On DEN-SRV1, create the folder **C:\Test** and share it with permissions of **Full Control** to **Everyone**.
4. On DEN-DC1, click **Start**, point to **Administrative Tools**, and then click **Performance**.
5. Click the graph and press CTRL+E to clear the existing counters.
6. Click **System Monitor**, and then add the following counters:
   a. Network Interface\Bytes Sent/sec
   b. Network Interface\Bytes Total/sec
   c. Server\Bytes Received/sec
7. Record the information for the following counters:
   a. Network Interface\Bytes Sent/sec _____
   b. Network Interface\Bytes Total/sec _____
   c. Server\Bytes Received/sec _____
8. Start Task Manager, and then click the **Networking** tab.
9. Record the Network Utilization: _____

10. Open a command prompt, and then type the following commands:

    D:

    CD \2275\Practices\Mod03

    Connect DEN-SRV1

    (This program copies files from DEN-SRV1 to DEN-DC1 to create a network load. This simulates a busy file server.)

11. Switch to report view, and then record the information for the following counters:

    a. Network Interface\Bytes Sent/sec _____

    b. Network Interface\Bytes Total/sec _____

    c. Server\Bytes Received/sec _____

12. Record the Network Utilization shown in Task Manager: _____

13. Do any of these counters indicate the presence of a bottleneck? If so, which counter?

    _____

14. Close the Performance Microsoft Management Console (MMC) and Task Manager.

15. Log off of DEN-DC1 and DEN-SRV1.

Important Do not shut down the virtual machines.

Lesson: Monitoring Best Practices

- Guidelines for Using Counters and Thresholds
- Best Practices for Monitoring Server Performance
- Process for Troubleshooting Performance
- Other Monitoring and Management Tools

Introduction

Performance monitoring is a powerful tool for troubleshooting and ensuring server performance. To best use it, you should understand in what situations certain counters should be used as well as other monitoring best practices.

Lesson objectives

After completing this lesson, you will be able to:

- Describe the guidelines for using counters and thresholds.
- Use best practices for monitoring server performance.
- Explain the process that you can use to troubleshoot performance.
- Describe additional troubleshooting tools.

Guidelines for Using Counters and Thresholds

Subsystem	Counter	Threshold
Memory	• Monitor page faults • Monitor available RAM • Monitor committed bytes	• Over 5 per second • 4 MB or less of RAM • More than physical RAM
Processor	• % Processor time, % Privileged Time, % User Time • System: Processor Queue Length • Server Work Queues: Queue Length	• Above 85% • Above 2 • Above 2
Disk	• % Disk Time • Current Disk Queue Length	• If more than 90%, check for excessive paging • Greater than 3
Network	• Server: Bytes Total/sec, Network Interface: Bytes Total/sec	• Higher than the baseline number

Introduction

Deviations from your baseline provide the best indicator of performance problems. You can also check for various types of bottlenecks by monitoring the counters for each subsystem and checking them against the recommended thresholds.

Memory bottlenecks

Check for memory bottlenecks by monitoring the following counters:

Counter	Threshold	Action
Page faults	Sustained page fault rates greater than 5 per second	Add more memory to the server
Available RAM	4 megabytes (MB) or less of RAM	Add more memory to the server
Committed bytes	Less than physical RAM	Add more memory to the server

Processor bottlenecks

Check for processor bottlenecks by monitoring the following counters:

Counter	Threshold	Action
% Processor time, % Privileged Time, % User Time	Consistently above 85%	Upgrade your current processor or add another processor
System: Processor Queue Length, Server Work Queues: Queue Length	Greater than 2	Upgrade your current processor or add another processor

Disk bottlenecks

Check for disk bottlenecks by monitoring the following counters:

Counter	Threshold	Action
% Disk Time	More than 90%,	Check for excessive paging (memory bottleneck). If excessive paging is not the problem, replace the disk with a faster unit
Current Disk Queue Length	Greater than 3	Upgrade the hard disk

Network bottlenecks

Check for network bottlenecks by monitoring the following counters:

Counter	Threshold	Action
Server: Bytes Total/sec, Network Interface: Bytes Total/sec	Greater than the baseline numbers	Upgrade the network adapters or the physical network

Best Practices for Monitoring Server Performance

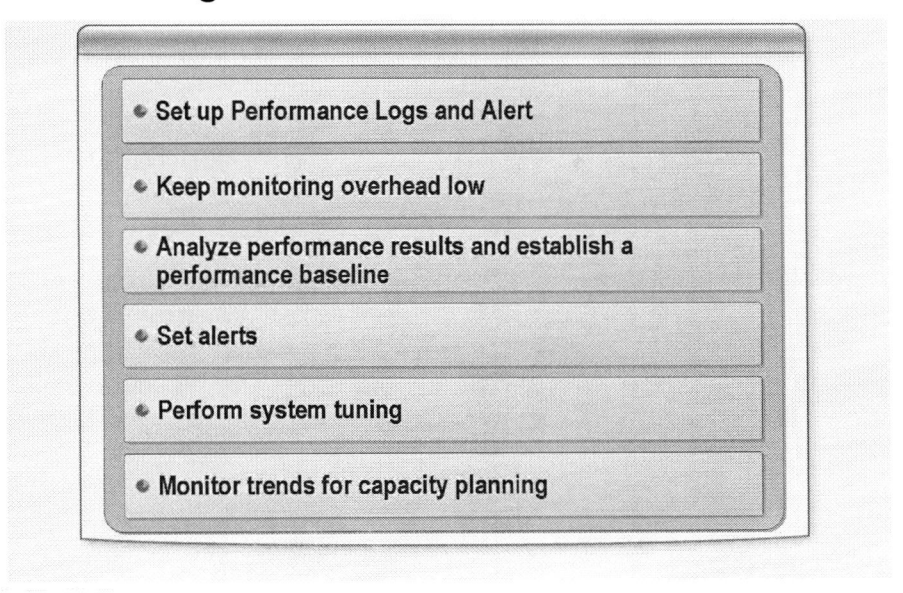

- Set up Performance Logs and Alert
- Keep monitoring overhead low
- Analyze performance results and establish a performance baseline
- Set alerts
- Perform system tuning
- Monitor trends for capacity planning

Introduction

Use the following best practices when you monitor the performance of a server.

Performance Logs and Alerts

- Set up Performance Logs and Alerts to monitor your server.

    Set up Performance Logs and Alerts to report data for the recommended counters at regular intervals, such as every 10 to 15 minutes. Retain logs over extended periods of time, store data in a database, and query the data to report on and analyze the data as needed for overall performance assessment, trend analysis, and capacity planning.

    For best results, perform the following tasks before starting System Monitor or Performance Logs and Alerts on the computer that you want to monitor for diagnostic purposes:

    - Stop screen-saver programs.
    - Turn off services that are not essential or relevant to monitoring.
    - Increase the paging file to physical memory size plus 100 MB.

Low overhead
- Keep monitoring overhead low.

  In general, the performance tools are designed for minimal overhead. However, you may find that the overhead increases under each of the following conditions:
  - You are running System Monitor in graph view.
  - You selected an option other than the default, current value, for a report view.
  - You are sampling at very frequent intervals, less than three seconds apart.
  - Many objects and counters are selected.

  Other aspects of performance tool operation that affect performance include file size and disk space that is used by log files. To reduce file size and related disk space usage, extend the update interval. Also, log on to a disk other than the one you are monitoring. Frequent logging also adds demand on disk I/O.

  If monitoring overhead is a concern, run only the Performance Logs and Alerts service; do not monitor by using a System Monitor graph.

  During remote logging, frequent updating can slow performance due to network transport. In this case, it is recommended that you log continuously on remote computers but upload logs infrequently, for example, once a day.

Performance baseline
- Analyze performance results and establish a performance baseline.

  Review logged data by using the System Monitor graph or by exporting it for printing. Compare the values against the counter thresholds to verify that resource usage or other activity is within acceptable limits. Set your baseline according to the level of performance that you consider satisfactory for your typical workload.

Alerts
- Set alerts.

  Set alerts according to the counter values that you consider unacceptable, as defined by baseline evaluation.

System tuning
- Perform system tuning.

  Tune system settings and workload to improve performance, and repeat monitoring to examine tuning results.

Trends

- Monitor trends for capacity planning, and add or upgrade components.

  Maintain logged data in a database, and observe changes to identify changes in resource requirements. After you observe changes in activity or resource demand, you can identify where you may require additional resources.

Process for Troubleshooting Performance

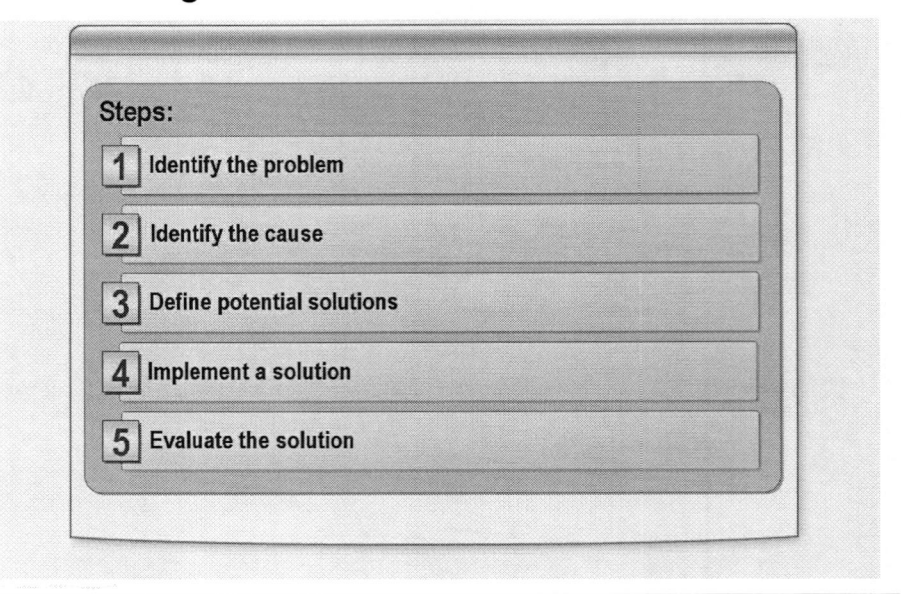

Steps:
1. Identify the problem
2. Identify the cause
3. Define potential solutions
4. Implement a solution
5. Evaluate the solution

Introduction

Troubleshooting performance is a skill set that network administrators use to find the source of performance problems and fix them. Many network administrators perform this process intuitively. However, troubleshooting is a skill that can be learned.

Troubleshooting process

Effective troubleshooting is performed as consistent process that can be applied to performance problems.

The troubleshooting steps are:

- Identify the problem
- Identify the cause
- Define potential solutions
- Implement a solution
- Evaluate the solution

Identify the problem

Accurate identification of the problem is essential to creating a valid solution. If a user has identified a problem, such as a slow application, be sure to investigate under exactly what circumstances the problem occurred. It is almost impossible to fix a problem that is not repeatable.

When identifying the problem, consider the following:

- Does the problem affect one user or many?
- Does the problem affect one workstation or many?
- Does the problem affect one server or many?
- Does the problem affect one network segment, or all network segments?
- Does the problem occur each day at a specific time?
- Are other processes, such as a backup, running at the same time this problem occurs?
- Has anything been changed recently in the environment? For example, did you install a new service pack, or new network equipment, or deploy a new application.

Identify the cause

To fix a problem you must understand why it is occurring. When troubleshooting performance this is where you identify what subsystem is acting as a bottleneck. Comparing current performance data to the baseline performance data will identify the subsystem.

When identifying the cause, be sure to monitor all subsystems and consider the relationship between them. For example, a high number of disk requests may indicate a shortage of RAM rather than a disk problem.

It may be possible to further investigate and identify a particular process that is causing a problem. For example, if CPU utilization is high you can use Task Manager to identify the process.

Define potential solutions

Once a cause has been identified, research potential solutions. Depending on the situation, this may include visiting the Microsoft Knowledge Base and vendor knowledge bases as well as past experience.

If you cannot find information that exactly describes your situation, then look for similar problems. A strong understanding of hardware, the operating systems, and your applications will help in this process.

Implement a solution

The list of potential solutions should be prioritized based on how easy they are to implement and how likely they are to fix the problem. It is often better to try a few quick fixes before a long involved solution even if they are less likely to solve the problem.

Implement only one potential solution at a time. This ensures that you understand exactly what fixed the problem. If a fix is understood then it is repeatable and can be performed again if required for other servers or applications.

Evaluate the solution

If the solution has fixed the problem then the troubleshooting process is complete, and the solution should be documented. Documenting the problem and the solution ensures that it can be fixed quickly if it or a similar problem occurs in the future.

Often it takes several attempts to fix a problem. If the solution did not fix the problem then undo the changes that were made as part of the solution and implement the next highest priority solution. If the problem is partially fixed then evaluate whether this solution needs to be combined with another solution to completely fix the problem.

If new information about the problem or the cause of the problem was learned then this should be taken into account before implementing the next solution.

After the problem appears to be fixed, test the solution thoroughly. Also, continue to monitor the affected systems after implementing the solution to ensure that the solution did not cause other problems.

Other Monitoring and Management Tools

> - **Microsoft Operations Manager 2005**
>   - Performance analysis for enterprise environments
>   - Centralized and scalable
>   - Flexible reporting
> - **Systems Management Server 2003**
>   - Manages Windows servers and workstations
>   - Deploys applications
>   - Hardware and software inventory

Introduction

The Performance snap-in is an excellent solution for monitoring Windows Server 2003 in small and mid-sized businesses. However, additional enterprise level solutions are available for monitoring performance and other server management tasks.

Two enterprise level monitoring tools from Microsoft are Microsoft Operations Manager 2005 (MOM) and Systems Management Server 2003.

MOM 2005

MOM 2005 provides comprehensive event and performance management, proactive monitoring and alerting, reporting and trend analysis, and system and application specific knowledge and tasks to improve the manageability of Windows-based servers and applications.

MOM 2005 features include:

- Centralized data collection and monitoring.
- Scalable to manage thousands of entities.
- Flexible built-in reporting that can filter millions of events to locate the important information.
- Accurate data collection over unreliable and slow networks via agents.
- A security framework that requires less permissions for monitoring than the Performance snap-in.
- Database of knowledge base articles that provides solutions to known problems.

Systems Management Server 2003

Systems Management Server 2003 is a solution for managing Windows servers and workstations. The main features of Systems Management Server are:

- Application deployment.
- Hardware and software inventory.
- Security patch management.
- Support for mobile clients.
- Integration with existing Windows Management Services, including Windows XP Remote Assistance.

Note You can also use Server Performance Advisor to analyze performance bottlenecks. You can download Server Performance Advisor from the Server Performance Advisor V1.0 page on the Microsoft Download Center Web site.

Lab: Monitoring Server Performance

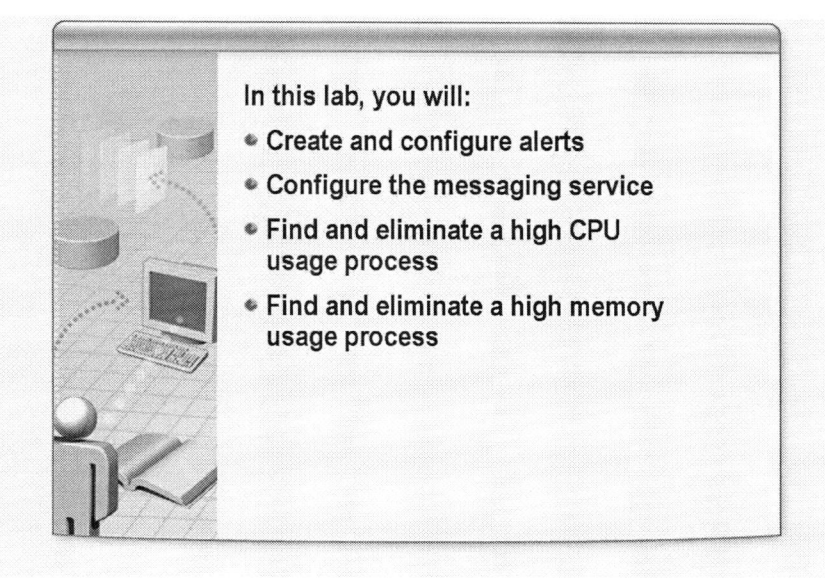

Objectives

After completing this lab, you will be able to:

- Create and configure alerts.
- Configure the messaging service.
- Find and eliminate a high CPU usage process.
- Find and eliminate a high memory usage process.

Instructions

Ensure that the DEN-DC1 virtual machine is running.

Scenario

You are the systems administrator for an organizational unit on a large network. Recently, users have been complaining that access to the department server is slow. After doing some initial research, you believe that poorly written applications are using too much CPU time and memory. You are configuring alerts to indicate when the problem is occurring so you can find the offending processes.

Estimated time to complete this lab: 20 minutes

Exercise 1
Create and Configure Alerts

In this exercise, you will create an alert that sends a network message when CPU utilization is too high.

Tasks	Specific instructions
1. Log on to your computer.	- Log on to DEN-DC1 as **Administrator** with a password or **Pa$$w0rd**.
2. Create a performance console.	a. Start **Performance**. b. Clear the System Monitor. c. Add Processor\% Processor Time. d. Add Memory\Available MBytes.
3. Create a high CPU Utilization alert for over 80% processor time.	a. Create an alert named **HighCPU**. b. Add **Processor\% Processor Time**. c. Configure a limit of over **80**.
4. Configure HighCPU to send a network message.	- Select Send a network message to Administrator.
5. Create a low memory alert for less than 100 MB free.	a. Create an alert named **LowMem**. b. Add **Memory\Available MBytes**. c. Configure a limit of under **100**.
6. Configure LowMem to send a network message.	- Select Send a network message to Administrator.

Exercise 2
Configure the Messaging Service

In this exercise, you will enable the messenger service.

Tasks	Specific instructions
1. Open Computer Management.	a. Click **Start**, point to **Administrative Tools**, and then click **Computer Management**. b. Expand the **Services and Applications** node. c. Click **Services**.
2. Enable the messenger service.	a. Change the **Startup type** for the **Messenger** service to **Automatic**. b. Start the **Messenger** service. c. Close Computer Management.

Exercise 3
Finding a High CPU Usage Process

In this exercise, you will find the high CPU usage process and stop it.

Tasks	Specific instructions
1. Test the high CPU usage alert.	a. Start the following program: **D:\2275\Practices\Mod03\cpustres.exe** b. In the **CPU Stress** dialog box, change the activity for **Thread 1** to **Maximum**. c. View the CPU utilization in the performance console. d. A dialog box will appear indicating that CPU utilization exceeds 80%. e. Stop the **HighCPU** alert.
2. Find the high CPU usage process.	a. Open **Task Manager**. b. Click the **Processes** tab. c. Sort the processes by CPU utilization. d. End the high CPU usage process. e. Close Task Manager.

Exercise 4
Finding a High Memory Usage Process

In this exercise, you will find the high memory usage process and stop it.

Tasks	Specific instructions
1. Test the high CPU usage alert.	a. Start the following program: **D:\2275\Practices\Mod03\leakyapp.exe** b. In the **My Leaky App** dialog box, click **Start Leaking**. c. View Available MBytes in the performance console. d. A dialog box will appear indicating that Available Mbytes is less than 100 MB. e. Stop the **LowMem** alert.
2. Find the high CPU usage process.	a. Open **Task Manager**. b. Click the **Processes** tab. c. Sort the processes by **Mem Utilization**. d. End the high memory usage process. e. Close Task Manager.
3. Complete the lab exercise.	a. Close all programs and shut down all computers. Do not save changes. b. To prepare for the next module, start the DEN-DC1 and DEN-SRV1 virtual computers.

THIS PAGE INTENTIONALLY LEFT BLANK

Module 4: Maintaining Device Drivers

Contents

Overview	1
Lesson: Configuring Device Driver Signing Options	2
Lesson: Using Device Driver Rollback	15

Information in this document, including URL and other Internet Web site references, is subject to change without notice. Unless otherwise noted, the example companies, organizations, products, domain names, e-mail addresses, logos, people, places, and events depicted herein are fictitious, and no association with any real company, organization, product, domain name, e-mail address, logo, person, place or event is intended or should be inferred. Complying with all applicable copyright laws is the responsibility of the user. Without limiting the rights under copyright, no part of this document may be reproduced, stored in or introduced into a retrieval system, or transmitted in any form or by any means (electronic, mechanical, photocopying, recording, or otherwise), or for any purpose, without the express written permission of Microsoft Corporation.

The names of manufacturers, products, or URLs are provided for informational purposes only and Microsoft makes no representations and warranties, either expressed, implied, or statutory, regarding these manufacturers or the use of the products with any Microsoft technologies. The inclusion of a manufacturer or product does not imply endorsement of Microsoft of the manufacturer or product. Links are provided to third party sites. Such sites are not under the control of Microsoft and Microsoft is not responsible for the contents of any linked site or any link contained in a linked site, or any changes or updates to such sites. Microsoft is not responsible for webcasting or any other form of transmission received from any linked site. Microsoft is providing these links to you only as a convenience, and the inclusion of any link does not imply endorsement of Microsoft of the site or the products contained therein.

Microsoft may have patents, patent applications, trademarks, copyrights, or other intellectual property rights covering subject matter in this document. Except as expressly provided in any written license agreement from Microsoft, the furnishing of this document does not give you any license to these patents, trademarks, copyrights, or other intellectual property.

© 2005 Microsoft Corporation. All rights reserved.

Microsoft, Active Directory, ActiveX, Authenticode, BizTalk, IntelliMirror, MSDN, PowerPoint, Windows, Windows Media, Windows NT, and Windows Server are either registered trademarks or trademarks of Microsoft Corporation in the United States and/or other countries.

All other trademarks are property of their respective owners.

Overview

- **Configuring Device Driver Signing Options**
- **Using Device Driver Rollback**

Introduction

To function properly, each device that is attached to a computer requires software, known as a device driver, to be installed on the computer. Every device requires a device driver to communicate with the operating system. Device drivers that are used with the Microsoft® Windows® operating systems are typically provided by Microsoft and the device manufacturer.

This module introduces you to concepts and procedures that will help you maintain device drivers.

Objectives

After completing this module, you will be able to:

- Configure device driver signing.
- Restore the previous version of a device driver.

Lesson: Configuring Device Driver Signing Options

- What Is a Device?
- What Is a Device Driver?
- What Are Device Driver Properties?
- What Is a Signed Device Driver?
- Group Policy Setting for Unsigned Device Drivers
- Practice: Configuring Device Driver Signing Options

Introduction

This lesson introduces devices, device drivers, device driver signing, and Group Policy driver signing settings. This lesson also describes how to configure device driver signing manually and by using Group Policy objects.

Lesson objectives

After completing this lesson, you will be able to:

- Explain devices and types of devices.
- Explain the purpose of a device driver.
- Determine device driver properties.
- Explain signed device drivers.
- Describe the Group Policy settings for managing device drivers.
- Configure device driver signing options manually.

What Is a Device?

> - **A device is any piece of equipment that can be attached to a computer**
>   - Examples: Video card, printer, joystick, network adapter, modem card
>
> - **Devices can be divided into two groups:**
>   - Plug and Play
>   - Non–Plug and Play

Definition

A device is any piece of equipment that can be attached to a computer.

Examples of devices

Some examples of devices are a video card, a printer, a joystick, a network adapter, a modem card, and other peripheral equipment.

Types of devices

Devices can be divided into two groups:

- Plug and Play

    Plug and Play is a combination of hardware and software support that enables a computer system to recognize and adapt to hardware configuration changes with little or no user intervention.

    You can add or remove Plug and Play devices dynamically, without manually changing the configuration. With Plug and Play, you can be confident that all devices will work together and that the computer will function correctly after you add or remove the device.

    Some Plug and Play devices are hot pluggable, which means they can be attached and removed without turning on the computer. Most Universal Serial Bus (USB) devices are hot-pluggable.

    For most internal devices such as network cards you must turn off the computer to install the device, and then restart the computer to initialize the device.

    In Microsoft Windows Server™ 2003, Plug and Play support is optimized for computers that have an Advanced Configuration and Power Interface (ACPI) BIOS. ACPI devices are defined by the ACPI specification, a hardware and software interface specification that combines and enhances the Plug and Play and Advanced Power Management (APM) standards.

Most devices manufactured since 1995 are Plug and Play devices.

> **Note** For more information about Plug and Play, see the white paper, *Plug and Play*, under **Additional Reading** on the Web page on the Student Materials compact disc.

- Non–Plug and Play

    Plug and Play support depends on both the hardware device and the device driver. If the device driver does not support Plug and Play, its devices behave as non–Plug and Play devices, regardless of any Plug and Play support that is provided by the hardware. If the drivers are not Plug and Play–compatible, you will need to install and configure the drivers manually. Be sure to use the latest drivers that include Plug and Play support to avoid hardware resource conflicts.

What Is a Device Driver?

> - **A device driver is:**
>   - A program that allows a specific device to communicate with the operating system
>   - Loaded automatically when a computer is started
> - **Use Device Manager to:**
>   - Identify, install, and update device drivers
>   - Roll back to the previous version of a device driver
>   - Disable, enable, and uninstall devices

Definition

A device driver is a software program that allows a specific device, such as a modem, network adapter, or printer, to communicate with the operating system.

Scenario

For example, you are a systems administrator for a department in a large organization. The department recently acquired three new color printers. Users are complaining that all three color printers produce prints that are blurred and grainy. You suspect that the printer device driver is at fault. To solve the problem, you visit the Web site of the printer manufacturer, download the latest device driver for the printer, and then install it on the printer server.

Key concepts

The following key concepts describe device drivers:

- A device driver is loaded automatically when a computer is started.
- Before Windows can use a device that is attached to your system, the appropriate device driver must be installed.
- If a device is listed in the Windows Catalog, a device driver for that device is usually included with Windows.

    The Windows Server Catalog is a list of hardware that Microsoft compiles for specific products, including Windows Server 2003 and Windows 2000 Server. It includes the hardware devices and computer systems that are tested by Microsoft as compatible with that version of the product.

Note The Windows Catalog is updated as new hardware becomes available, so always check "Products Designed for Microsoft Windows—Windows Catalog and HCL" on the Microsoft Windows Web site for the latest version.

- Device drivers must be obtained from the device manufacturer if they are not available in Windows.
- You can use Device Manager, the administrative tool, to:
  - Identify the device drivers that are loaded for each device, and obtain information about each device driver.
  - Change resources such as interrupt requests (IRQs), which are assigned to devices.
  - Install updated device drivers.
  - Roll back to the previous version of a device driver.
  - Determine whether the hardware on your computer is working properly.
  - Disable, enable, and uninstall devices.
  - Print a summary of the devices that are installed on your computer.

Note Device Manager manages devices on a local computer only. On a remote computer, Device Manager works only in read-only mode.

Note After you load the device driver onto your system, Windows configures the properties and settings for the device. Although you can manually configure device properties and settings, you should let Windows do it most of the time. When you manually configure properties and settings, the settings become fixed, which means that Windows cannot modify them in the future if a problem arises or there is a conflict with another device.

What Are Device Driver Properties?

Device driver property	Description
Driver Name	Name of the driver file and its location
Driver Provider	Name of the company that provided the driver to Microsoft
Driver Date	Date that the driver was written
Driver Version	Version number of the driver
Digital Signer	Name of the entity that tested and verified the driver to be working properly

Introduction

One of your duties as a systems administrator may be to monitor the Web sites of hardware vendors to look for updated device drivers and then install them on your server computer. Before installing an updated device driver, you must document the properties of the device driver, such as name, date, and version.

Device driver properties

The following five properties are associated with every device driver:

- *Driver Name.* The physical name of the driver file and its location.
- *Driver Provider.* The name of the company that provided the driver to Microsoft.
- *Driver Date.* The date that the driver was written.
- *Driver Version.* The version number of the driver. The first version is typically named 1.0.
- *Digital Signer.* The name of the entity that tested and verified that the driver works properly.

Module 4: Maintaining Device Drivers

Example

The properties of a driver for a system device named Intel 21140-Based PCI Fast Ethernet Adapter (Generic) are shown in the following table.

Property	Description
Driver Name	C:\Windows\System32\drivers\dc21x4.sys
Driver Provider	Microsoft
Driver Date	10/1/2002
Driver Version	5.5.4.0
Digital Signer	Microsoft Windows Publisher

Note To view information about a device driver, open Device Manager, double-click the type of device that you want to view, and then, on the **Driver** tab, click **Driver Details**.

What Is a Signed Device Driver?

> - The digital signature indicates that the device driver meets a certain level of testing and that it has not been altered
> - Use signed device drivers to ensure the performance and stability of your system
> - To ensure that device drivers and system files remain in their original, digitally-signed state, Windows provides:
>   - Windows File Protection
>   - System File Checker
>   - File Signature Verification

Introduction

Each device driver and operating system file that is included with Windows has a digital signature. The digital signature indicates that the driver or file meets a certain level of testing and that it was not altered or overwritten by another program's installation process.

An administrator can configure Windows to respond to an unsigned device driver in one of three ways:

- Ignore device drivers that are not digitally signed, and install them without warning.
- Display a warning when it detects device drivers that are not digitally signed.
- Prevent users from installing device drivers that are not digitally signed.

Tip Driver signing can be configured manually on each individual server. However, using Group Policy is more efficient.

Why use signed device drivers?

Using signed device drivers helps to ensure the performance and stability of your system. Also, it is recommended that you use only signed device drivers for new and updated device drivers.

Note Software for hardware products that display the Designed for Microsoft Windows XP logo or Designed for Microsoft Windows Server 2003 logo has a digital signature from Microsoft. This digital signature indicates that the product was tested for compatibility with Windows and has not been altered since testing.

Tools and components to maintain the digital signature of a device driver

Windows includes the following tools and components to ensure that your device drivers and system files remain in their original, digitally-signed state:

- Windows File Protection

    Windows File Protection prevents the replacement of protected system files, such as .sys, .dll, .ocx, .ttf, .fon, and .exe files. Windows File Protection is a component that runs in the background and protects all files that are installed by the Windows Setup program.

    Windows File Protection checks the file's digital signature to determine whether the new file is the correct version. If the file is not the correct version, Windows File Protection either replaces the file from the backup that is stored in the Dllcache folder or from the Windows Server 2003 compact disc. If Windows File Protection cannot locate the appropriate file, it prompts you for the location.

    By default, Windows File Protection is always enabled and allows digitally signed files to replace existing files. Currently, signed files are distributed through Windows Service Packs, hotfix distributions, operating system upgrades and Windows Update.

- System File Checker

    System File Checker, **sfc**, is a command-line tool that scans and verifies the versions of all protected system files after you restart your computer. System File Checker replaces overwritten files with the correct system files that are provided by Microsoft. It is part of the Windows File Protection feature of Windows Server 2003. System File Checker also checks and repopulates the Dllcache folder.

    If the Dllcache folder becomes damaged or unusable, use **sfc** with the **/purgecache** switch to repair its contents. Most .sys, .dll, .exe, .ttf, .fon, and .ocx files on the Windows Server 2003 compact disc are protected.

    The following table lists the various **sfc** switches and their descriptions.

Switch	Description
/scannow	Scans all protected system files immediately
/scanonce	Scans all protected system files at the next system start
/scanboot	Scans all protected system files at every start
/revert	Returns scan to default setting.
/purgecache	Purges the file cache and scans all protected system files immediately
/cachesize=x	Sets the file cache size, in megabytes
/?	Displays this list

    Note To start a system file check, click **Start**, click **Run**, and then type **sfc /scannow**.

- File Signature Verification

    The system files and device driver files that are provided with Windows XP and the Windows Server 2003 family of products have a Microsoft digital signature. The digital signature indicates that the files are original, unaltered system files or that they are approved by Microsoft for use with Windows.

    By using File Signature Verification, you can identify signed and unsigned files on your computer and view the name, location, modification date, type, and version number.

    Note To start File Signature Verification, click **Start**, click **Run**, type **sigverif**, and then click **OK**.

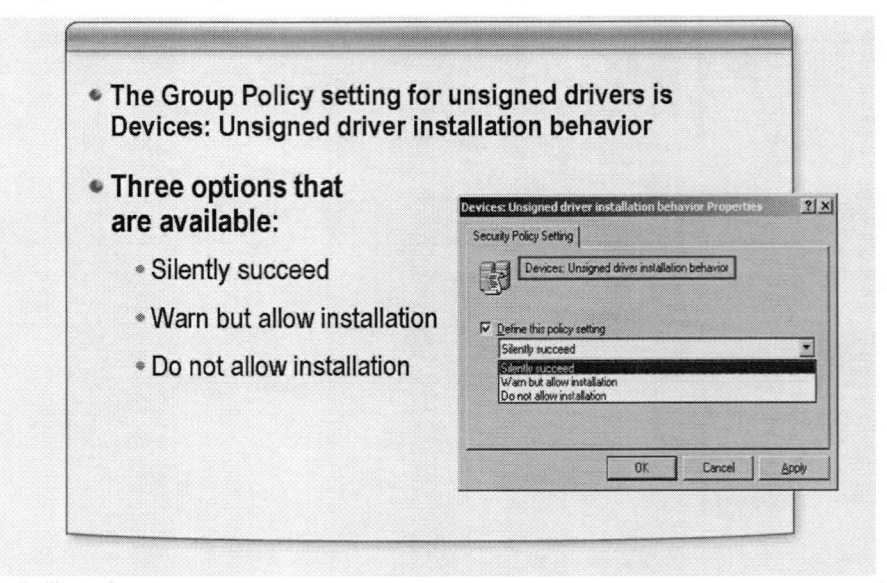

Group Policy Setting for Unsigned Device Drivers

- The Group Policy setting for unsigned drivers is **Devices: Unsigned driver installation behavior**
- Three options that are available:
  - Silently succeed
  - Warn but allow installation
  - Do not allow installation

Introduction

The Group Policy setting for unsigned device drivers is **Devices: Unsigned driver installation behavior**. You can use it to allow users to install unsigned drivers, to warn users before they install unsigned device drivers, and to prevent users from installing unsigned device drivers.

Example of using Group Policy

You are a systems administrator for an organization that does not allow users to install unsigned device drivers on their computers. The organization has more than 1,000 computers, so enforcing this rule by manually configuring each computer is an impractical solution. The most efficient way to enforce this rule is to automate the setting by configuring Group Policy.

Group Policy options

The **Unsigned driver installation behavior** Group Policy setting has three options:

- *Silently succeed.* Allows the user to install an unsigned device driver without receiving a warning.
- *Warn but allow installation.* Allows the user to install an unsigned device driver, but a warning about installing unsigned device drivers is displayed.
- *Do not allow installation.* Prevents the installation of unsigned device drivers.

Note Settings configured in Group Policy override settings configured locally for computers that are members of an Active Directory® directory service domain.

Practice: Configuring Device Driver Signing Options

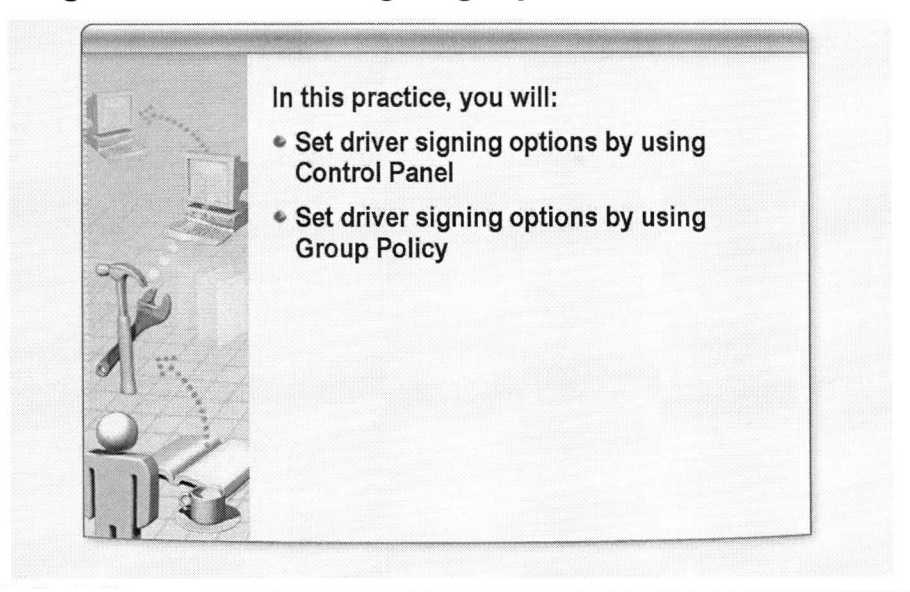

Objective

In this practice, you will:

- Set driver signing options by using Control Panel
- Set driver signing options by using Group Policy

Instructions

Ensure that the DEN-DC1 virtual machine is running.

Practice

▶ **Set driver signing options by using Control Panel**

1. Log on to DEN-DC1 as **Administrator** with a password of **Pa$$w0rd**.
2. Click **Start**, point to **Control Panel**, and then click **System**.
3. Click the **Hardware** tab.
4. Click **Driver Signing**.
5. Click **Block – Never install unsigned driver software** and then click **OK**.
6. Click **Device Manager**.
7. Expand **Mice and other pointing devices**, right-click **VM Additions PS/2 Port Mouse**, and then click **Update Driver**.
8. Click **No, not this time**, and click **Next**.
9. Click **Install from a list or specific location (Advanced)**, and then click **Next**.
10. Click **Don't search. I will choose the driver to install**, and then click **Next**.
11. Click **Have Disk**, in the **Copy manufacturers files from** box, type **D:\2275\Practices\Mod04**, and then click **OK**. Notice that the driver is not digitally signed.
12. Click **Next**.
13. Click **Yes** to confirm the device installation.

14. A **Hardware Installation** dialog box appears, indicating that the driver cannot be installed. Click **OK**.
15. Click **Finish** and close **Device Manager**.
16. Click **OK** to close **System Properties**.

▶ **Set driver signing options by using Group Policy**

1. Click **Start**, point to **Administrative Tools**, and then click **Group Policy Management**.
2. Expand **Forest: Contoso.msft**, expand **Domains**, and then expand **Contoso.msft**.
3. Right-click **Contoso.msft** and click **Create and Link a GPO Here**.
4. In the **Name** box, type **DriverSigning**, and click **OK**.
5. In the left pane, right-click **DriverSigning** and click **Edit**.
6. Under **Computer Configuration**, expand **Windows Settings**, expand **Security Settings**, expand **Local Policies**, and then click **Security Options**.
7. In the right pane, double-click **Devices: Unsigned driver installation behavior**.
8. Select the **Define this policy setting** check box, click **Warn but allow installation** in the drop-down list, and then click **OK**.
9. Close **Group Policy Object Editor** and close **Group Policy Management**.
10. Click **Start**, click **Run**, type **gpupdate**, and then click **OK**.
11. Log off of DEN-DC1.

Important Do not shut down the virtual machine.

Lesson: Using Device Driver Rollback

- **What Is Device Driver Rollback?**
- **Uninstalling Devices and Device Drivers**
- **Practice: Using Device Driver Rollback**

Introduction

If a device stops functioning after you install an updated device driver for the device, you can use the Roll Back Driver feature to restore the previous version of the driver. By using this feature, you can avoid spending hours searching for a copy of the original driver that was installed.

This lesson describes how to restore, update, and uninstall device drivers.

Lesson objectives

After completing this lesson, you will be able to:

- Explain device driver rollback.
- Describe the effects of uninstalling device drivers and devices.
- Restore a previous version of a device driver and update device driver.

What Is Device Driver Rollback?

- After updating device drivers, you might encounter problems
- If a problem occurs, you can revert to the previous version by using Roll Back Driver
- You cannot:
  - Roll back beyond one driver version
  - Roll back printer drivers
  - Simultaneously roll back drivers for all functions of a multifunction device

Introduction

Updating one or more device drivers can cause problems. For example, a device can stop functioning, a stop error may be displayed, and startup problems can occur. To prevent problems from occurring after you upgrade a device driver, avoid using beta or unsigned device drivers. These device drivers might not be fully tested for compatibility with Windows Server 2003.

Why use device driver rollback?

If a problem occurs immediately after you update a device driver, you can restore the previous version by using the Roll Back Driver feature in Device Manager. If the problem prevents you from starting Windows Server 2003 in normal mode, you can roll back device drivers in safe mode.

Note You must be logged on as an administrator or a member of the Administrators group to roll back a driver, or you must have been delegated this authority.

Driver rollback limitations

When using device driver rollback, be aware of the following limitations:

- You can roll back only one driver version. For example, you cannot restore the second to the last version of a driver.
- You cannot roll back printer drivers because Device Manager does not support or display printer properties.
- You cannot simultaneously roll back device drivers for all functions of a multifunction device. You must roll back each driver separately. For example, for a multifunction device that provides audio and modem functionality, you must roll back the modem driver and the audio driver separately.

Uninstalling Devices and Device Drivers

- Uninstalling a device driver does not delete it from disk
- Remove a Plug and Play device to uninstall it
- Disable a device to remove it temporarily

Introduction

When you use Device Manager to uninstall a device driver, the device driver is removed from memory but not from the hard disk. Until you remove the device, Windows automatically reloads the driver the next time the computer is restarted.

Uninstalling a Plug and Play device

You uninstall a Plug and Play device by disconnecting or removing the device from your computer. Some devices, such as cards that plug into the motherboard, require that you turn off the computer first. To ensure that you uninstall a Plug and Play device properly, consult the device manufacturer's installation and removal instructions.

Uninstalling devices vs. disabling devices

If you want a Plug and Play device to remain attached to a computer without being enabled, you can disable the device instead of uninstalling it.

When you disable a device, the device stays physically connected to your computer, but Windows updates the system registry so that the device drivers for the disabled device are no longer loaded when you start your computer. The device drivers are available again when you enable the device.

Disabling devices is useful if you must switch between two hardware devices, such as a networking card and a modem, or if you need to troubleshoot a hardware issue.

Note To enable or disable devices, open Device Manager, double-click the type of device that you want to enable or disable, right-click the specific device you want, and then click **Enable** or **Disable**.

Practice: Using Device Driver Rollback

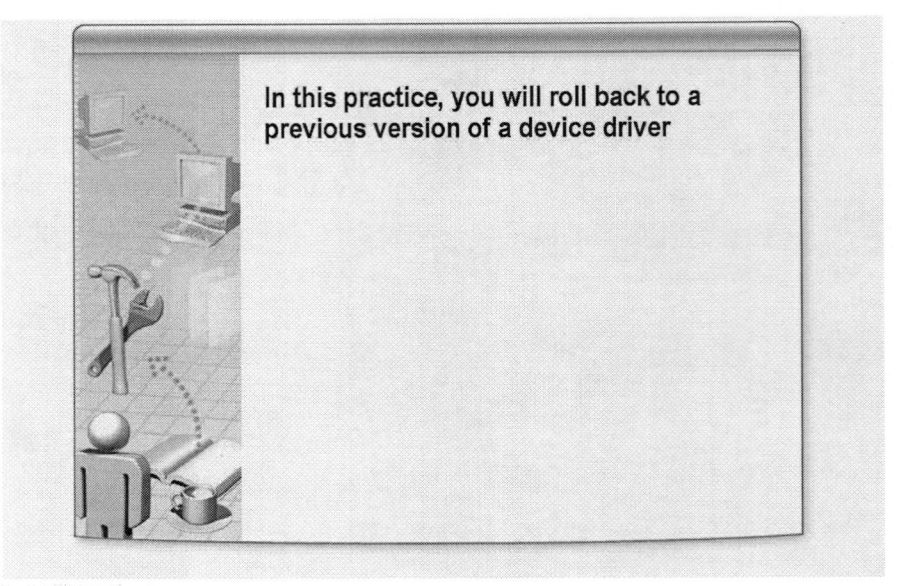

Objective

In this practice, you will:

- Roll back to a previous version of a device driver.

Instructions

Ensure that the DEN-DC1 virtual machine is running.

Practice

▶ **Roll back to a previous version of a device driver**

1. Log on to DEN-DC1 as **Administrator** with a password of **Pa$$w0rd**.
2. Click **Start**, point to **Control Panel**, and then click **System**.
3. Click the **Hardware** tab.
4. Click **Driver Signing**.
5. Click **Warn-Prompt me each time to choose an action** and then click **OK**.
6. Click **Device Manager**.
7. Expand **Mice and other pointing devices**, right-click **VM Additions PS/2 Port Mouse**, and then click **Update Driver**.
8. Click **No, not this time**, and then click **Next**.
9. Click **Install from a list or specific location (Advanced)**, and then click **Next**.
10. Click **Don't search. I will choose the driver to install**, and then click **Next**.
11. Click **Have Disk**, and, in the **Copy manufacturers files from** box, type **D:\2275\Practices\Mod04**, and then click **OK**.
12. Click the **Microsoft PS/2 Mouse**. Notice that the driver is not digitally signed.
13. Click **Next**.

14. Click **Yes** to confirm the device installation.

15. A **Hardware Installation** dialog box appears, indicating that the driver has not passed logo testing. Click **Continue Anyway**.

16. If prompted to insert the Windows Server 2003, Enterprise Edition CD-ROM then complete the following.

    a. In the **Copy files from** box, type **C:\Win2K3\i386**.

    b. Click **OK**.

17. Click **Finish**.

18. In device manager, right-click **Microsoft PS/2 Mouse**, and then click **Properties**.

19. Click the **Driver** tab, and click **Roll Back Driver**.

20. Click **Yes** to confirm.

21. Click **Close**.

22. Do not restart the computer if prompted.

▶ **To prepare for the next module**

1. Close all programs and shut down all computers. Do not save changes.

2. Start the DEN-DC1 and DEN-SRV2 virtual computers.

Note Shut down the virtual machine and do not save changes.

Module 5: Managing Disks

Contents

Overview	1
Lesson: Preparing Disks	2
Lesson: Managing Disk Properties	13
Lesson: Managing Mounted Drives	20
Lesson: Converting Disks	24
Lesson: Creating Volumes	31
Lesson: Creating Fault-Tolerant Volumes	38
Lesson: Importing a Foreign Disk	49
Lab: Managing Disks	52

Information in this document, including URL and other Internet Web site references, is subject to change without notice. Unless otherwise noted, the example companies, organizations, products, domain names, e-mail addresses, logos, people, places, and events depicted herein are fictitious, and no association with any real company, organization, product, domain name, e-mail address, logo, person, place or event is intended or should be inferred. Complying with all applicable copyright laws is the responsibility of the user. Without limiting the rights under copyright, no part of this document may be reproduced, stored in or introduced into a retrieval system, or transmitted in any form or by any means (electronic, mechanical, photocopying, recording, or otherwise), or for any purpose, without the express written permission of Microsoft Corporation.

The names of manufacturers, products, or URLs are provided for informational purposes only and Microsoft makes no representations and warranties, either expressed, implied, or statutory, regarding these manufacturers or the use of the products with any Microsoft technologies. The inclusion of a manufacturer or product does not imply endorsement of Microsoft of the manufacturer or product. Links are provided to third party sites. Such sites are not under the control of Microsoft and Microsoft is not responsible for the contents of any linked site or any link contained in a linked site, or any changes or updates to such sites. Microsoft is not responsible for webcasting or any other form of transmission received from any linked site. Microsoft is providing these links to you only as a convenience, and the inclusion of any link does not imply endorsement of Microsoft of the site or the products contained therein.

Microsoft may have patents, patent applications, trademarks, copyrights, or other intellectual property rights covering subject matter in this document. Except as expressly provided in any written license agreement from Microsoft, the furnishing of this document does not give you any license to these patents, trademarks, copyrights, or other intellectual property.

© 2005 Microsoft Corporation. All rights reserved.

Microsoft, Active Directory, ActiveX, Authenticode, BizTalk, IntelliMirror, MSDN, PowerPoint, Windows, Windows Media, Windows NT, and Windows Server are either registered trademarks or trademarks of Microsoft Corporation in the United States and/or other countries.

All other trademarks are property of their respective owners.

Overview

- Preparing Disks
- Managing Disk Properties
- Managing Mounted Drives
- Converting Disks
- Creating Volumes
- Creating Fault-Tolerant Volumes
- Importing a Foreign Disk

Introduction

One of the tasks that you perform when administering a server is managing disks. You will need to understand the Microsoft® Windows Server™ 2003 tools that are available to set up and manage disks and disk drives. This understanding also allows users to employ advanced features, such as creating a mounted drive and importing a foreign disk.

This module covers these tasks and describes how to use the tools to manage and set up disks.

Objectives

After completing this module, you will be able to:

- Initialize and partition a disk.
- View and update disk properties.
- Manage mounted drives.
- Convert a disk from basic to dynamic and from dynamic to basic.
- Create volumes on a disk.
- Create fault-tolerant volumes.
- Import disks.

Lesson: Preparing Disks

- What Is Disk Management?
- What Is the DiskPart Tool?
- What Is a Partition?
- Multimedia: What Are the Differences Between the FAT, FAT32, and NTFS File Systems?
- Best Practices for Preparing Disks
- Practice: Preparing Disks

Introduction

When you install a new disk, Windows Server 2003 recognizes it and configures it as a basic disk. A basic disk is the default storage medium and provides limited configuration capabilities.

This lesson describes how to partition a basic disk by using Disk Management and the DiskPart command-line tool. It also explains how file system attributes affect disks and how to use the file systems when you configure disks.

Lesson objectives

After completing this lesson, you will be able to:

- Describe the function of Disk Management.
- Describe the function of DiskPart.
- Describe partitions.
- Distinguish among FAT (file allocation table), FAT32, and the NTFS file system.
- Describe best practices for preparing disks.
- Prepare disks.

What Is Disk Management?

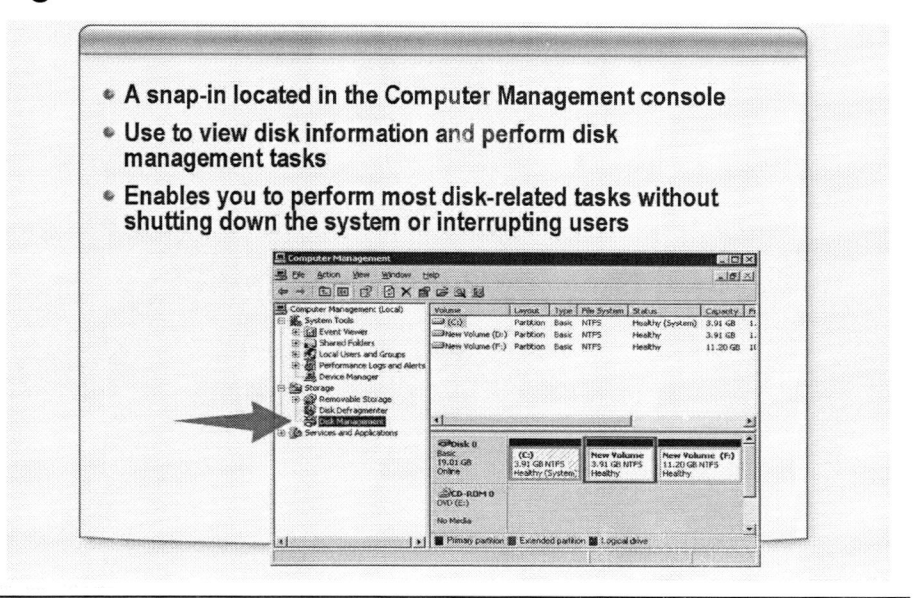

- A snap-in located in the Computer Management console
- Use to view disk information and perform disk management tasks
- Enables you to perform most disk-related tasks without shutting down the system or interrupting users

Introduction

Disk Management, a Microsoft Management Console (MMC) snap-in, is a system utility that consolidates all your disk management tasks for both local and remote administration of Windows Server 2003. Because Disk Management is an MMC snap-in, it uses the interface, menu structure, and shortcut menus that you are accustomed to using. You can gain access to Disk Management in the Computer Management console, or you can create a separate console for it.

Perform disk management tasks

You can use Disk Management to configure and manage your storage space and perform all your disk management tasks. You can also use Disk Management to convert disk storage type, create and extend volumes, and perform other disk management tasks, such as managing drive letters and paths and maintaining Windows Server 2003.

Most disk management tasks can be performed without restarting the system or interrupting users.

Local and remote administration

When you create a separate console and add the Disk Management snap-in, you can focus the snap-in either on the local computer or on another computer for remote administration of that computer. To manage disks, you must be a member of the Backup Operators group or the Administrators group on the server being managed, or you must have been delegated the appropriate authority. If the computer is joined to a domain, members of the Domain Admins group can perform this procedure. As a security best practice, consider using the **Run as** command to perform disk management tasks.

For example, you can create a console to which you add multiple Disk Management snap-ins, each focused on a different remote computer. You can then manage the disk storage of all the computers from that single console.

What Is the DiskPart Tool?

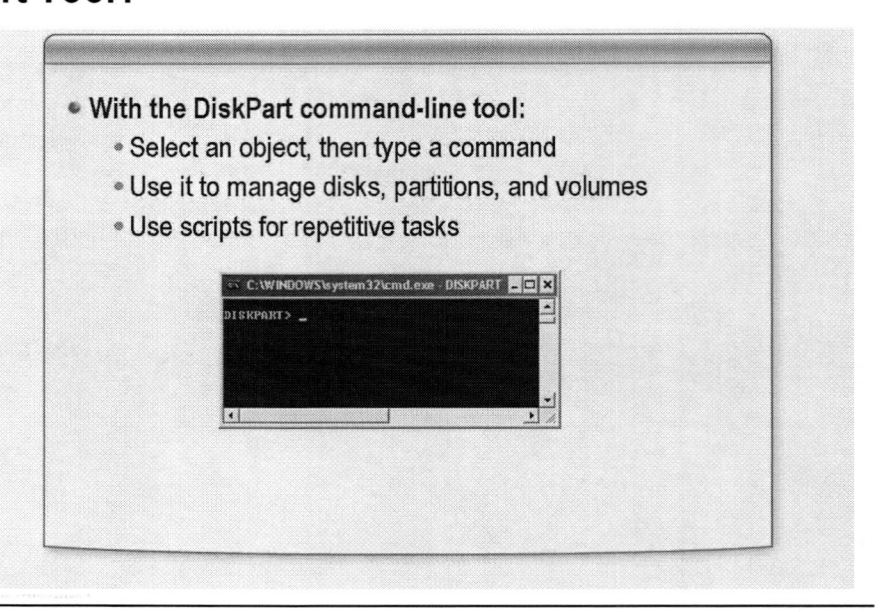

- With the DiskPart command-line tool:
  - Select an object, then type a command
  - Use it to manage disks, partitions, and volumes
  - Use scripts for repetitive tasks

Introduction

By using the DiskPart command-line tool, you can perform many disk management tasks from the command line. Use DiskPart to perform disk-related tasks as an alternative to using Disk Management.

Use DiskPart to manage objects

DiskPart is a text-mode command interpreter that enables you to manage objects, such as disks, partitions, and volumes, by using scripts or direct input from a command prompt. Administrators often write scripts to perform repetitive tasks.

Give an object focus

Before you can use a DiskPart command, you must first list and then select an object that you want to manage to give it focus. When an object has focus, any DiskPart command that you type acts on that object.

You can list the available objects and discover an object's number or drive letter by using the **list disk**, **list volume**, and **list partition** commands. The **list disk** and **list volume** commands display all the disks and volumes that are on the computer. Conversely, the **list partition** command displays only those partitions on the disk that have focus. When you use the list commands, an asterisk (*) appears next to the object with focus.

You select an object by using its number or drive letter, such as disk 0, partition 1, volume 3, or volume C. When you select an object, the focus remains on that object until you select a different object. For example, if the focus is set on disk 0 and you select volume 8 on disk 2, the focus shifts from disk 0 to disk 2, volume 8.

DiskPart example

The following table shows an example of using the **diskpart** command to focus on a particular disk.

Command	Description	Response
C:\diskpart	Type **diskpart** on the command line.	Microsoft DiskPart version 5.2 Copyright © 1999-2001 Microsoft Corporation. On computer: DEN-DC1
DISKPART> list disk	Type **list disk** to request a list of disks on the server. A list of disks, their status, size, and unallocated space appears.	Disk ### Status Size Free Dyn Gpt Disk 0 Online 37 GB 0 B
DISKPART> **select disk 0**	Type **select disk** *n* to focus on the selected disk. Disk 0 is now selected. The object with focus has an asterisk.	DISKPART> list disk Disk ### Status Size Free Dyn Gpt * Disk 0 Online 37 GB 0 B

Partition and volume focus

On a basic disk, the partition focus and volume focus are the same. If you change the focus on one item, you change the focus on the other.

Note For more information about the DiskPart tool, search for DiskPart in the Windows 2003 Server Help and Support Center.

What Is a Partition?

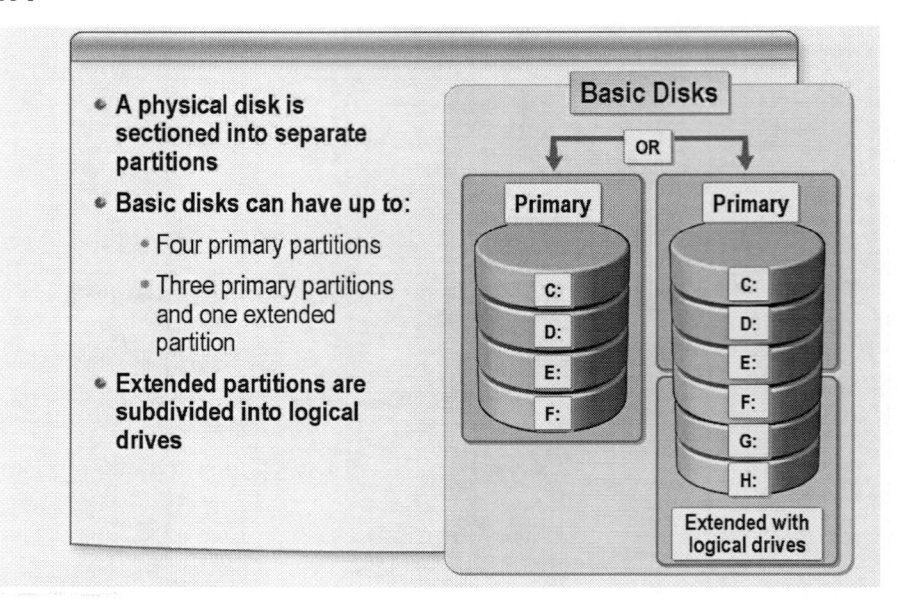

- A physical disk is sectioned into separate partitions
- Basic disks can have up to:
  - Four primary partitions
  - Three primary partitions and one extended partition
- Extended partitions are subdivided into logical drives

Basic Disks

Primary: C:, D:, E:, F:

OR

Primary: C:, D:, E:, F:, G:, H: (Extended with logical drives)

Introduction

Disk partitioning is a way to divide a basic physical disk into sections so that each section, or *partition*, functions as a separate unit. You can use partitioning to divide the hard disk drive into several drive letters so that it is easier to organize data files. Each partition is usually assigned a different drive letter such as C or D. Volume mount points, which do not require a drive letter, can also be used instead of, or in addition to, drive letters. After you create a partition, you must format it with a file system before you can store data on the partition.

Partition example

An administrator who wants to keep applications separate from the system files can use partitioning to set up a drive letter for the application files and another drive letter for the system files.

Initialize a disk

When you attach a new disk to your computer, you must first initialize the disk before you can create partitions. When you first start Disk Management after installing a new disk, a wizard appears that provides a list of the new disks that are detected by the operating system. When you complete the wizard, the operating system initializes the disk by writing a disk signature, the end of sector marker (also called a signature word), and a master boot record (MBR). If you cancel the wizard before the disk signature is written, the disk status remains Not Initialized.

Primary partitions

You create primary partitions on a basic disk. A basic disk can have as many as four primary partitions or three primary partitions and one extended partition. A primary partition cannot be subdivided. An extended partition can be divided into logical drives.

Note For more information about partitions, see Appendix B, "Partition Styles," on the Student Materials compact disc.

Logical drives

Logical drives are similar to primary partitions, except that you can create as many as 24 logical drives per disk but are limited to four primary partitions per disk. You can format a logical drive and assign a drive letter to it.

Extended partitions	You can create an extended partition only on a basic disk. Unlike a primary partition, an extended partition is not formatted with a file system. Instead, you create one or more logical drives in the extended partition and then format them with a file system.
Format a disk	You must format a disk before you can use it. Formatting a disk configures the partition with a file allocation table. Formatting prepares the disk for reading and writing. When you format a disk, the operating system erases all the file allocation tables on the disk, tests the disk to verify that the sectors are reliable, marks bad sectors, and creates internal address tables that it later uses to locate information.
Delete a partition	Deleting a partition destroys all the data in the partition. The partition is then restored to an unallocated space. If you are deleting an extended partition, you must delete all its logical drives on the disk before deleting the partition.
	Note Specialized data recovery utilities are able to recover most data even after a partition has been deleted.
Assign drive letters	Windows Server 2003 allows the static assignment of drive letters to partitions, volumes, and CD-ROM drives. This means that you assign a drive letter to a specific partition, volume, or CD-ROM drive. It is often convenient to assign drive letters to removable devices in such a way that the devices appear after the permanent partitions and volumes on the computer.
	Note The drive letter assigned to a partition can be changed, with the exception of the C drive. The drive letter of the system or boot volume cannot be changed.
Manage drive letters	You can use as many as 24 drive letters, from C through Z. Drive letters A and B are reserved for floppy-disk drives. However, if you have only one floppy-disk drive, you can use the letter B for a network drive. When you add a new hard disk to an existing computer system, it will not affect drive letters already assigned.
	Important Before you delete or create partitions on a hard disk, back up the disk contents, because creating and deleting partitions destroys any existing data. As with any major change to disk contents, it is recommended that you back up the entire contents of the hard disk before working with partitions, even if you plan to make no changes to any of the partitions.

Multimedia: What Are the Differences Between the FAT, FAT32, and NTFS File Systems?

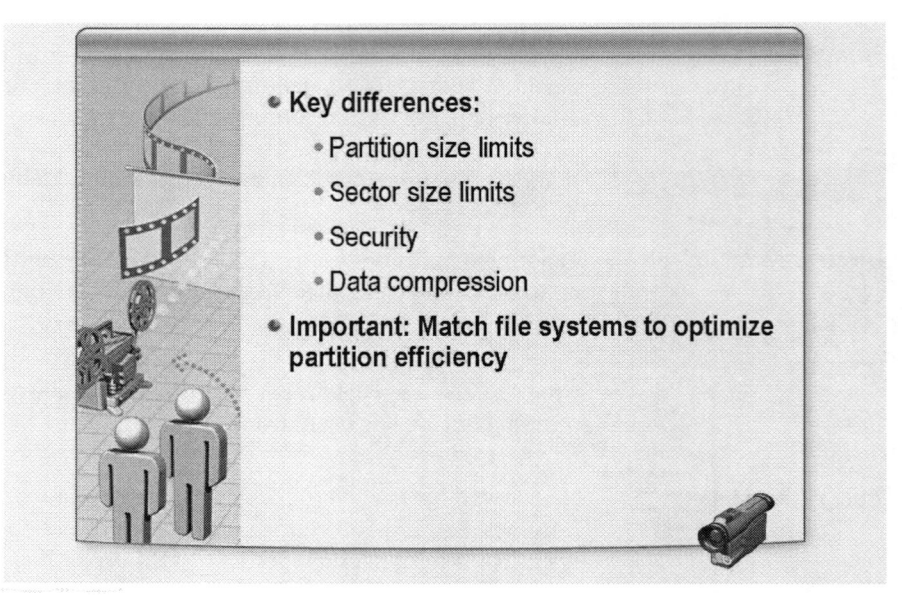

- **Key differences:**
  - Partition size limits
  - Sector size limits
  - Security
  - Data compression
- **Important: Match file systems to optimize partition efficiency**

Introduction

Windows supports three main file systems: FAT (file allocation table), FAT32, and NTFS. This topic describes the main features and uses of each.

Key file system features

The following table summarizes the key features of the three file systems.

	FAT	FAT32	NTFS
Max partition size	4 gigabytes (GB)	32 GB	2 terabytes
Sector size	16 kilobytes (KB) to 64 KB	As low as 4 KB	As low as 4 KB
Security	File attributes	File attributes	File, folder, and encryption
Compression	None	None	Files, folders, and drives

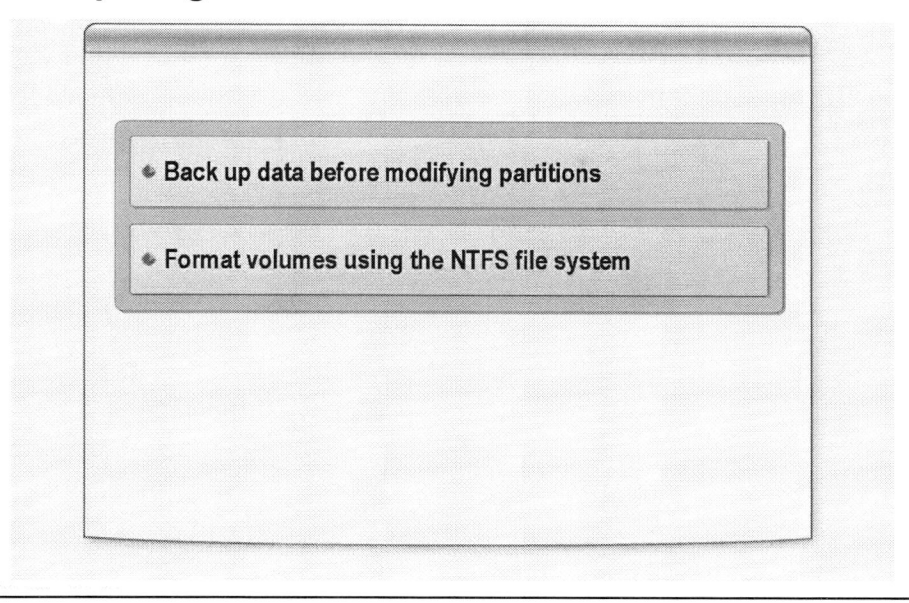

Best Practices for Preparing Disks

- Back up data before modifying partitions
- Format volumes using the NTFS file system

Introduction

It is important to be aware of the best practices for preparing disks. Adhering to these best practices ensures that data is not lost and that all file system features are available.

Back up data

Because deleting or creating partitions or volumes destroys any existing data, be sure to back up the disk contents beforehand. As with any major change to disk contents, it is recommended that you back up the entire contents of the hard disk before working with partitions or volumes.

Format volumes using the NTFS file system

Many features in the Windows Server 2003 family of operating systems, such as file and folder permissions, encryption, large volume support, and sparse file management, require the NTFS file system format. Be prepared by formatting your volumes by using the NTFS file system.

Practice: Preparing Disks

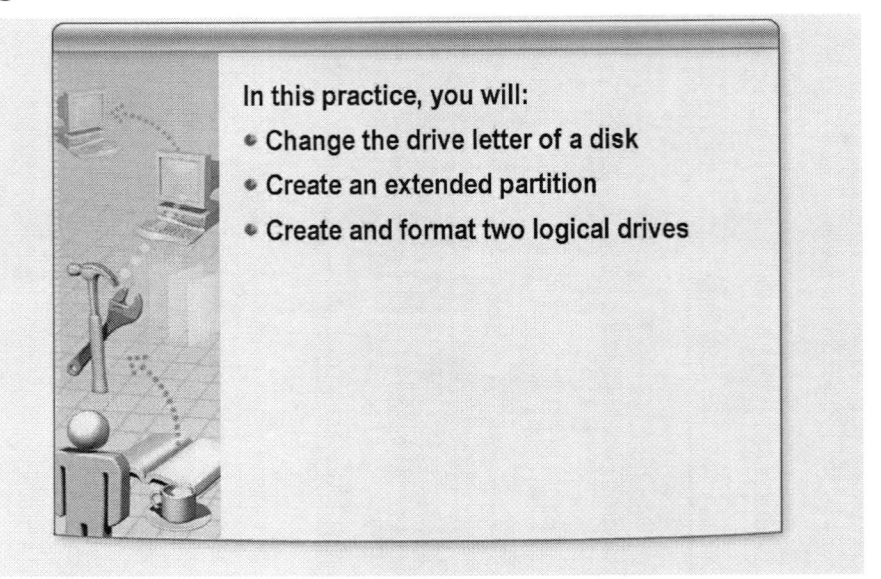

Objective

In this practice, you will:

- Change the drive letter of a disk.
- Create an extended partition.
- Create and format two logical drives.

Instructions

Ensure that the DEN-DC1 and the DEN-SRV2 virtual machines are running.

Practice

▶ **Change the drive letter of a disk**

1. On DEN-SRV2, log on as **Administrator** with a password of **Pa$$w0rd**.
2. Click **Start**, point to **Administrative Tools**, and then click **Computer Management**.
3. Maximize the Computer Management window to see all the information.
4. Click **Disk Management**.
5. In the **Initialize and Convert Disk Wizard** welcome page, Click **Next**.
6. In the **Select Disks to Initialize** page, click **Next**.
7. In the **Select Disks to Convert** page, do not select any disks.
8. Click **Next** and then **Finish**.
9. Right-click **CD-ROM 0** and then click **Change Drive Letter and Paths**.
10. Click **Change**.
11. In the drop down list, click **Z** and then click **OK**.
12. Click **Yes** to close the **Confirm** dialog box.

▶ **Create an extended partition**

1. Right-click the unallocated space in **Disk 1** and then click **New Partition**.
2. Click **Next** to start the **New Partition Wizard**.
3. Click **Extended partition** and then click **Next**.
4. In the **Partition size in MB** box, type **4000**, and then click **Next**.
5. Click **Finish**.
6. Close Computer Management.

▶ **Create and format two logical drives**

1. Click **Start**, click **Run**, type **cmd**, and then click **OK**.
2. Type **diskpart /?** and then press ENTER.
3. Type **diskpart** and then press ENTER.
4. Type **list disk** and then press ENTER.
5. Type **select disk 1** and then press ENTER.
6. Type **list partition** and then press ENTER.
7. Type **select partition 1** and then press ENTER.
8. Type **create partition logical size=1500** and then press ENTER.
9. Type **create partition logical size=2000** and then press ENTER.
10. Type **list partition** and then press ENTER.
11. Type **select partition 2** and then press ENTER.
12. Type **assign letter=d** and then press ENTER.
13. Type **select partition 3** and then press ENTER.
14. Type **assign letter=e** and then press ENTER.
15. Type **exit** and then press ENTER.
16. Close the command prompt.
17. Click **Start**, point to **Administrative Tools**, and then click **Computer Management**.
18. Click **Disk Management**.
19. Right-click **(D:)**, and then click **Format**.
20. In the **Volume label** box, type **FAT32**.
21. In the **File system** box, click **FAT32**.
22. Select the **Perform a quick format** check box and then click **OK**.
23. Click **OK** to continue.
24. Right-click **(E:)**, and then click **Format**.
25. In the **Volume label** box, type **NTFS**.
26. In the **File system** box, click **NTFS**.

27. Select the **Perform a quick format** check box and then click **OK**.
28. Click **OK** to continue.
29. Close Computer Management.

Important Do not shut down the virtual machines.

Lesson: Managing Disk Properties

- What Are Disk Properties?
- What Is the Convert Utility?
- Practice: Managing Disk Properties

Introduction

This lesson explains disk properties. Systems administrators use the information in disk properties when they replace the hard disk in a server.

Lesson objectives

After completing this lesson, you will be able to:

- Describe disk properties.
- Convert FAT and FAT32 file systems to the NTFS file system.
- Manage disk properties.

What Are Disk Properties?

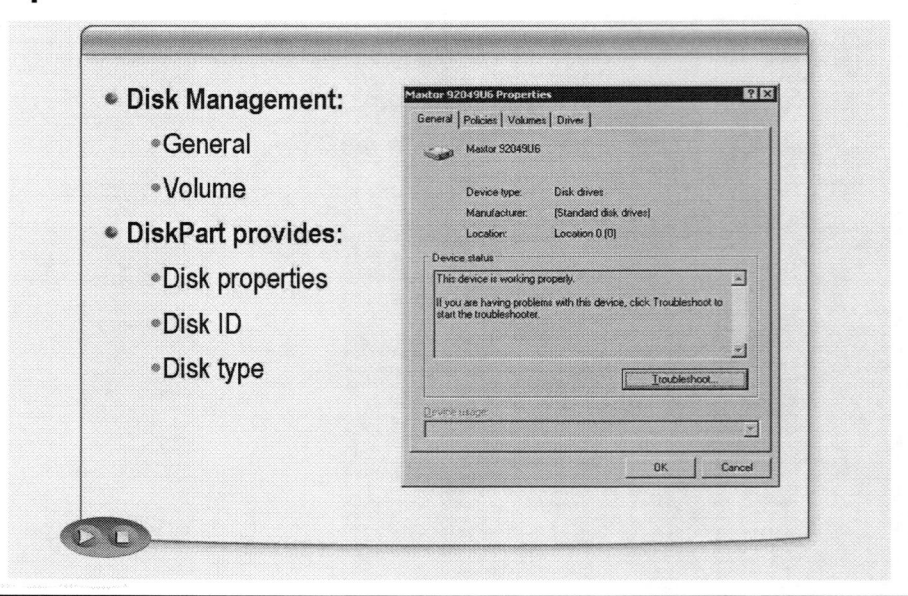

- **Disk Management:**
    - General
    - Volume
- **DiskPart provides:**
    - Disk properties
    - Disk ID
    - Disk type

Definition

You can use either Disk Management or DiskPart to view disk properties, which contain information about the physical disk and the volumes that it contains.

Use of disk properties information

Use the information in disk properties when you replace a hard disk or to verify that a specific disk is installed on a server.

Latest disk information

Disk properties provide the latest available information about the disk. You can access this information by using DiskPart or by using Disk Management to open the **Properties** dialog box for the disk. The following tabs in the **Properties** dialog box display disk properties:

- *General.* Provides the model number and the location of the disk.
- *Volumes.* Provides the disk number, type (basic or dynamic), status, partition style, capacity, unallocated space, and reserved space of the disk.

In addition to the information in Disk Management, DiskPart provides the Disk ID and whether it is Integrated Device Electronics (IDE), Advanced Technology Attachment (ATA), or Small Computer System Interface (SCSI).

To understand how this data is used, imagine that you need to order a replacement for a failed hard disk. As systems administrator, you must know the model, type, and capacity of the original disk. You use DiskPart or Disk Manager to discover the disk properties to document this information ahead of time. After installing the new disk, you configure it with the disk number, partitions, unallocated space, and volume type of the failed disk before restoring data.

Rescan disks

In most cases, Disk Management will automatically recognize new hard disks when they are added to a computer. If Disk Management does not recognize that new hard disks are in the system, you must rescan the disks. When Disk Management rescans disk properties, it scans all attached disks for changes to the disk configuration. It also updates information about removable media, CD-ROM drives, basic volumes, file systems, and drive letters. Rescanning disks is most commonly required for hot-swappable drives that are added while Windows Server 2003 is running.

What Is the Convert Utility?

- Converts FAT and FAT32 volumes to NTFS
- All data is preserved
- No reboot is required for most volumes

Introduction

The NTFS file system is recommended for all servers. It implements advanced features such as security and fault-tolerant volumes that are not available in FAT or FAT32.

Convert file systems

The **Convert** command –line utility is used to convert existing FAT or FAT32 volumes to NTFS. All files are left intact after the migration process.

When data volumes are converted to NTFS a reboot is not required. However, the system and boot volumes cannot be converted while the operating system is running. When the **Convert** utility is used on the system or boot volumes then the conversion is scheduled to occur during the next reboot.

Convert syntax

The syntax for the **Convert** utility is:

Convert [*volume*] **/fs:ntfs** [**/v**] [**cvtarea:***FileName*] [**/nosecurity**] [**/x**]

Option	Description
volume	The name of the volume to be converted. For example, C:.
/fs:ntfs	Specifies that the volume be converted to NTFS. This is required.
/v	Specifies verbose mode.
/cvtarea:*FileName*	Specifies a file that serves a place holder for the Master File Table (MFT) and other NTFS metadata. This may result in a less fragmented file system after conversion. This file must exist before running the convert command. It is recommended that this file is 1KB in size for each file and directory in the system.
/nosecurity	Specifies that everyone has access to the files.
/x	Dismounts the volume if necessary before conversion. This will override open files.

Practice: Managing Disk Properties

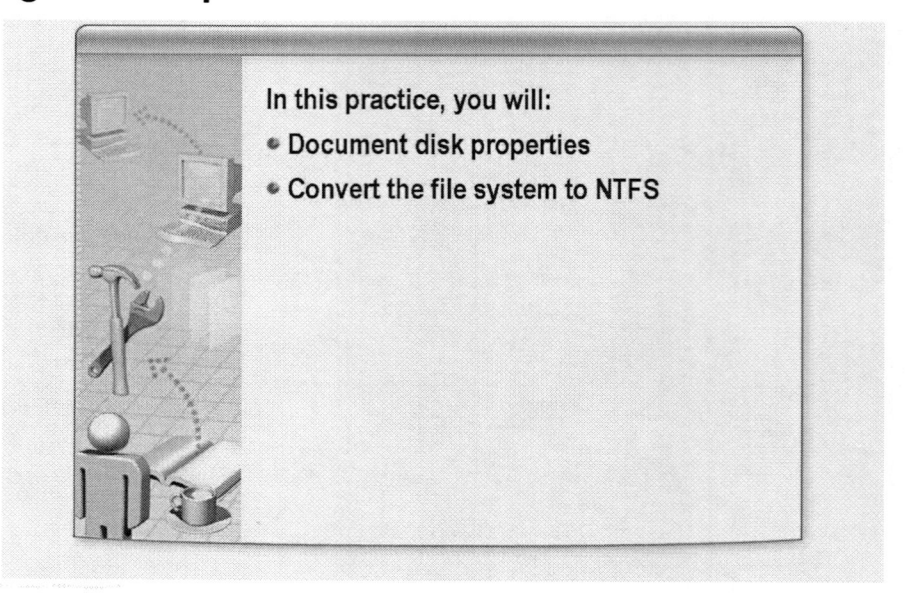

Objective

In this practice, you will:

- Document disk properties
- Convert the file system to NTFS.

Instructions

Ensure that the DEN-DC1 and the DEN-SRV2 virtual machines are running.

Practice

▶ **Document disk properties**

1. On DEN-SRV2, click **Start**, point to **Administrative Tools**, and then click **Computer Management**.
2. Click **Disk Management**.
3. Right-click **Disk 1** and then click **Properties**.
4. Click the **Volumes** tab.
5. Record the following information:

    Disk number: _____

    Disk type: _____

    Partition style: _____

    Drive capacity: _____

    Number of volumes: _____

    Capacity of D: _____

    Capacity of E: _____

6. Click **Cancel**.
7. Close Computer Management.

▶ Convert the file system to NTFS

1. Click **Start**, click **Run**, type **cmd**, and then click **OK**.
2. Type **convert d: /fs:ntfs** and then press ENTER.
3. Type **FAT32** and then press ENTER.
4. Type **diskpart** and then press ENTER.
5. Type **list disk** and then press ENTER.
6. Type **select disk 1** and then press ENTER.
7. Type **detail disk** and then press ENTER. Notice that the D drive is now using the NTFS file system.
8. Type **Exit** and then press ENTER.
9. Close the command prompt.

Important Do not shut down the virtual machines.

Lesson: Managing Mounted Drives

- What Is a Mounted Drive?
- What Is the Purpose of a Mounted Drive?
- Practice: Managing Mounted Drives

Introduction

Using mounted drives can help you manage and organize data on your server. For example, to provide a more intuitive name for your drive, you can use a mounted drive to add a drive description of an existing partition. Use a mounted drive when you have two drives of related data that logically belong on one drive. Also, mounted drives help you manage the limited number of drive letters that you have to work with on a hard disk.

Lesson objectives

After completing this lesson, you will be able to:

- Describe a mounted drive.
- Describe how to use a mounted drive.
- Manage a mounted drive.

What Is a Mounted Drive?

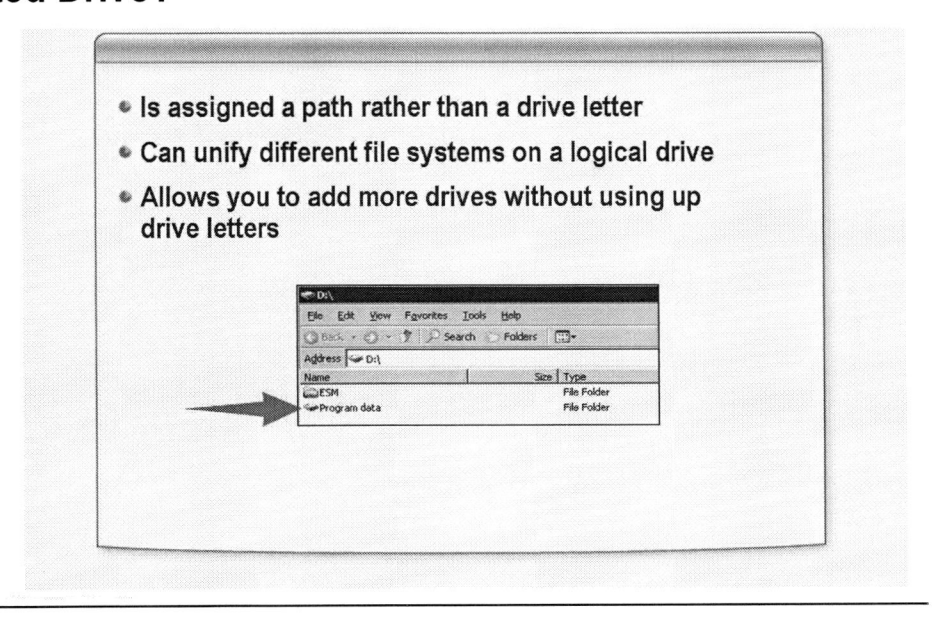

- Is assigned a path rather than a drive letter
- Can unify different file systems on a logical drive
- Allows you to add more drives without using up drive letters

Definition

A mounted drive is a self-contained unit of storage that is administered by an NTFS file system. You can use Disk Management to mount a local drive to any empty folder on a local NTFS volume rather than to a drive letter. This method is similar to creating a shortcut that points to a disk partition or volume.

Assigns drive path not drive letter

When you mount a local drive to an empty folder on an NTFS volume, Disk Management assigns a path, rather than a letter, to the drive. Mounted drives are not subject to the 26-drive limit that is imposed by drive letters, so you can use mounted drives to access more than 26 drives on your computer. Windows Server 2003 ensures that drive paths retain their association to the drive, so you can add or rearrange storage devices without causing the drive path to fail.

Unifies disparate file systems

By using mounted drives, you can unify into one logical file system disparate file systems such as NTFS 5.0, a 16-bit FAT file system, an ISO-9660 file system on a CD-ROM drive, and so on. Neither users nor applications need information about the volume on which a specific file resides. A complete path provides all the information required to locate a specified file. You can rearrange volumes, substitute volumes, or subdivide one volume into many volumes without requiring users or applications to change settings.

What Is the Purpose of a Mounted Drive?

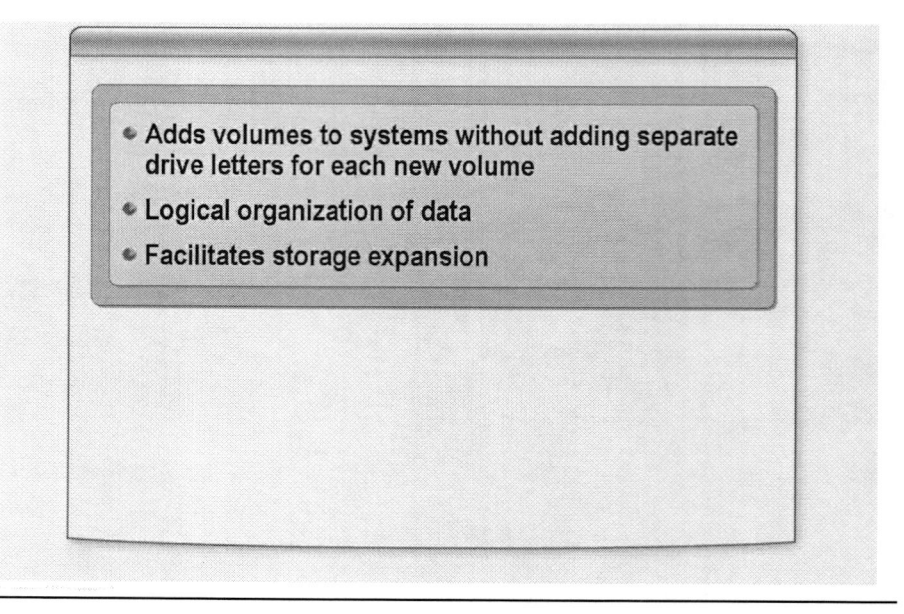

> - Adds volumes to systems without adding separate drive letters for each new volume
> - Logical organization of data
> - Facilitates storage expansion

Introduction

Using NTFS mounted drives is a convenient way to add volumes to a computer when no drive letters are available. Also, you can add space to a volume by mounting other disks as folders on the volume instead of replicating the volume on a larger disk.

Add volumes to systems

You can add new volumes to your system without adding separate drive letters for each new volume. Doing this makes it easier to manage your drive letters.

Create multiple mounted drives per volume

You can create multiple mounted drives per volume. For example, the volume storing project data can be mounted at several points where it is logical to access the date.

Manage data storage

Mounted drives help you manage data storage that is based on the work environment and system usage. For example, if the drive letter holding user data is low on disk space, you can mount a new partition to a folder name to expand the volume. Any data that should be in the mounted volume must be copied there after the volume is mounted.

Deleting a mount point

When you delete a mount point, all the files and folders remain on the drive that was mounted. For example, if you mounted drive F as C:\Temp, after you delete the mount point, the files and folders that you copied to C:\Temp are still available on drive F.

Examples of using a mounted drive

You can use a mounted drive as a gateway to a volume. When you create a volume as a mounted drive, users and applications can refer to the mounted drive by either the path of the mounted drive, such as C:\mnt\Ddrive, or a drive letter, such as D.

For example is an application server currently has a drive C that is near its capacity, a drive D that stores data, and an empty drive E. The application uses the C:\Temp folder extensively. You can mount drive E to C:\Temp to provide additional space for temporary files. The C:\Temp folder must be empty when you mount drive E to it.

Practice: Managing Mounted Drives

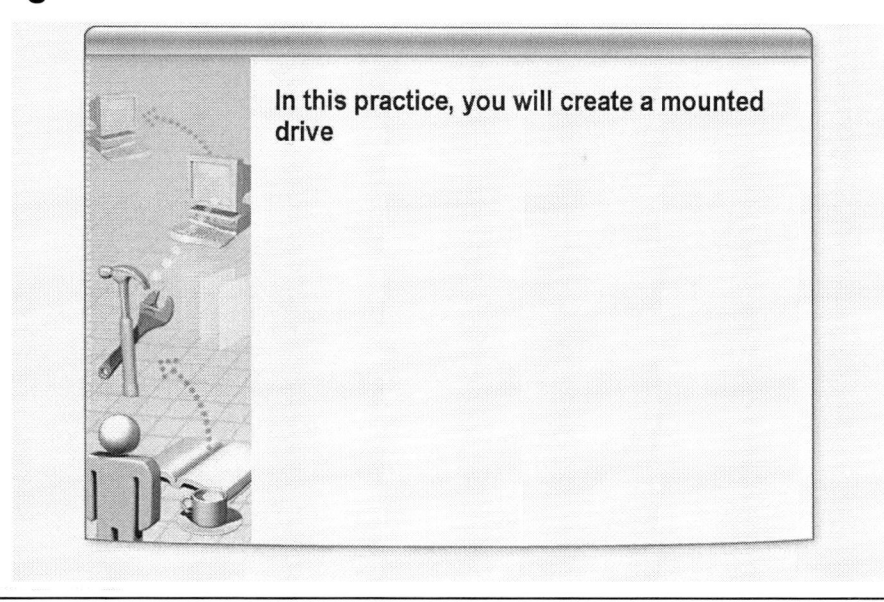

Objective

In this practice, you will

- Create a mounted drive.

Instructions

Ensure that the DEN-DC1 and the DEN-SRV2 virtual machines are running.

Practice

▶ **Create a mounted drive**

1. On DEN-SRV2, create a folder called **C:\Program Files\BigApp**.
2. Click **Start**, point to **Administrative Tools**, and then click **Computer Management**.
3. Click **Disk Management**.
4. Right-click the unallocated space on **Disk 2** and then click **New Partition**.
5. Click **Next**, and click **Next** again.
6. In the **Partition size in MB** box, type **3000**, and then click **Next**.
7. Click **Mount in the following empty NTFS folder**, type **C:\Program Files\BigApp** in the box, and then click **Next**.
8. In the **Volume label** box, type **Mount**, select the **Perform a quick format** check box, and then click **Next**.
9. Click **Finish**.
10. Close Disk Management.
11. View the folder **C:\Program Files\BigApp** in Windows Explorer. Notice the icon that is used to indicate a mount point.
12. Close Windows Explorer.

Important Do not shut down the virtual machines.

Lesson: Converting Disks

- Basic Disks vs. Dynamic Disks
- Results of Dynamic Disk Conversion
- Practice: Converting Disks

Introduction

Windows Server 2003 supports disks configured as basic disks and dynamic disks. When a new disk is installed, it is recognized and configured as a basic disk. It is important to be aware of the benefits gained by converting to a dynamic disk.

Lesson objectives

After completing this lesson, you will be able to:

- Describe the differences between basic and dynamic disks.
- Describe the results of a conversion to a dynamic disk.
- Convert a basic disk to a dynamic disk.

Basic Disks vs. Dynamic Disks

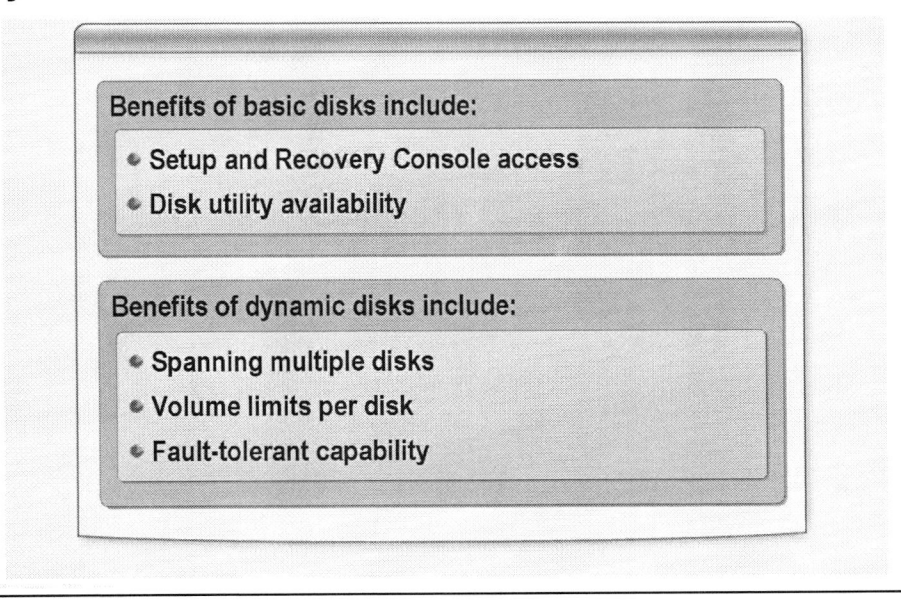

> **Benefits of basic disks include:**
> - Setup and Recovery Console access
> - Disk utility availability
>
> **Benefits of dynamic disks include:**
> - Spanning multiple disks
> - Volume limits per disk
> - Fault-tolerant capability

Introduction

A basic disk is the default disk type for Windows Server 2003. A basic disk provides you with limited capabilities for setting up your disks.

Dynamic disks provide you with more flexibility for setting up your hard disk than basic disks provide. For example, you can implement fault tolerance on a dynamic disk but not on a basic disk.

Benefit of basic disks

Basic disks can be partitioned and formatted during the text-based portion of the Windows Server 2003 installation and in the Recovery Console. Dynamic disks cannot. In addition because basic disks are well understood, there are a wide range of disk recovery utilities to repair disk corruption problems.

Note Removable storage can only be configured as a basic disk.

Benefits of dynamic disks

The benefits of dynamic disks are:

- A dynamic disk can be used to create volumes that span multiple disks.
- There is no limit on the number of volumes that can be configured on a dynamic disk.
- Dynamic disks are used to create fault-tolerant disks that ensure data integrity when hardware failures occur.

Convert basic disks to dynamic disks

You must convert basic disks to dynamic disks to perform the following tasks:

- Create and delete simple, spanned, striped, mirrored, and RAID-5 volumes.
- Extend a simple or spanned volume.
- Repair mirrored or RAID-5 volumes.
- Reactivate volumes that span more the one disk.

Example of using dynamic disks

When you need to reduce the risk of lost data and downtime, store your data on a RAID-5 volume. To create a RAID volume, you must use dynamic disks.

Results of Dynamic Disk Conversion

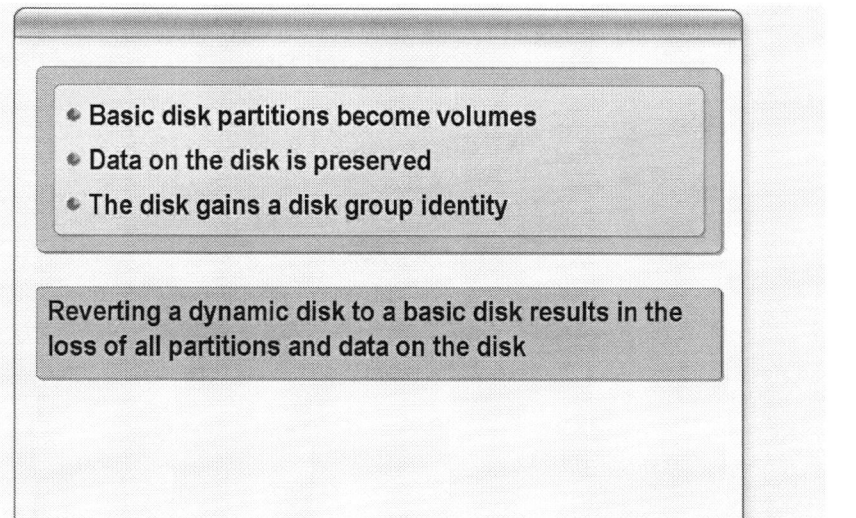

- Basic disk partitions become volumes
- Data on the disk is preserved
- The disk gains a disk group identity

Reverting a dynamic disk to a basic disk results in the loss of all partitions and data on the disk

Conversion results

You can convert a disk from basic to dynamic storage at any time without losing data. When you convert a disk from basic to dynamic, the existing partitions on the basic disk become volumes.

Note It is recommended that you always back up data before performing any major configuration of hardware storage devices.

Disk groups

All dynamic disks in a computer are members of a single disk group. Each disk in a disk group stores replicas of the same configuration data. This configuration data is stored in a 1-megabyte (MB) region at the end of each dynamic disk.

The first disk group name used by each computer is the computer name with the suffix Dg0. In the rare event that all dynamic disks in a disk group are removed then a new disk group will be created based on the computer name and the incremented suffix Dg1.

Note The name of dynamic disk groups is used by Windows in the background and is not visible through management utilities. However it can be viewed in the registry key KEY_LOCAL_MACHINE\SYSTEM\CurrentControlSet\Services\dmio\Boot Info\Primary Disk Group\Name

Disk Group identity

During conversion, Windows initializes the disk with a disk group identity and a copy of the current configuration of the disk group. Windows also adds dynamic volumes to the configuration, which represents the old partitions and fault-tolerant structures on the disk. If there are no existing Dynamic/Online disks, then a new disk group is automatically in the background. If there are existing Dynamic/Online disks, the new disk is automatically added to the existing disk group.

Revert to a basic disk

Reverting a dynamic disk to a basic disk erases all data from the drive. Even partitions must be newly created on the resulting basic disk.

To retain data when you revert to a basic disk, you must back up dynamic volumes and restore the data after partitions have been recreated on the basic disk.

Practice: Converting Disks

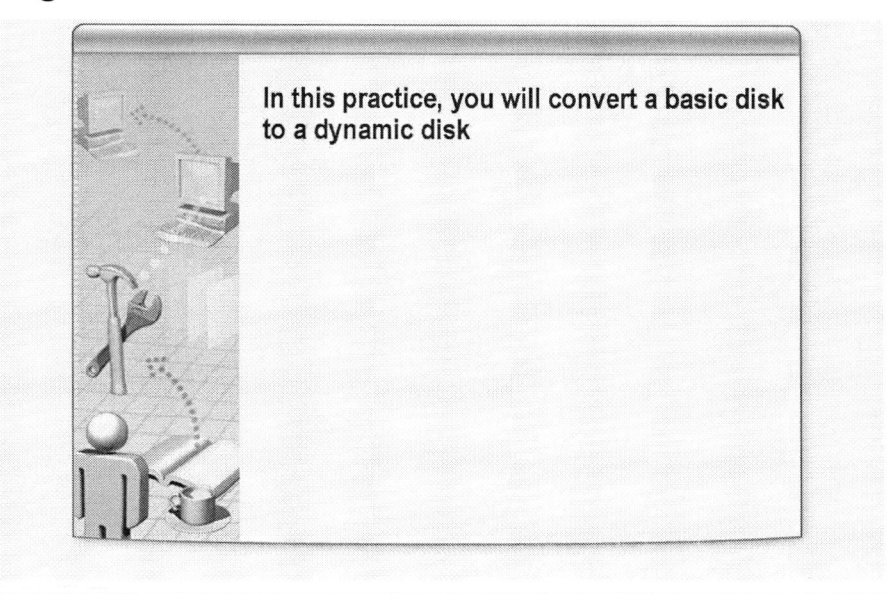

Objective

In this practice, you will

- Convert a basic disk to a dynamic disk.

Instructions

Ensure that the DEN-DC1 and the DEN-SRV2 virtual machines are running.

Practice

▶ **Convert a basic disk to a dynamic disk**

1. On DEN-SRV2, click **Start**, point to **Administrative Tools**, and then click **Computer Management**.
2. Click **Disk Management**.
3. Right-click **Disk 1** and then click **Convert to Dynamic Disk**.
4. Click **OK**.
5. Click **Convert**.
6. Click **Yes** and click **Yes** again. Notice that D: and E: become simple volumes.
7. Close Computer Management.
8. Click **Start**, click **Run**, type **cmd**, and then click **OK**.
9. Type **diskpart** and then press ENTER.
10. Type **list disk** and then press ENTER.
11. Type **select disk 2** and then press ENTER.
12. Type **convert dynamic** and then press ENTER.
13. Type **select disk 0** and then press ENTER.

14. Type **convert dynamic** and then press ENTER. Notice that you must reboot to convert this drive.
15. Type **Exit** and then press ENTER.
16. Close the command prompt and restart the server.

Important Do not shut down the virtual machines.

Lesson: Creating Volumes

- What Is a Simple Volume?
- What Is an Extended Volume?
- What Is a Spanned Volume?
- What Is a Striped Volume?
- Practice: Creating Volumes

Introduction

Dynamic disks provide features that basic disks do not provide, such as the ability to create volumes that span multiple disks. All volumes on dynamic disks are known as dynamic volumes.

Lesson objectives

After completing this lesson, you will be able to:

- Describe the characteristics of a simple volume.
- Describe the characteristics of an extended volume.
- Describe the characteristics of a spanned volume.
- Describe the characteristics of a striped volume.
- Create volumes.

What Is a Simple Volume?

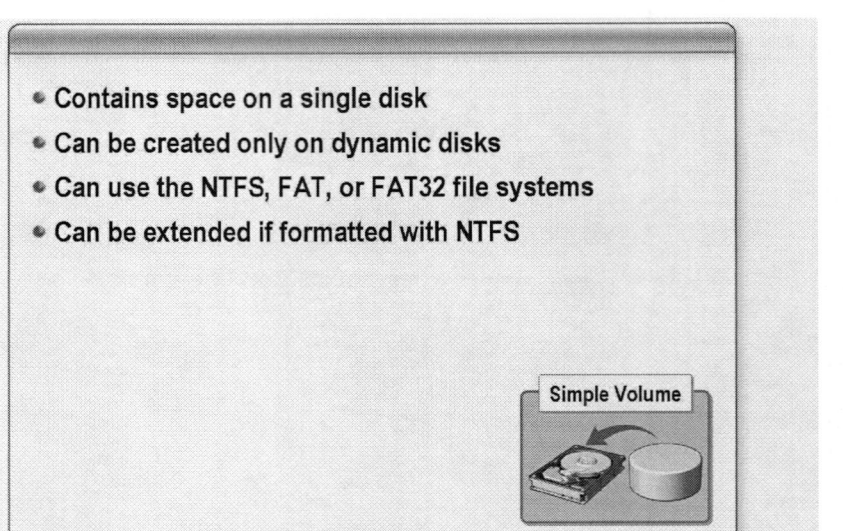

- Contains space on a single disk
- Can be created only on dynamic disks
- Can use the NTFS, FAT, or FAT32 file systems
- Can be extended if formatted with NTFS

Definition

A simple volume is a single volume that resides on a dynamic disk. You can create a simple volume from unallocated space on a dynamic disk. A simple volume is similar to a partition, except it does not have the size limits that a partition has, nor is there a restriction on the number of volumes that you can create on a single disk.

Simple volume file formats

A simple volume uses the NTFS, FAT, or FAT32 file system formats. However, you can extend a simple volume only if it is formatted with the version of NTFS that is used in Microsoft Windows® 2000 or the Windows Server 2003 family of operating systems. Also, you can add space to, or extend, a simple volume after you create it.

Use a simple volume for all basic data storage

You can use a simple volume for all data storage until you need more space on your disks. To gain more space, you can create an extended volume with unused space on the same disk, or create a spanned volume with unused space on a different dynamic disk.

What Is an Extended Volume?

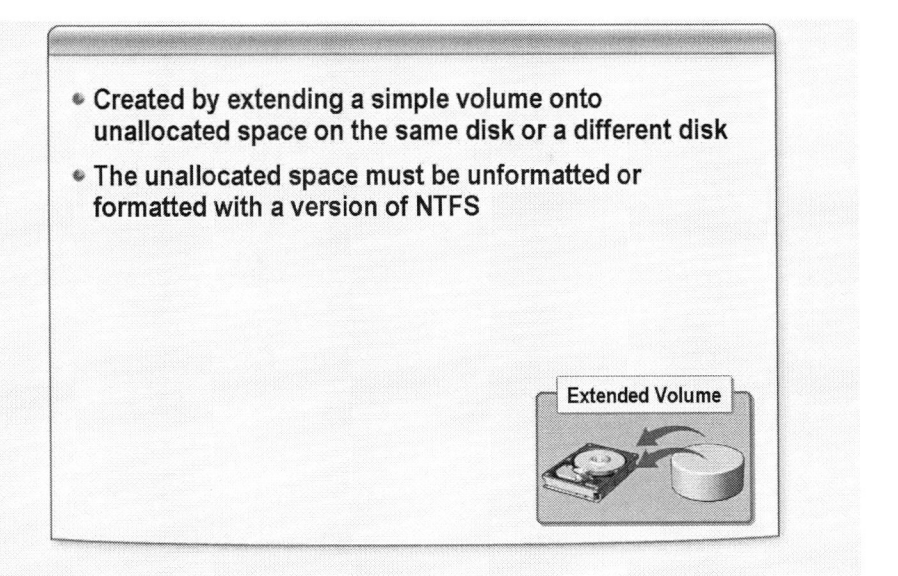

- Created by extending a simple volume onto unallocated space on the same disk or a different disk
- The unallocated space must be unformatted or formatted with a version of NTFS

Extended Volume

Definition	You can increase the size of an existing simple volume by extending the volume onto unallocated space on the same disk or a different disk. To extend a simple volume, the volume must be unformatted or formatted with the version of NTFS that is used in Windows 2000 or the Windows Server 2003 family of operating systems.
Additional hard disk space	To make additional space available without reconfiguring your hard disks, you can add space to an existing volume on your hard disk. Exceptions include any volume that contains a system partition, the boot partition, or an active paging file.
Example of using extended volumes	Your organization has increased the number of products it sells and needs additional storage capacity for their new marketing brochures. The current storage capacity available to marketing is 2 GB. The marketing manager predicts that need will exceed this capacity in six months. After auditing the hard disk storing the marketing brochures, you find 6 GB of unallocated space. You extend the volume devoted to marketing by including 3 GB from the unallocated space.

Important You cannot extend a simple or spanned volume that was originally created as a basic volume and converted to a dynamic volume on Windows 2000. This applies if you upgraded from Windows 2000 to the Windows Server 2003 family, or if you move a disk containing a simple or spanned volume that was originally created as a basic volume and converted to a dynamic disk from a computer running Windows 2000 to a computer running the Windows Server 2003 family.

What Is a Spanned Volume?

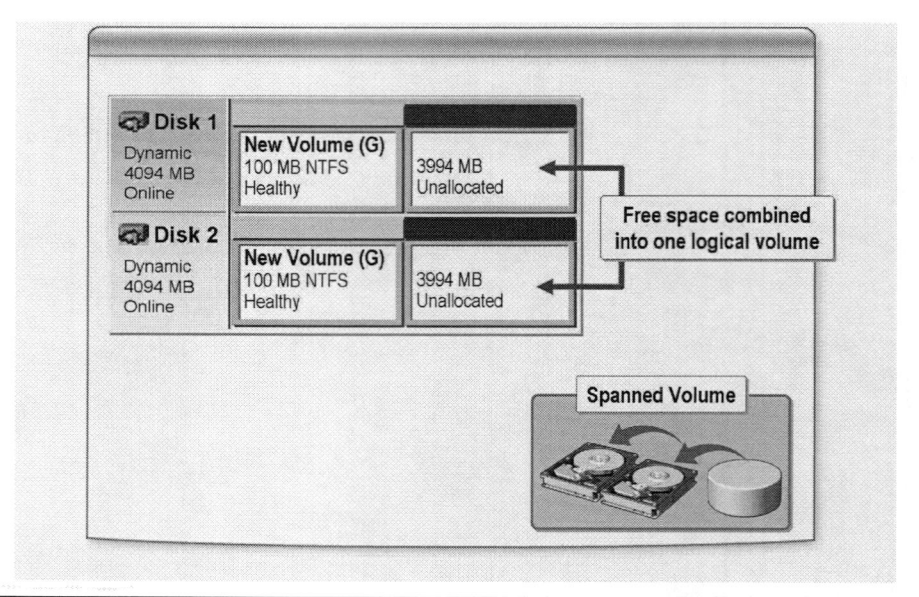

![Diagram showing Disk 1 and Disk 2, both Dynamic 4094 MB Online, each with New Volume (G) 100 MB NTFS Healthy and 3994 MB Unallocated. Free space combined into one logical volume forms a Spanned Volume.]

Definition	A spanned volume is a simple volume that includes a single logical volume and uses unallocated space that is available on other dynamic disks on the computer. By using spanned volumes, you can use your storage space more efficiently. After a volume is extended, you must delete the entire spanned volume to delete a part of it.
Spanned volume file formats	You can create a spanned volume only by using the NTFS file system. Spanned volumes do not offer fault tolerance. If one of the disks that contain a spanned volume fails, the entire volume fails and all the data is lost. A volume that spans two disks is twice as likely to fail as a simple volume on a single disk.
	Caution Use of spanned volumes is not recommended because spanned volumes have a higher risk of failure than simple or extended volumes.
Increase storage size	You can use spanned volumes to increase storage size when you must create a volume but do not have enough unallocated space for the volume on a single disk. By combining sections of unallocated space from multiple disks, you can create one spanned volume.
Example of a spanned volume	Your organization hires 100 college interns every summer. The interns are provided with an old server to use for their work. The interns estimate they will need 10 GB of storage on their D drive in the next month. You want to add the storage to their assigned drive, but the drive has only 240 MB of unused space. You find that the interns' server has 15 GB of unallocated space on a different dynamic disk. You can span the D drive to include 10 GB of storage from the other disk.
	Note A spanned volume does not increase disk performance. The reason is that a spanned volume does not fill the second disk until the first disk is full.

What Is a Striped Volume?

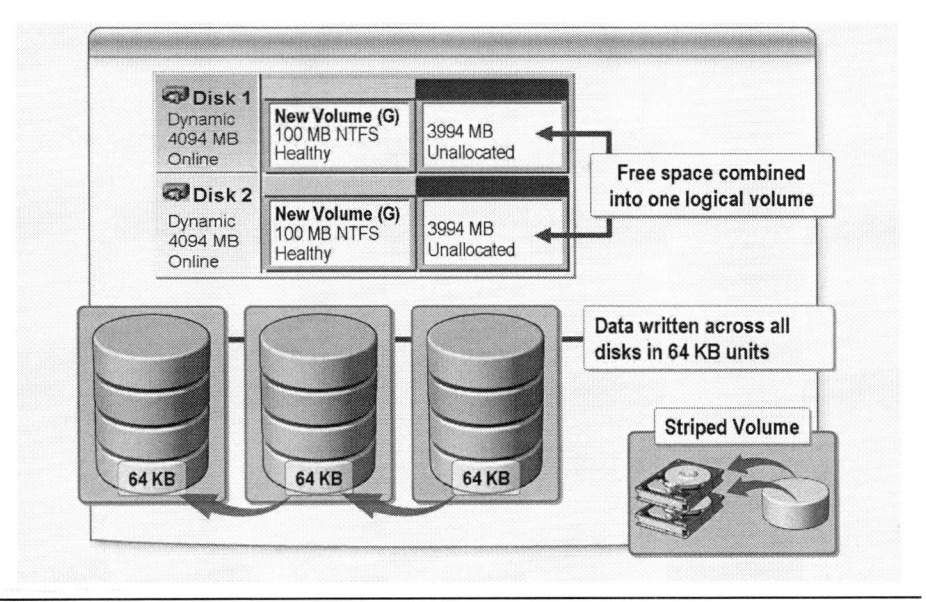

Definition

A striped volume stores data on two or more physical disks by combining areas of free space into one logical volume on a dynamic disk. Striped volumes, also known as RAID-0, contain data that is distributed across multiple dynamic disks. Striped volumes cannot be extended or mirrored.

Blocks of data

Data that is written to the stripe set is divided into blocks that are called *stripes*. These stripes are written simultaneously to all drives in the stripe set. The major advantage of disk striping is speed. Data can be accessed on multiple disks by using multiple drive heads, which improves performance considerably.

Caution Striped volumes do not provide fault tolerance. The loss of a single disk results in the loss of the entire striped volume. Use of striped volumes is not recommended because striped volumes have a higher risk of failure than simple or extended volumes.

Striped volumes performance

Striped volumes offer the best performance of all the disk strategies because data that is written to a striped volume is simultaneously written to all disks at the same time rather than sequentially. Consequently, disk performance is faster on a striped volume than on any other type of disk configuration.

Striped volume uses

Use a striped volume when you:

- Load program images, dynamic-link libraries (DLLs), or run-time libraries.
- Want to provide the best performance for high usage files that can be easily restored, for example page files.

Example of striped volumes

Use striped volumes for page files because striped volumes provide the best performance for high usage files.

Practice: Creating Volumes

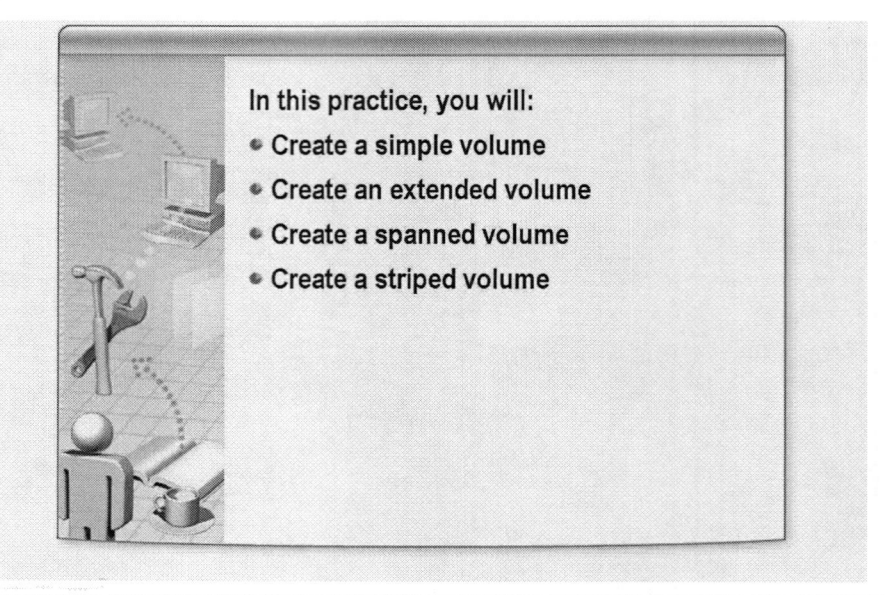

Objective

In this practice, you will:

- Create a simple volume.
- Create an extended volume.
- Create a spanned volume.
- Create a striped volume.

Instructions

Ensure that the DEN-DC1 and the DEN-SRV2 virtual machines are running.

Practice

▶ **Create a simple volume**

1. On DEN-SRV2, log on as **Administrator** with a password of **Pa$$w0rd**. If you are prompted to restart your computer click **No**.
2. Click **Start**, point to **Administrative Tools**, and then click **Computer Management**.
3. Click **Disk Management**.
4. Right-click the unallocated space on **Disk 2** and then click **New Volume**.
5. Click **Next**.
6. Click **Simple** and then click **Next**.
7. In the **Select the amount of space in MB** box, type **500**, and then click **Next**.
8. Click **Next** to accept the default drive letter of F.
9. Select the **Perform a quick format** check box and then click **Next** to format the volume as NTFS.
10. Click **Finish**.

▶ Create an extended volume

1. Right-click **New Volume (F:)** and then click **Extend Volume**.
2. Click **Next**.
3. Click **Remove All** and then double-click **Disk 2**.
4. In the **Select the amount of space in MB** box, type **250**, and then click **Next**.
5. Click **Finish**.

▶ Create a spanned volume

1. Right-click **New Volume (F:)** and then click **Extend Volume**.
2. Click **Next**.
3. Click **Remove All** and then double-click **Disk 1**.
4. In the **Select the amount of space in MB** box, type **250**, and then click **Next**.
5. Click **Finish**.

▶ Create a striped volume

1. Right-click the unallocated space on **Disk 1** and then click **New Volume**.
2. Click **Next**.
3. Click **Striped** and then click **Next**.
4. Add both **Disk 1** and **Disk 2** to the **Selected** box.
5. In the **Amount of space in MB** box, type **500**, and then click **Next**. Notice that this takes 500MB from each disk selected.
6. Click **Next** to accept the default drive letter of G.
7. In the **Volume Label** box, type **Striped**, select the **Perform a quick format** check box, and then click **Next**.
8. Click **Finish**.
9. Close Computer Management.

Important Do not shut down the virtual machines.

Lesson: Creating Fault-Tolerant Volumes

- What Is Fault Tolerance?
- What Is a Mirrored Volume?
- What Is a RAID-5 Volume?
- Software RAID vs. Hardware RAID
- What Is External Storage?
- Practice: Creating Fault-Tolerant Volumes

Introduction

The loss of a hard disk because of mechanical or electrical failure is a common computer disaster. If you experience this problem before implementing fault tolerance, your only option for recovering the data on the failed drive is to use disaster-recovery methods, such as a backup. Even with successful data recovery, there is significant loss in time, access to the data, and diverted resources.

Understanding the management of fault-tolerant volumes in Microsoft Windows Server 2003 can help you protect data against disk failure.

Lesson objectives

After completing this lesson, you will be able to:

- Describe fault tolerance.
- Describe the characteristics of a mirrored volume.
- Describe the characteristics of a RAID-5 volume.
- Describe the difference between hardware RAID and software RAID.
- Describe types of external storage.
- Create fault-tolerant volumes.

What Is Fault Tolerance?

> - The ability to survive hardware failure
> - Fault-tolerant volumes provide data redundancy
> - Fault-tolerant volumes require dynamic disks
> - Fault-tolerant volumes are not a replacement for backups

Definition

Fault tolerance is the ability of computer hardware or software to ensure data integrity when hardware failures occur. Fault-tolerant features appear in many server operating systems and include mirrored volumes (RAID-1) and RAID-5 volumes.

Fault-tolerant volumes provide data redundancy. With data redundancy, a computer writes data to multiple disks, so that if one disk fails, the information is still available.

Dynamic disks

Fault-tolerant volumes in Windows Server 2003 are only available on dynamic disks.

Backups

Although the data is available and current in a fault-tolerant system, you should still make backup copies to protect the information. Backups are required to recover from corrupted fault-tolerant systems, accidental file deletions, fire, theft, or other physical disasters. Backups are also required for offsite storage.

What Is a Mirrored Volume?

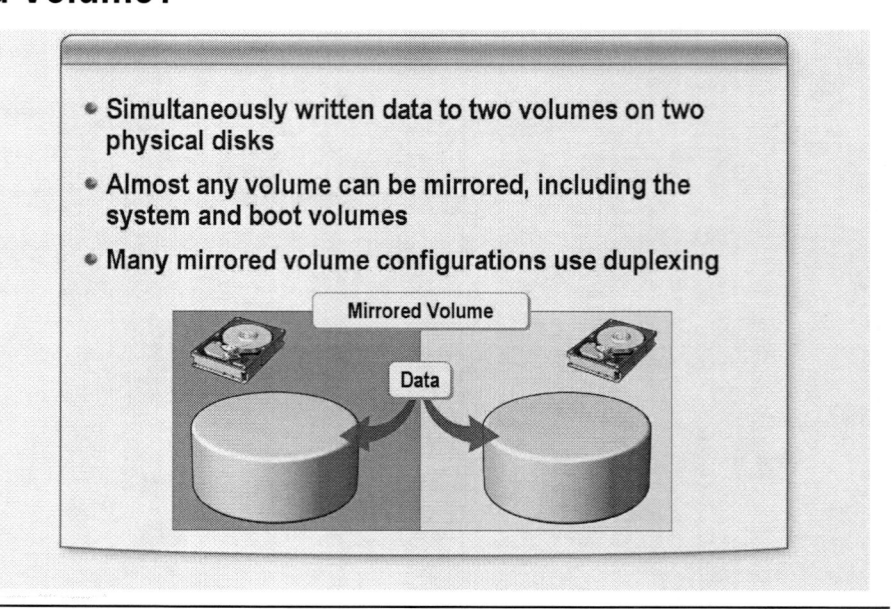

- Simultaneously written data to two volumes on two physical disks
- Almost any volume can be mirrored, including the system and boot volumes
- Many mirrored volume configurations use duplexing

Definition

A mirrored volume is a fault-tolerant volume that provides data redundancy by using two copies, or mirrors, of the volume to duplicate the data stored on the volume. All data that is written to one mirrored volume is written to the other mirrored volumes too. Each mirrored volume is located on a separate physical disk. Mirrored volumes are also known as RAID-1 volumes.

Almost any volume can be mirrored

Almost any volume can be mirrored, including the system and boot volumes. You cannot extend a mirrored volume to increase the size of the volume later.

Mirroring is popular for the system and boot volumes because either disk from the system can be used to boot the system. However, the **boot.ini** command file may need to be edited to reference the remaining drive properly.

How does mirroring work?

If one of the physical disks fails, the data on the failed disk becomes unavailable, but the system continues to operate by using the unaffected disk. When one of the mirrors in a mirrored volume fails, the other disk continues to operate, but it is no longer fault-tolerant.

To prevent potential data loss, you must recover the mirrored volume as soon as possible. First, you must tell the system that the lost mirrored drive is gone permanently by breaking the mirrored volume. After breaking the mirror, the system recognizes the remaining volume as a simple volume. You can then create a mirrored volume with unused free space of equal or greater size on another disk.

If you are using duplexing, use identical disks and controllers, especially if you plan to mirror the system or boot volumes.

Failed disk status	The status of the failed volume appears in Disk Management as **Failed Redundancy**, and one of the disks appears as **Offline, Missing,** or **Online (Errors)**.
	Warning If a disk continues to appear as **Online (Errors)**, it may be about to fail. You should replace the disk as soon as possible.
Many mirrored volumes use duplexing	Because dual-write operations can degrade system performance, many mirrored volume configurations use *duplexing*, where each disk in the mirrored volume resides on its own disk controller. A duplexed mirrored volume has the best data reliability because the entire input/output (I/O) subsystem is duplicated. This means that if one disk controller fails, the other controller, and thus the disk on that controller, continues to operate normally. If you do not use two controllers, a failed controller makes both mirrors in a mirrored volume inaccessible until the controller is replaced.

What Is a RAID-5 Volume?

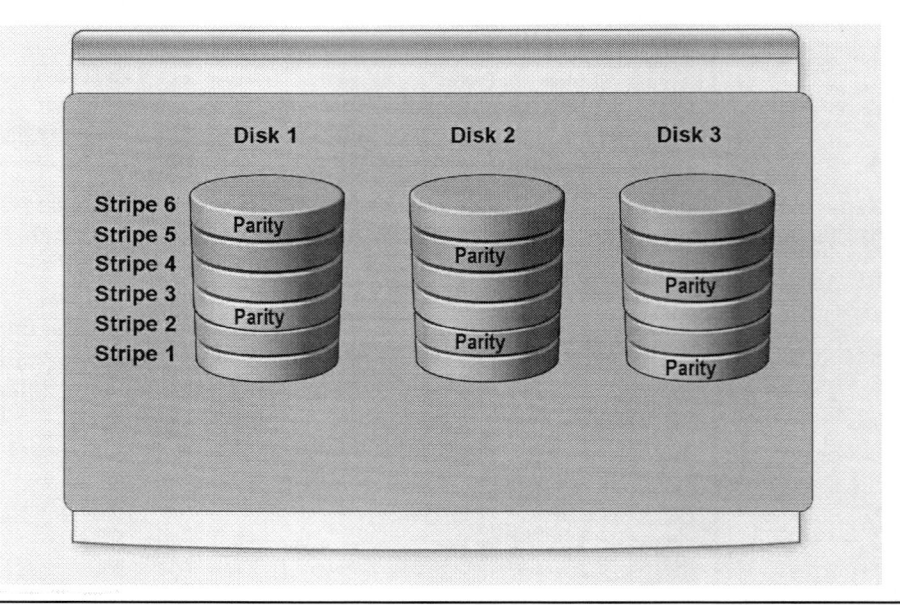

Definition	Windows Server 2003 supports fault tolerance through striped volumes with parity, more commonly referred to as RAID-5. Parity is a mathematical method of determining the number of odd and even bits in a number or series of numbers, which can be used to reconstruct data if one number in a sequence of numbers is lost.
	In a RAID-5 volume, Windows Server 2003 achieves fault tolerance by adding a parity-information stripe to each disk partition in the volume. If a single disk fails, Windows Server 2003 can use the data and parity information on the remaining disks to reconstruct the data that was on the failed disk.
RAID-5 and disk performance	The performance of a RAID-5 volume is faster than a single disk or mirrored volume because the reading and writing of data is spread across multiple hard disks. However, the calculation of parity information increases load on the CPU. This calculation makes RAID-5 volumes slower than striped volumes.

Note The read performance of RAID-5 volumes is reduced significantly when a drive is missing. This forces the missing data to be calculated from parity information whenever it is read.

What happens when a member fails	When one member of a RAID-5 volume fails, the other members continue to operate even though the volume is no longer fault-tolerant. To prevent potential data loss, you must recover the RAID-5 volume as soon as possible.
	The status of the failed volume appears in Disk Management as **Failed Redundancy**, and one of the disks appears as **Offline**, **Missing**, or **Online (Errors)**.

Warning If a disk continues to appear as **Online (Errors)**, it may be about to fail. You should replace the disk as soon as possible.

Module 5: Managing Disks 43

Cost advantage over mirrored volumes

RAID-5 volumes have a cost advantage over mirrored volumes because disk usage is optimized. A mirrored volume uses 50 percent of its storage capacity for redundant data. A RAID-5 volume uses one disk of storage capacity for parity information. The more disks that are used in a RAID-5 volume, the more efficient it is.

The following table show how the amount of space that is required for the parity stripe decreases with the addition of more disks. In this example, disks are 20 GB.

Number of Disks	Total Disk Space	Disk Space for Data	Percentage lost to parity
3	60 GB	40 GB	33%
4	80 GB	60 GB	25%
5	100 GB	80 GB	20%

Note A RAID-5 volume requires a minimum of three disks and can use as many as 32 disks.

Important A software-implemented RAID-5 volume cannot contain the boot or system partition.

Software RAID vs. Hardware RAID

RAID Type	Benefits
Software RAID	• Configured in Disk Management • Requires dynamic disks • Used mostly in smaller organizations • Failed mirrors may require boot.ini changes • Can move disks to any computer running Windows 2003 Server
Hardware RAID	• Configured with vendor utilities • Does not require dynamic disks • Higher performance • Does not require boot.ini changes • Can expand existing RAID-5 volumes

Introduction

Mirroring and RAID-5 volumes can be implemented either with software or hardware. Windows Server 2003 provides software-based mirroring and RAID-5. Hardware-based mirroring and RAID-5 require a RAID disk controller or external storage.

Management

Software RAID is configured using the Disk Management snap-in that is available in Computer Management. This capability is part of the Windows Server 2003 operating system.

Hardware RAID uses a specialized disk controller to perform all RAID functions. This isolates the RAID volumes completely from the operating system. Problems with the operating system will not affect the volumes.

Management of the RAID controller and its volumes can typically be done through Windows-based management software provided by the vendor or through a BIOS-level utility embedded in the card. Hardware RAID volumes appear as a single disk when viewed in Disk Management.

Dynamic disks

The software RAID in Windows Server 2003 requires that disks be dynamic disks. Hardware RAID can use dynamic disks or basic disks because the operating system is isolated from the RAID process.

Performance

The server CPU is used to perform any parity calculations that need to be made. This can be a significant performance drain when RAID-5 volumes are used.

All the parity calculations for hardware RAID are performed by the RAID controller. Therefore there is no extra load on the CPU of the server. Hardware RAID has better performance than software RAID.

Implementations	Small organizations are the most likely to use software RAID, which is less expensive because no specialized hardware is required.
	Mid-sized and large organizations use hardware RAID almost exclusively. Even many smaller organizations use hardware RAID. Even lower-end servers now have the option to include a SCSI RAID controller for only a few hundred dollars. IDE or Serial Advanced Technology Attachment (SATA) RAID controllers targeted at small companies cost even less.
Failed boot or system partitions	The initial startup of Windows Server 2003 does not recognized mirrored volumes. If the boot partition is on a mirrored volume then Windows starts from one of the two drives as specified in the **boot.ini** command file. Later in the boot process that Windows recognizes, the mirrored volume uses it. If a disk in a mirrored volume holding the boot partition fails, then the Advanced RISC Computing (ARC) path in the **boot.ini** file that points to the operating system may need to be modified.
	When hardware RAID is used for mirroring, there is no need to modify the **boot.ini** file when a mirrored volume fails. The RAID card automatically boots from the available drive. However, the driver for the RAID card will place events in the System event log to indicate that there is a problem.
Moving volumes	With software RAID the disks can be moved to any computer running Windows Server 2003 and they will be recognized.
	If a hardware RAID controller fails, it may be difficult to get access to the data. A RAID volume from one brand or model or RAID controller cannot typically be moved and attached to another. You may need to use the exact same brand and model of controller. Even firmware revisions on a controller can be an issue.
Volume expansion	The software RAID included with Windows Server 2003 cannot expand existing volumes. The data must be moved to a new larger volume. If the existing disks are required for the new volume then data must be backed up and then restored after the new volume is created.
	Most hardware RAID controllers can expand existing RAID-5 volumes and striped volumes without losing data. After attaching a new disk, you can instruct the RAID controller to add the new disk to the RAID array.

What Is External Storage?

- External and auxiliary disk space
- External Array
- Storage Area Network (SAN)
- Network Attached Storage (NAS)

Definition

External storage is disk-based storage that is located physically outside the server. External storage offers the obvious benefit of increase storage capacity, some also offer easier reconfiguration.

External array

An external array (also directly attached storage) is a hardware device that holds external hard drives and is typically attached to the server through a SCSI cable. Storing disks in an external box makes it easier to move disks to a new server in the case of a hardware failure. In addition they often hold a larger number of disks than a server.

Some external arrays are simple devices that just physically hold disks. Others are more sophisticated and provide mirroring and RAID-5 capabilities in the external array.

SAN

A storage area network (SAN) is a network dedicated to hosting disk space. The connection between the servers and the disk storage is usually a fiber channel. One large central disk storage unit provides the disk for all servers. Most SANs are configured to use RAID-5.

In addition to being scalable to multiple terabytes in size, SANs are very flexible. Disk space can be taken from one server and reassigned to another very easily.

NAS

Network attached storage (NAS) is a device specialized for file sharing on the network. NAS devices are different from external arrays or SANs in that NAS devices run an operating system such as Microsoft Windows Storage Server 2003. NAS devices appear as a file server on the network and can act as a member server in a Windows network. Most NAS devices are capable of mirroring or RAID-5.

In some cases, NAS devices can be configured to so that they perform file serving for other servers. A file request is sent to a Windows server and that request is mapped to the NAS device. The path to the Windows server effectively acts as an alias to the NAS device.

NAS devices are easy to administer. There are very few options to configure on the device because it is configured and optimized for file sharing only.

Note Windows Storage Server 2003 is a NAS device based on the Windows Server 2003 operating system. For more information about this device, see the Windows Storage Server 2003 Web site.

Practice: Creating Fault-Tolerant Volumes

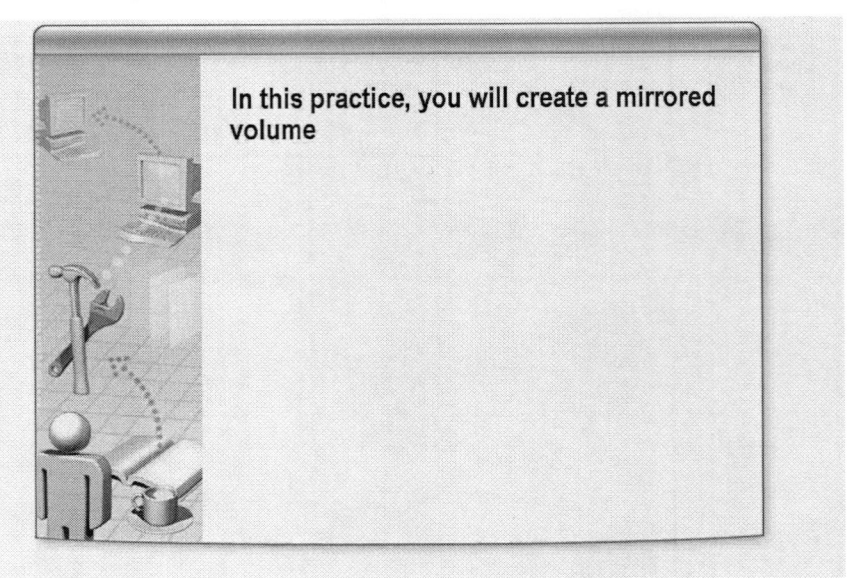

Objective

In this practice, you will create:

- Create a mirrored volume

Instructions

Ensure that the DEN-DC1 and the DEN-SRV2 virtual machines are running.

Practice

▶ **Create a mirrored volume**

1. On DEN-SRV2, click **Start**, point to **Administrative Tools**, and then click **Computer Management**.
2. Click **Disk Management**.
3. Right-click the unallocated space on **Disk 1** and then click **New Volume**.
4. Click **Next**.
5. Click **Mirrored** and then click **Next**.
6. Double-click **Disk 2** to select it.
7. In the **Select the amount of space in MB** box, type **500**, and then click **Next**.
8. Click **Next** to accept the default drive letter H.
9. In the **Volume label** box, type **Mirrored**, select the **Perform a quick format** check box, and then click **Next**.
10. Click **Finish**.
11. Close all open windows.

Important Do not shut down the virtual machines.

Lesson: Importing a Foreign Disk

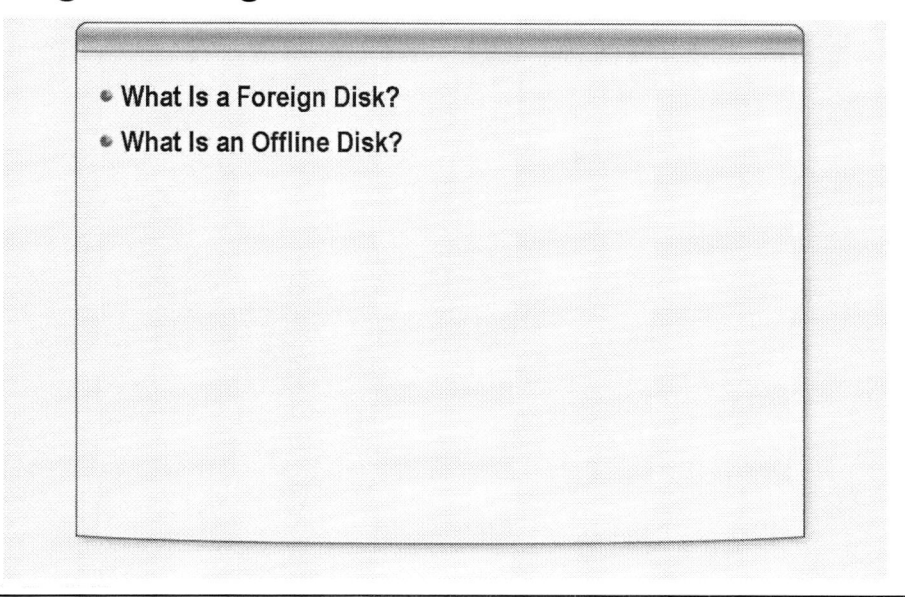

- What Is a Foreign Disk?
- What Is an Offline Disk?

Introduction

You can move a disk from another system or within the same system by importing it. After the disk is imported, Disk Management refers to it as a foreign disk. To manage foreign disks, you must understand the characteristics of a foreign disk, as well as what happens if a foreign disk is not imported properly.

Lesson objectives

After completing this lesson, you will be able to:

- Describe the characteristics of a foreign disk.
- Describe what causes an offline disk.
- Import a foreign disk.

What Is a Foreign Disk?

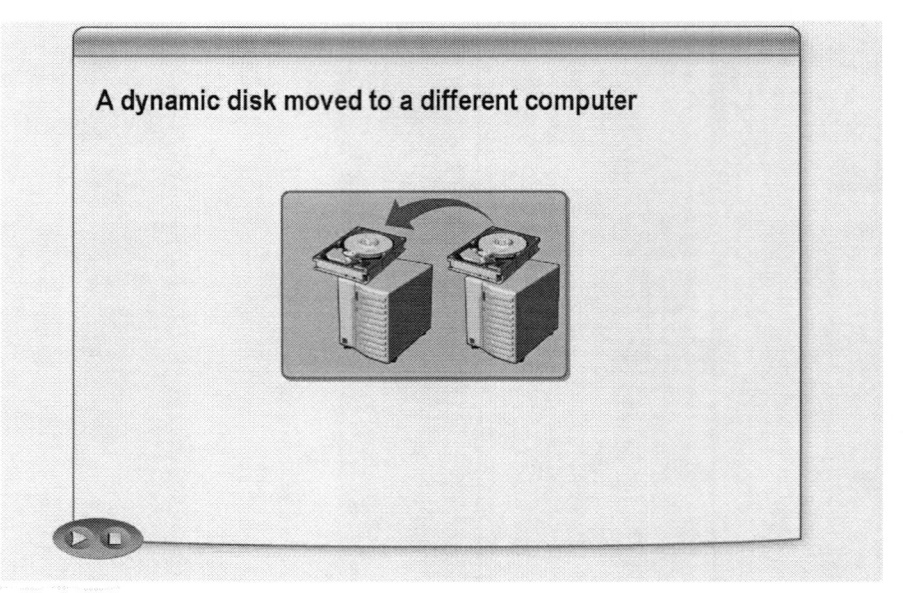

A dynamic disk moved to a different computer

Introduction

When you move a dynamic disk from one computer to another, Windows Server 2003 automatically considers the disk a *foreign disk*. When Disk Manager indicates the status of a new disk as foreign, you must import the disk before you can access volumes on the disk.

Foreign Disks

You can move dynamic disks to Windows Server 2003 from any computer running Windows 2000, Windows XP Professional, or Windows XP 64-bit Edition, or from another computer running Windows Server 2003.

Each dynamic disk is assigned to a disk group that is based on the computer name. When a dynamic disk is moved to a different computer that already has dynamic disks, then the disk group names do not match. Windows Server 2003 identifies the moved disk as a foreign disk because of the disk group-name mismatch. Importing a foreign disk rewrites the disk group name to match the existing dynamic disks in the system.

Volumes status

When you move all the disks that contain parts of a volume from one computer to another at the same time, the volume and its data are identical to the original state after the import. All simple volumes on any moved disks are recovered to their original state if the disks have been rescanned.

On a spanned or striped volume, if you move only some disks from one system to another, the volume is disabled during import. The volume also becomes disabled on the original system. So long as you do not delete the volume on either the original or the target system, you can move the remaining disks later. When all disks are moved over, the volume is recovered to its original state.

All disks containing a RAID-5 volume should be moved at the same time. A RAID-5 volume will be functional with all disks except one moved. This is effectively the same as if a single disk has failed. The final disk will show as a missing disk and should be moved as soon as possible.

Both disks in a mirrored volume should be moved at the same time. If the two disks are moved at different times, then it is possible that the operating system will overwrite the newer disk with the older disk.

What Is an Offline Disk?

- A disk management status option
- A corrupt or intermittently unavailable dynamic disk
- A failed foreign disk

Introduction

Disk Management displays the Offline status when a dynamic disk is not accessible. The inaccessible disk may be corrupted or intermittently unavailable. The Offline status also appears if you attempt to import a foreign dynamic disk, but the operation fails. An error icon appears on the offline disk. The Offline status appears only for dynamic disks.

Remove a disk

When you remove a dynamic disk from a computer, the remaining online dynamic disks retain information about it and its volumes. Disk Management displays the removed disk as a Dynamic/Offline disk named Missing. You can remove this disk entry by removing all volumes on that disk and then using the **Remove Disk** command that is associated with that disk.

Foreign disks
Reactivate or rescan an offline disk

Reactivating or rescanning an offline disk changes the disk status from Offline to **OK**.

Note For more information about troubleshooting a foreign disk, see Appendix C, "Foreign Disks Volume Status in Disk Management," on the Student Materials compact disc.

Lab: Managing Disks

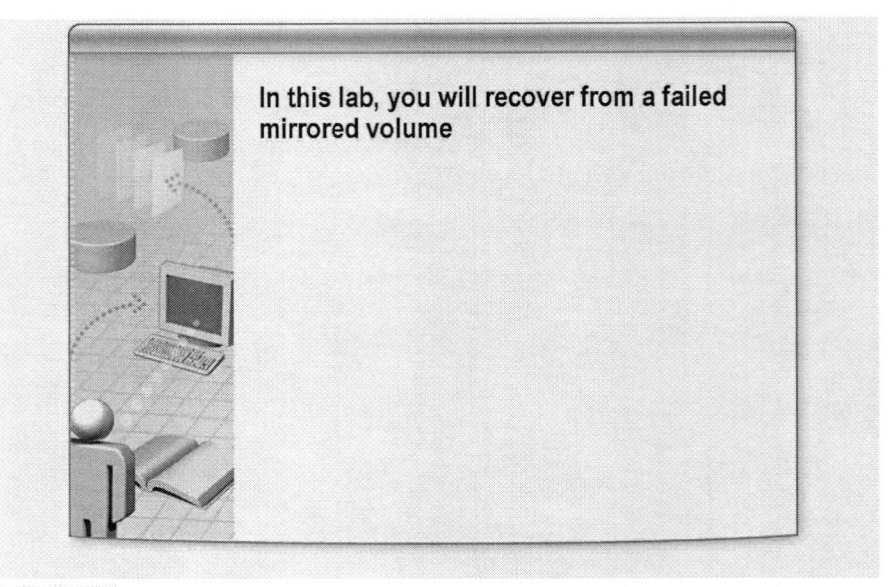

Objectives

After completing this lab, you will be able to:

- Recover from a failed mirrored drive.

Scenario

You are the systems administrator for a large organization and responsible for several servers. Your management software has alerted you to a drive failure on DEN-SRV2. You have replaced the hard drive and now must repair the mirrored volume that has been affected.

Estimated time to complete this lab: 15 minutes

Exercise 1
Recovering from a Failed Mirrored Drive

In this exercise, you will recover from a failed mirrored drive.

Tasks	Specific instructions
1. Replace the failed disk.	a. Shut down DEN-SRV2. b. In the **Close** dialog box, select **Save undo disk changes** (Do not choose Commit changes to the virtual hard disk). c. In the **Virtual PC Console**, select **DEN-SRV2**, and click **Settings**. d. Click **Hard Disk 2**. e. In the **Virtual hard disk file** box, type **C:\Program Files\Microsoft Learning\2275\DEN-SRV2-Disk2-New.vhd**, and click **OK**. If you receive a warning about the undo disk, click **Continue**. f. Start the DEN-SRV2 virtual machine.
2. Log on to the server.	▪ Log on to DEN-SRV2 as **Administrator** with a password of **Pa$$w0rd**.
3. Import the new disk.	a. Open **Computer Management**. b. Click **Disk Management**. c. Use the **Initialize and Convert Disk Wizard**.
4. Break the Mirror for Mirrored (H:).	▪ Remove the Mirror located on the missing disk.
5. Add a new mirror disk.	▪ Add a mirror to Mirrored (H:) on Disk 1.
6. Complete the lab exercise.	a. Close all programs and shut down all computers. Do not save changes. b. To prepare for the next module, start the DEN-DC1 and DEN-CL1 virtual computers.

THIS PAGE INTENTIONALLY LEFT BLANK

Module 6: Managing Data Storage

Contents

Overview	1
Lesson: Managing File Compression	2
Lesson: Configuring File Encryption	13
Lesson: Configuring EFS Recovery Agents	26
Lesson: Implementing Disk Quotas	32
Lab: Managing Data Storage	38

Information in this document, including URL and other Internet Web site references, is subject to change without notice. Unless otherwise noted, the example companies, organizations, products, domain names, e-mail addresses, logos, people, places, and events depicted herein are fictitious, and no association with any real company, organization, product, domain name, e-mail address, logo, person, place or event is intended or should be inferred. Complying with all applicable copyright laws is the responsibility of the user. Without limiting the rights under copyright, no part of this document may be reproduced, stored in or introduced into a retrieval system, or transmitted in any form or by any means (electronic, mechanical, photocopying, recording, or otherwise), or for any purpose, without the express written permission of Microsoft Corporation.

The names of manufacturers, products, or URLs are provided for informational purposes only and Microsoft makes no representations and warranties, either expressed, implied, or statutory, regarding these manufacturers or the use of the products with any Microsoft technologies. The inclusion of a manufacturer or product does not imply endorsement of Microsoft of the manufacturer or product. Links are provided to third party sites. Such sites are not under the control of Microsoft and Microsoft is not responsible for the contents of any linked site or any link contained in a linked site, or any changes or updates to such sites. Microsoft is not responsible for webcasting or any other form of transmission received from any linked site. Microsoft is providing these links to you only as a convenience, and the inclusion of any link does not imply endorsement of Microsoft of the site or the products contained therein.

Microsoft may have patents, patent applications, trademarks, copyrights, or other intellectual property rights covering subject matter in this document. Except as expressly provided in any written license agreement from Microsoft, the furnishing of this document does not give you any license to these patents, trademarks, copyrights, or other intellectual property.

© 2005 Microsoft Corporation. All rights reserved.

Microsoft, Active Directory, ActiveX, Authenticode, BizTalk, IntelliMirror, MSDN, PowerPoint, Windows, Windows Media, Windows NT, and Windows Server are either registered trademarks or trademarks of Microsoft Corporation in the United States and/or other countries.

All other trademarks are property of their respective owners.

Overview

- Managing File Compression
- Configuring File Encryption
- Configuring EFS Recovery Agents
- Implementing Disk Quotas

Introduction

One of your tasks as a systems administrator is to manage the data that you will store on network storage devices. To manage data storage, you can compress files and folders to decrease their size, thereby reducing the amount of space that they use. In this module, you will learn when and how to compress files and folders.

To manage data, you must also understand encryption. In this module, you will learn about Encrypting File System (EFS). EFS stores data with a level of security higher than NTFS permissions.

When using EFS, you need a way to recover files when passwords are lost or an account is deleted. In this module, you will learn how to configure an EFS recovery agent.

You will also learn how to administer disk quotas. You use disk quotas to limit the amount of storage space that is available to users on servers running Microsoft® Windows Server™ 2003.

Objectives

After completing this module, you will be able to:

- Manage NTFS file compression.
- Configure file encryption.
- Configure an EFS recovery agent.
- Implement disk quotas.

Lesson: Managing File Compression

- What Is File Compression?
- What Is the compact Command?
- What Are the Effects of Moving and Copying Compressed Files and Folders?
- Best Practices for Compressing Files or Folders
- Practice: Managing File Compression

Introduction

Compressing files and folders decreases their size and reduces the amount of space they use on drives and removable storage devices. Microsoft Windows Server 2003 supports two types of compression: NTFS compression and compression using the Compressed (zipped) Folders feature.

In this lesson, you will learn about these features and how to use them. You will also learn the best practices that are associated with compressing files and folders.

Lesson objectives

After completing this lesson, you will be able to:

- Describe file compression.
- Describe the **compact** command-line tool.
- Describe the effects of moving and copying compressed files and folders.
- Describe the best practices for compressing files and folders.
- Compress a file or folder on an NTFS partition.

What Is File Compression?

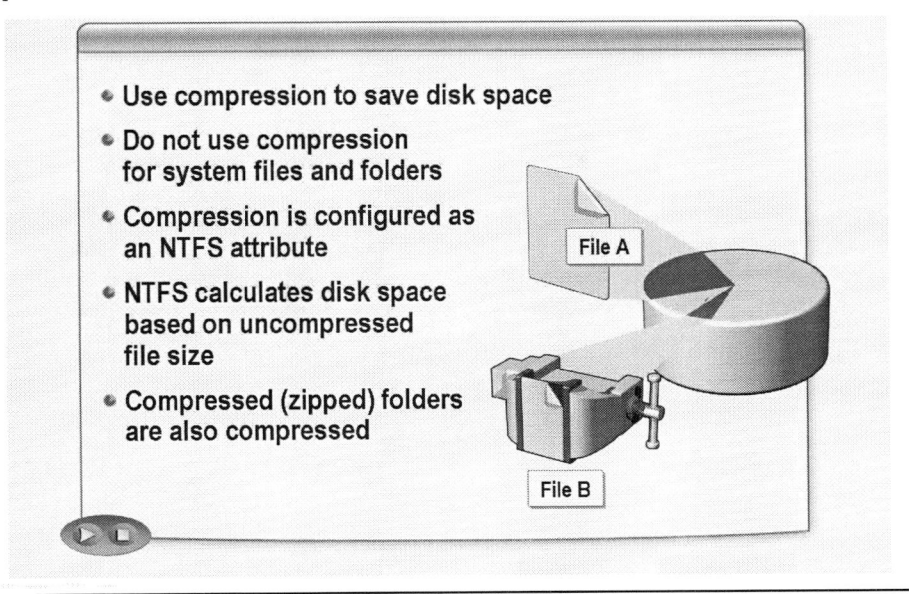

- Use compression to save disk space
- Do not use compression for system files and folders
- Compression is configured as an NTFS attribute
- NTFS calculates disk space based on uncompressed file size
- Compressed (zipped) folders are also compressed

Introduction

Use compression when you need more space on your hard-disk drive. Compressing files, folders, and programs decreases their size and reduces the amount of space they use on drives or removable storage devices. You can also compress disk drives.

Windows supports two types of compression: NTFS file compression and Compressed (zipped) Folders. You use Microsoft Windows® Explorer to configure both types.

Uses of compression

You will get the most compression from text files, bitmap files, spreadsheets, and presentation files. You will have less compression with graphic and video files that are already compressed. Avoid compressing system folders and files because this affects the server performance.

NTFS file compression

Volumes, folders, and files on an NTFS volume are either compressed or uncompressed. Compression is configured as an attribute of a file or folder. New files created in a compressed folder are compressed by default. A file can be compressed but have an uncompressed file within it. The compression state of a folder does not necessarily reflect the compression state of files within that folder. For example, you can uncompress some of or all the files in a compressed folder.

When an application or an operating system command requests access to a compressed file, Windows Server 2003 automatically uncompresses the file. When you close or save a file, Windows Server 2003 compresses it again.

Space allocation

When files are copied, NTFS calculates disk space based on the size of the uncompressed file. This is important because files are uncompressed during the copy process and the system must be sure there is enough space. If you copy a compressed file to an NTFS partition that does not have enough space for the uncompressed file, an error message notifies you that there is not enough disk space for the file.

Compressed (zipped) Folders

Files and folders that are compressed using the Compressed (zipped) Folders feature can be compressed on FAT, FAT32, and NTFS drives. A zipper icon identifies files and folders that are compressed by using this feature.

You can open files directly from these compressed folders, and you can run some programs directly from these compressed folders without uncompressing them. You can also move these compressed files and folders to any drive or folder on your computer, the Internet, or your network, and they are compatible with other file-compression programs and files.

Compressing folders by using Compressed (zipped) Folders does not affect the overall performance of your computer. CPU utilization rises only when Compressed (zipped) Folders are accessed to compress a file.

Comparison of compression methods

The two compression methods are compared in the following table.

Attribute	NTFS file compression	Compressed (zipped) Folders
File system	NTFS	NTFS or FAT, FAT32
Compressible objects	Files, folders, and drives	Files and folders
User interaction	Transparent, when saving a file to a folder that is compressed	Manual
Performance	Decrease if system files are compressed	No decrease
Password protection	No	Yes
Encrypt	No	Yes
Change display color	Yes	No

What Is the compact Command?

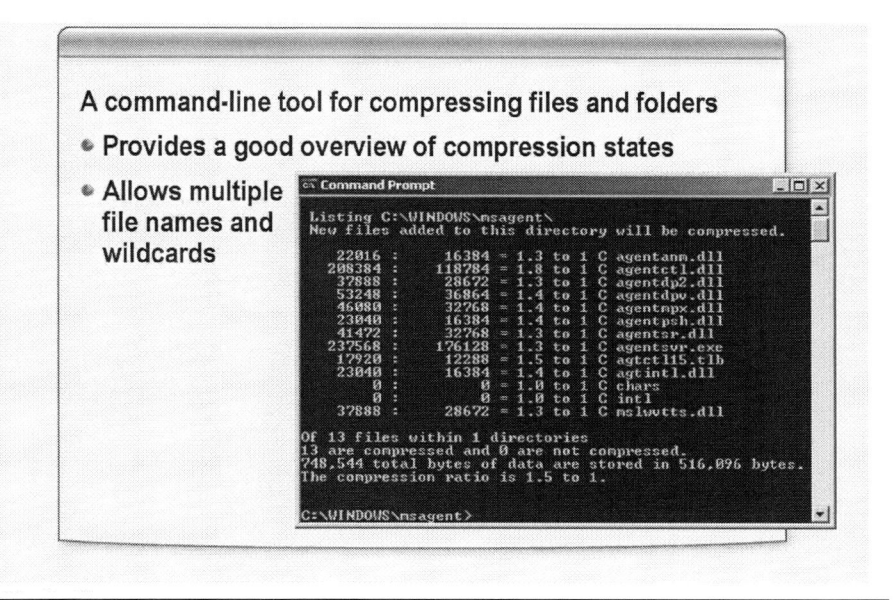

* A command-line tool for compressing files and folders
* Provides a good overview of compression states
* Allows multiple file names and wildcards

Definition

Another tool for compressing files and folders is the **compact** command-line tool. This tool allows administrators to write batch scripts to compress files, which can then be scheduled to run at certain times.

Displays compression state of directory

When used without parameters, **compact** displays the compression state of the current directory and any files that it contains. For example, you can use the following command line to compress all files and folders in the Internet Information Services (IIS) directory:

compact /c c:*IIS****.***

Example using multiple parameters

You can use multiple file names and wildcards with **compact**. You must, however, insert spaces between multiple parameters, as shown in the following example:

compact /C | /U] [/S[:*dir***]] [/A] [/I] [/F] [/Q]** [*filename* [...]

Each parameter is listed and described in the following table.

Parameter	Description
/C	Compresses the files specified. Directories are marked so that files added afterward are compressed.
/U	Uncompresses the specified files. Directories are marked so that files added afterward are not compressed.
/S	Performs the specified operation on files in the specified directory and all subdirectories. The default value is the current directory.
/A	Displays files with the hidden or system attributes. These files are omitted by default.
/I	Continues performing the specified operation even after errors occur. By default, **compact** stops when an error is encountered.
/F	Forces the compress operation on all specified files, even those that are already compressed. Files that are already compressed are skipped by default.
/Q	Reports only the most essential information about the specified pattern, file, or directory. Specifies a pattern, file, or directory.

What Are the Effects of Moving and Copying Compressed Files and Folders?

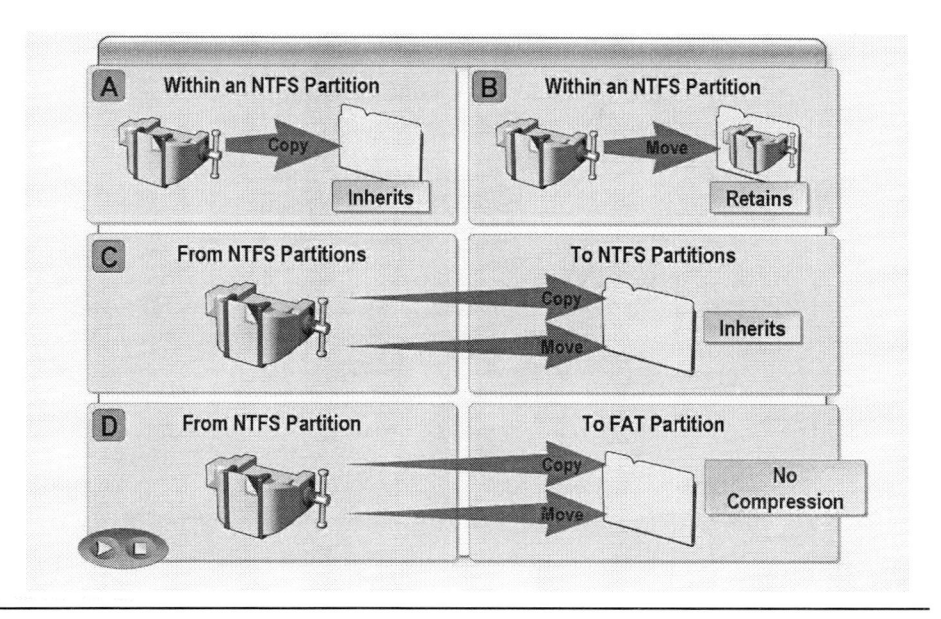

Introduction	Moving and copying compressed files and folders can change their compression state. This lesson examines several move and copy situations and provides you with some basic rules to help you predict outcome.
Copy within an NTFS partition	When you copy a file or folder within an NTFS partition, the file or folder inherits the compression state of the target folder. For example, if you copy a compressed file or folder to an uncompressed folder, the file or folder is automatically uncompressed.
Move within an NTFS partition	When you move a file or folder within an NTFS partition, the file or folder retains its original compression state. For example, if you move a compressed file or folder to an uncompressed folder, the file remains compressed.
Copy between NTFS partitions	When you copy a file or folder between NTFS partitions, the file or folder inherits the compression state of the target folder.
	When copying an NTFS file or a folder to a NTFS folder, the file or folder takes on the compression attribute of the target folder. For example, if you copy a compressed file to an uncompressed folder, the file is uncompressed when it is copied to the folder.
Move between NTFS partitions	When you move a file or folder between NTFS partitions, the file or folder inherits the compression state of the target folder. Because Windows Server 2003 treats a move between partitions as a copy and then a delete operation, the files inherit the compression state of the target folder.

Copying files or folders on NTFS volumes

When you copy a file to a folder that already contains a file of the same name, the copied file takes on the compression attribute of the target file, regardless of the compression state of the folder.

Moving and copying files between FAT16, FAT32, and NTFS volumes

Compressed files that are copied to a FAT or FAT32 partition are uncompressed. This is because compression is not supported on FAT or FAT32 volumes. The same applies to floppy disks because they cannot be formatted with NTFS.

When files are moved or copied from a FAT or FAT32 partition to an NTFS partition, they inherit the compression attribute of the folder into which they are copied.

Note Unlike NTFS compressed folders and files, Compressed (zipped) Folders can be moved and copied without change between volumes, drives, and file systems. This is because using the Compressed (zipped) Folders creates a new file (with the extension .zip) that is actually copied or moved. The original files retain their attributes and location unless otherwise modified.

Best Practices for Compressing Files or Folders

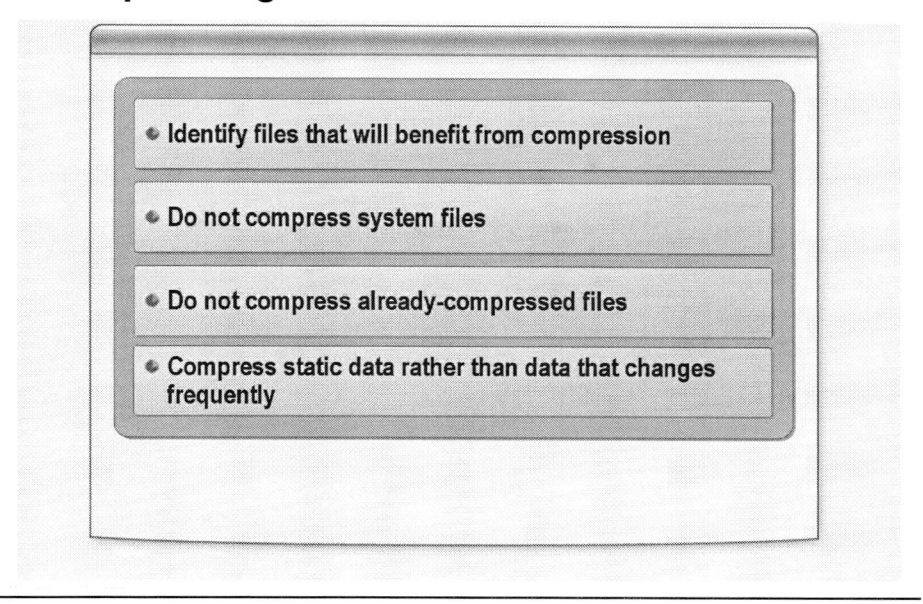

- Identify files that will benefit from compression
- Do not compress system files
- Do not compress already-compressed files
- Compress static data rather than data that changes frequently

Introduction

Some files compress better than others, and some files present problems when they are compressed. Consider the following best practices for managing compression on NTFS partitions.

Identify files that will benefit from compression

Because some file types can be compressed more than others, determine which file types to compress based on the anticipated size of the compressed file. For example, because Windows bitmap files contain more redundant data than application executable files, this file type can be compressed more than an .exe file. Bitmaps can often be compressed to less than 50 percent of the original file size, whereas an application file can rarely be compressed to less than 75 percent of its original size.

Do not compress system files

Do not compress system files. If system files are compressed, system performance will suffer because Windows must uncompress the files whenever they are accessed.

Do not compress already compressed file

Do not compress files that are already compressed. This wastes system time and yields no additional disk space.

Compress static data

Compress static data rather than data that changes frequently. Compressing and uncompressing files burdens the system. By choosing to compress files that are accessed infrequently, you minimize the amount of system time that is dedicated to compression and uncompression activities.

Practice: Managing File Compression

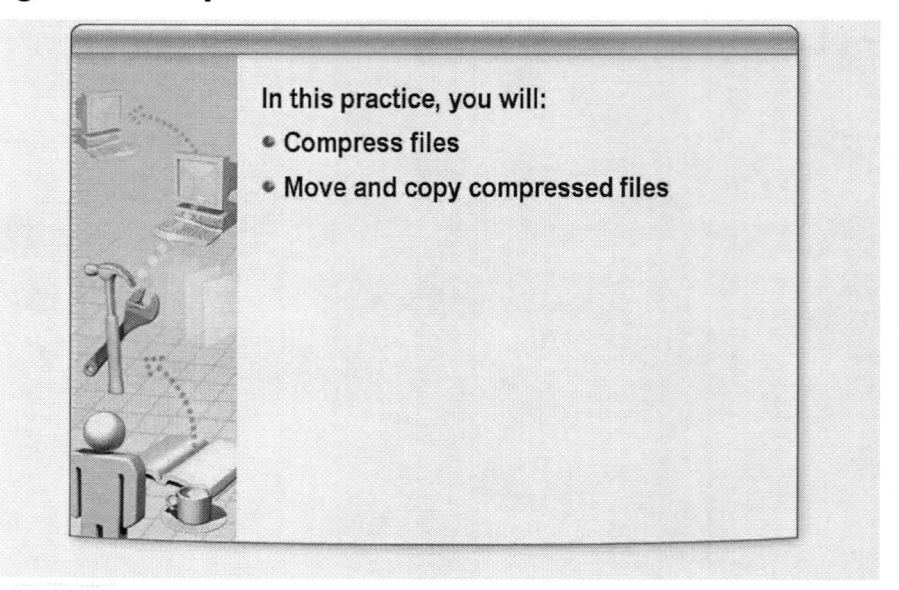

Objective

In this practice, you will:

- Compress files.
- Move and copy compressed files.

Instructions

Ensure that the DEN-DC1 virtual machine is running.

Practice

▶ **Compress files**

1. Log on as **Administrator** with a password of **Pa$$w0rd**.
2. Open Windows Explorer.
3. Browse to **D:\2275\Practices\Mod06\Data\Compressed**.
4. Right-click **Compressed** and then click **Properties**.
5. Note the **Size on disk** parameter: _____
6. Click **Advanced**.
7. Check the **Compress contents to save disk space** check box, and then click **OK**.
8. Click **Apply**, and then click **OK** to confirm that you want the changes to be made to this folder and all subfolders and files.
9. Note the **Size on disk** parameter:_____
10. How much room did you gain by compressing the tax folders? _____ %.
11. Click **OK**. Notice that the compressed files are now blue.

Practice

▶ **Move and copy compressed files**

1. In Windows Explorer, perform the following file operations in the **D:\2275\Practices\Mod06\Data\Compressed** folder:

File	Action	Destination
C-copybtwn.txt	Copy	C:\Uncompressed
C-copywithin.txt	Copy	D:\2275\Practices\Mod06\Data\Uncompressed
C-movebtwn.txt	Move	C:\Uncompressed
C-movewithin.txt	Move	D:\2275\Practices\Mod06\Data\Uncompressed

2. Record the file compression state results in the following table.

   The drives in the exercise represent NTFS-formatted volumes on the same computer.

File	Action	Volume	Folder	File
C-copybtwn.txt	Copy	Different	Uncompressed	
C-copywithin.txt	Copy	Same	Uncompressed	
C-movebtwn.txt	Move	Different	Uncompressed	
C-movewithin.txt	Move	Same	Uncompressed	

3. In Windows Explorer, perform the following file operations in the **D:\2275\Practices\Mod06\Data\Uncompressed** folder:

File	Action	Destination
UC-copybtwn.txt	Copy	C:\Compressed
UC-copywithin.txt	Copy	D:\2275\Practices\Mod06\Data\Compressed
UC-movebtwn.txt	Move	C:\Compressed
UC-movewithin.txt	Move	D:\2275\Practices\Mod06\Data\Compressed

Module 6: Managing Data Storage

4. Record the file compression state results in the following table.

   The drives in the exercise represent NTFS-formatted volumes on the same computer.

File	Action	Volume	Folder	File
UC-copybtwn.txt	Copy	Different	Compressed	
UC-copywithin.txt	Copy	Same	Compressed	
UC-movebtwn.txt	Move	Different	Compressed	
UC-movewithin.txt	Move	Same	Compressed	

5. Close all open windows and log off of DEN-DC1.

▶ **To prepare for the next practice**
- Start the DEN-CL1 virtual machine.

Important Do not shut down the virtual machines.

Lesson: Configuring File Encryption

- What Is EFS Encryption?
- What Is Public-Key Encryption?
- How EFS Uses Encryption
- How EFS Uses Certificates
- What Are the Effects of Moving and Copying Encrypted Files or Folders?
- Sharing an Encrypted Folder
- Practice: Configuring File Encryption

Introduction

An intruder who has physical access to a computer can easily install a new operating system and bypass the security of the existing operating system. If you realize that the operating system controls access to sensitive data, then you can see the risk to sensitive data. You can add an additional layer of security by encrypting these files with Encrypting File System (EFS). An encrypted file's data is protected even if an intruder has full access to the computer's data storage.

In this lesson, you will learn about encryption, as well as how to manage encryption. You will also learn the effects of moving and copying encrypted files.

Lesson objectives

After completing this lesson, you will be able to:

- Describe EFS file encryption.
- Describe public-key encryption.
- Describe how EFS uses encryption
- Describe how EFS uses certificates.
- Describe the effects of moving and copying encrypted files or folders.
- Describe sharing an encrypted folder.
- Configure file encryption.

What Is EFS Encryption?

> EFS encryption makes data unintelligible without a decryption key
> - EFS encrypts data
> - Encryption keys are automatically generated if required
> - Opening and saving encrypted files is transparent to users
> - Use the **cipher** command to display or alter encryption of folders and files on NTFS volumes

Introduction

An attacker can gain access to a shared system by starting a different operating system. An attacker can also steal a computer, remove the hard disk, install the disk in another system, and gain access to the stored files. Files that are encrypted by using Encrypting File System (EFS), however, appear as unintelligible characters when the attacker does not have the decryption key.

EFS provides file level encryption

EFS provides encryption for files created on NTFS volumes. By using EFS, you bar access to sensitive or confidential data to anyone without a decryption key.

Use EFS to encrypt data

Encryption and decryption are the primary tasks of EFS. The default configuration of EFS requires no administrative effort; users can begin encrypting files immediately. EFS automatically generates an encryption key pair for a user if one does not exist.

Encryption and decryption options available

Several encryption and decryption options are available to users. Users can encrypt and decrypt files by using Windows Explorer, by using the **cipher** command, or by using the shortcut menu accessed by right-clicking a file or folder.

Encrypted folder contents

Folders that are marked for encryption are not actually encrypted. Only the files in the folder are encrypted, as well as any new files that are created in or moved to the folder.

Use EFS to access encrypted data

Authorized users with the appropriate key may access encrypted files just as they do unencrypted files. Thus, when a user accesses an encrypted file that is stored on disk, the user can read the contents of the file in the normal way. When the user saves the file on disk again, EFS saves the changes as encrypted. The process for opening, modifying, and saving encrypted files is completely transparent.

Note Unauthorized users attempting to access encrypted files will get an access denied message.

Use EFS to decrypt data

You can decrypt a file by clearing the **Encryption** check box in the file's **Properties** dialog box. After it is decrypted, the file remains decrypted until you encrypt it again. There is no automatic re-encryption of a file, even if it exists in a directory that is marked as encrypted.

Authorized users with the appropriate key can decrypt a file either by clearing the **Encryption** check box in the **Properties** dialog box for the file, or by using the **cipher** command.

Display or alter encryption on NTFS volumes with the cipher command

Use the **cipher** command to display or alter the encryption of folders and files on NTFS volumes. Used without parameters, **cipher** displays the encryption state of the current folder and any files it contains.

Parameters of cipher

You can use the **cipher** command with the parameters in the following table to perform the listed tasks.

Example, to encrypt all files in the current directory: **cipher /e /a *.***.

Parameters	Task description
Use **cipher** with no parameters or with the name of a specific file or folder.	Display the encryption status of files and folders
/e	Set the encryption attribute for folders in the current directory
/e /a	Encrypt files in the current directory
/d	Remove the encryption attribute from folders in the current directory
/d /a	Decrypt files in the current directory
/?	Display all the options that are available with **cipher**

What Is Public-Key Encryption?

- Public key
- Private key
- Certification authorities
- Automated certificate creation

Definition

Public-key encryption, also called *asymmetric encryption*, is an encryption method that uses a public key and private key to encrypt data. Public keys used by a particular user are available to anyone. Private keys must be kept secret by the account that has encrypted the file. A matched public key and private key is referred to as a *key pair*.

Public key characteristics

- Public-key encryption has the following characteristics: Anyone can encrypt data by using a public key, which is available as public information. However, only one account possesses the corresponding private key, so only that account can decrypt the data.
- The account that uses the private key generates the key pair.
- A key pair is created by using a program that generates keys. For example, EFS can be used to create a key pair to encrypt files on your domain.
- The public key, an attribute of the certificate, is widely distributed, in locations such as the Active Directory® directory service, to ensure that other users can obtain the public key for both encryption and digital signing of data.

Private key characteristics

- The private key is never exposed to network users, and is protected either in a user or computer profile, or on a physical device such as a smart card.

Note EFS uses the public key only for encryption.

Certification authorities

A certification authority (CA) creates certificates for public key cryptography. Windows Server 2003 has the ability to act as a certification authority. When a Windows Server 2003 is used as the certification authority for EFS certificates, the entire certificate creation process can be automated.

How EFS Uses Encryption

> - **Symmetric encryption protects the file**
>   - Symmetric encryption is strong and fast
> - **Public-key encryption protects the symmetric key**
>   - A copy is stored for each user
>   - A copy is stored for the recovery agent

Introduction

EFS uses a combination of public-key and symmetric-key encryption to ensure that files are protected from all but the most computationally impracticable methods of attack. A symmetric key is used to encrypt the file. Public-key encryption is used to protect the symmetric key.

Symmetric encryption

Symmetric encryption uses the same key to encrypt a file and decrypt a file. This type of encryption is faster and stronger than public key encryption. However, the difficulty of securing the key during a cross-network transfer requires additional security for the symmetric key.

Symmetric is the typical method of encrypting large amounts of data.

Protecting symmetric keys

EFS uses public key encryption to protect the symmetric key that is required to decrypt the file contents. Each user certificate contains a public key that is used to encrypt the symmetric key. Then only the user with the private key can access the symmetric key.

The file encryption process is described below:

1. When a user encrypts a file, EFS generates a file-encryption key (FEK) to encrypt the data. The FEK is encrypted with the user's public key, and the encrypted FEK is then stored with the file. This ensures that only the user who holds the matching EFS Encryption private key can decrypt the file. After a user encrypts a file, the file remains encrypted for as long as it is stored on the disk.

2. To decrypt files, the user can open the file, remove the encryption attribute, or decrypt the file by using the **cipher** command. When this occurs, EFS decrypts the FEK by using the user's private key, and then decrypts the data by using the FEK.

Note In addition to the user that encrypted the file, additional copies of the symmetric key are encrypted with the public key of the recovery agent and any other authorized users.

How EFS Uses Certificates

> * Certificate identifies user
> * EFS generates a certificate
>   * Requests from CA
>   * Self-signed if CA not available
> * EFS renews certificates if required

Introduction

Each user who logs on to a computer running Windows 2000 or later can encrypt files. The first time the user encrypts a file, EFS generates a unique certificate and key pair for the user. Unless a user sets up sharing for selected users, no one else can access the user's encrypted files.

What is a certificate?

A certificate is a digital statement issued by an authority that vouches for the identity of the certificate holder. A certificate binds a public key to the identity of the person, computer, or service that holds the corresponding private key. Certificates are used by a variety of public key security services and applications to provide authentication, data integrity, and secure communications across networks such as the Internet.

How EFS Uses Certificates

EFS must find a certificate for a user before it will allow the user to access an encrypted file. The method that EFS uses to find and employ certificates to open an encrypted file is described below.

1. When a user sets the encrypted attribute for a file or folder, EFS attempts to locate the user's certificate in the personal certificate store.

2. If the user does not have a certificate that has been authorized for use with EFS, EFS requests a certificate from an available enterprise certification authority (CA).

3. If an enterprise CA is not available, EFS automatically generates its own self-signed certificate for the user.

If the EFS user certificate expires, EFS ensures that the certificate is renewed if possible or, if not, that a new public-private key pair and a new public-key certificate are issued for the user the next time an EFS operation is performed for that user. The private key from an expired certificate can still be used to access previously encrypted files, but the public key from an expired certificate cannot be used to encrypt new files.

What Are the Effects of Moving and Copying Encrypted Files and Folders?

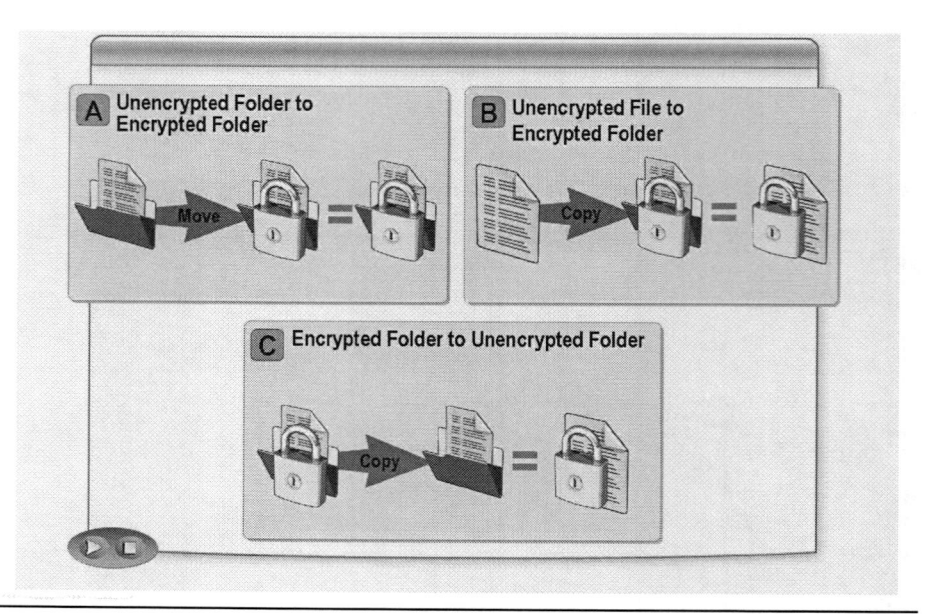

Introduction

All files and folders that are created in a folder marked for encryption are automatically encrypted. Moving and copying encrypted files and folders can change the encryption state of the file or folder This discussion will help you understand the effects of these actions.

Effect of moving encrypted files

If you move a file from an unencrypted folder to an encrypted folder, the file is encrypted.

Effect of copying encrypted files

If you copy an unencrypted file to an encrypted folder, the copied file is encrypted. If you copy an encrypted file from an encrypted folder to an unencrypted folder, the file remains encrypted.

If your access allows you to decrypt a file and you copy the encrypted file from an NTFS volume to a FAT or FAT32 volume, the file becomes unencrypted. If you copy a file from a FAT volume to an encrypted folder on an NTFS volume, the file becomes encrypted. If your access does not allow you to decrypt a file and you attempt to copy or move it to a FAT or FAT32 partition you will receive an access denied error message.

After you encrypt a folder, all files and subfolders that are added to the folder will be encrypted.

Note For more information about encryption, see the white paper, *EFS*, under **Additional Reading** on the Student Materials compact disc.

Sharing Encrypted Files

- Encrypted files can be shared with local, domain, and trusted domain users
- Groups cannot be authorized for access
- Any user with access can add other users
- Self-signed certificates are difficult for sharing

Introduction

Users can share encrypted files with other local, domain, and trusted domain users. Files can be shared locally on a computer or on the network. Authorizing access to encrypted files is a separate process from NTFS or share permissions. Sharing access to encrypted files involves the configuration of both file system access control list (ACL) permissions, and EFS permissions.

Groups

Because there is no method for issuing a certificate and assigning a key pair for a group, groups cannot be authorized for accessing encrypted files. Only individual user accounts have authorized access to encrypted files.

Authorization

Any user who is authorized to decrypt a file can authorize other users to access the file. Granting access is not limited to the file owner. Caution users to share files only with trusted accounts, because those accounts can authorize other accounts. Removing the Write permission from a user or user group mitigates risk.

Certificates

EFS sharing requires that the users who will be authorized to access the encrypted file have EFS certificates. These certificates can be located in roaming profiles or in the user profiles on the computer on which the file to be shared is stored, or they can be stored in and retrieved from Active Directory.

Self-signed certificates created by EFS are difficult to use for sharing encrypted files because the certificates are stored only on the computer that stores the encrypted files. When files are encrypted on a remote server, a profile is created for the encrypting user on the remote server, and a self-signed certificate is stored there. Each user must import the self-signed certificates of other users to give them access. The file must be exported from the remote server.

If your organization is going to be sharing encrypted files you should configure a certification authority to issue EFS certificates. This provides a central trusted source for certificates and eliminates the need to import user certificates.

Practice: Configuring File Encryption

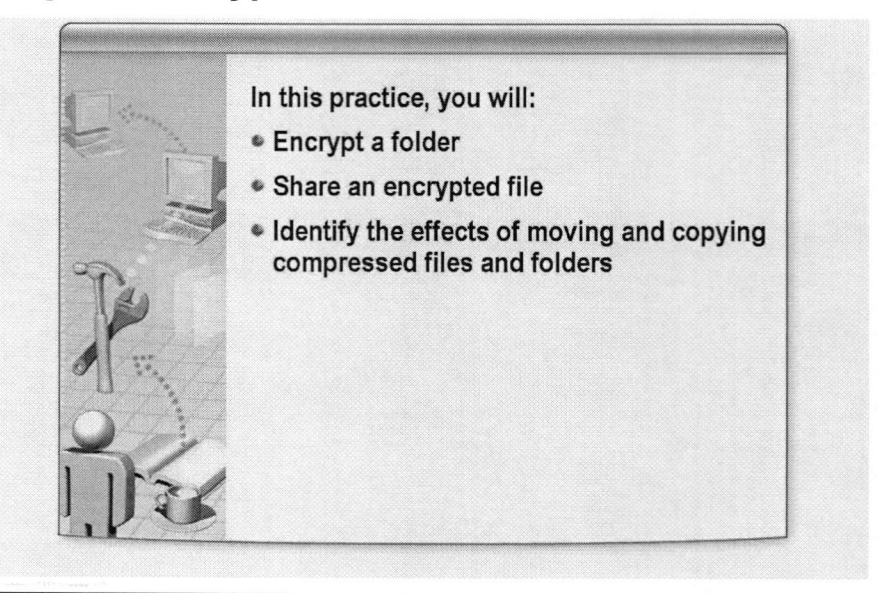

Objective

In this practice, you will:

- Encrypt a folder.
- Share an encrypted file.
- Identify the effects of moving and copying compressed files and folders.

Instructions

Ensure that the DEN-DC1 and DEN-CL1 virtual machines are running.

Practice

▶ **Encrypt a folder**

1. On DEN-CL1, log on as **EFS1** with a password of **Pa$$w0rd**.
2. Open Windows Explorer.
3. Browse to **\\DEN-DC1\Data**.
4. Right-click the **Encrypted** folder and then click **Properties**.
5. Click **Advanced**.
6. Check the **Encrypt contents to secure data** check box, and then click **OK**.
7. Click **Apply**.
8. In the **Confirm Attribute Changes** dialog box, click **OK** to confirm that you want the changes to be made to this folder and all subfolders and files.
9. Click **OK**. Notice that the **Encrypted** folder text is colored green.
10. Log off as **EFS1**.
11. Log on to DEN-CL1 as **EFS2** with a password of **Pa$$w0rd**.
12. Open Windows Explorer.
13. Browse to **\\DEN-DC1\Data\Encrypted**.

Module 6: Managing Data Storage

14. Double-click **E-copybtwn** to open it.
15. Although Notepad opens, access to the file contents is denied. Click **OK** to close the dialog box.
16. Close all open windows.

Practice

▶ **Share an encrypted file**

1. On DEN-DC1, log on as **Administrator** with a password of **Pa$$w0rd**.
2. Click **Start**, click **Run**, type **mmc**, and then click **OK**.
3. Add the Certificates snap-in.
    a. Click **File** and then click **Add/Remove Snap-in**.
    b. Click **Add**.
    c. Double-click **Certificates,** and click **Finish**.
    d. Click **Close** and then click **OK**.
4. Expand **Certificates – Current User**, expand **Trusted People**, and then click **Certificates**.
5. Right-click **EFS1**, point to **All Tasks,** and click **Export**.
6. Click **Next** to start the Certificate Export Wizard.
7. Click **Next** to accept the default export format.
8. In the **File name** box, type **D:\2275\Practices\Mod06\Data\EFS1key.cer** and then click **Next**.
9. Click **Finish**.
10. Click **OK**.
11. On DEN-CL1, open Windows Explorer.
12. Browse to **\\DEN-DC1\Data**.
13. Double-click **EFS1key** and then click **Install Certificate**.
14. Click **Next** to start the Certificate Import Wizard.
15. Click **Next** to let Windows automatically select the certificate store. It will be placed in Trusted People.
16. Click **Finish**. Click **OK**.
17. In the **Certificate** dialog box, click **OK**.
18. In Windows Explorer, browse to **\\DEN-DC1\Data\Encrypted**.
19. Create a text file named **Shared**.
20. Open **Shared**, enter your name, save the file and close Notepad.
21. Right-click **Shared** and then click **Properties**.
22. Click **Advanced**, and then click **Details**.
23. Click **Add**, click **EFS1**, and then click **OK**. Notice that EFS1 and EFS2 are both listed as users.
24. Click **OK** three times to close all dialog boxes.
25. Close Windows Explorer.
26. Log off of DEN-CL1.

Practice

▶ **Identify the effects of moving and copying encrypted files and folders**

1. On DEN-DC1, in Windows Explorer, perform the following file operations in the **D:\2275\Practices\Mod06\Data\Encrypted** folder:

File	Action	Destination
E-copybtwn.txt	Copy	C:\Unencrypted
E-copywithin.txt	Copy	D:\2275\Practices\Mod06\Data\Unencrypted
E-movebtwn.txt	Move	C:\Unencrypted
E-movewithin.txt	Move	D:\2275\Practices\Mod06\Data\Unencrypted

2. Record the file encryption state results in the following table.

   The drives in the exercise represent NTFS-formatted volumes on the same computer.

File	Action	Volume	Folder	File
E-copybtwn.txt	Copy	Different	Unencrypted	
E-copywithin.txt	Copy	Same	Unencrypted	
E-movebtwn.txt	Move	Different	Unencrypted	
E-movewithin.txt	Move	Same	Unencrypted	

3. In Windows Explorer, perform the following file operations in the **D:\2275\Practices\Mod06\Data\Unencrypted** folder:

File	Action	Destination
UE-copybtwn.txt	Copy	C:\Encrypted
UE-copywithin.txt	Copy	D:\2275\Practices\Mod06\Data\Encrypted
UE-movebtwn.txt	Move	C:\Encrypted
UE-movewithin.txt	Move	D:\2275\Practices\Mod06\Data\Encrypted

4. Record the file encryption state results in the following table.

   The drives in the exercise represent NTFS-formatted volumes on the same computer.

File	Action	Volume	Folder	File
UE-copybtwn.txt	Copy	Different	Encrypted	
UE-copywithin.txt	Copy	Same	Encrypted	
UE-movebtwn.txt	Move	Different	Encrypted	
UE-movewithin.txt	Move	Same	Encrypted	

5. Close all open windows.

Important Do not shut down the virtual machines.

Lesson: Configuring EFS Recovery Agents

- What Is an EFS Recovery Agent?
- Recovering Encrypted Files
- Practice: Configuring EFS Recovery Agents

Introduction

When a user account is deleted the associated certificate is lost as well. Without a recovery agent, that user cannot access encrypted files.

Lesson objectives

After completing this lesson, you will be able to:

- Describe a recovery agent.
- Describe how to recover an encrypted file.
- Export and import a recovery key.

What Is an EFS Recovery Agent?

> - Authorized to decrypt data
> - Required when users are deleted
> - Required when local user passwords are reset
> - The recovery key can be exported

Definition

A recovery agent is an individual who is authorized to decrypt data that was encrypted by another user. Recovery agents do not need any other permissions to function in this role. The default recovery agent is the domain administrator. However, this can be delegated to any user.

Uses of data recovery

Data recovery is might be necessary when you need access to data encrypted by an employee who leaves or who loses the private key. Data recovery is available through the Encrypting File System (EFS) as a part of the overall security policy for the system. If your file encryption certificate and associated private key is lost through disk failure, damage, or other reason, the person who is the designated recovery agent can recover the data.

Caution When the password for a local user is reset by an administrator, Windows XP or Windows Server 2003 is unable to read the private key stored in the user's profile. They key must be recovered from a backup or a recovery agent must recover the files.

Special certificates and private key

Each recovery agent has a special certificate and associated private key that allows data recovery wherever the recovery policy applies. If you are the designated recovery agent, you should be sure to use the **Export** command in Certificates in the Microsoft Management Console (MMC) to back up the recovery certificate and the associated private key to a secure location.

After backing them up, you should use Certificates in MMC to delete the recovery certificate. Then, when you need to perform a recovery operation for a user, you should first restore the recovery certificate and associated private key using the **Import** command from Certificates in MMC. After recovering the data, you should again delete the recovery certificate. You do not have to repeat the export process.

Recovering Encrypted Files

- Log on as recovery agent
- Recovery policies define the recovery agent
- Default recovery agent is the domain Administrator account
- Back up the recovery key

Introduction

To recover encrypted files, you must understand which user is configured as the recovery agent. After this is accomplished, log on as that user and decrypt the files.

Recovery policies

A recovery policy is configured locally for stand-alone computers. For computers that are part of a network, a recovery policy is configured at the domain, organizational unit, or individual computer level. These recovery policies apply to all computers running Windows 2000, Windows XP, and Windows Server 2003 operating systems. A certification authority (CA) issues recovery certificates; you use Certificates in Microsoft Management Console (MMC) to manage them.

In a domain environment, the domain Administrator account is automatically configured as a recovery agent.

Adding a recovery agent

The recovery agent is defined through Group Policy. The default recovery agent is defined in the Default Domain Policy. The administrator is the default recovery agent.

When a new recovery agent is added through Group Policy, it is automatically added to all newly encrypted files. However, it is not automatically added to existing encrypted files. The recovery agent for a file is set at the time that the file is encrypted. Therefore an encrypted file must be accessed and saved to update the recovery agent.

Note The best way to update the recovery agent for many files is by using the **cipher /u** command.

Backing up the recovery key

There are two reasons to back up the recovery key:

1. To secure against system failure. The domain administrator key that is used by default for EFS recovery is stored only on the first domain controller in the domain. If anything were to happen to this domain controller, then EFS recovery would be impossible.

2. To make the recovery key portable. The recovery key is not automatically available to the recovery agent on all computers. The recovery key must be installed in the profile of the recovery agent. If roaming profiles are used, then the key will be available to the recovery agent on any computer. However, if roaming profiles are not used, then exporting and importing the recovery key is a method to update the profile of the recovery agent on a particular computer.

Practice: Configuring EFS Recovery Agents

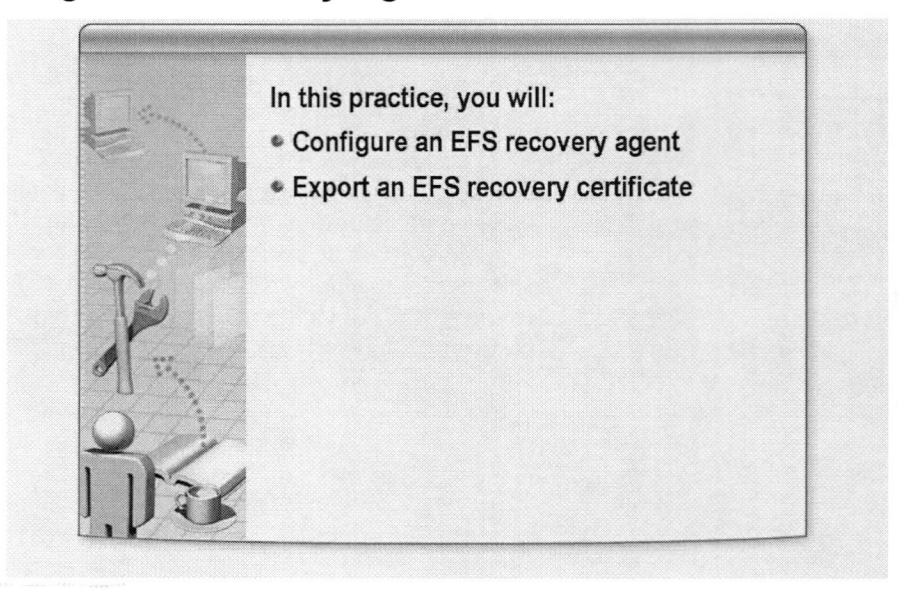

Objective

In this practice, you will:

- Configure an EFS recovery agent.
- Export an EFS recovery certificate.

Instructions

Ensure the DEN-DC1 and DEN-CL1 virtual machines are running.

Practice

▶ **Configure an EFS recovery agent**

1. On DEN-DC1, log on as **EFS2** with a password of **Pa$$w0rd**.
2. Click **Start**, click **Run**, type **cmd**, and then click **OK**.
3. Type **cipher /r:\\DEN-DC1\data\EFS2recovery** and then press **ENTER**. Type Enter when prompted for a password. This command creates a .cer file to be imported as the recovery agent in Group Policy and a .pfx file to be imported in the profile of the user performing data recovery.
4. Close the command prompt.
5. Log off of DEN-DC1.
6. Log on to DEN-DC1 as the **Administrator** with a password of **Pa$$w0rd**.
7. On DEN-DC1, click **Start**, point to **Administrative Tools**, and then click **Group Policy Management**.
8. Expand **Forest: Contoso.msft**, expand **Domains**, expand **Contoso.msft**, and then click **Default Domain Policy**.
9. Read the **Group Policy Management Console** dialog box that appears, check the **Do not show this message again** check box, and then click **OK**.
10. Right-click **Default Domain Policy** and click **Edit**.
11. Under **Computer Configuration**, expand **Windows Settings**, expand **Security Settings**, expand **Public Key Policies**, and then click **Encrypting File System**.

Module 6: Managing Data Storage

12. Right-click **Encrypting File System** and click **Add Data Recovery Agent**.
13. Click **Next** to start the **Add Recovery Agent Wizard**.
14. Click **Browse Folders** and select **D:\2275\Practices\Mod06\Data\EFS2recovery**, and then click **Open**.
15. Click **Yes** to install the certificate and then click **Next**.
16. Click **Finish**.
17. Close the **Group Policy Object Editor**.
18. Close **Group Policy Management**.

Practice

▶ **Export an EFS recovery certificate**

1. Click **Start**, click **Run**, type **mmc**, and then click **OK**.
2. Add the Certificates snap-in.
   a. Click **File** and click **Add/Remove Snap-in**.
   b. Click **Add**.
   c. Double-click **Certificates,** and then click **Finish**.
   d. Click **Close** and then click **OK**.
3. Expand **Certificates – Current User**, expand **Personal**, and then click **Certificates**.
4. Right-click the certificate with an intended purpose of **File Recovery**, point to **All Tasks**, and then click **Export**.
5. Click **Next** to start the **Certificate Export Wizard**.
6. Click **Yes, export the private key** and then click **Next**.
7. Click **Next** to accept the default file format.
8. In the **Password** and **Confirm password** boxes, type **Pa$$w0rd** and then click **Next**.
9. In the **File name** box, type **D:\2275\Practices\Mod06\Data\AdminRecovery.pfx** and click **Next**.
10. Click **Finish**.
11. Click **OK**.
12. Close the MMC and do not save console settings.
13. Close all open windows on DEN-DC1 and DEN-CL1.

Important Do not shut down the virtual machines.

Caution An EFS recovery key should always be exported directly to removable media and stored in a safe location. Data-recovery tools could be used recover the exported recovery key after it has been deleted if it is stored on a server hard drive.

Lesson: Implementing Disk Quotas

- Multimedia: What Are Disk Quotas?
- What Are Disk-Quota Settings?
- Practice: Implementing Disk Quotas

Introduction

Use disk quotas to manage server resources. Quotas do this by limiting user storage space. You can also use disk quotas to track disk usage by users. In this lesson, you will learn how to use disk quotas and how to set up disk entries.

Lesson objectives

After completing this lesson, you will be able to:

- Explain disk quotas.
- Describe disk-quota settings.
- Implement disk quotas.

Multimedia: What Are Disk Quotas?

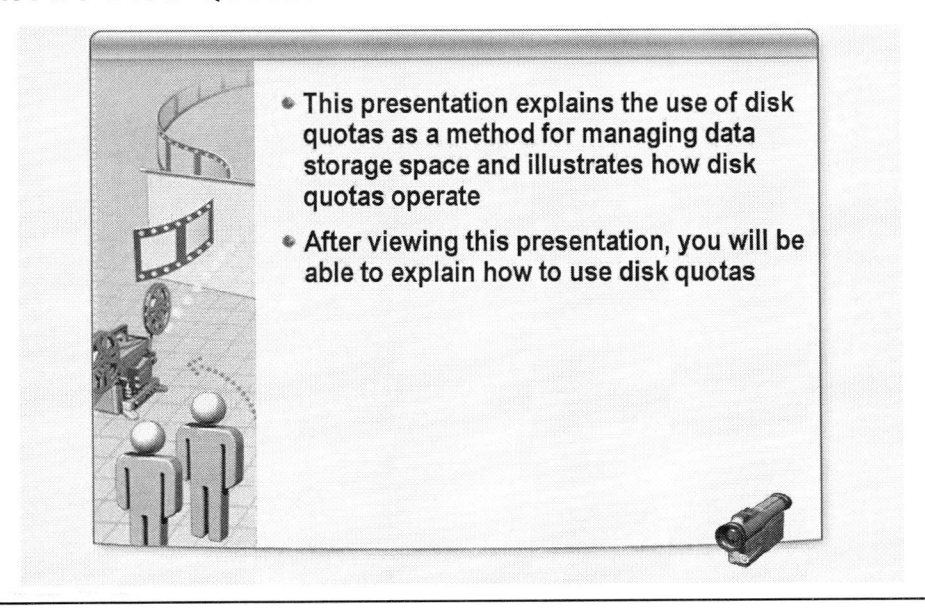

- This presentation explains the use of disk quotas as a method for managing data storage space and illustrates how disk quotas operate
- After viewing this presentation, you will be able to explain how to use disk quotas

File location

To view the *What Are Disk Quotas?* presentation, open the Web page on the Student Materials compact disc, click **Multimedia**, and then click the title of the presentation.

Do not open this presentation unless the instructor tells you to.

What Are Disk-Quota Settings?

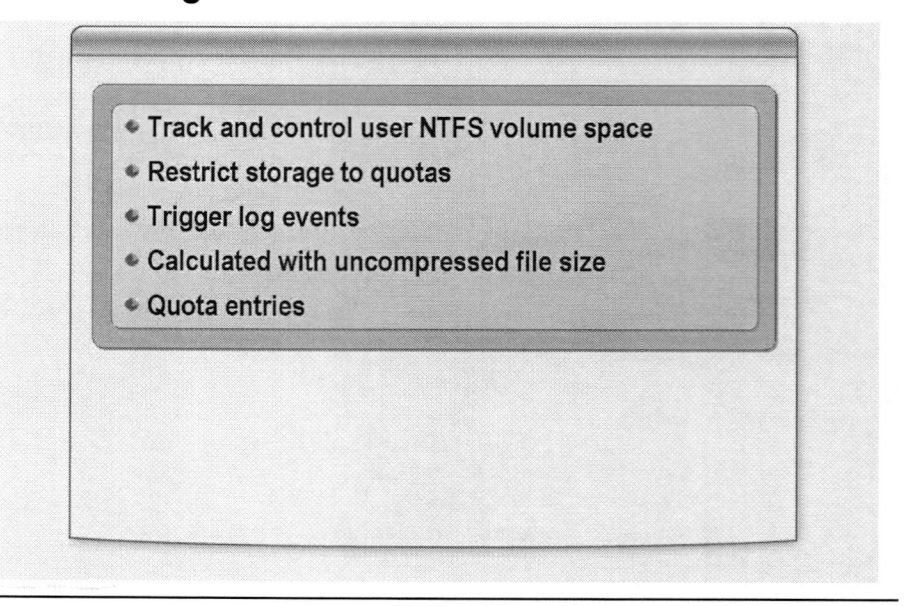

> - Track and control user NTFS volume space
> - Restrict storage to quotas
> - Trigger log events
> - Calculated with uncompressed file size
> - Quota entries

Introduction

Administrators must manage the always increasing demand for data storage. You can use disk-quota settings to monitor and manage disk usage. Quotas prevent users from writing additional data to a disk volume after they exceed their quota.

Use disk quotas to track disk space

Quotas need not limit space. You can also use quotas to track the disk-space use of each user. When you do limit space, you can specify whether to log an event when users exceed quota limits or quota warning levels.

Note Quotas are tracked per volume or partition. If there are multiple network fie shares on a volume, then the quotas apply to the sum of all file shares.

Enable quotas on volumes

You can enable quotas on local volumes, network volumes, and removable drives if they are formatted by using NTFS. When you enable disk quotas for a volume, volume usage is automatically tracked for all users from that point on.

File compression does not prevent exceeding quota limits

You cannot use file compression to increase storage capacity within a limit because compressed files are tracked based on their uncompressed size. For example, Windows counts a 50-megabyte (MB) file compressed to 40 MB as 50 MB.

CPU overhead and administration

Enabling disk quotas requires a minimal amount of CPU overhead and no administration after the initial configuration.

Set quotas on remote volumes	You can set quotas on a remote volume by mapping to it by using Windows Explorer or My Computer. You can manage NTFS volumes on remote computers running Windows 2000 and Windows Server 2003. The volumes must be formatted by using NTFS and must be shared from the root folder of the volume.
Overriding quotas for individuals	When quota settings are configured for a volume, they are the default quota values for each user. You can override the quota settings on a per user basis by configuring a quota entry to override the quota settings. For example, you can allow several individual engineers increased quota sizes because they are storing large technical drawings. By default, there is a quota entry for Administrators group allowing unlimited file storage.

Practice: Configuring Quota Limits

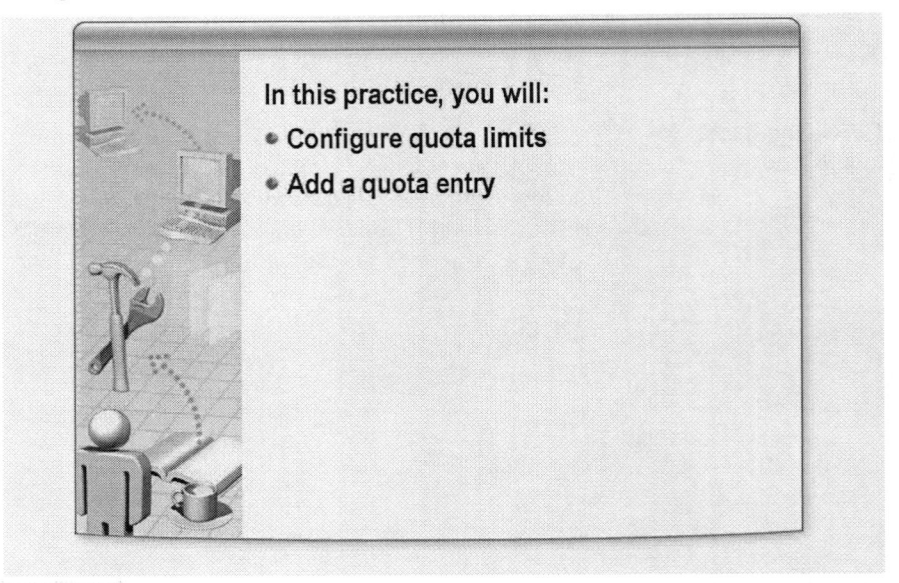

Objective

In this practice, you will:

- Configure quota limits.
- Add a quota entry.

Instructions

Ensure that the DEN-DC1 and DEN-CL1 virtual machines are running.

Practice

▶ **Configure quota limits**

1. On DEN-DC1, Click **Start** and then click **My Computer**.
2. Right-click **Allfiles (D:)** and click **Properties**.
3. Click the **Quota** tab.
4. Check the **Enable quota management** check box.
5. Check the **Deny disk space to users exceeding quota limit** check box.
6. Click **Limit disk space to**, type **100** in the box, and click **MB** in the drop-down list.
7. In the **Set warning level to** box, type **90**, and click **MB** in the drop-down list.
8. Check the **Log event when a user exceeds their quota limit** check box.
9. Check the **Log event when a user exceeds their warning level** check box.
10. Click **OK** and click **OK**.

Practice

▶ **Add a quota entry**

1. Right-click **Allfiles (D:)** and click **Properties**.
2. Click the **Quota** tab.

3. Click **Quota Entries**. This is a list of individual quota entries that overrides the defaults set in the previous steps.
4. Click **Quota** and then click **New Quota Entry**.
5. Type **Administrator**, click **Check Names**, and then click **OK**.
6. Click **Do not limit disk usage** and then click **OK**.
7. Close the **Quota Entries for Allfiles (D:)** window.
8. Click **OK**, and then close all open windows.
9. Log off of DEN-DC1 and DEN-CL1.

Important Do not shut down the virtual machines.

Lab: Managing Data Storage

Objectives

After completing this lab, you will be able to:

- Troubleshoot disk-quota entries.
- Recover an encrypted file.

Instructions

Ensure that the DEN-DC1 and DEN-CL1 virtual machines are running.

Scenario

You are the systems administrator for an organizational unit on a large network. After arriving at work one morning, you receive the following requests from your manager:

- You have implemented quotas on data volumes to control the volume of data users were storing. One user, Paul West, is attempting to copy some files between two folders and is getting an error message. Paul needs to copy these files and you must enable him to do so.

- Another systems administrator has deleted some user profiles from the DEN-DC1 server. He did not realize that EFS (without a certification authority) stores encryption keys in profiles on the server with the encrypted files. You must recover these files for the users.

Estimated time to complete this lab: 20 minutes

Exercise 1
Troubleshooting Disk-Quota Entries

You need to configure a disk quota entry for Paul West.

Tasks	Specific instructions
1. Configure a disk-quota entry for Paul West.	a. Log on to DEN-DC1 as **Administrator** with a password of **Pa$$w0rd**. b. Use My Computer to open the properties of **Allfiles (D:)**. c. Click the **Quota** tab in the **Allfiles (D:) Properties** dialog box. d. Configure **Paul West** as a quota entry. e. Configure a limit of **10MB** and warning of **5MB**.
2. Test the disk space as Paul West.	a. Log on to DEN-CL1 as **Paul** with a password of **Pa$$w0rd**. b. Copy **File1**, **File2**, and **File3** from **\\DEN-DC1\Data\Quota** to **\\DEN-DC1\Data\Quota\Project 1**.
3. On DEN-DC1, view the quota status.	a. On DEN-DC1, in **System** event viewer, find the event with source **ntfs**. Notice that a user has hit their threshold limit. b. Copy **File4** and **File5** into the **Project1** folder. You should now get an error message stating that there is not enough free space.
4. Allow Paul West unlimited disk space.	a. Change the Paul West quota entry to unlimited. b. Copy all of the files from the **\\DEN-DC1\Data\Quota** to **\\DEN-DC1\Data\Quota\Project 1**. The copy task should be successful. c. Close all open windows.

Exercise 2
Recovering an Encrypted File

In this exercise, you recover an encrypted file.

Tasks	Specific instructions
1. Create an encrypted file logged on as **Paul West**.	a. Ensure that you are logged on to DEN-CL1 as **Paul** with a password of **Pa$$w0rd**. b. Create a text file in **\\DEN-DC1\Data\Encrypted** named **Recover.txt**. c. Put some information in the text file. d. Log off of DEN-CL1.
2. On DEN-DC1, log on as **Administrator** and Delete the Paul West profile.	a. Log on to DEN-DC1 as **Administrator** with a password of **Pa$$w0rd**. b. Open **System Properties**. c. Delete the **Paul West** profile. d. Restart DEN-DC1.
3. On DEN-CL1, open Recover.txt.	a. Log on to DEN-CL1, as **Paul**. b. Attempt to open the **\\DEN-DC1\Data\Encrypted\Recover.txt** file. This action will fail because the profile with the private key required for decryption is missing. c. Close all open windows.
4. On DEN-DC1, decrypt the file.	a. Log on to DEN-DC1 as **Administrator** with a password of **Pa$$w0rd**. b. Browse to **D:\2275\Practices\Mod06\Data\Encrypted**. c. Decrypt **Recover.txt**.
5. On DEN-CL1, open Recover.txt.	▪ On DEN-CL1, as Paul, attempt to open the **\\DEN-DC1\Data\Encrypted\Recover.txt** file. This action will be successful because the file is decrypted.
6. Encrypt Recover.txt	a. Encrypt the file again. b. Close all windows and log off.
7. Complete the lab exercise.	a. Close all programs and shut down all computers. Do not save changes. b. To prepare for the next module, start the DEN-DC1 virtual computer.

Module 7: Managing Disaster Recovery

Contents

Overview	1
Lesson: Preparing for Disaster Recovery	2
Lesson: Backing Up Data	7
Lesson: Scheduling Backup Jobs	25
Lesson: Restoring Data	32
Lesson: Configuring Shadow Copies	37
Lesson: Recovering from Server Failure	50
Lab: Managing Disaster Recovery	64
Course Evaluation	69

Information in this document, including URL and other Internet Web site references, is subject to change without notice. Unless otherwise noted, the example companies, organizations, products, domain names, e-mail addresses, logos, people, places, and events depicted herein are fictitious, and no association with any real company, organization, product, domain name, e-mail address, logo, person, place or event is intended or should be inferred. Complying with all applicable copyright laws is the responsibility of the user. Without limiting the rights under copyright, no part of this document may be reproduced, stored in or introduced into a retrieval system, or transmitted in any form or by any means (electronic, mechanical, photocopying, recording, or otherwise), or for any purpose, without the express written permission of Microsoft Corporation.

The names of manufacturers, products, or URLs are provided for informational purposes only and Microsoft makes no representations and warranties, either expressed, implied, or statutory, regarding these manufacturers or the use of the products with any Microsoft technologies. The inclusion of a manufacturer or product does not imply endorsement of Microsoft of the manufacturer or product. Links are provided to third party sites. Such sites are not under the control of Microsoft and Microsoft is not responsible for the contents of any linked site or any link contained in a linked site, or any changes or updates to such sites. Microsoft is not responsible for webcasting or any other form of transmission received from any linked site. Microsoft is providing these links to you only as a convenience, and the inclusion of any link does not imply endorsement of Microsoft of the site or the products contained therein.

Microsoft may have patents, patent applications, trademarks, copyrights, or other intellectual property rights covering subject matter in this document. Except as expressly provided in any written license agreement from Microsoft, the furnishing of this document does not give you any license to these patents, trademarks, copyrights, or other intellectual property.

© 2005 Microsoft Corporation. All rights reserved.

Microsoft, Active Directory, ActiveX, Authenticode, BizTalk, IntelliMirror, MSDN, PowerPoint, Windows, Windows Media, Windows NT, and Windows Server are either registered trademarks or trademarks of Microsoft Corporation in the United States and/or other countries.

All other trademarks are property of their respective owners.

Overview

- Preparing for Disaster Recovery
- Backing Up Data
- Scheduling Backup Jobs
- Restoring Data
- Configuring Shadow Copies
- Recovering from Server Failure

Introduction

This module helps you prepare for a computer disaster. Microsoft® Windows Server™ 2003 includes several features that support data loss prevention. It also includes tools that allow you recover when data loss occurs. Understanding these features is essential to developing and implementing an effective disaster protection and recovery plan.

Objectives

After completing this module, you will be able to:

- Prepare for disaster recovery.
- Back up data.
- Schedule backup jobs.
- Restore data.
- Configure a shadow copy.
- Recover from server failure.

Lesson: Preparing for Disaster Recovery

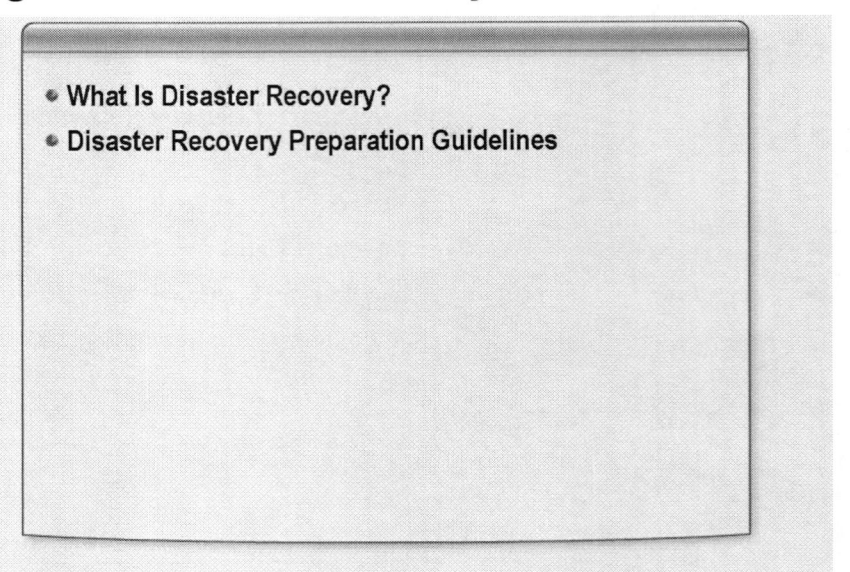

- What Is Disaster Recovery?
- Disaster Recovery Preparation Guidelines

Introduction

This lesson introduces the components of disaster recovery and the methods of recovering data after a disaster occurs. This lesson also provides recommended guidelines that will help you to develop your own disaster recovery plan.

Lesson objectives

After completing this lesson, you will be able to:

- Describe recovery plan components.
- List the guidelines for creating a disaster recovery plan.

What Is Disaster Recovery?

> - Resuming operations after a disaster
> - Implementing a disaster recovery plan:
>   - Replacing damaged components
>   - Restoring data
>   - Testing before resuming

Introduction

A sudden catastrophic loss of data is a computer disaster. The business world depends on mission-critical data more than ever. As a result, organizations place greater emphasis on protecting their information assets from data loss and server failure.

Disaster recovery

Disaster recovery is the process that allows normal business operations to resume as quickly as possible after a disaster. Disaster recovery seeks to restore data and services to the state before the disaster occurred.

Disaster-recovery considerations

For each operating system and application that you introduce to your environment, answer the following questions about disaster recovery:

Disaster-recovery item	Considerations
Recovery plan	• What are the possible failure scenarios? • What data is critical? • How often should you perform backups? • How long will you save the backups? • How fast must data be restored from backup to prevent unacceptable downtime? • Where will you store the backups to allow access by the appropriate people? • If the responsible systems administrator is gone, is there someone else who knows the proper passwords and procedures to perform backups and, if necessary, to restore the system?

(*continued*)

Disaster recovery item	Considerations
Hardware	• How many, what kind, and where are individual computer components, such as hard disks and controllers, processors, and RAM? • How many, what kind, and where are external components such as routers, bridges, switches, cables, and connectors? • Are the critical hardware and services redundant?
Data restoration	• To what storage device, will you send the backup? • When will you perform backups, while users are working, or when the system is offline? • Will you perform the backups manually or schedule them to be performed automatically? • How long will you save the backups? • How often is the critical data updated?
Testing	• How will you verify automated backups ? • How will you ensure the usability of backups?

Determine questions based on your situation

This is not a complete list; you must determine other questions based on your particular situation.

Disaster-Recovery Preparation Guidelines

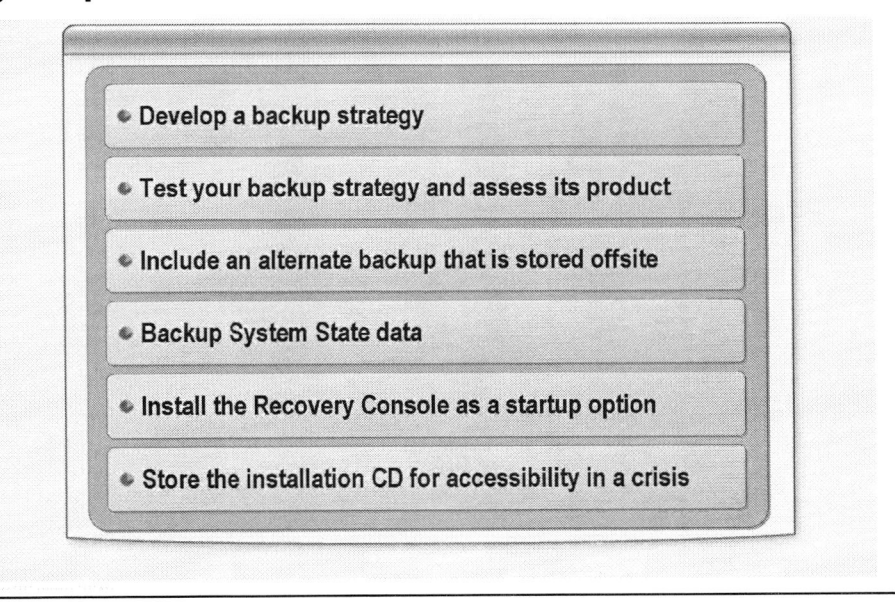

- Develop a backup strategy
- Test your backup strategy and assess its product
- Include an alternate backup that is stored offsite
- Backup System State data
- Install the Recovery Console as a startup option
- Store the installation CD for accessibility in a crisis

Introduction

You should develop and thoroughly test a disaster recovery plan. When testing the plan, apply the results to as many failure scenarios as possible.

Guidelines

Use the following guidelines to prepare for disaster recovery:

- Create a disaster recovery plan for performing regular backup operations.

    Review and incorporate a plan for backing up all your files on a regular basis. Keep a log of every update in your disaster-recovery plan.

- Test your backup files and your backup plan.

    Testing your backup files and recovery plan is an important part of being prepared for disaster recovery. Testing must include the following tasks:

    - Test your uninterruptible power supply (UPS) on the computers running Windows Server 2003 and on hubs, routers, and other network components.
    - Perform full or partial restorations from your daily, weekly, and monthly backup media.

- Keep two sets of backed-up files: one onsite, for accessibility, and one offsite, for security.

    The backup should be available for restoration to another computer. This can be achieved with network shared folders or with removable media.

    If possible, make a copy of your backup sets every day and store them separately, one onsite and one offsite. That way, if a catastrophic event, such as a fire, destroys all your computers and onsite backup sets, you can restore all your data later. If all your backups are offsite, then the restore process will be very time-consuming because every time you need to recover a file, you must get the backup files from the offsite location.

- Create a backup of the System State data.

    System State data is the collection of system-specific data used by Windows Server 2003 to load, configure, and run the operating system. (System State data is discussed in more detail later on in this module) Create a backup copy of the System State data in case the hard disk on the server fails and cannot be recovered. This backup is required to properly restore your operating system to a new hard disk.

- Install the Recovery Console as a startup option.

    The Recovery Console is a minimal version of the Windows Server 2003 operating system that you can use to start Windows Server 2003 when severe startup problems prevent the server from booting. To allow rapid access to the Recovery Console in a crisis, install the Recovery Console on your computer. This adds the Recovery Console to the list of available operating systems.

- Keep the installation CD-ROM accessible.

    Keep the installation CD-ROM where it can be easily found. You can start the computer from the CD-ROM and then use the Recovery Console or Automated System Recovery.

Lesson: Backing Up Data

- Overview of Backing Up Data
- Who Can Back Up Data?
- What Is System State Data?
- What Is the Backup Utility?
- Types of Backup
- What Is ntbackup?
- What Is Automated System Recovery?
- Practice: Backing Up Data

Introduction

Backing up your data prevents data loss when the original files are lost. Windows Server 2003 includes a backup utility, Backup, that backs up data by copying designated files to storage media. You can also use Windows Server 2003 to back up your server by using Automated System Recovery.

Lesson objectives

After completing this lesson, you will be able to:

- Describe the process of backing up data.
- List those who can back up data.
- Describe the backup of System State data.
- Describe the Backup utility.
- List the various types of backup.
- Describe the **ntbackup** command-line tool.
- Describe an Automated System Recovery set.
- Backup files.

Overview of Backing Up Data

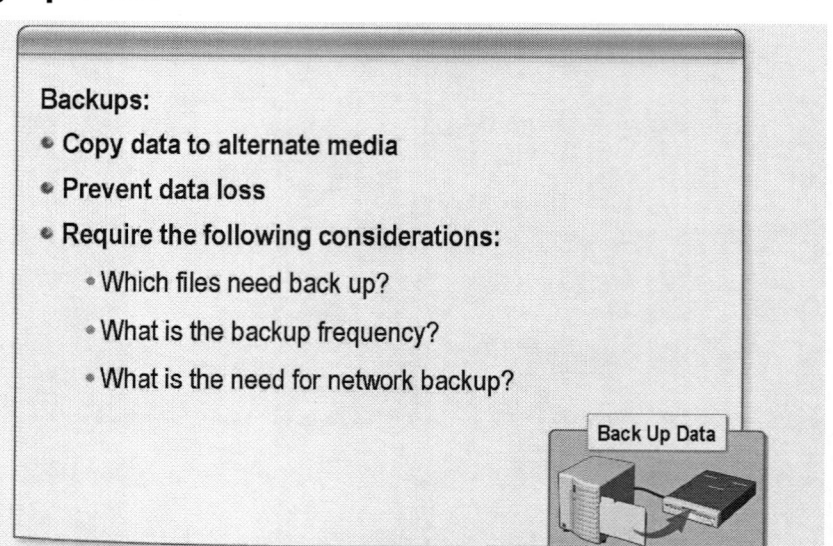

> **Backups:**
> - Copy data to alternate media
> - Prevent data loss
> - Require the following considerations:
>   - Which files need back up?
>   - What is the backup frequency?
>   - What is the need for network backup?
>
> Back Up Data

Introduction

Backup is a single process of copying files and folders from one location to another. Regularly backing up the data on server and client computer hard disks prevents data loss due to disk-drive failures, power outages, virus infections, and other such incidents. If a data loss occurs, and you have performed regular backups based on careful planning, you can restore the lost data, whether it is in one file or on an entire hard disk.

Types of data to back up

The general rule for backing up is, if you cannot get along without it, back it up.

Critical data is the information that your organization needs to survive. If files are accidentally lost or corrupted, you can use the most recent backup to restore this data.

System State data defines the configuration of the server's operating system. If accidental changes occur or if System State data is lost, you can restore System State data from a backup.

How frequently to back up

The following factors determine backup frequency:

- How critical is the data to the organization? You back up critical data more often than data of less importance.
- How frequently is the data changed? For example, if users create or modify reports only on Fridays, a weekly backup for these files is sufficient.

When to use a network backup

Perform a network backup when the critical data is stored on multiple servers. The following table describes the advantages and disadvantages of a network backup.

Advantages	Disadvantages
Backs up the entire network	Users must copy their important files to the servers
Requires less storage	Cannot back up the registry on remote computers
Less media to manage	Increases network traffic
One user can back up data	Requires greater planning and preparation

Who Can Back Up Data?

> - File owners and users with read permissions
> - Users with rights to the backup files and directories
> - Groups on local servers:
>   - Administrators
>   - Backup operators
>   - Server operators

Introduction

You must have certain permissions or user rights to back up and restore files and folders.

Permissions and user rights

To successfully back up and restore data on a computer running Windows Server 2003, you must have the appropriate permissions and user rights, as described in the following list:

- Users can back up the files and folders for which they have assigned ownership, as well the files they have permission to read.

- Users that are assigned the Backup Files and Directories right are able to backup files on the specified servers.

- Users that are assigned the Restore Files and Directories right are able to restore files on the specified servers.

- Members of the local or domain local Administrators, Backup Operators, and Server Operators groups can back up and restore all files, regardless of the assigned NTFS permissions. Server operators can back up all domain controllers. By default, members of these groups have the following user rights: Backup Files and Directories and the Restore Files and Directories.

Restrict access

You can restrict access to a backup by selecting **Allow only the owner and the Administrator access to the backup data** in the **Backup Job Information** dialog box. If you select this option, only an administrator or the person who created the backup file can restore the files and folders.

Separate backup and restore user rights

For security reasons, many organizations prefer to separate the backup and restore user rights into two groups as follows:

1. Create a Backup group and a Restore group by using Active Directory Users and Computers.
2. Add one set of members to the Backup group and another set of members to the Restore group.
3. Assign the Backup group the right to **Backup files and directories** using a Group Policy object (GPO).
4. Assign the Restore group the right to **Restore files and directories** using a GPO.

Location of the Backup files and directories GPO setting

The Backup files and directories GPO setting and Restore files and directories GPO setting are located in the following area of a group policy object:

Computer Configuration

    Windows Settings

        Security Settings

           Local Policies

                User Rights Assignment

What Is System State Data?

System-specific data that must be backed up as a unit	
Component	**Included in System State**
Registry	Always
Boot files, including system files	Always
Certificate Services database	If it is a Certificate Services server
Active Directory directory service	If it is a domain controller
SYSVOL Directory	If it is a domain controller
Cluster service information	If it is within a cluster
IIS metadirectory	If it is installed
System files that are under Windows File Protection	Always

Definition

The System State is the collection of system-specific data that must be backed up as a unit and is maintained by the operating system. The computer uses these system files to load, configure, and run the operating system.

System State components

Backup refers to the following system files as the System State data.

Component	Included in System State?
Registry	Always
Boot files, Com+ Class Registration, including the system files	Always
Certificate Services database	If Certificate Services is installed
Active Directory® directory service	If it is a domain controller
SYSVOL directory	If it is a domain controller
Cluster service information	If it is within a cluster
IIS metadirectory	If IIS is installed
System files that are under Windows File Protection	Always

Back up System State data

When you back up or restore the System State data, all the System State data for the relevant system is backed up or restored. You cannot back up or restore individual components of the System State data because of dependencies among the System State components. However, you can restore the System State data to an alternate location. If you do this, only the registry files, SYSVOL directory files, Cluster database information files, and system boot files are restored to the alternate location. Active Directory, the Certificate Services database, and the COM+ Class Registration database are not restored if you designate an alternate location when you restore the System State data.

Note To restore system state data on a domain controller you must start the computer in Directory Services Restore Mode.

What Is the Backup Utility?

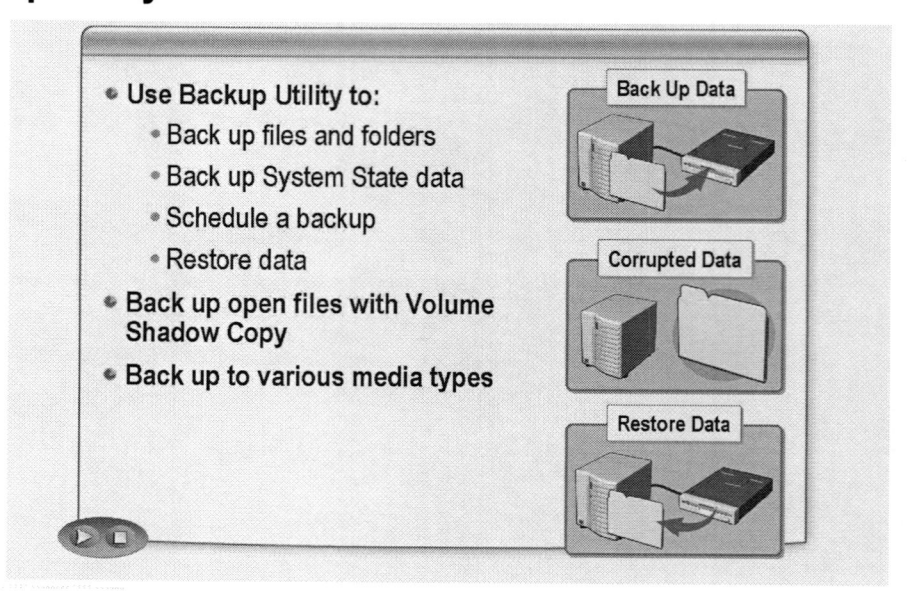

- **Use Backup Utility to:**
  - Back up files and folders
  - Back up System State data
  - Schedule a backup
  - Restore data
- **Back up open files with Volume Shadow Copy**
- **Back up to various media types**

Introduction

The Windows Server 2003 backup utility, Backup, is designed to protect data from accidental loss resulting from the failure of your hardware or storage media.

Use to manage backup

You can use Backup to:

- Back up files and folders.
- Back up System State data.
- Schedule a backup job.
- Restore data.

You can use the Backup Wizard to back up the entire contents of a server, selected portions of the server contents, or the System State data.

Volume shadow copy

You can use Backup to create shadow copy backups of volumes and exact copies of files, including all open files. For example, databases that are held open exclusively and files that are open due to operator or system activity are backed up during a volume shadow copy backup. In this way, files that changed during the backup process are copied correctly.

Volume shadow copy backups ensure that:

- Applications can continue to write data to the volume during a backup.
- Open files are not omitted during a backup.
- Backups can be performed at any time, without locking out users.

Some applications manage storage consistency differently while files are open, which can affect the consistency of the files in the backup. For critical applications, consult the application documentation or your provider to gain a complete understanding of the recommended backup method. When doubt occurs during a backup, quit the application and resolve any questions before performing the backup.

Volume shadow copy is enabled by default. If you disable this option, some files that are open or in use during the backup might be skipped. It is recommended that you do not disable this option.

Storage devices The Backup utility supports a variety of storage devices and media, including tape drives, logical drives, removable disks, and recordable CD-ROM drives.

Types of Backup

- Some backup types use the archive attribute
- Some backup types work together

Type	Files backed up	Clears archive attribute
Normal or Full	Selected files and folders	Yes
Copy	Selected files and folders	No
Differential	Selected files and folders that were modified after the last normal backup	No
Incremental	Selected files and folders that changed after the last normal or incremental backup	Yes
Daily	Selected files and folders that changed during the day	No

Introduction

Because system needs vary greatly, Windows Server 2003 provides five backup alternatives in the Backup utility. The table below describes each alternative and specifies which data is backed up.

Backup archive attributes

Some backup types use the **archive** attribute, which indicates that a file was modified since the last backup. When a file is modified, the **archive** attribute is set to show that the file needs to be backed up. If these files are backed up by Normal or Incremental, the **archive** attribute is cleared or reset.

Backup types

Backup provides five backup types: Normal, Copy, Differential, Incremental, and Daily. Each of these backup types targets specific file categories for backup, such as files that have changed since the last backup or all files in a specific folder.

The following table presents the backup types, the function of each type, whether the backup type clears **archive** attributes, and tips for using the backup type.

Type	Description
Normal	Backs up all selected files, regardless of the setting of the **archive** attribute, and clears the archive attribute on each backed up file.
	If the file is modified later, the archive attribute is reset to indicate that the file needs to be backed up.
	To establish a baseline for future backups, perform a Normal backup the first time you create a backup set.
Copy	Identical to a Normal backup except that it does not change the **archive** attribute, which allows you to perform other types of backups on the files later.
	Use a Copy backup to create an additional backup tape or disk without disturbing the **archive** attributes.

(*continued*)

Type	Description
Differential	Creates backup copies of files that have changed since the last backup. The presence of the **archive** attribute indicates that the file was modified and only files with this attribute are backed up. However, the **archive** attribute on files is not modified. This allows you to perform other types of backups on the files later.
	Because a Differential backup does not clear archive attributes, if you perform two Differential backups on a file, the file is backed up each time.
	Differential backups use more media than Incremental backups, but when you restore, you need only the media that contains the files from the Normal backup and the most recent Differential backup. The Differential backup method is slower than the Incremental backup method for backup but faster for restore.
Incremental	Designed to create backups of files that have changed since the most recent normal or Incremental backup. The presence of the **archive** attribute indicates that the file was modified, and only files with this attribute are backed up. When a file is backed up, the **archive** attribute is cleared.
	Because an Incremental backup clears **archive** attributes, if you perform two Incremental backups in a row on a file, the file is not backed up the second time.
	Incremental backups use the minimum amount of media and also save time in a backup by not copying all of the files that have changed since the last full backup. However, restoring a disk after Incremental backups may be inconvenient because some files needing restoration will be on the Normal backup and other files will be on the Incremental backups. The Incremental method backs up faster than the Differential method but restores more slowly.
Daily	Backs up files by using the modification date on the file itself; the Daily method disregards the current state of the archive attribute. The Daily backup does not change the **archive** attributes of files. If a file was modified on the same day as the backup, the file is backed up.

Important Your backup plan can combine various backup types. If you combine backup types, it is critically important to understand the **archive** attribute. Incremental and Differential backups check for and rely on the **archive** attributes.

Backup scenarios

You perform a normal backup on Monday and Incremental backups on Tuesday through Friday. If your disk fails on Saturday, you must restore the hard disk with Monday's backup and then complete the restore process by using the Tuesday-through-Friday backups in the order that they were written.

You perform a normal backup on Monday and differential backups on Tuesday through Friday. If your disk fails on Saturday, you must restore the hard disk using Monday's backup followed by Friday's backup.

Workers in your organization are required to save their work to a server every hour. Management wants to limit the amount of data that is lost due to a server failure to one hour. To accomplish this, you perform a normal backup on Monday, a differential backup the other four days, and a daily backup every hour.

What Is ntbackup?

> - Use the ntbackup command-line tool to:
>   - Back up System State data
>   - Back up files
>   - Back up using batch files
> - Understand the ntbackup limitations
>   - Backs up whole folders, not selected files
>   - Does not accommodate wildcard characters

Definition

In addition to Backup, Windows Server 2003 provides a command-line tool, **ntbackup**, that you can use to back up and restore data. Just like Backup, it can back up files and folders, as well as System State data. However, unlike Backup, **ntbackup** can be used in batch files.

Use the command prompt or batch file

You can perform backup operations from a command prompt or from a batch file by using the **ntbackup** command, followed by various parameters.

Bach files have two important limitations when used to back up your data:

- When using the **ntbackup** command, you can back up entire folders only. You cannot designate individual files for backup. However, you can designate a backup selection file (.bks file) from the command line, which contains a list of files that you want to back up. You must use the GUI version of the Backup utility to create backup selection files.

- The **ntbackup** command does not support the use of wildcard characters. For example, typing ***.txt** does not back up files with a .txt extension.

Ntbackup syntax

To back up files by using **ntbackup**:

- At the command-line prompt, type:

    ntbackup backup [systemstate] "**@bks** *file name*" **/J** {"*job name*"} [**/P** {"*pool name*"}] [**/G** {"*guid name*"}] [**/T** { "*tape name*"}] [**/N** {"*media name*"}] [**/F** {"*file name*"}] [**/D** {"*set description*"}] [**/DS** {"*server name*"}] [**/IS** {"*server name*"}] [**/A**] [**/V:**{**yes**|**no**}] [**/R:**{**yes**|**no**}] [**/L:**{**f**|**s**|**n**}] [**/M** {*backup type*}] [**/RS:**{**yes**|**no**}] [**/HC:**{**on**|**off**}] [**/SNAP:**{**on**|**off**}]

- To back up the System State to E:\SysState.bkf:

    ntbackup backup systemstate /J SysState /F E:\SysState.bkf

- To backup the C:\MOC directory:

ntbackup backup C:\MOC /J MOC /F E:\MOC.bkf

Parameter	Definition
systemstate	Initiates a backup of the System State data. When you select this option, the backup type is forced to normal or copy.
@bks *file name*	Specifies the name of the backup selection file (.bks file) to be used for this backup operation. The at (@) character must precede the name of the backup selection file. A backup selection file contains information about the files and folders you have selected for backup. You must create the file by using the graphical user interface (GUI) version of Backup.
/J {"*job name*"}	Specifies the job name to be used in the backup report. The job name usually describes the files and folders you are backing up in the current backup job.
/P {"*pool name*"}	Specifies the media pool from which you want to use media. This is usually a subpool of the Backup media pool, such as 4mm DDS. If you select this parameter, you cannot use the /A, /G, /F, or /T command-line options.
/G {"*guid name*"}	Overwrites or appends to this tape. Do not use this switch in conjunction with **/P**.
/T {"*tape name*"}	Overwrites or appends to this tape. Do not use this switch in conjunction with **/P**.
/N {"*media name*"}	Specifies the new tape name. Do not use **/A** with this switch.
/F {"*file name*"}	Logical disk path and file name. Do not use the **/P, /G,** or **/T** switch with this switch.
/D {"*set description*"}	Specifies a label for each backup set.
/DS {"*server name*"}	Backs up the directory service file for the specified Microsoft Exchange server.
/IS {"*server name*"}	Backs up the Information Store file for the specified Microsoft Exchange server.
/A	Performs an append operation. Use either **/G** or **/T** with this switch. Do not use this switch in conjunction with **/P**.

(*continued*)

Parameter	Definition
/V:{yes|no}	Verifies the data after the backup is complete.
/R:{yes|no}	Restricts access to this tape to the owner or members of the Administrators group.
/L:{f|s|n}	Specifies the type of log file: **f**=full, **s**=summary, **n**=none (no log file is created).
/M {*backup type*}	Specifies the backup type. It must be one of the following: normal, copy, differential, incremental, or daily.
/RS:{yes|no}	Backs up the migrated data files located in Remote Storage. The **/RS** command-line option is not required to back up the local Removable Storage database that contains the Remote Storage placeholder files. When you back up the %systemroot% folder, Backup automatically backs up the Removable Storage database as well.
/HC:{on|off}	Uses hardware compression, if available, on the tape drive.
/SNAP:{on|off}	Specifies whether the backup should use a volume shadow copy.

Note For more information about how to use **ntbackup** command-line parameters, see Microsoft Knowledge Base article 814583 on the Microsoft Help and Support Web site.

What Is Automated System Recovery?

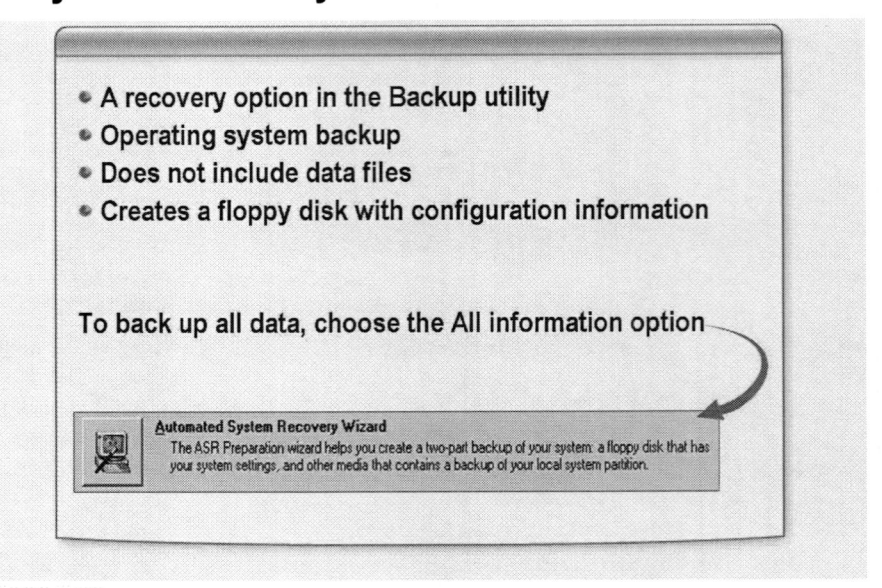

- A recovery option in the Backup utility
- Operating system backup
- Does not include data files
- Creates a floppy disk with configuration information

To back up all data, choose the All information option

Automated System Recovery Wizard
The ASR Preparation wizard helps you create a two-part backup of your system: a floppy disk that has your system settings, and other media that contains a backup of your local system partition.

Introduction

Automated System Recovery (ASR), in the Backup utility, helps you to recover a system that does not start. ASR contains two parts: backup and recovery. ASR also creates a floppy disk that is used to store disk configurations during the ASR recovery procedure.

ASR restores operating system

Typically, after installing or upgrading to Windows Server 2003, you create a set of ASR disks. The ASR process enables you to restore an installation of Windows Server 2003 to the condition of the operating system at the time that you created the ASR backup set.

ASR Backup Wizard

The ASR Backup Wizard backs up the System State data, system services, and the boot and system volumes. The ASR Backup Wizard also creates a floppy disk, which contains information about the backup, the disk configurations, including basic and dynamic volumes, and the restore procedure. The ASR Backup Wizard does not back up volumes other than the boot and system volumes.

Backup or Restore Wizard

The Backup or Restore Wizard provides several backup options. The **All information on this computer** option backs up all data on the computer in addition to the System State data and the operating system components. This option also creates a system recovery disk that you can used to restore Windows in case of a disk failure.

Practice: Backing Up Data

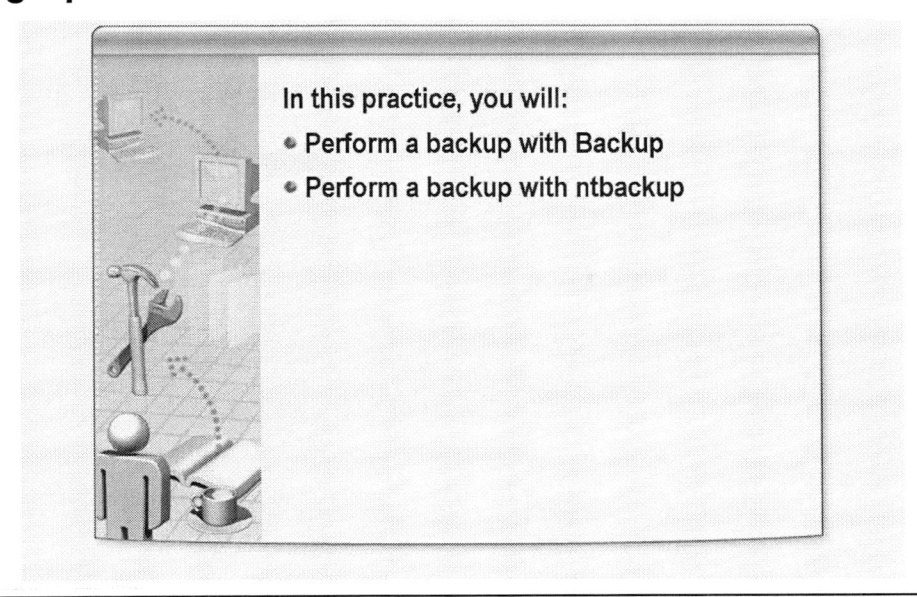

Objective

In this practice, you will:

- Perform a backup with Backup
- Perform a backup with ntbackup

Instructions

Ensure that the DEN-DC1 virtual machine is running.

Practice

▶ **Perform a backup with Backup**

1. Log on to DEN-DC1 as **Administrator** with a password of **Pa$$w0rd**.
2. Click **Start**, point to **All Programs**, point to **Accessories**, point to **System Tools**, and click **Backup**.
3. Click **Advanced Mode** and click the **Backup** tab.
4. Expand **D:\2275\Practices**, and then check the **MOD07** check box.
5. In the **Backup media or file name** box, type **D:\MOD07.bkf**
6. Click **Start Backup**.
7. Click **Replace the data on the media with this backup** and click **Start Backup**.
8. When the backup is complete, click **Report**.
9. Read the report then close Notepad.
10. Click **Close** and close Backup.

Practice

▶ **Perform a backup with ntbackup**

1. Open a command prompt.
2. In the command window, type:

   ntbackup backup D:\2275\Practices\Mod07 /j ntbackup /f d:\MOD072.bkf

   This command backs up the **D:\2275\Practices\Mod07** folder as **D:\MOD072.bkf**.
3. Verify the backup completed.
   a. Type **D:** and press ENTER.
   b. Type **dir** and press ENTER. **MOD072.bkf** should be listed and the same size as **MOD07.bkf**.
4. Close the command prompt.

Important Do not shut down the virtual machine.

Lesson: Scheduling Backup Jobs

- What Is a Scheduled Backup Job?
- What Are Scheduled Backup Options?
- Best Practices for Backup
- Practice: Scheduling Backup Jobs

Introduction

A systems administrator responsible for backing up files and folders must take care to schedule backups appropriately. Using your organization's backup plan, schedule your backups so that they contain the most complete and up-to-date set of files by using the most efficient method.

Lesson objectives

After completing this lesson, you will be able to:

- Describe a scheduled backup job.
- List backup schedule options.
- List best practices for backup.
- Schedule a backup job by using Backup.

What Is a Scheduled Backup Job?

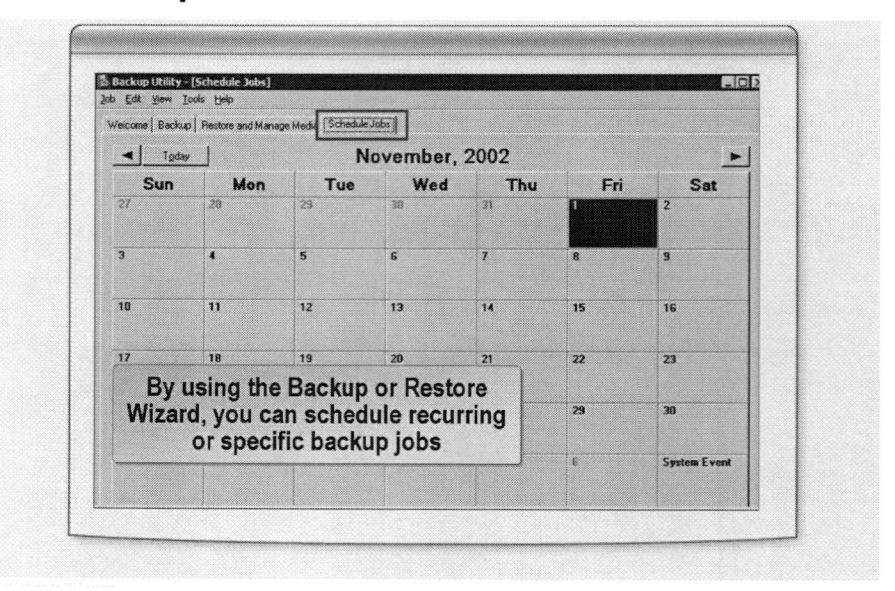

By using the Backup or Restore Wizard, you can schedule recurring or specific backup jobs

Introduction

Most backups occur outside of regular business hours; it is a good practice to perform backups on a consistent and predictable schedule. Backups are ideal to run as scheduled jobs because they are routine work done at inconvenient times. Scheduling backups ensures that they are not forgotten and avoid requiring staff at odd hours.

Two ways to schedule a backup job

Try to schedule a backup job to occur at regular intervals or during periods of relative inactivity on a network.

You can schedule a backup job two ways:

- When you create a new backup job in Backup
- By using the **Scheduled Jobs** tab in Backup to schedule a previously saved backup job

What Are Scheduled Backup Options?

Schedule options	Executes the job:
Once	At a specific time on a specified date
Daily	At a specified time each day
Weekly	At a specified time on specified weekdays
Monthly	At a specified time on a specified day each month
At startup	The next time the system is started
At logon	The next time the job owner logs on
When idle	After the system is idle for a specified period

Introduction Windows Server 2003 provides several options to help you schedule your backup job.

Backup options The following table describes the options that are available for scheduling backup jobs.

Schedule options	Executes the job:
Once	At a specified time on a specified date
Daily	At a specified time each day
Weekly	At a specified time on each specified day of the week
Monthly	At a specified time on a specified day each month
At system startup	The next time the system is started
At logon	The next time the job owner logs on
When idle	After the system is idle for a specified period

Best Practices for Backup

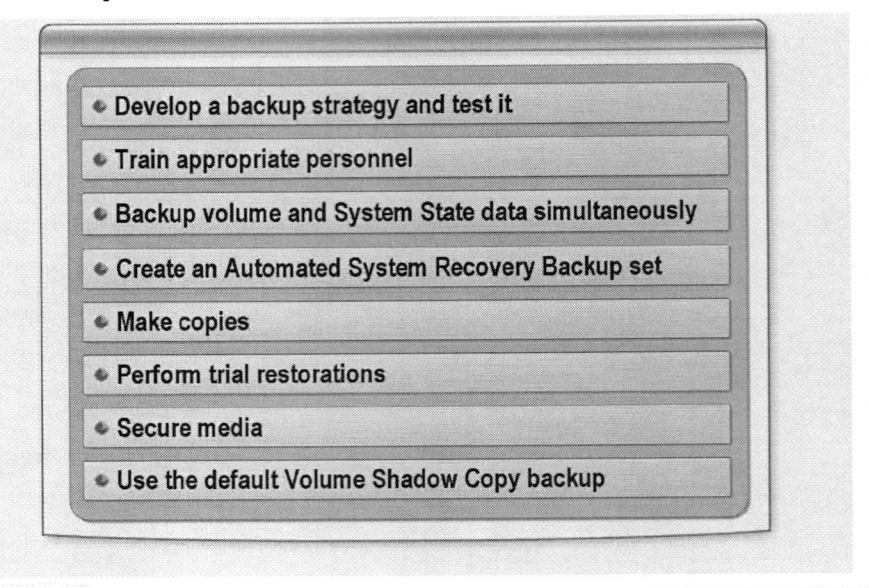

> - Develop a backup strategy and test it
> - Train appropriate personnel
> - Backup volume and System State data simultaneously
> - Create an Automated System Recovery Backup set
> - Make copies
> - Perform trial restorations
> - Secure media
> - Use the default Volume Shadow Copy backup

Introduction

You can protect your organization from data loss with a backup plan that employs the backup best practices.

Best practices

Apply these best practices as you develop your backup plan:

- Develop backup strategies and test them.

    A good plan ensures that you can quickly recover your data if it is lost.

- Train appropriate personnel.

    On minimum-security and medium-security networks, assign backup rights to one user, by using Group Policy, and assign restore rights to a different user. Identify and train alternate administrators with rights to perform the restore tasks when the administrator is unavailable.

    On a high-security network, only administrators should restore files.

- Back up volumes and the System State data at the same time. This action allows you to be prepared in the unlikely event of a disk failure.

- Create an Automated System Recovery backup set.

    Always create an Automated System Recovery (ASR) backup set when the operating system changes, for example, whenever you install new hardware and drivers or apply a service pack. An ASR backup set can help you to recover from a server failure. ASR protects only the System State files, so you must back up data volumes separately.

- Create a backup log.

    Always create a backup log for each backup, and then print the logs for reference. Keep a book of logs to help you locate specific files. The backup log is helpful when you restore data; you can print it or read it from any text editor. Also, if the media containing the backup set catalog is corrupted, the printed log can help you locate a file.

- Make copies of the backup media.

    Keep at least three copies of the media. Keep at least one copy offsite in a properly controlled environment.

- Perform trial restorations.

    Perform a trial restoration on a regular basis to verify that your files are properly backed up. A trial restoration can uncover hardware or media corruption problems that do not show up when you verify software.

- Secure media.

    Secure the media. It is possible for someone to access the data from a stolen medium by restoring the data to another server for which they are an administrator.

- Use the default Volume Shadow Copy backup.

    Do not disable the default Volume Shadow Copy backup method. If you disable this method, open files that are being used by the system during the backup process will be skipped during the backup.

Practice: Scheduling Backup Jobs

Objective

In this practice, you will:

- Schedule a backup job using the Backup Wizard.

Instructions

Ensure that DEN-DC1 virtual machine is running.

Practice

▶ **Schedule a backup job by using the Backup Wizard**

1. Click **Start**, point to **All Programs**, point to **Accessories**, point to **System Tools**, and click **Backup**.
2. Click **Advanced Mode**, and then click the button beside **Backup Wizard (Advanced)**.
3. Click **Next** to begin the Backup Wizard.
4. Click **Back up selected files, drives, or network data** and click **Next**.
5. Expand **My Computer**, expand **D:\2275\Practices**, check the **MOD07** check box, and click **Next**.
6. In the **Choose a place to save your backup** box, click **D:**.
7. In the **Type a name for this backup** box, type **MOD07**, and click **Next**.
8. Click the **Advanced** button.
9. Click **Next** to select a normal backup.
10. Check the **Verify data after backup** check box and click **Next**.
11. Click **Replace the existing backups** and click **Next**.
12. Click **Later**, type **MOD073** in the **Job name** box, and click **Set Schedule**.
13. Change the **Start time** to 5 minutes from now and click **OK**.
14. In the **Run as** box, type **CONTOSO\Administrator**, type **Pa$$w0rd** in the **Password** and **Confirm password** boxes, and then click **OK**.

Module 7: Managing Disaster Recovery 31

15. Click **Next**.
16. In the **Run as** box, type **CONTOSO\Administrator**, type **Pa$$w0rd** in the **Password** and **Confirm password** boxes, and then click **OK**.
17. Click **Finish**.
18. Close Backup.
19. Click **Start**, point to **Control Panel**, point to **Scheduled Tasks**, and click **MOD073**. This is the task that runs the backup job you just created.
20. Read the options in the **Run** box. These options correspond with options you selected when creating the backup job.
21. Click **Cancel** and wait for the backup job to run.

Important Do not shut down the virtual machine.

Lesson: Restoring Data

- What Is Restoring Data?
- Guidelines for Restoring Data
- Practice: Restoring Data

Introduction

The second part of the disaster recovery process involves restoring the backup data.

Lesson objectives

After completing this lesson, you will be able to:

- Describe how to restore data.
- Describe guidelines for restoring data.
- Restore data with Backup.

What Is Restoring Data?

> Restoring data rewrites:
> - Files and folders
> - System State data
>
> The ASR Restore:
> - Reads recovery data for disk configuration
> - Restores book disk signatures, volumes, and partitions
> - Installs a recovery version of Windows
> - Initiates the restore from backup

Introduction

When you use Backup to create a duplicate copy of the data on your hard disk and then archive the data on another storage device, such as a hard disk or a tape, you can use the Restore feature in Backup to easily restore the data.

Restore files and folders

Using Backup, you can restore the archived files and folders to your hard disk or any other disk that you can access.

Back up and restore data on FAT or NTFS volumes

You can use Backup to back up and restore data on either FAT (file allocation table) or NTFS file system volumes. However, restore data backed up from an Windows Server 2003 NTFS volume, to a Windows Server 2003 NTFS volume. This practice avoids the loss of both data and file and folder features, such as permissions, Encrypting File System (EFS) settings, disk quota information, mounted drive information, and Remote Storage information.

Restore System State data

You can use Backup to restore the System State data. If the System State data was backed up on a computer and that computer system fails, you can rebuild the computer with the original Windows Server 2003 compact disc and the System State data.

ASR Restore

You can access the restore part of ASR by pressing F2 when prompted in the text mode portion of Windows setup. ASR reads the disk configurations from the floppy disk and restores the entire disk signatures, volumes, and partitions on the disks that are required to start the computer. ASR then installs a simple installation of Windows and automatically starts to restore from backup by using the ASR backup set that you created by using the ASR Backup Wizard.

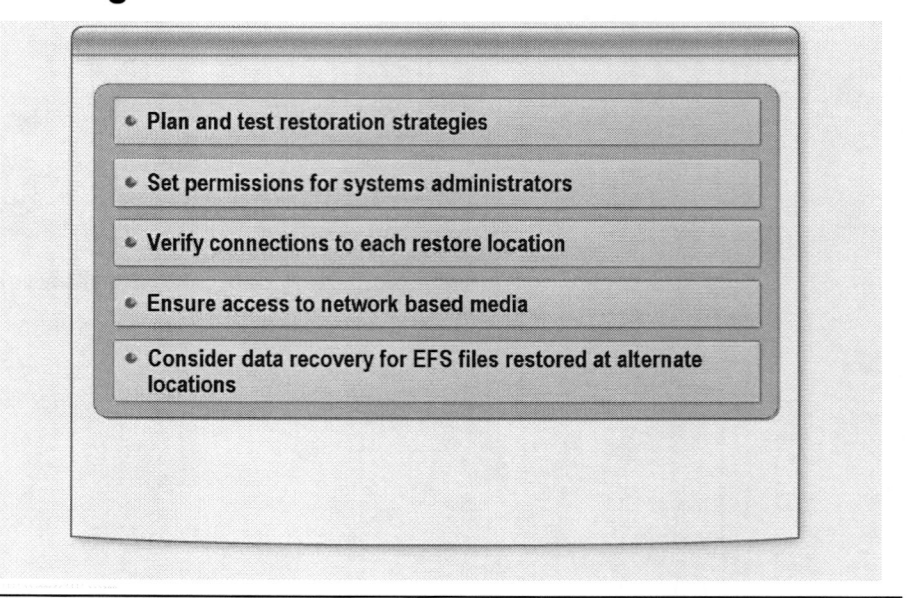

Guidelines for Restoring Data

- Plan and test restoration strategies
- Set permissions for systems administrators
- Verify connections to each restore location
- Ensure access to network based media
- Consider data recovery for EFS files restored at alternate locations

Introduction

After backing up your files and employ the best practices while developing a backup plan, you must create a restoration plan. The following checklist includes recommended best practices for creation of your organization's restoration plan.

Guidelines for restoring data

Restoration plan best practices include the following:

- Develop restoration strategies and test them.

    Remember to keep a record of your backup and restoration plans for reference in the event of data loss.

- Be sure that all appropriate systems administrators have the necessary permissions.

- Verify that you can connect to all shared folders on computers under your restoration plan.

    You can use the default user rights of the Backup Operators group to restore your organization's data and system files, or you can segregate backup and restore permissions by individuals.

- Ensure that you have access to network-based media and to the server where the data is to be restored.

    As part of your restoration plan, be sure to test your access to the storage media with the backed-up files.

- To restore files manually, use the Backup utility and select the appropriate files or folders.

    Because you may need to restore only certain files, use the Backup utility to test the procedure that you will use to select and restore only those files.

- If you are restoring EFS files on a system where the private key for the encrypted data is inaccessible, send the files to a designated recovery agent.

    For files that are inaccessible due to encryption, perform a test by sending the files to a designated recovery agent.

Practice: Restoring Data

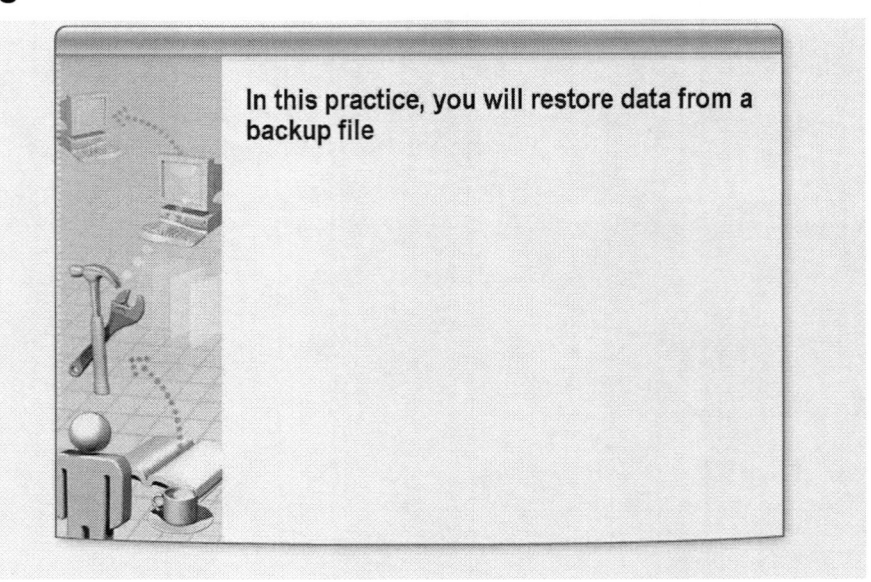

Objective
- In this practice, you will restore data from a backup file.

Instructions

Ensure that the DEN-DC1 virtual machine is started.

Practice

▶ **Restore data from a backup file**

1. Open Windows Explorer, and delete the **D:\2275\Practices\MOD07** folder.
2. Click **Start**, point to **All Programs**, point to **Accessories**, point to **System Tools**, and then click **Backup**.
3. Click **Advanced Mode** and click the **Restore and Manage Media** tab.
4. On the **Restore and Manage Media** tab, expand **File**, expand **MOD07.bkf**, and expand **D:**. You can see that only the MOD07 folder structure exists in this backup.
5. Check the **D:** check box, and then click **Start Restore**.
6. Click **OK**.
7. When "Restore is complete" appears in the **Restore Progress** dialog box, click **Close**, and then close the Backup utility.
8. In Windows Explorer, press F5 to refresh the screen, and then verify that the **D:\2275\Practices\MOD07** folder has been restored.
9. Close Windows Explorer.

▶ **To prepare for the next practice**
- Start the DEN-CL1 virtual machine.

Important Do not shut down the virtual machine.

Lesson: Configuring Shadow Copies

- What Are Shadow Copies?
- Previous Versions Client Software for Shadow Copies
- Shadow Copy Scheduling
- What Is Restoring Shadow Copies?
- Best Practices for Using Shadow Copies
- Practice: Configuring Shadow Copies

Introduction

In Windows Server 2003, you can use Shadow Copies of Shared Folders as a data recovery tool. The Previous Versions client software saves iterative versions of files and folders.

Lesson objectives

After completing this lesson, you will be able to:

- Describe shadow copies.
- Describe the Previous Versions client software for shadow copies.
- Describe scheduling shadow copies.
- Describe restoring shadow copies.
- List best practices for using shadow copies.
- Configure Shadow Copies.

What Are Shadow Copies?

> - Shadow copies provide iterative versions of network folders
> - Use shadow copies to:
>   - Recover files
>   - Review previous versions
> - Shadow copies are:
>   - Enabled per volume
>   - Not a replacement for regular backups
>   - Allocated storage limits versions

Definition A shadow copy is a feature of the Windows Server 2003 family that provides point-in-time, read-only copies of files on network shares. With Shadow Copies of Shared Folders, you can view the contents of network folders as they existed at various points in time. To view Shadow Copies of Shared Folders, you must install the client software.

Shadow copy scenarios You can use shadow copies in the following three scenarios:

- Recover files that were accidentally deleted.

    This scenario is the network equivalent of a short-term local backup and restore. If a user accidentally deletes a file, the user can open a previous version of the file and copy it to a safe location.

- Recover files that were accidentally overwritten.

    Shadow Copies of Shared Folders can be very useful in environments where new files are commonly created by opening an existing file, making modifications, and then saving the file with a new name. For example, you might open a financial-modeling spreadsheet, make modifications based upon new assumptions, and then save the spreadsheet with a new name to create a new spreadsheet. The problem arises when you forget to save the file by using a new name, thereby erasing the original work. You can use Shadow Copies of Shared Folders to recover the previous version of the file.

- Allow version-checking while working on documents.

    You can use Shadow Copies of Shared Folders during the normal work cycle to check the differences between two versions of a file. For example, you might want to know "What did this paragraph say this morning before I started to rewrite it?"

Shadow copy characteristics	The following characteristics apply to shadow copies: ■ Configuring shadow copies is not a replacement for creating regular backups. Shadow copies may not be able to recover corrupted files, and cannot recover files if a volume fails. ■ Shadow copies are read-only. You cannot edit the contents of a shadow copy. ■ Shadow copies are enabled on a per-volume basis. You cannot enable shadow copies on specific shared resources. ■ After shadow copies are enabled on a volume, shadow copies are enabled for all shared folders on that volume. ■ Shadow copies track changes to files, they do not make copies of files.
Shadow copies storage	The minimum amount of storage space for shadow copies is 100 megabytes (MB). The default maximum storage size is 10 percent of the source volume or the volume being copied, but you can change the maximum size at any time. When the storage limit is reached, the oldest versions of the shadow copies are deleted and cannot be restored.
Allocate storage space	When determining the amount of space to allocate for storing shadow copies, you must consider how many files are being changed, the size of the files, and the number of changes being performed. If too little space is allocated, some previous versions will be lost.
Store shadow copies on a different volume	You can also store shadow copies on a different storage volume. However, changing the storage volume deletes the shadow copies. To avoid this problem, verify that the storage volume that you initially select is large enough to handle your present and future needs.

Note For more information about shadow copies, see the Volume Shadow Copy Presentation on the Microsoft Web site.

Previous Versions Client Software for Shadow Copies

- **Previous Versions client software is stored on the server**
  %systemroot%\system32\clients\twclient\x86 directory
- **Use to access previous versions of files**

Introduction

The ability to access shadow copies of files is not built into client computers. The Previous Versions client software must be installed on each client that requires access to shadow copies of files.

Client software for shadow copies

The installation files for the Previous Versions client software are located on the server in the %Systemroot%\system32\clients\twclient\x86 directory. You can distribute the client software in a variety of ways; consider the various options before deployment. Windows Server 2003 provides several tools, such as Group Policy, that can make deploying and maintaining the client software easier.

Viewing shadow copies

Shadow copies are snapshots of files taken at a specific point in time to retain multiple versions. Shadow copies are not available for files stored on client computers, only Windows Server 2003. Shadow copies can be viewed from both servers and clients.

Locations of shadow copy views

Access to shadow copies differs between server and client.

- On the server, access shadow copies of shared folders through the **Shadow Copies** tab of the **Local Disk Properties** dialog box.
- On the client, access shadow copies (called previous versions) through the **Previous Versions** tab of the shared folder **Properties** dialog box.

Alert users

It is recommended that you place the client software on a shared resource and then send an e-mail message to users that describes the function of the software and how to install it.

For example, you may want to inform users that:

- A new feature, Previous Versions, is enabled on the following file share: *\\server\sharedresource*.

- Files are scheduled to be copied at 7:00 A.M. and noon, Monday through Friday. Remember that these copies do not reflect modifications made to these files after these copy times.

- Saving your work frequently is still the best way to ensure that your work is not lost.

- To use Previous Versions, install the client software located at *\\server\sharedresource* and double-click **twclient.msi**.

Note For more information about installing software using Group Policy, see Course 2279, *Planning, Implementing, and Maintaining a Microsoft Windows Server 2003 Active Directory Infrastructure*.

Shadow Copy Scheduling

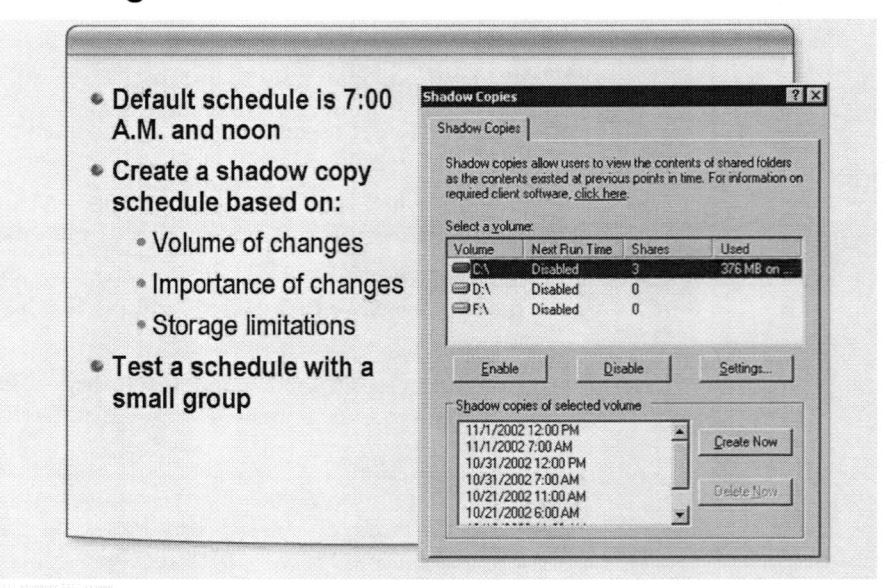

- **Default schedule is 7:00 A.M. and noon**
- **Create a shadow copy schedule based on:**
  - Volume of changes
  - Importance of changes
  - Storage limitations
- **Test a schedule with a small group**

Introduction

When you enable Shadow Copies of Shared Folders, a default schedule is created. Although this schedule may work for your organization, evaluate the work habits of your users to confirm its suitability to your needs.

Create a shadow copy schedule

Consider how many changes there are to your data and how important it is to capture them all. The default schedule is 7:00 A.M. and noon, daily. In most organizations this schedule captures changes before daily work begins and again during the lull at lunch hour. However, if the work day starts at 6 A.M., you may want to change the first shadow copy to 5 A.M. If losing a half day of changes would severely affect your users, you might want to create a shadow copy every hour.

If you increase the number of scheduled shadow copies, consider how often copies can be added without requiring additional storage. Before deploying Shadow Copies of Shared Folders, it is recommended that you create a plan that specifies where to store the shadow copies and what the storage limits are. You can store up to 64 shadow copies per volume. When this limit is reached, the oldest shadow copy is deleted and cannot be retrieved.

Deploy a small test group

You may want to create an initial schedule and deploy it for a small group to test whether your schedule creates enough shadow copies while staying within your storage limits. Also, consider asking your users about their work habits and when they think that a shadow copy would be beneficial. For example, if there is a shift change at 3 P.M., that would be a good time to capture changes.

Scenario

You have enabled Shadow Copies for Shared Folders on all file servers and are using the default schedule. Your organization has a flexible schedule that allows employees to work any time between 7:00 A.M. and 7:00 P.M. Many users create files between noon and 7:00 P.M.

Question: Are these files protected by shadow copies if users save them every hour?

Answer: The files of users who modify and save their files between noon and 7:00 P.M. are not saved by shadow copies until 7:00 A.M. the next day. To protect their files, set up a schedule to create shadow copies of their files every hour from 7:00 A.M. to 7:00 P.M. every weekday. Depending on storage limits, this schedule provides the users with up to five days of shadow copies.

What Is Restoring Shadow Copies?

A server saved copy of a file or folder is restored to the client

Characteristics of Shadow Copies	
If...	Then
No previous versions	The file was not modified after the last save
Restoring a folder	The current version is deleted
Restoring a file	File permissions are not changed
Properties does not include a Previous Versions tab	Shadow copies might not be enabled
Copying a file	File permissions are set to default

Introduction

After you create a shadow copy, you can use it to restore shared files and folders to a previous version.

Note You can restore a shadow copy only from a client.

Restored files and folders using previous versions

If no previous versions are listed on the Previous Versions tab, the file has not changed since the oldest copy was made.

Restoring overwrites the current version

Restoring a previous version overwrites the current version. If you restore a previous version of a folder, the folder is restored to its state at the date and time that you selected. Any changes that you made to files in the folder before that time are lost.

If you do not want to delete the current version, use the **Copy** command to copy the previous version to a different location.

Example of a previous version folder

For example, the current version of a folder contains files A, B, and C. The previous version of the folder contained only files A and B. After you restore the previous version, the folder contains the previous version of file A, the previous version of file B, and the current version of file C.

File permissions are not changed

When you restore a file, the file permissions are not changed. Permissions remain the same as they were before you restored the file. When you copy a previous version of a file, the permissions are set to the default permissions for the directory where the copy of the file is placed.

Best Practices for Using Shadow Copies

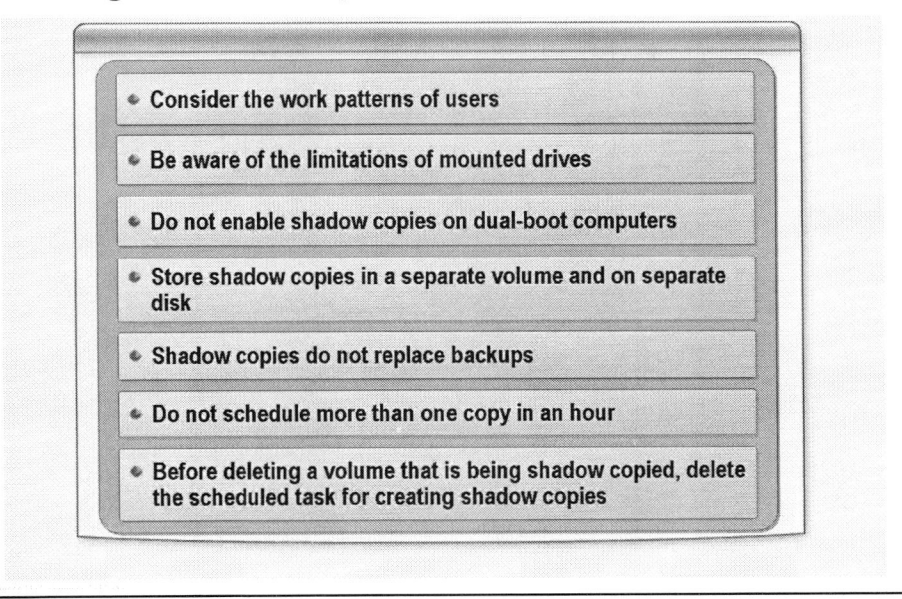

- Consider the work patterns of users
- Be aware of the limitations of mounted drives
- Do not enable shadow copies on dual-boot computers
- Store shadow copies in a separate volume and on separate disk
- Shadow copies do not replace backups
- Do not schedule more than one copy in an hour
- Before deleting a volume that is being shadow copied, delete the scheduled task for creating shadow copies

Introduction

Shadow copies can help you restore lost or corrupt data files. Best practices are designed to help you gain the maximum benefit from this important resource.

Best practices

Consider these best practices when you configure shadow copies and create a shadow copy schedule:

- Adjust the shadow copy schedule to fit the work patterns of your users.
- Be aware of mounted drive limitations.

    Mounted drives are not included when shadow copies are made for a volume. If you want shadow copies enabled on a mounted drive, it must be done separately from the volume to which the drive is mounted. Clients cannot access previous versions on a mounted drive if it is through a share with mount points. However, clients can access previous versions if they have access through a share on the mounted drive.

    Note For more information about Volume Shadow copies and mounted drives see Microsoft Knowledge Base article 812547 on the Microsoft Help and Support Web site.

- Do not enable shadow copies on computers with a dual-boot configuration.

    If you have enabled a dual-boot configuration on a computer running an earlier operating system (such as Microsoft Windows NT® 4.0), the shadow copies that persist during the reboot may be corrupted and unusable when the computer is started in Windows Server 2003.

- Select a separate volume on another disk as the storage area for shadow copies.

    Using a separate volume on another disk provides better performance and is recommended for heavily used file servers.

- Creating shadow copies is not a substitute for regular backups.

    Use Backup in coordination with shadow copies to provide your best restoration scenario.

- Do not schedule copies to occur more often than once per hour. The default schedule is set for 7:00 A.M. and noon. If you decide that you need copies to be made more often, make sure you allot enough storage space and that you do not schedule copies to be made so often that server performance is degraded.

- If you delete the volume but not the shadow copy task, the scheduled task fails and an Event ID: 7001 error is written to the event log. Delete the shadow copy task before deleting the volume to avoid filling the event log with these errors.

Practice: Configuring Shadow Copies

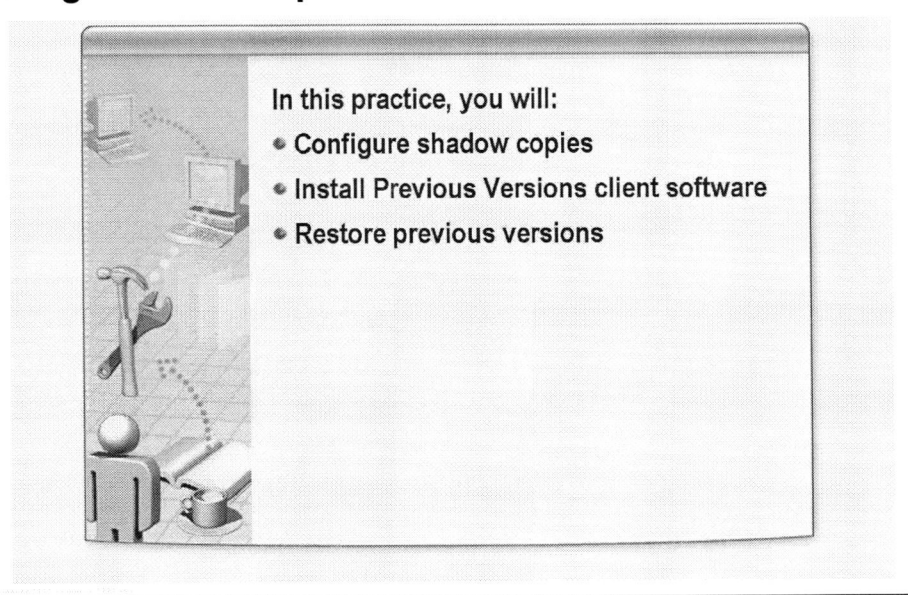

Objective

In this practice, you will:

- Configure shadow copies.
- Install Previous Versions client software.
- Restore previous versions.

Instructions

Ensure that the DEN-DC1 and DEN-CL1 virtual machines are running.

Practice

▶ **Configure shadow copies**

1. On DEN-DC1, click **Start**, point to **Administrative Tools**, and click **Computer Management**.
2. Right-click **Shared Folders**, point to **All Tasks**, and then click **Configure Shadow Copies**.
3. Click the **D:** volume and then click **Enable**.
4. In the **Enable Shadow Copies** dialog box, click **Yes**.
5. Click **Settings**, and then click **Schedule**.
6. Check the **Sat** and **Sun** check boxes. This configures a 7 A.M. shadow copy to also run on Saturday and Sunday.
7. In the Schedule drop-down list, click item **2**. This selects the 12 P.M. shadow copy schedule.
8. Check the **Sat** and **Sun** check boxes. This configures the 12 P.M. shadow copy to also run on Saturday and Sunday.
9. Click **OK** and click **OK**.
10. Click **OK** and close **Computer Management**.

Module 7: Managing Disaster Recovery

Practice

▶ **Install Previous Versions client software**

1. On DEN-DC1, click **Start**, point to **Administrative Tools**, and click **Computer Management**.
2. Expand **Shared Folders**, right-click **Shares**, and click **New Share**.
3. Click **Next**, in the **Folder path** box, type **C:\Windows\system32\clients\twclient\x86**, and then click **Next**.
4. Type **ShadowClient** in the **Share name** box, and click **Next**.
5. Click **Finish** and click **Close**.
6. Close **Computer Management**.
7. On DEN-CL1, log on as **Administrator** with a password of **Pa$$w0rd**.
8. Click **Start**, click **Run**, type **\\DEN-DC1\ShadowClient\twcli32.msi** and then click **OK**.
9. Click **Finish** and then log off of **DEN-CL1**.
10. Log on to DEN-CL1 as **Paul** with the password of **Pa$$w0rd**.

Practice

▶ **Restore previous versions**

1. On DEN-CL1, click **Start**, click **Run**, type **\\DEN-DC1\Data**, and then click **OK**.
2. Create a text file named **Shadow**.
3. Double-click **Shadow** to edit it, type **Version1**, save the file, and close Notepad.
4. On DEN-DC1, click **Start**, point to **Administrative Tools**, and click **Computer Management**.
5. Right-click **Shared Folders**, point to **All Tasks**, and then click **Configure Shadow Copies**.
6. Click the **D:** volume and click **Create Now**. This forces a shadow copy to be taken. This is done in the classroom because the default schedule for shadow copies is 7A.M. and 12 noon only.
7. Click **OK** and close **Computer Management**.
8. On DEN-CL1, double-click **Shadow** to edit it, add a second line **Version2**, save the file, and close Notepad.
9. Right-click **Shadow** and click **Properties**.
10. Click the **Previous Versions** tab. Notice that the previous version is here.
11. Click **Copy**, click **My Documents**, and click **Copy**.
12. Click **OK**.
13. In Windows Explorer, click **My Documents**.

14. Double-click **Shadow** to edit it. This is the original version of the file.
15. Close **Notepad** and close the Explorer window.

Important Do not shut down the virtual machines.

▶ **To prepare for the next practice**
- To prepare for the next practice, start the DEN-SRV1 virtual machine.

Lesson: Recovering from Server Failure

- What Is Safe Mode?
- What Are Safe Mode Options?
- What Is Last Known Good Configuration?
- What Is the Recovery Console?
- What Is a Windows Startup Disk?
- How Startup Files Function
- Selecting Disaster-Recovery Methods
- Practice: Recovering from Server Failure

Introduction

If a server fails, Windows Server 2003 provides you with several options for restoring the computer. Understanding these options and their functions can help you to restore a server to working condition.

Lesson objectives

After completing this lesson, you will be able to:

- Explain safe mode and when it is appropriate.
- Describe safe mode options.
- Explain Last Known Good Configuration and when its use is appropriate.
- Describe the Recovery Console and when its use is appropriate.
- Describe the Windows startup disk.
- Explain how startup files function.
- Explain how to select a disaster-recovery method.
- Use server recovery methods.

What Is Safe Mode?

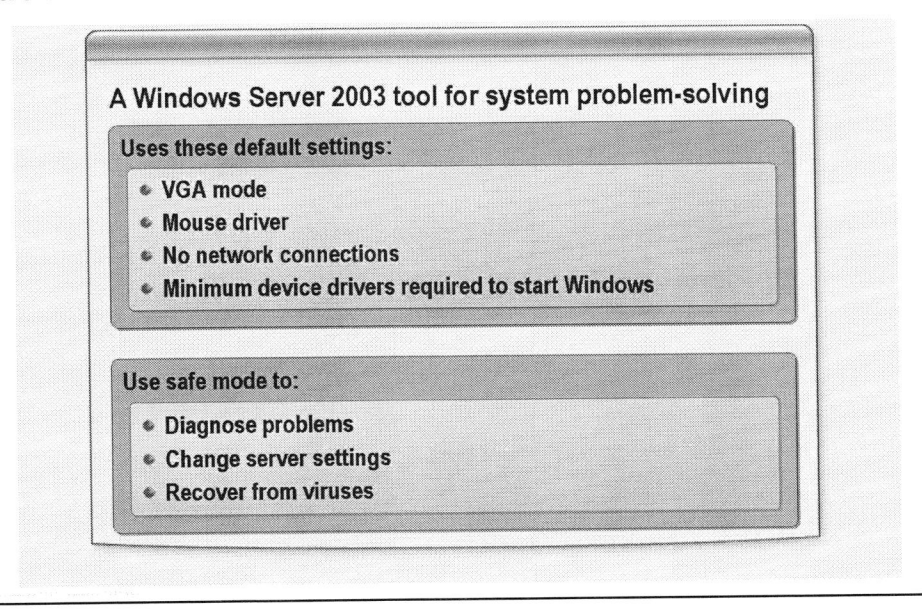

> **A Windows Server 2003 tool for system problem-solving**
>
> **Uses these default settings:**
> - VGA mode
> - Mouse driver
> - No network connections
> - Minimum device drivers required to start Windows
>
> **Use safe mode to:**
> - Diagnose problems
> - Change server settings
> - Recover from viruses

Definition

If your computer does not start, you may be able to start it in safe mode. In this mode, Windows uses default settings, video graphics adapter (VGA) mode, the mouse driver, no network connections, and only the device drivers required to start Windows.

Start a computer using Safe Mode

If your computer does not start after you install new software, new hardware, or a new driver, you may be able to start it with minimal services in safe mode and then change your computer settings, remove newly installed software from startup, or remove a hardware driver that is causing the problem. If necessary, you can reinstall a service pack or the entire operating system.

Use Safe Mode to diagnose problems

Safe mode helps you diagnose problems. If a symptom does not reappear when you start in safe mode, you can eliminate the default settings and minimum device drivers as possible causes. If a newly added device or a changed driver is causing problems, you can use safe mode to remove the device or reverse a change.

Safe mode is often used when recovering from a virus infection. Starting only the minimum drivers ensures that a virus is not in memory when the system is cleaned.

What Are Safe Mode Options?

Option	Description	Use
Safe Mode	Loads only basic files and drivers	When Windows is not starting in Normal mode
Safe Mode with Networking	Loads only basic files and drivers, plus network connections	To access troubleshooting tools that are on the network
Safe Mode with Command Prompt	Loads only basic files, drivers, and a command prompt interface	When Safe Mode will not start properly

Introduction

There are three different Safe Mode options in the Advanced Startup Options that you can use to troubleshoot problems. Each option is suited to a different set of circumstances.

Note To display the advanced startup options, press F8 during the operating system selections phase of the startup process in Windows Server 2003.

Safe Mode

Safe Mode loads only the basic devices and drivers that are required to start the computer, including the mouse, keyboard, mass storage devices, base video, and the standard, default set of system services. This option also creates a log file.

This mode is used to troubleshoot most problems because it provides access to all of the standard GUI administrative tools while minimizing the running services. Typical problems include poorly written drivers and bad services. In Safe Mode, drivers can be changed and services can be disabled.

The Windows installer service is not functional in Safe Mode, so installing and removing most applications is not possible.

Safe Mode with Networking

Safe Mode with Networking loads the same basic set of drivers and services as Safe Mode, but also includes networking drivers. This option also creates a log file.

This mode is used when network drivers are not suspect and troubleshooting tools on the network are required. For instance, a computer may need to obtain a virus removal tool from a network file share.

Safe Mode with Command Prompt

Safe Mode with Command Prompt loads the same basic set of drivers and services as Safe Mode, but does not load the GUI. This option also creates a log file.

This mode is typically used only when Safe Mode is unable to start properly. If Safe Mode with Command Prompt starts properly and Safe Mode does not then there is likely a problem with the display subsystem in Windows.

What Is Last Known Good Configuration?

- Restores registry information and drivers
- Resolves startup problems after a change
- Does not solve problems caused by corrupted or missing drivers or files
- Logging on updates the Last Known Good Configuration

Definition

The Last Known Good Configuration startup option uses the registry information and drivers that Windows saved at the last successful logon. When you use this option to start a server, any changes made to driver settings or other system settings since the last successful logon are lost. Use this option only when the configuration is incorrect.

Registry restore

When Last Known Good Configuration is selected, the information for the registry subkey HKEY_LOCAL_MACHINE\SYSTEM\CurrentControlSet is restored. Also, if you updated any device drivers, using Last Known Good Configuration restores the previous drivers.

Resolve startup problems

Using Last Known Good Configuration can help you resolve startup or stability problems. For example, if a Stop error occurs immediately after you install a new application or device driver, you can restart the computer and use Last Known Good Configuration to recover from the problem. It does not solve problems that are caused by corrupted or missing drivers or files.

Updating Last Known Good Configuration

Windows Server 2003 only updates Last Known Good Configuration information in the registry when the operating system starts in normal mode and a user logs on successfully.

Logging on to the computer in safe mode does not update the Last Known Good Configuration. Therefore, using Last Known Good Configuration remains an option if you cannot resolve your problem by using safe mode.

What Is the Recovery Console?

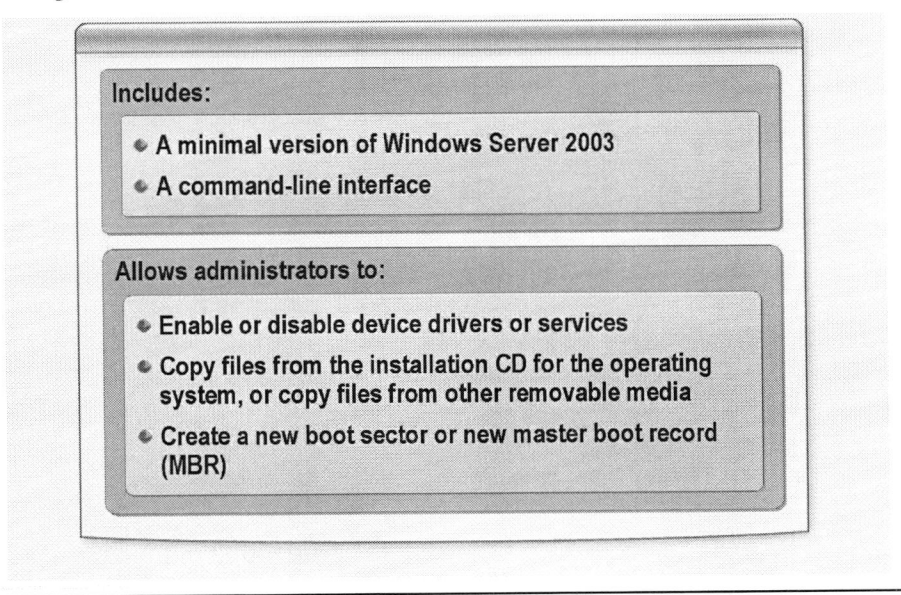

Includes:
- A minimal version of Windows Server 2003
- A command-line interface

Allows administrators to:
- Enable or disable device drivers or services
- Copy files from the installation CD for the operating system, or copy files from other removable media
- Create a new boot sector or new master boot record (MBR)

Definition

The Recovery Console is a minimal version of the Windows Server 2003 operating system that you can use to start Windows Server 2003 when severe startup problems prevent the server from booting. It provides a command-line interface and a set of commands that you can use to repair damaged system components, such as a damaged boot sector, that prevent you from starting the computer any other way.

Starting the Recovery Console

You can start the Recovery Console from the Windows Server 2003 Setup program or from the operating system section screen at startup. To start the Recovery Console from the Windows Server 2003 Setup program, boot the computer using the Windows Server 2003 compact disk. When prompted to choose whether to set up Windows Server 2003 or repair an existing installation, select the repair option.

The Recovery Console must be manually installed into the operating system selection screen. To install the Recovery Console locally, run **D:\i386\winn32.exe /cmdcons**, where D: is your CD-ROM drive.

If Windows Server 2003 has been updated with Service Pack 1 then the Recovery Console must be installed from updated installation files. For more information see Microsoft Windows Server 2003 Service Pack 1 Installing and Deploying Updates on the Windows Server 2003 Web site.

Logging in

When you start the Recovery Console, you must specify which installation of Windows Server 2003 you wish log on to, even on a server with a single-boot configuration. Then, you must log on using the local Administrator account.

On a domain controller, the local Administrator account is often referred to as the Directory Services Restore Mode (DSRM) administrator and the password is set when Active Directory® directory service is installed. This password is not synchronized with the domain Administrator account. In Windows Server 2003, use **ntdsutil** to reset the DSRM administrator password. In Windows 2000, use **setpwd** to reset the DSRM administrator password.

Use to perform repair tasks

You use the Recovery Console to perform the following repair tasks:

- Enable and disable services that prevent Windows Server 2003 from starting.
- Read and write files on a local drive, including drives that are formatted with the NTFS file system. The Recovery Console recognizes and enforces NTFS permissions.
- Format hard disks.
- Repair a boot sector.
- Copy files and system files from a floppy disk or compact disc.

Recovery Console commands

When you run the Recovery Console, you can get help on the available commands by typing **help** at the command prompt and then pressing ENTER.

The following table describes the commands available in the Recovery Console.

Command	Description
attrib	Displays the attributes of the files in the current folder
batch	Executes commands specified in a text file
bootcfg	Repairs boot configuration and recovery
chdir (cd)	Displays the name of the current folder or changes the current folder
chkdsk	Checks a disk and displays a status report
cls	Clears the screen
copy	Copies a single file to another location
delete (del)	Deletes one or more files
dir	Displays a list of files and subfolders in a folder
disable	Disables a system service or a device driver
diskpart	Manages partitions on your hard disks
enable	Starts or enables a system service or a device driver
exit	Exits the Recovery Console and restarts your computer
expand	Expands a compressed file
fixboot	Writes a new partition boot sector onto the system partition
fixmbr	Repairs the master boot record of the partition boot sector
format	Formats a disk
help	Displays a list of the commands that you use in the Recovery Console
listsvc	Lists all available services and drivers on the computer
logon	Logs on to a Windows Server 2003 installation
map	Displays the drive letter mappings
mkdir (Md)	Creates a folder
more	Displays a text file

(continued)

Command	Description
rmdir (rd)	Deletes a folder
rename (ren)	Renames a single file
systemroot	Sets the current folder to the Systemroot folder of the system to which you are currently logged on
type	Displays a text file

What Is a Windows Startup Disk?

- **Allows Windows startup on a computer with a faulty boot sequence**
  - Damaged boot sector
  - Damaged master boot record (MBR)
  - Missing or damaged Ntldr or Ntdetect.com files
  - Incorrect Ntbootdd.sys driver
- **Includes:**
  - Ntldr
  - Ntdetect.com
  - Boot.ini
  - Ntbootdd.sys

Definition

A Windows startup disk allows you to start the operating system on a computer running Windows Server 2003 that has a faulty boot sequence.

Use a Windows startup disk to work around the following startup problems:

- Damaged boot sector
- Damaged master boot record (MBR)
- Missing or damaged Ntldr or Ntdetect.com files
- Incorrect Ntbootdd.sys driver

The Windows startup disk must include the Ntldr, Ntdetect.com, and Boot.ini files. It may also require ntbootdd.sys, which is the device driver for your hard disk controller renamed to ntbootdd.sys.

Note The attributes of the Ntldr, Ntdetect.com, and Boot.ini files are typically set to system, hidden, and read-only. You do not have to reset these attributes for the startup disk to work, but you must reset them if you copy these files to the hard disk.

Using the Windows startup disk

To use a Windows startup disk, place it in the floppy drive and boot from it. After starting the system from the floppy disk Windows is loaded from the hard drive.

A Windows startup disk was a common repair tool in Windows NT. However, the Recovery Console eliminates the need for a Windows startup disk. The Recovery Console allows the necessary access to repair all of the problems that a Windows startup disk solves.

How Startup Files Function

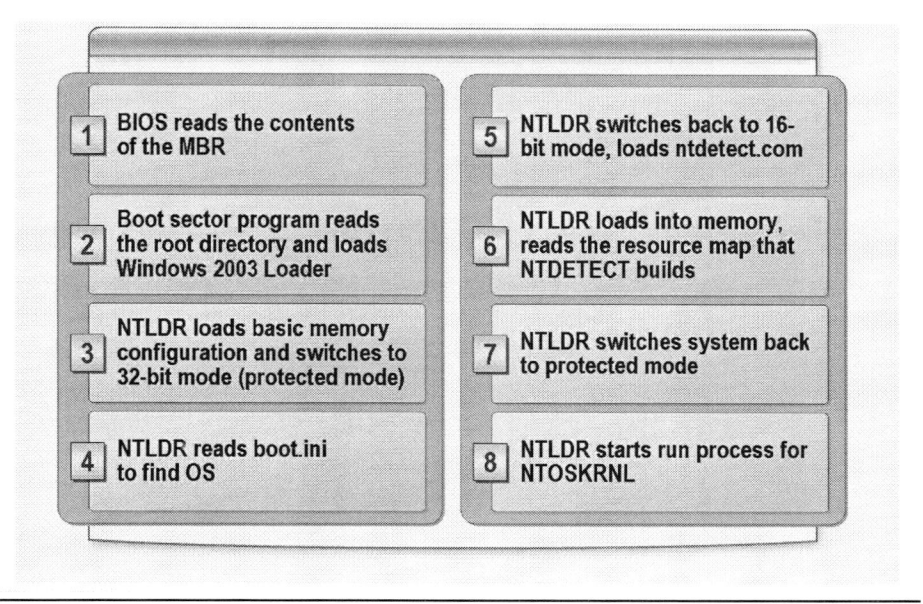

1. BIOS reads the contents of the MBR
2. Boot sector program reads the root directory and loads Windows 2003 Loader
3. NTLDR loads basic memory configuration and switches to 32-bit mode (protected mode)
4. NTLDR reads boot.ini to find OS
5. NTLDR switches back to 16-bit mode, loads ntdetect.com
6. NTLDR loads into memory, reads the resource map that NTDETECT builds
7. NTLDR switches system back to protected mode
8. NTLDR starts run process for NTOSKRNL

Introduction

If your server fails to start, and you must start the computer temporarily, start it by using the Windows startup disk. If the problem is caused by one of the three boot files, you will be able to run the server normally.

Function of the boot files

The boot files function as follows.

1. After the power-on self test (POST) loads the system BIOS into memory, the BIOS reads the contents of the master boot record (MBR). The MBR takes control, finds the active partition, and loads the boot sector from the active partition.

2. The boot sector program reads the root directory and loads Windows Server 2003 Loader (NTLDR).

3. NTLDR loads the basic memory configuration and switches to 32-bit mode (protected mode). NTLDR then places itself into high memory to free as much memory space as possible.

4. NTLDR reads boot.ini to find the operating system. If boot.ini is not present, NTLDR assumes that Windows Server 2003 is in the C:\Windows directory.

5. NTLDR switches back to 16-bit mode and loads ntdetect.com, which is a 16-bit application. NTDETECT determines the computer's physical environment. This determination occurs every time Windows Server 2003 starts, so the environment can change for each boot.

6. NTLDR loads into memory and reads the resource map that NTDETECT builds.

7. NTLDR switches the system back to protected mode. NTLDR then sets up the ring 0 mode for the kernel and loads the proper kernel (NTOSKRNL) for the computer. NTLDR pulls in the proper Hardware Abstraction Layer (HAL) and all boot drivers. Everything that NTDETECT collects becomes the HKEY_LOCAL_MACHINE/HARDWARE Registry key.

8. NTLDR starts the run process for NTOSKRNL.

Selecting Disaster-Recovery Methods

Tool	Use When
Safe Mode	A problem prevents the normal Windows Server 2003 startup
Last Known Good Configuration	The configuration is incorrect
Backup	You need to create a duplicate copy of data on your hard drive and then archive the data on another storage device
Recovery Console	You cannot fix the problems by using one of the startup methods
Automated System Recovery (ASR)	Other repair operations fail

Introduction

To recover your system, you can use Safe Mode, Last Known Good Configuration, Backup, Recovery Console, ASR, or some combination of these tools, as well as others such as shadow copies. Follow the recommended best practices when you use these disaster recovery solutions.

Disaster recovery tools

The following table lists disaster recovery tools in the preferred order of use, from tools that present little or no risk to data, to those that might cause data loss.

Disaster recovery tool	Function
Safe Mode	Use when a problem prevents Window Server 2003 from starting normally.
	Safe mode is a startup option that disables startup programs and nonessential services to create an environment that is useful for troubleshooting and diagnosing problems.
Last Known Good Configuration	Use only in cases of incorrect configuration. By using Last Known Good Configuration, you recover by reverting back to a previous configuration that worked. This also serves to remove the most recent driver and registry changes.
Backup	Use Backup to create a duplicate copy of data on your hard drive and then archive the data on another storage device.
	Backup is a tool for saving and restoring data, including System State data.

Module 7: Managing Disaster Recovery 61

(*continued*)

Disaster recovery tool	Function
Recovery Console	Use if you cannot fix the problems by using one of the startup methods.
	The Recovery Console is used if Windows cannot be started.
Automated System Recovery (ASR)	Use to restore an operating system from a backup.
	Use this option instead of reinstalling Windows because ASR restores system settings and critical files on the system and boot partitions.
	Because the ASR process formats disks, consider this a last resort to be used when other repair operations such a restoring system state or the Recovery Console are not effective.

Note For more information about how to select the correct recovery tool or combination of tools to correct the specific disaster you encounter, see Appendix D, "Which Recovery Tool Do I Use?"

Practice: Recovering from Server Failure

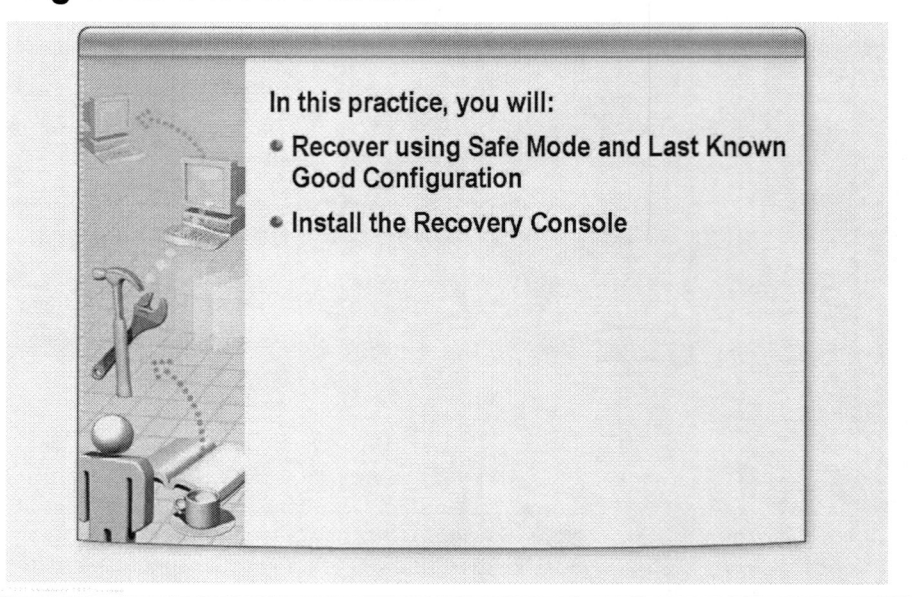

Objective

In this practice, you will:

- Recover using Safe Mode and Last Known Good Configuration
- Install the Recovery Console

Instructions

Ensure the DEN-DC1 and DEN-SRV1 virtual machines are running.

Practice

▶ **Recover using Safe Mode and Last Known Good Configuration**

1. Log on to DEN-SRV1 as **Administrator** with a password of **Pa$$w0rd**.
2. On DEN-SRV1, click **Start**, click **Run** dialog box, type **\MOC\2275\Practices\Mod07\install.bat** and then click **OK**.
3. After the computer restarts, log on as Administrator.
4. Note the unusual behavior. What does the computer do?

   _____

5. When the computer restarts, press **F8** to access the Windows Advanced Options Menu.
6. Select **Last Known Good Configuration** and press ENTER.
7. Press ENTER to start Windows Server 2003, Enterprise Edition
8. Log on as **Administrator**.
9. Did this work? Why or why not?

   _____

10. When the computer restarts, press F8 to access the Windows **Advanced Options** Menu.
11. Select **Safe Mode** and press ENTER.
12. Press ENTER to start the computer.
13. Log on as **Administrator**.
14. Click **OK** to close the **Safe Mode** dialog box.
15. Did this work? Why or why not?

---

16. Click **Start** menu and click **Search**.
17. In the **All or part of the file name** box, type **bootme**, and click **Search**.
18. In the **Search Results** dialog box, delete the **bootme** file in the Windows folder.
19. Restart your computer, and then log on as **Administrator**. Does the problem appear to be solved?

▶ **Install the Recovery Console**

1. On DEN-DC1, click **Start**, click **Run** dialog box, type **C:\win2k3\i386\winnt32.exe /cmdcons** and then click **OK**. A copy of the Windows Server 2003 installation CD-ROM is located in C:\win2k3.
2. Click **Yes** to install the Recovery Console.
3. Click **Skip this step and continue installing Windows** and click **Next**.
4. Click **OK** to close the **Windows Server 2003, Enterprise Edition Setup** dialog box.
5. Restart **DEN-DC1**.
6. When the computer restarts, select **Microsoft Windows Recovery Console** and press ENTER.
7. Type **1** and press ENTER to select C:\WINDOWS as the Windows Server 2003 installation.
8. Type **Pa$$w0rd** as the password and press ENTER.
9. Type **help** and press ENTER.
10. Press the SPACEBAR to scroll through the list.
11. Type **listsvc** and press ENTER.
12. Press the SPACEBAR to scroll through the list.
13. Type **dir** and press ENTER.

14. Press the SPACEBAR to scroll through the list.
15. Type **exit** and press ENTER to exit the Recovery Console and restart Windows.

Important Do not shut down the virtual machines.

Lab: Managing Disaster Recovery

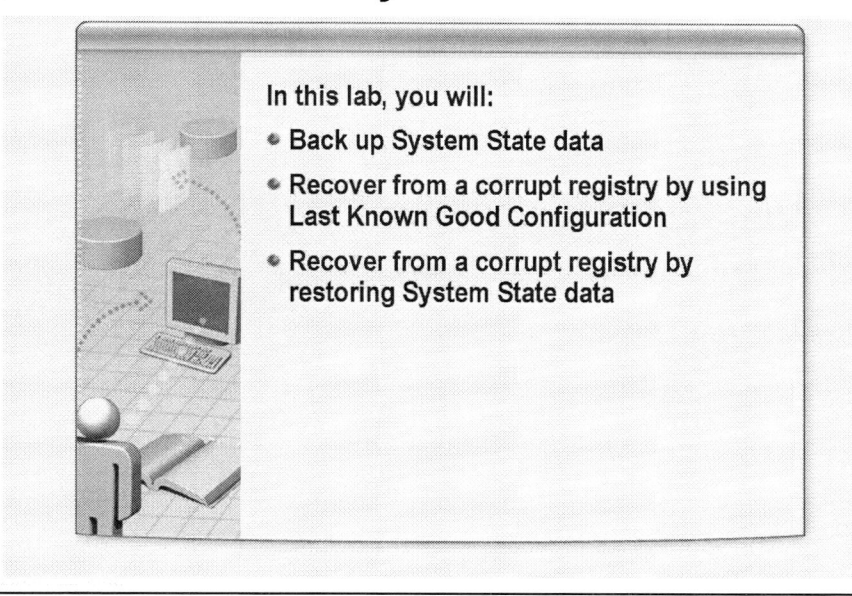

In this lab, you will:
- Back up System State data
- Recover from a corrupt registry by using Last Known Good Configuration
- Recover from a corrupt registry by restoring System State data

Objectives

After completing this lab, you will be able to:

- Back up System State data.
- Recover from a corrupt registry by using Last Known Good Configuration.
- Recover from a corrupt registry by restoring System State data.

Instructions

Ensure that the DEN-DC1 and DEN-SRV1 virtual machines are running.

Estimated time to complete this lab: 50 minutes

Exercise 1
Backing Up the System State Data

In this exercise, you will use the Backup Wizard to back up the System State data for your computer.

Tasks	Specific instructions
1. Back up the System State data.	a. Log on to DEN-DC1 as **Administrator** with a password of **Pa$$w0rd**. b. Start **Backup** in **Advanced** mode. c. On the **Backup** tab, select **System State**. d. Save the backup as **D:\SysState.bkf**. e. Start the backup. f. When the backup completes, close the **Backup Utility**.

Exercise 2
Recovering from a Corrupt Registry by Using Last Known Good Configuration

In this exercise, you will recover from a nonresponsive computer. The cause of this problem was the installation of a software package that modified the registry. (The source for this exercise is Microsoft Knowledge Base article 317246.)

Tasks	Specific instructions
1. Install the software.	a. Log on to DEN-SRV1 as **Administrator** with a password of **Pa$$w0rd**. b. Using Windows Explorer, browse to **C:\MOC\2275\Labfiles\Lab07** and then double-click **inst_01.bat**.
? What happens when the computer restarts?	
? What do you need to do to recover from this disaster?	
2. Repair the system.	a. Reset the virtual machine from the Action menu. b. Access the Windows Advanced Options menu. c. Choose the appropriate recovery method. d. Repair the system.
3. Log on as **Administrator**.	▪ Log on as **Administrator** with a password of **Pa$$w0rd**.

Exercise 3
Recovering from a Corrupt Registry by Restoring System State Data

In this exercise, you will recover from a nonresponsive mouse. The cause of this problem was the installation of a software package that modified the registry. (The source for this exercise is Microsoft Knowledge Base article 317246.)

Tasks	Specific instructions
1. Install the software.	a. On DEN-DC1, open Windows Explorer, browse to **D:\2275\Labfiles\Lab07**, and then double-click **inst_04.bat**. b. When the computer restarts, log on to the domain as **Administrator**.
❓ What do you need to do to recover from this disaster?	
2. Recover from a corrupt registry using Last Known Good Configuration.	a. Press **CTRL+ESC** to open the **Start** menu and restart the computer. b. Access the Windows **Advanced Options** menu. c. Select **Last Known Good Configuration** to resolve this problem. d. Log on to the domain using the **Administrator** account. Did this resolve the problem?
3. Recover from a corrupt registry by restoring System State data using the keyboard. Use the following keys to navigate in the Backup program: ALT+TAB CTRL+ESC TAB ENTER CTRL+TAB SPACEBAR Up arrow Down arrow Right arrow Left arrow	a. Access the Windows **Advanced Options** menu. b. Select **Directory Services Restore Mode**. c. Open the **Start** menu by pressing CTRL+ESC. d. Use the arrow keys to start **Backup**. e. Use keyboard commands to restore the system state backup **D:\SysState.bkf**.
4. Confirm the problem is fixed.	▪ Log on as **Administrator** with a password of **Pa$$w0rd**.
5. Complete the lab exercise.	a. Close all programs and shut down all computers. Do not save changes. b. To prepare for the next module, start the DEN-DC1 virtual computer.

Course Evaluation

Your evaluation of this course will help Microsoft understand the quality of your learning experience.

At a convenient time before the end of the course, please complete a course evaluation, which is available on the Metrics That Matter page of the Knowledge Advisors Web site at http://www.metricsthatmatter.com/MTMStudent/ClassListPage.aspx?&orig=6&VendorAlias=survey.

Microsoft will keep your evaluation strictly confidential and will use your responses to improve your future learning experience.

THIS PAGE INTENTIONALLY LEFT BLANK

Module 8: Software Maintenance Using Windows Server Update Services

Contents

Overview	1
Lesson: Introduction to Windows Server Update Services	3
Lesson: Installing and Configuring Windows Server Update Services	11
Lesson: Managing Windows Server Update Services	20
Lab: Maintaining Software by Using Windows Server Update Services	33

Information in this document, including URL and other Internet Web site references, is subject to change without notice. Unless otherwise noted, the example companies, organizations, products, domain names, e-mail addresses, logos, people, places, and events depicted herein are fictitious, and no association with any real company, organization, product, domain name, e-mail address, logo, person, place or event is intended or should be inferred. Complying with all applicable copyright laws is the responsibility of the user. Without limiting the rights under copyright, no part of this document may be reproduced, stored in or introduced into a retrieval system, or transmitted in any form or by any means (electronic, mechanical, photocopying, recording, or otherwise), or for any purpose, without the express written permission of Microsoft Corporation.

The names of manufacturers, products, or URLs are provided for informational purposes only and Microsoft makes no representations and warranties, either expressed, implied, or statutory, regarding these manufacturers or the use of the products with any Microsoft technologies. The inclusion of a manufacturer or product does not imply endorsement of Microsoft of the manufacturer or product. Links are provided to third party sites. Such sites are not under the control of Microsoft and Microsoft is not responsible for the contents of any linked site or any link contained in a linked site, or any changes or updates to such sites. Microsoft is not responsible for webcasting or any other form of transmission received from any linked site. Microsoft is providing these links to you only as a convenience, and the inclusion of any link does not imply endorsement of Microsoft of the site or the products contained therein.

Microsoft may have patents, patent applications, trademarks, copyrights, or other intellectual property rights covering subject matter in this document. Except as expressly provided in any written license agreement from Microsoft, the furnishing of this document does not give you any license to these patents, trademarks, copyrights, or other intellectual property.

© 2005 Microsoft Corporation. All rights reserved.

Microsoft, Active Directory, ActiveX, Authenticode, BizTalk, IntelliMirror, MSDN, PowerPoint, Windows, Windows Media, Windows NT, and Windows Server are either registered trademarks or trademarks of Microsoft Corporation in the United States and/or other countries.

All other trademarks are property of their respective owners.

Overview

- Introduction to Windows Server Update Services
- Installing and Configuring Windows Server Update Services
- Managing Windows Server Update Services

Introduction

This module introduces Microsoft® Windows Server Update Services (WSUS), a tool for managing and distributing software updates that resolve known security vulnerabilities and other stability issues in Microsoft Windows® 2000 and newer operating systems, as well as other Microsoft applications. This module also describes how to install the client and server components of WSUS. It also provides necessary information about managing the WSUS infrastructure.

Objectives

After completing this module, you will be able to:

- Describe Microsoft WSUS.
- Install and configure servers to use WSUS.
- Manage WSUS.

Lesson: Introduction to Windows Server Update Services

- Multimedia: Windows Server Update Services
- What Is Microsoft Update?
- What Is Automatic Updates?
- What Is Windows Server Update Services?
- Windows Server Update Services Process

Introduction

Traditionally, systems administrators keep systems up-to-date by frequently checking the Microsoft Update Web site or the Microsoft Security Web site for software updates. Administrators manually download available updates, test the updates in their environments, and then distribute the updates manually or by using their traditional software-distribution tools.

By using WSUS, administrators can perform these tasks automatically.

This lesson describes WSUS and explains how it works with Microsoft Update and Automatic Updates.

Lesson objectives

After completing this lesson, you will be able to:

- Describe WSUS.
- Describe Microsoft Update.
- Describe Automatic Updates.
- Describe how WSUS is used.
- Describe the WSUS process.

Module 8: Software Maintenance Using Windows Server Update Services 3

Multimedia: Windows Server Update Services

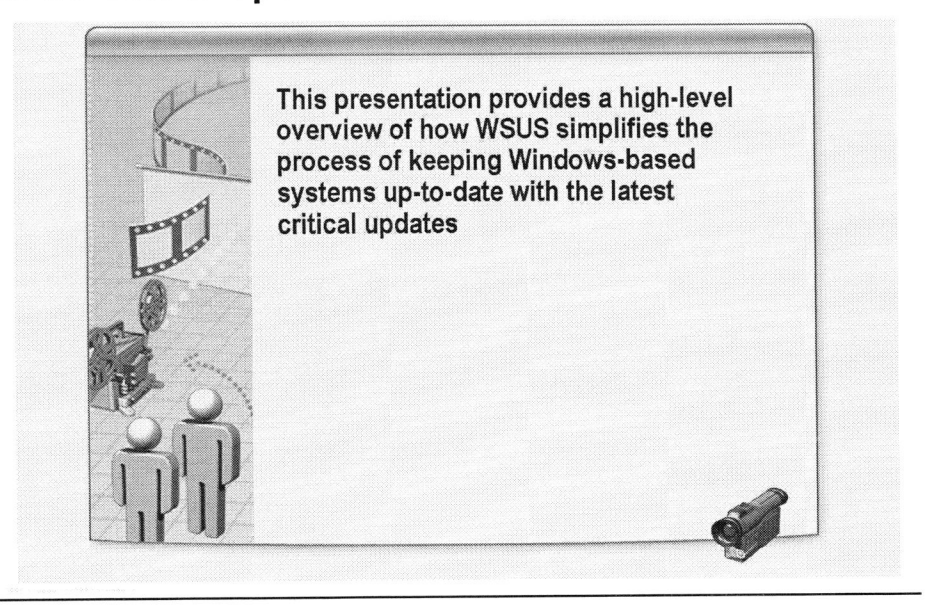

This presentation provides a high-level overview of how WSUS simplifies the process of keeping Windows-based systems up-to-date with the latest critical updates

File location	To view the *Windows Server Update Services* presentation, open the Web page on the Student Materials compact disc, click **Multimedia**, and then click the title of the presentation.

What Is Microsoft Update?

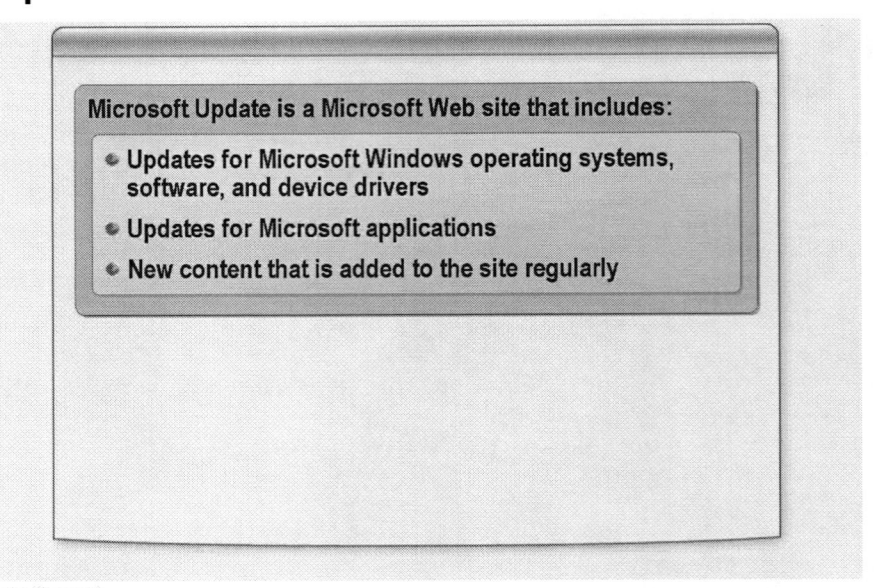

> **Microsoft Update is a Microsoft Web site that includes:**
> - Updates for Microsoft Windows operating systems, software, and device drivers
> - Updates for Microsoft applications
> - New content that is added to the site regularly

Definition

Microsoft Update is a Web site that helps keep your systems up-to-date. Use Microsoft Update to obtain updates for Windows operating systems and applications, updated device drivers, and software. New content is added to the site regularly, so you can always get the most recent updates to help protect your server and the client computers on your network.

What are updates?

Updates can include security fixes, critical updates, and critical drivers. These updates resolve known security and stability issues in Microsoft Windows 2000, Windows XP, and Windows Server™ 2003 operating systems. The Microsoft Update site also has updates for applications such as Microsoft Office, Microsoft Exchange Server and Microsoft SQL Server.

Update categories

The categories for the Windows operating system updates are:

- *Critical updates*. Security fixes and other important updates to keep computers current and networks secure.
- *Recommended downloads*. Latest Windows and Microsoft Internet Explorer service packs and other important updates.
- *Windows tools*. Utilities and other tools that are provided to enhance performance, facilitate upgrades, and ease the burden on systems administrators.
- *Internet and multimedia updates*. Latest Internet Explorer releases, upgrades to Microsoft Windows Media® Player, and more.
- *Additional Windows downloads*. Updates for desktop settings and other Windows features.
- *Multilanguage features*. Menus and dialog boxes, language support, and Input Method Editors for a variety of languages.
- Deployment guides and other software-related documents are also available.

What Is Automatic Updates?

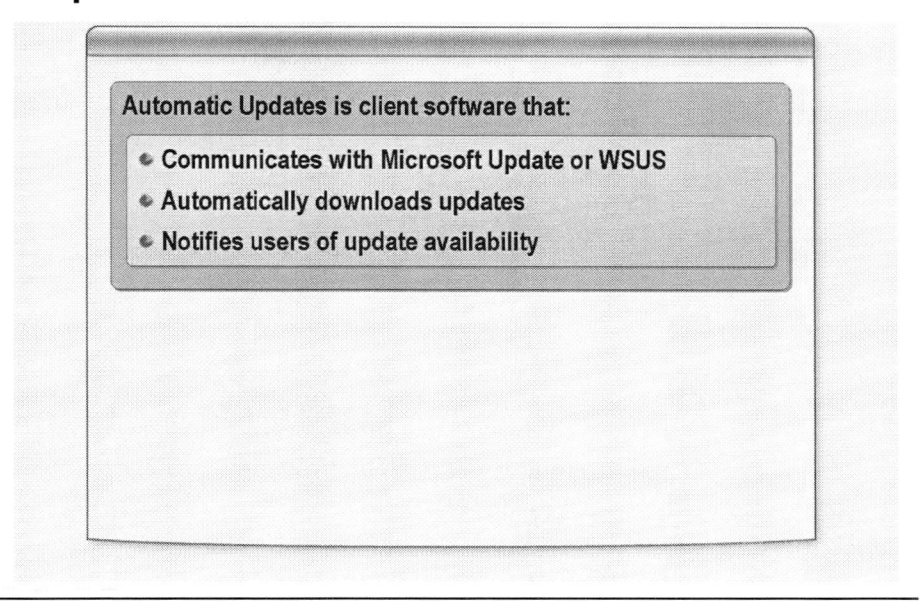

> **Automatic Updates is client software that:**
> - Communicates with Microsoft Update or WSUS
> - Automatically downloads updates
> - Notifies users of update availability

Definition

Automatic Updates is a configurable option in Windows. It can download and install operating system updates without any user intervention. The updates can be downloaded from the Microsoft Update Web site or a WSUS server. Configuration of Automatic Updates can be controlled centrally by the administrator.

Automatic Update options

Automatic Updates gives you flexibility to decide how and when updates will be installed. The options are:

- *Automatic*. Updates downloaded automatically and installed at a scheduled time. This option installs updates for all users and is recommended. If the computer is turned off at the scheduled update time, Windows will install the updates the next time you start your computer. This option is recommended.

- *Download updates for me, but let me choose when to install them*. Updates are downloaded automatically, but they are not installed until an administrator chooses to install them.

- *Notify me but do not automatically download or install them*. Updates are not downloaded or installed automatically. The notifications are only shown to administrators logged on to the local machine.

- *Turn off Automatic Updates*. There will be no notifications when updates are available for your computer. This option is not recommended.

Notification of available updates

After a download is complete, an icon appears in the notification area with a message that the updates are ready to be installed. When you click the icon or message, Automatic Updates guides you through the installation process.

If you choose not to install a specific update that has been downloaded, Windows deletes its files from your computer. If you later change your mind, you can download it by opening the **System Properties** dialog box, clicking the **Automatic Updates** tab, and then clicking **Offer updates again that I've previously hidden**.

Note If required, the version of Automatic Updates is upgraded the first time a WSUS server is contacted.

Digital signatures

To ensure that the programs you download from Microsoft Update are from Microsoft, all files are digitally signed. The purpose of digital signatures is to ensure the authenticity and integrity of the signed files. Automatic Updates installs a file only if it contains this digital signature.

Automatic Updates client deployment

The following operating systems include the required version of Automatic Updates:

- Windows 2000 Service Pack 3 (SP3)
- Windows XP SP1
- Windows Server 2003

Note For more information about deploying Windows Server Update Services, see the white paper, *Deploying Microsoft Windows Server Update Services*, under **Additional Reading** on the Web page on the Student Materials compact disc.

What Is Windows Server Update Services?

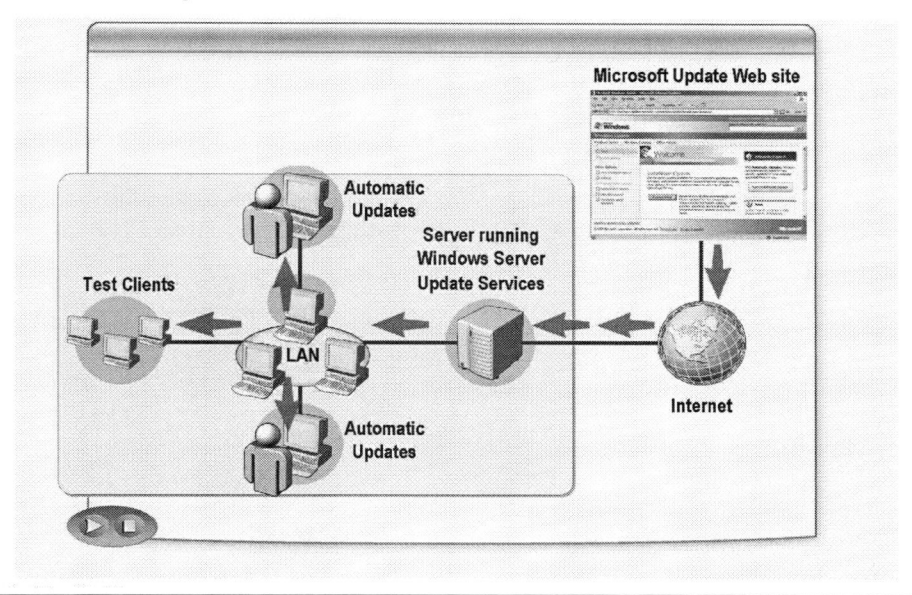

Definition

WSUS is an optional component for Windows 2000 Server or Window Server 2003 that can be downloaded from the Microsoft Web site. It acts as a central point on your network for distributing updates to workstations and server.

Supported software

WSUS has the ability to deliver updates for all Microsoft products. However, at this time, WSUS provides updates for the following:

- Windows 2000 and newer operating systems
- Microsoft Office
- Exchange Server
- SQL Server

Server component

You install the server component of WSUS on a server running Windows 2000 Server or Windows Server 2003 inside your corporate firewall. The firewall must be configured to allow your internal server to synchronize content with the Microsoft Update Web site whenever critical updates for Windows are available. The synchronization can be automatic, or the administrator can perform it manually.

Synchronized updates must be approved before they can be installed by client computers. This allows testing of updates with corporate applications before distribution. This is a key benefit over Microsoft Update.

Client component

Automatic Updates is the client software that downloads and installs updates from a WSUS server. The client must be configured with the location of a WSUS server. The location can be configured through registry edits or through Group Policy. Using Group Policy is strongly recommended.

Note WSUS is not intended to serve as a replacement for enterprise software-distribution solutions, such as Microsoft Systems Management Server or Microsoft Group Policy–based software distribution. Many customers use solutions such as Microsoft Systems Management Server for complete software management, including responding to security and virus issues, and these customers should continue using these solutions. Advanced solutions such as Microsoft Systems Management Server provide the ability to deploy all software throughout an enterprise, in addition to providing administrative controls that are critical for medium-size and large organizations.

Windows Server Update Services Process

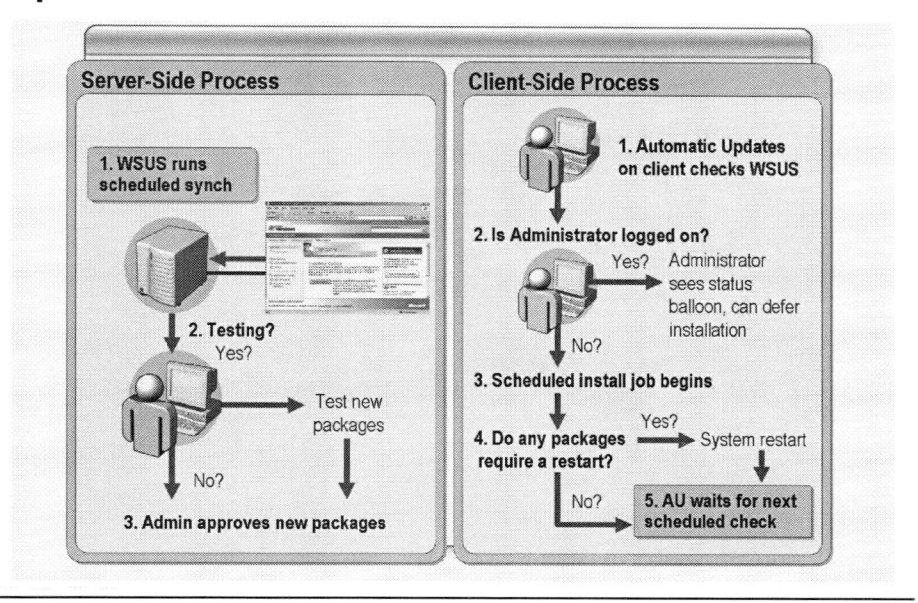

Introduction

The process for using WSUS involves both the server running WSUS and the client computers on a network. If both are configured, the administrator can review the update packages and approve them for installation.

Server-side processes

The server-side process occurs as follows:

1. The server running WSUS runs a scheduled synchronization with Microsoft Update and receives new update packages.

2. The systems administrator reviews the new packages and determines whether testing is required.

    a. If testing is required, the administrator sends the new packages to be tested. This can be done by manually by downloading the updates on a test system or approving the updates for a test group.

    b. If testing is not required, the administrator proceeds to step 3.

3. Administrator approves the new packages of updates.

Client-side processes

The client-side process occurs as follows:

1. Automatic Updates on client computers check the server running WSUS daily and download new approved updates packages from either the server running WSUS or the Microsoft Update Web site.

2. At the scheduled update time, Automatic Updates checks to determine whether the administrator is logged on.

    a. If logged on, the administrator sees a status balloon on the desktop and decides whether to defer or run the installation.

    b. If the administrator is not logged on, step 3 is performed.

Note By using Group Policy, you can configure Automatic Updates to allow nonadministrative users to defer installing updates.

3. The scheduled installation job begins, and Automatic Updates installs new or changed packages.
4. Automatic Updates checks whether the new packages require a restart of the server or client.
    a. If a restart is required, the system restarts after all the packages are installed.
    b. If no restart is required, the installation is completed.
5. Automatic Updates waits for the next scheduled check.

Lesson: Installing and Configuring Windows Server Update Services

- WSUS Deployment Scenarios
- Server Requirements for Windows Server Update Services
- Automatic Updates Configuration
- Practice: Installing and Configuring Windows Server Update Services

Introduction

WSUS consists of both client-side and server-side components to provide a basic solution to critical update management.

This lesson explains how to install and configure the client-side and server-side components of WSUS.

Lesson objectives

After completing this lesson, you will be able to:

- Describe WSUS deployment scenarios.
- Describe server hardware and software requirements for WSUS.
- Describe Automatic Updates configuration.
- Install and configure WSUS.

WSUS Deployment Scenarios

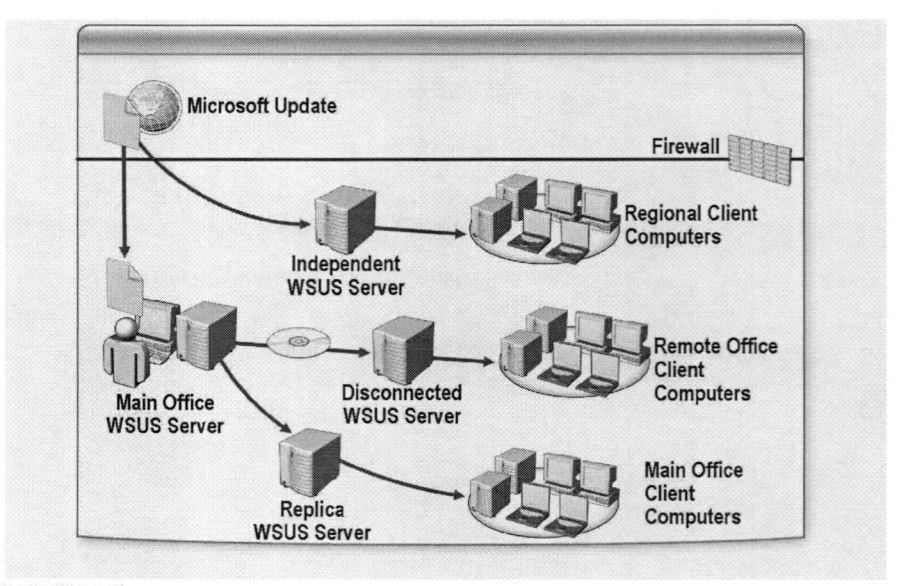

Introduction

To allow for varied situations, you can deploy a WSUS server in several scenarios. You can choose the deployment scenario that is most appropriate for your organization. The decision factors may include the number of locations in your network or the speed of your Internet connection.

Single WSUS server

In a single-site network, a single WSUS server can be sufficient to support as many as 5,000 clients. This is suitable for most single-site networks.

Independent WSUS servers

In a multiple-site network, you can configure multiple independent WSUS servers are each location. This requires that each site use its own Internet connection to download the updates. Having each site download its own updates reduces the load on wide-area network (WAN) links as compared to using a centralized server to download updates.

Independent WSUS servers are also managed independently. This scenario is best suited to organizations with distributed IT support.

Replica WSUS servers

Another option for multiple-site networks it to use replica WSUS servers. Replica WSUS servers download their updates and configuration information from a central WSUS server. This allows the approval of updates to be centralized for multiple servers.

In this scenario, only one server is exposed to the Internet and it is the only server that downloads updates from Microsoft Update. This server is set up as the upstream server—the source from which the replica server synchronizes.

Disconnected WSUS servers

For organizations that do not allow servers to communicate directly with the Internet, you can deploy disconnected WSUS servers. In this scenario, you can set up a server running WSUS that is connected to the Internet but isolated from rest of the network. After downloading, testing, and approving the updates on the isolated server, an administrator would then export the update metadata and content to external storage, and then, from the external storage, import the update metadata and content to servers running WSUS within the intranet.

Server Requirements for Windows Server Update Services

- **Hardware requirements**
  - Pentium III 1GHz or higher
  - 1 GB of RAM
  - 30 GB of hard disk space
- **Software requirements**
  - Windows 2000 Server or Windows Server 2003
  - IIS 5.0 or later
  - BITS
  - Microsoft .NET Framework 1.1 SP1
  - Internet Explorer 6.0 SP1 or later

Introduction

You install the server component of WSUS by using a Windows Installer package that installs the necessary server files and configures Internet Information Services (IIS). To ensure that your server can support WSUS, check the hardware and software capabilities of your server.

Hardware server requirements

The following are the recommended hardware requirements for a server with as many as 500 clients.

- Pentium III 1 gigahertz (GHz) or faster
- 1 gigabyte (GB) of RAM
- 1 GB of hard disk space on the system volume
- 30 GB of hard disk space for security packages
- Hard disks must be formatted with NTFS

Software server requirements

Each server running WSUS requires the following software:

- Windows 2000 Server or Windows Server 2003
- IIS 5.0 or later
- Windows SQL Server 2000 Desktop Engine (WMSDE) for deployments up to 500 clients
- Microsoft SQL Server 2000 for deployments over 500 clients
- Background Intelligent Transfer Service (BITS) 2.0

- Microsoft .NET Framework 1.1 Service Pack 1
- Internet Explorer 6.0 Service Pack 1 or later

Note WMSDE is included when WSUS is installed on Windows Server 2003. Deployments on Windows 2000 must use a free download of MSDE or Microsoft SQL Server 2000.

Note For more information about server requirements for WSUS, see the white paper, *Deploying Microsoft Windows Server Update Services*, under **Additional Reading** on the Web page on the Student Materials compact disc.

Automatic Updates Configuration

> * Configure Automatic Updates by using Group Policy
> * Requires updated wuau.adm administrative template
> * Requires:
>   * Windows 2000 SP3
>   * Windows XP SP1
>   * Windows Server 2003

Introduction

Group Policy is the most appropriate way to configure the settings for Automatic Updates. It allows configuration to be centralized and distributed to all WSUS client computers without any user interaction.

Updating Group Policy administrative templates

WSUS enables some Automatic Updates options that were not available in older versions of the Automatic Updates client. As a consequence, the default Group Policy settings that are included with Windows Server 2003 do not allow configuration of all the options in the current Automatic Updates client that is used with WSUS.

Group Policy settings are based on administrative templates (.adm files). These templates contain lists of registry keys, available options and descriptions. **Wuau.adm** is the template for Automatic Update settings. The latest version of **wuau.adm** is available in Windows XP SP2 and Windows Server 2003 SP1.

If a Group Policy object is created on a server without the latest version of **wuau.adm,** then some WSUS options will not be available.

Administrative control by using policies

Administrator-defined configuration options that are defined by Group Policy always take precedence over user-defined options. Also, **Automatic Updates** options in Control Panel are disabled on the target computer when administrative policies are set.

The Group Policy object (GPO) setting for Automatic Updates is located in the Computer Configuration\Administrative Templates\Windows Components\Windows Update folder.

Group Policy settings for Automatic Updates

Some of the Group Policy settings for Automatic Updates are:

- Specify intranet Microsoft update service location
- Automatic Updates detection frequency
- Allow Automatic Updates immediate installation
- Delay Restart for scheduled installations
- Allow nonadministrators to receive update notifications

Requirements for the client computer

Client computers must be running the updated Automatic Updates client and Windows 2000 (Service Pack 3), Windows XP (Service Pack 1), or Window Server 2003.

Practice: Installing and Configuring Windows Server Update Services

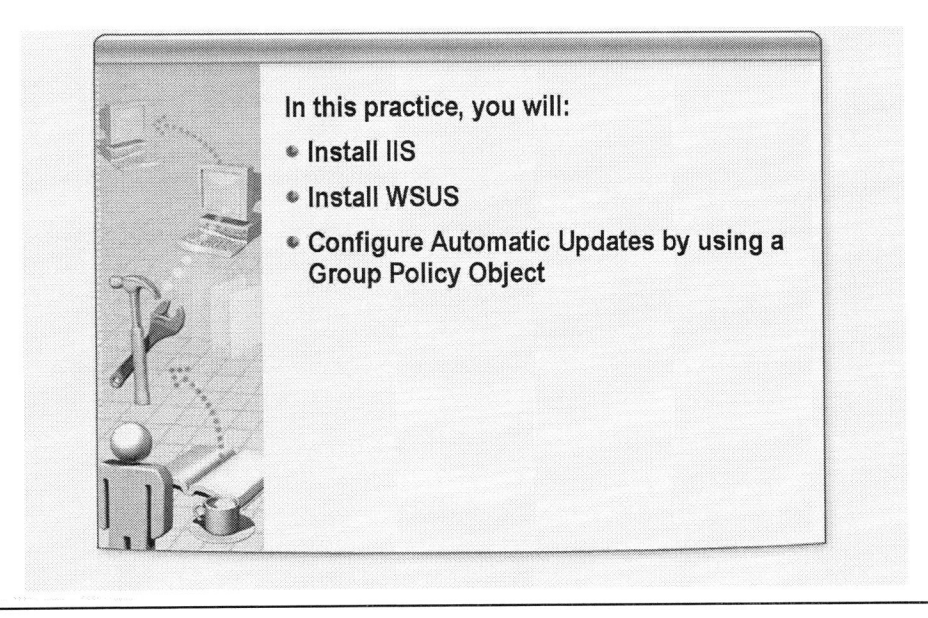

Objective

In this practice, you will:

- Install IIS.
- Install WSUS.
- Configure Automatic Updates by using a Group Policy object.

Instructions

Ensure that the DEN-DC1 virtual machine is running.

Practice

▶ **Install IIS**

1. Log on DEN-DC1 as **Administrator** with a password of **Pa$$w0rd**.
2. Click **Start**, point to **Control Panel**, and then click **Add or Remove Programs**.
3. Click **Add/Remove Windows Components**.
4. In the **Components** box, select the **Application Server** check box, and then click **Next**.
5. Click **Finish**.
6. Close Add or Remove Programs.

▶ Install WSUS

1. Open Windows Explorer.
2. Browse to **D:\2275\Practices\Mod08**.
3. Double-click **WSUSSetup**.
4. Click **Next** to begin the Microsoft Windows Server Update Services Setup Wizard.
5. Click **I accept the terms of the License agreement** and then click **Next**.
6. Ensure that the **Store updates locally** check box is selected and the path is configured for **D:\WSUS**, and then click **Next**.
7. Click **Next** to accept the default of **Install SQL Server desktop engine (Windows) on this computer**.
8. Ensure that **Use the existing IIS Default Web site** is selected and click **Next**. Take note of the Web sites used for management and obtaining updates.
9. Click **Next** to accept the default of this server being a standalone WSUS server.
10. Read the installation summary and then click **Next**. The installation will take about 10 minutes.
11. Click **Finish**.
12. Complete the **New Connection Wizard** with the following settings:
    - Connect to the Internet
    - Connect using a broadband connection that is always on.
13. Open **Internet Explorer**.
14. Check the **In the future, do not show this message** check box and click **OK**.
15. In the Address bar type **HTTP://DEN-DC1/Wsusadmin**. Press **Enter**.
16. In the **User name** box type **Administrator**, in the **Password** box type **Pa$$w0rd**, and click **OK**.
17. Add **http://DEN-DC1** to the list of trusted Web sites and close the Internet Explorer dialog box. Notice that this is the management interface for WSUS.
18. Close **Internet Explorer** and close all open windows.

▶ Configure Automatic Updates by using a Group Policy object

1. Click **Start**, point to **Administrative Tools**, and click **Group Policy Management**.
2. Expand **Forest: Contoso.msft**, expand **Domains**, and expand **Contoso.msft**.
3. Right-click **Contoso.msft** and click **Create and link a GPO here**.
4. In the **Name** box, type **WSUS** and then click **OK**.
5. Right-click **WSUS** and click **Edit**.

6. Under **Computer Configuration**, expand **Administrative Templates**, expand **Windows Components**, and click **Windows Update**.
7. Double-click **Configure Automatic Updates**.
8. Click **Enabled**, in the **Configure automatic updating** box, select **4 – Auto download and schedule the install**, and then click **OK**.
9. Double-click **Specify intranet Microsoft update service location**.
10. Click **Enabled**, type **http://DEN-DC1** in the **Set the intranet update service for detecting updates** box and the **Set the intranet statistics server** box, and click **OK**.
11. Close **Group Policy Object Editor**.
12. Close **Group Policy Management**.
13. Close all open windows.

▶ **To prepare for the next practice**
- Start the DEN-CL1 virtual machine.

Important Do not shut down the virtual machines.

Lesson: Managing Windows Server Update Services

- Windows Server Update Services Administration Web Site
- How Synchronization Works
- Managing Computer Groups
- Approving Updates
- Using Reports
- Backing Up and Restoring Windows Server Update Services
- Guidelines for Deploying Updates
- Practice: Managing Windows Server Update Services

Introduction

As an administrator, you decide whether to install updates immediately after they are downloaded, or to test the updates first. This lesson discusses how to view the synchronized content, as well as how to approve and install the updates.

It is important to have your WSUS configuration backed up and ready to restore in the event of a disaster. This lesson also describes what portions of WSUS need to be backed up and how to do it.

Lesson objectives

After completing this lesson, you will be able to:

- Describe the features and function of the WSUS administration Web site.
- Describe how synchronization works.
- Describe computer groups and how to manage them.
- Describe how updates are approved.
- Describe how to use reports.
- Describe the backup and restore process for WSUS.
- Describe guidelines for deploying updates.
- Manage WSUS.

Windows Server Update Services Administration Web Site

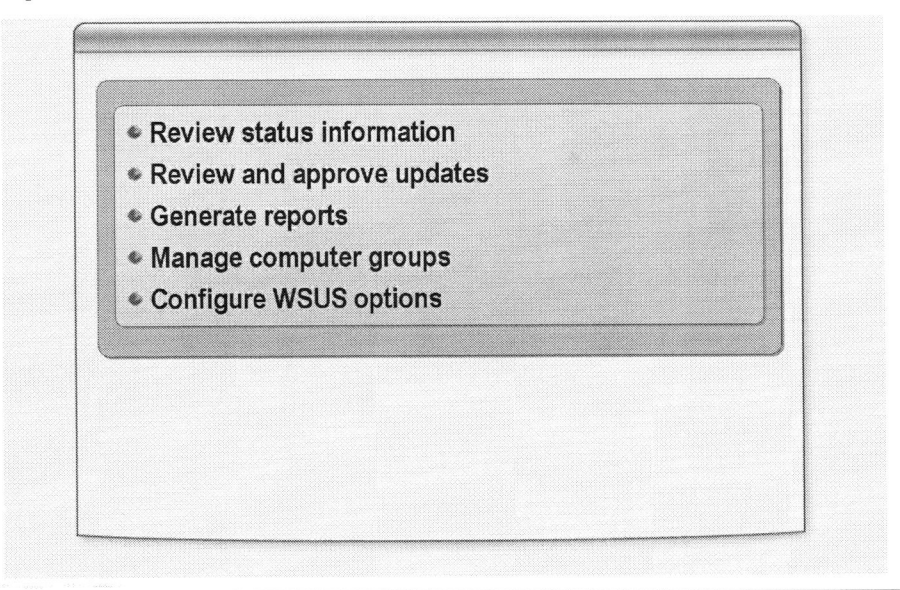

- Review status information
- Review and approve updates
- Generate reports
- Manage computer groups
- Configure WSUS options

Administrative tasks for managing WSUS

These are the five primary administrative tasks for managing WSUS.

- Review status information, such as computers requiring updates.
- Review and approve updates for distribution to clients.
- Generate reports on the status of updates, computers, synchronization, and WSUS settings.
- Manage computers and computer groups.
- Configure WSUS options for synchronization, automatic approval, and assigning computers to groups.

WSUS administrative Web site

All WSUS configuration is performed by using the WSUS administration Web site. The WSUS administration Web site is located at http://*servername*/WSUSAdmin, where *servername* is the DNS name of the server on which WSUS is installed.

You can access these pages on a corporate intranet by using Microsoft Internet Explorer 5.5 or later. If you try to connect to the administration Web site with a version of Internet Explorer earlier than version 5.5, an error page appears, reminding you to upgrade Internet Explorer.

Note To view this Web site, you must be a local administrator on a computer that is running WSUS.

How Synchronization Works

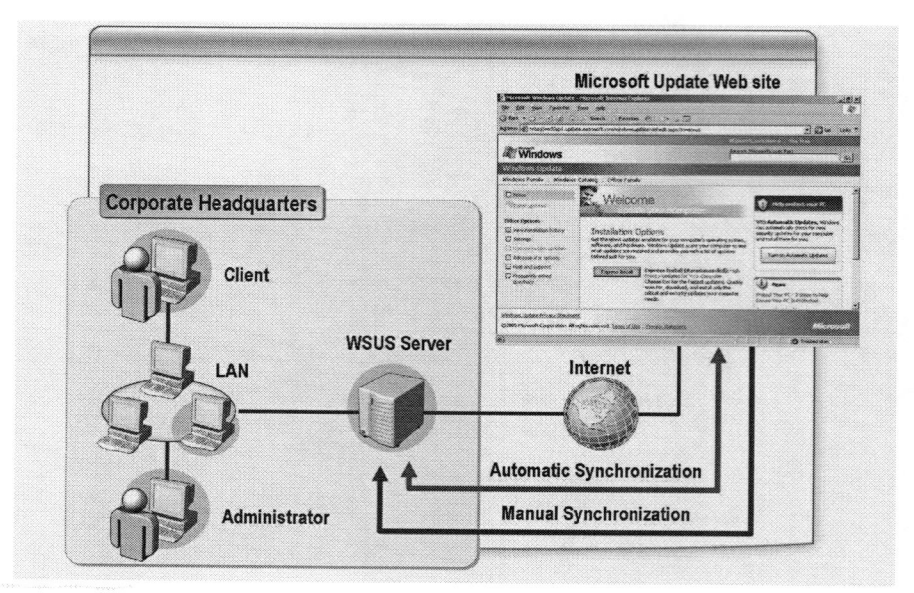

Introduction	Servers running WSUS are updated with a process called synchronization. This process compares the WSUS server software with the Microsoft Update Web site's latest release. Administrators can choose to configure these updates to proceed automatically or they can perform this process manually.
Synchronization schedule	The default setting for the synchronization schedule is manual. This means that an administrator must manually choose to download new updates to the WSUS server. This is appropriate for disconnected WSUS servers only. For other WSUS servers, synchronization should be scheduled.
	Schedule synchronization occurs once per day at a time selected by an administrator. Daily synchronization ensures that the WSUS server has the latest updates. After synchronization an administrator must still approve the updates before they are distributed to clients.
Products and update classifications	An administrator can select specific products and update classifications to limit unnecessary downloads. By default, only critical updates and security updates are downloaded.
	If a server is configured for WSUS, but requires a systems administrator to manually synchronize the updates, the updates remain on the Microsoft Update Web site until the administrator reviews and approves them.
Update source	You can synchronize content on your WSUS server from the Microsoft Update Web site or from another installation of WSUS. The update source you select will depend on how you have planned your deployment of WSUS. An independent WSUS server will synchronize content from the Microsoft Update Web site, while a branch office replica WSUS server will synchronize from a head-office WSUS server.
Update languages	You can limit the updates that are downloaded based on the language of the update. This reduces the bandwidth used for downloads and reduces disk space required for storing updates. The default configuration downloads updates in all languages.

Managing Computer Groups

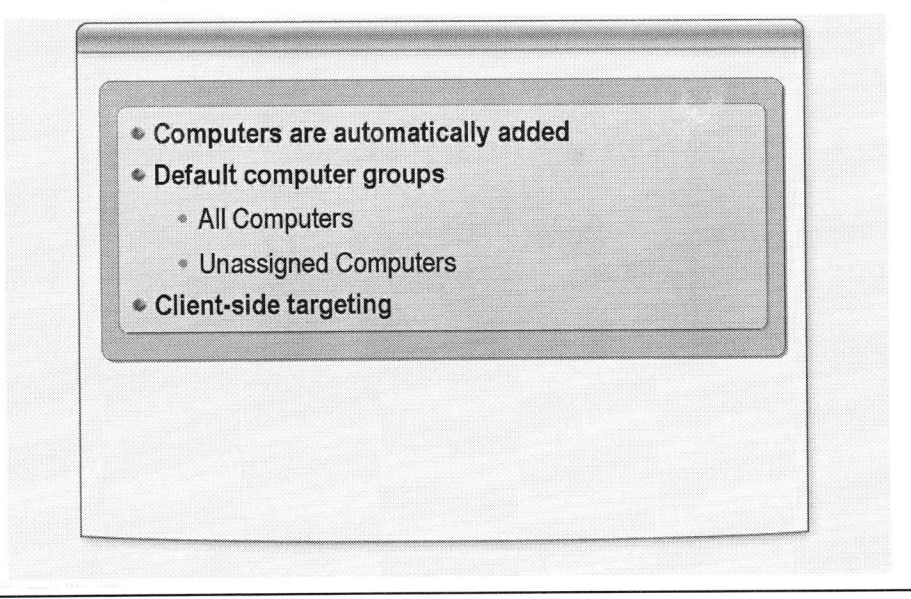

> - Computers are automatically added
> - Default computer groups
>   - All Computers
>   - Unassigned Computers
> - Client-side targeting

How computer groups are used	Computer groups are used by WSUS to control which updates are applied to which computers. This allows you to stage deployment of updates to reduce load on the network. Computer groups make it convenient to test updates on a few specific computers before distributing the updates to the entire organization.
Client computers	Client computers are listed on the Computers page of the WSUS administration site. They are automatically added to this page after they contact the WSUS server for the first time.
	A computer is never removed from WSUS server automatically. If you reconfigure a computer to use a different server, you must manually remove it from the original WSUS server.
Default computer groups	All new computers are added to the All Computers group and the Unassigned Computers group automatically. The All Computers group provides a convenient way to apply updates to every computer that is using a WSUS server. The Unassigned Computers group lets you see which computers using the WSUS server might be new and need to be added to a group. After computers are added to an administrator created group then they are no longer a part of Unassigned Computers.
Adding computers to computer groups	Computers can be added to groups manually in WSUS administration site or automatically through client-side targeting. Client-side targeting is done by using Group Policy settings. If the computers in your organization are organized into organization units (OUs) based on department, it is easy to configure a Group Policy for each OU that defines which computer group those computers should be a member of.

Approving Updates

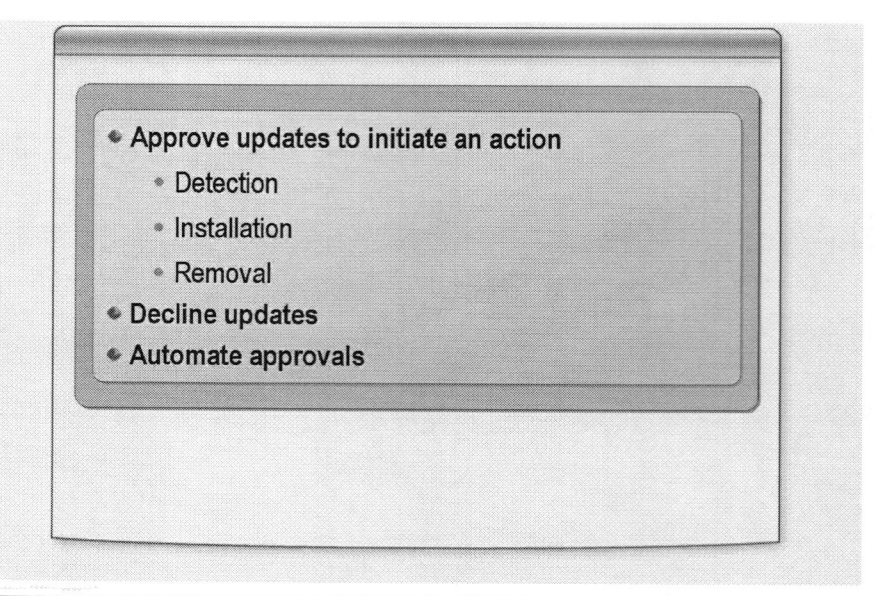

- **Approve updates to initiate an action**
  - Detection
  - Installation
  - Removal
- **Decline updates**
- **Automate approvals**

Introduction

After updates have been synchronized to a WSUS server, you must approve them to initiate a deployment action. When you approve an update, you are essentially telling WSUS what to do with it.

Approving an update

Your choices for approving an update are Install, Detect only, Remove, or Decline. When you approve an update, you specify a default approval setting for the All Computers group, and any necessary settings for each computer group in the **Approve Updates** dialog box. If you do not approve an update, its approval status remains Not approved and your WSUS server performs no action for the update. The exceptions to this are Critical Updates and Security Updates, which by default are automatically approved for detection after they are synchronized.

Detection

When you approve an update for detection, the update is not installed. Instead, WSUS checks whether the update is compliant with or needed by computers in the groups you specify for the **Detect only approval** option. The detection occurs at the scheduled time that the client computer communicates with the WSUS server.

After detection you can view how many computers do not have the update installed and need it. If the number of needed for an update is zero, then all client computers are up-to-date.

Installation

The **Install approval** option installs the update for selected computer groups. In a default installation of WSUS, updates are not downloaded to the WSUS server until they are approved for installation.

When an update is approved for installation, you can configure a deadline. The date specified in a deadline forces an update to be installed on client computers by that time. This overrides clients configured to only notify of available updates.

Removal	If an update causes problems after being approved for installation it can be removed by approving it for removal. This is particularly important if you have automated installation approval for certain classifications of updates.
Declining updates	You can choose to decline any updates that are not relevant for your environment. A declined update is removed from the list of available updates.
Automating approvals	The process for testing and approving new updates can be slow in many organizations. Some organizations have found that there is less risk in applying critical updates and security updates immediately than waiting for the testing process to be complete. This ensures that new viruses do not take advantage of flaws before updates are installed.
	WSUS has the ability to automatically approve updates for detection or installation. By default critical updates and security updates are approved for detection and WSUS updates are approved for installation. Automatic approvals can be configured to apply only to certain computer groups.

Using Reports

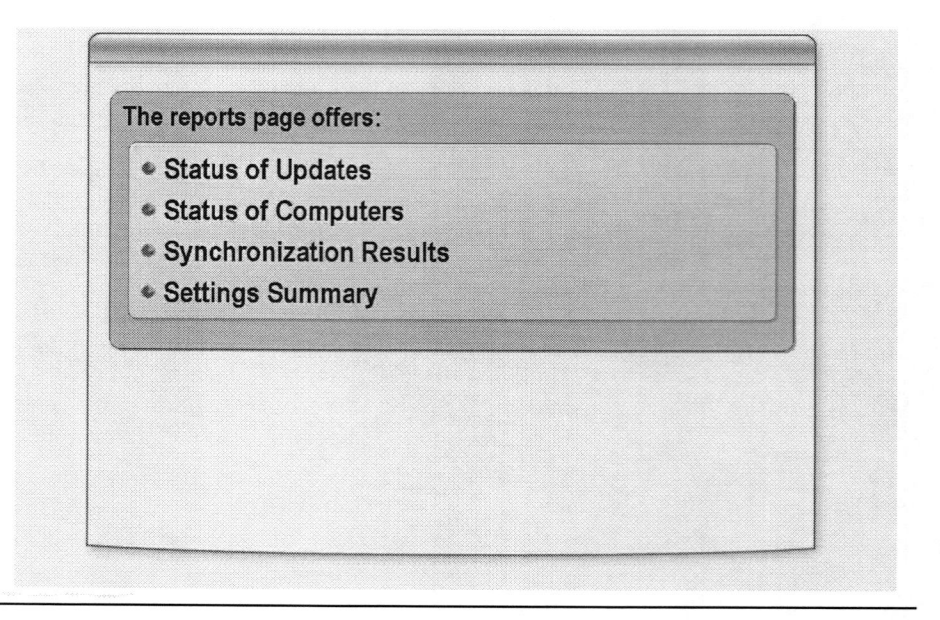

The reports page offers:
- Status of Updates
- Status of Computers
- Synchronization Results
- Settings Summary

Introduction

Reports provide a quick way to get an overview of an update status, computer status, synchronization results, and WSUS configuration. You can also print reports so that you can take them to status meetings and include them with network status reports.

Reports

The reports page offers four preconfigured reports:

- Status of Updates

    This report shows the status of updates for a particular computer group. For each update it shows how many computers have installed the update, need the update, or failed to install the update. This report can also be filtered based on update status such as updates that have failed to install.

- Status of Computers

    This report shows the status of updates on individual computers in a computer group. For each computer it shows how many updates are installed, needed or failed. This report can also be filtered based on update status such as computers with failed updates.

- Synchronization Results

    This report summarizes synchronization information including status of the last synchronization, synchronization errors, and new updates. This report can be filtered to limit the relevant timeframe.

- Settings Summary

    This report lists the current configuration of the WSUS server. This is useful for general documentation, comparing server configurations, and disaster recovery.

Backing Up and Restoring Windows Server Update Services

- **Use the Backup Utility**
- **Backup database**
  - Stop MSSQL$WSUS service
  - Contains metadata, configuration information, and client computer information
- **Updates folder**

Introduction

Although WSUS does not provide a built-in backup tool, you can use the Backup utility that is available on all servers running Windows 2000 or Windows Server 2003 to easily back up and restore both the WSUS database and update file storage folder.

WSUS database

When the WSUS database is backed up, the MSSQL$WSUS service should be stopped. If this service is running during a backup there is a risk the backup will be inconsistent.

The WSUS database contains the following information:

- Update metadata, including information about updates. Metadata is also where end-user license agreements (EULAs) are stored.

- WSUS server configuration information, which includes all settings for your WSUS server. These are options you specified through the WSUS console and settings configured by WSUS automatically during setup.

- Information about client computers, updates, and client interaction with updates. You can access this information through the WSUS console when you view status and run reports on update status and client computer status.

Note If you are using a full version of Microsoft SQL Server 2000 for your database, which is not installed by WSUS, you can use SQL Server Enterprise manager as an alternative to the Backup utility.

Updates folder

The updates folder contains all of the updates that have been downloaded and stored on the WSUS server. By default, update files are stored in the %systemdrive%\WSUS\WSUSContent folder on your WSUS server. If you have chosen to store update files on Microsoft Update, you do not have to back up the update file storage folder on your WSUS server.

Guidelines for Deploying Updates

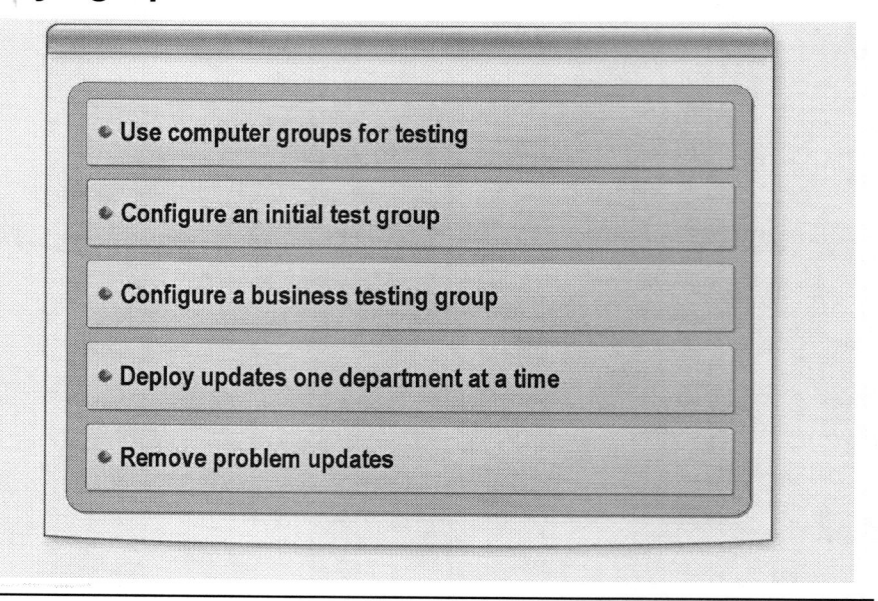

- Use computer groups for testing
- Configure an initial test group
- Configure a business testing group
- Deploy updates one department at a time
- Remove problem updates

Introduction

Due to the complex interdependencies between operating system components and corporate applications, it is strongly recommended that all updates be tested before deploying them to WSUS clients. This is particularly important for custom designed or in-house applications which may not be as well written as commercially available applications.

Guidelines

Use the following guidelines to install updates on the client computers on your network:

- Use computer groups for testing.

    Computer groups let you control which computers are approved to install updates. Using computer groups to install updates on test computers avoids the hassle of downloading updates for testing through a separate process.

- Configure an initial test group.

    Create a test group of nonproduction computers for testing updates. These computers should match your production environment as closely as possible. This initial testing can be performed by the IT group or designated business users. In this testing you can identify obvious problems with installation or functionality. At this stage a problem update will have no impact on production.

- Configure a business testing group.

    Recruit power users from different business groups to act as test groups before distributing updates to all users. Power users will be able to provide detailed functional testing of applications. This will catch application specific errors. At this stage a problem update will affect a limited group of users in production.

- Deploy updates one department at a time.

    Deploying updates to one department at a time will reduce the scope of a problem if an update causes a problem. Testing can also be done on a per department basis because they typically have unique applications.

- Remove problem updates.

    If an update causes problems, mark it for removal. This will uninstall the update. Be aware that some updates cannot be uninstalled.

Practice: Managing Windows Server Update Services

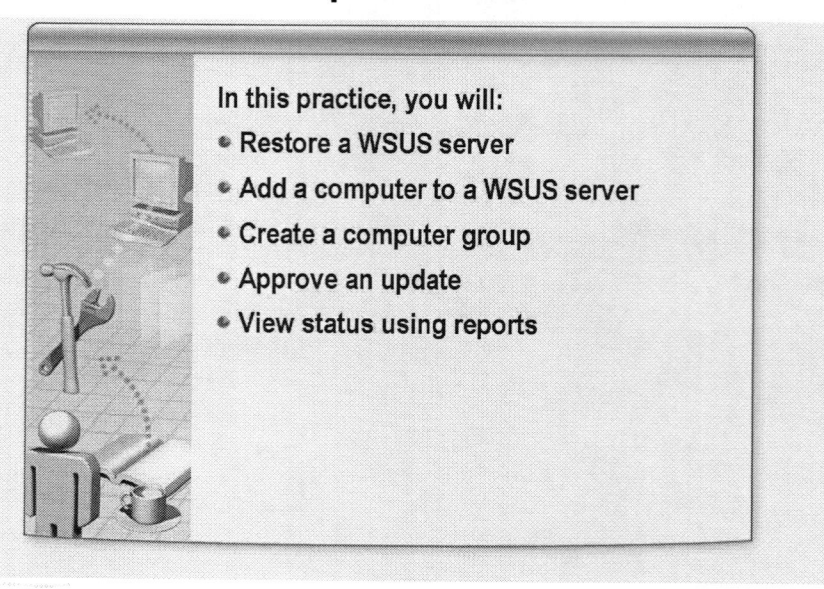

Objective

In this practice, you will:

- Restore a WSUS server.
- Add a computer to a WSUS server.
- Create a computer group.
- Approve an update.
- View status using reports.

Instructions

Ensure that the DEN-DC1 and DEN-CL1 virtual machines are running.

Practice

▶ **Restore a WSUS server**

1. If necessary, log on to DEN-DC1 as **Administrator** with a password of **Pa$$w0rd**.
2. Click **Start**, click **Run**, type **net stop mssql$wsus**, and then click **OK**.
3. Click **Start**, point to **All Programs**, point to **Accessories**, point to **System Tools**, and then click **Backup**.
4. Click **Advanced Mode** and click the **Restore and Manage Media** tab.
5. Click the **Tools** menu and then click **Options**.
6. Select **Always replace the file on my computer**. Click **OK**.
7. Right-click **File** and click **Catalog file**.
8. In the **Open** box, type **D:\2275\Practices\Mod08\WSUSBackup.bkf**, and then click **OK**.
9. Expand **File**, expand **WSUSBackup.bkf** and then select the check box next to **D: Allfiles**.

10. Click **Start Restore** and then click **OK**. This backup restores the updates folder that contains installation files for updates and the SQL database to the D: drive.
11. Click **Close** and close **Backup**.
12. Click **Start**, click **Run**, type **net start mssql$wsus**, and then click **OK**. Wait a couple of minutes before proceeding to the next step.

▶ **Add a computer to a WSUS server**

1. Log on to DEN-CL1 as **Administrator** with a password of **Pa$$w0rd**.
2. Click **Start**, click **Run**, type **cmd**, and then click **OK**.
3. Type **gpupdate /force** and press ENTER. This ensures that the latest Group Policy settings are applied to this computer.
4. Type **wuauclt.exe /detectnow** and press ENTER. This forces the Automatic Updates client to communicate with the WSUS server to register the computer.
5. Close the command prompt.

▶ **Create a computer group**

1. On DEN-DC1, click **Start**, point to **All Programs**, and click **Internet Explorer**.
2. In the **Address** Bar, type **http://DEN-DC1/WSUSadmin** and press ENTER.
3. In the **User name** box, type **administrator** and, in the **Password** box, type **Pa$$w0rd**, and then click **OK**.
4. Click **Computers**. Notice that DEN-CL1 is among the computers listed.
5. Click **Create a computer group**.
6. In the **Group name** box, type **HO-Clients**, and then click **OK**.
7. Click **den-cl1** and then click **Move the selected computer**.
8. In the **Computer group** box, click **HO-Clients**, and then click **OK**.
9. In the **Groups** area, click **HO-Clients**. Notice that DEN-CL1 is now in this computer group.

▶ **Approve an update**

1. On DEN-DC1, click **Updates**.
2. Scroll down and select **Security Update for Windows XP (KB885835)** and then click **OK** to the warning.
3. Click **Change approval**.
4. In the **Approval** box, select **Install**, and then click **OK**.
5. On DEN-CL1, click **Start**, click **Run**, type **wuauclt.exe /detectnow** and click **OK**. This forces DEN-CL1 to contact the WSUS server.

▶ **View status using reports**

1. On DEN-DC1, click **Reports**.
2. Click **Settings Summary**.
3. Scroll down and read the settings for your WSUS server.
4. Click **Reports**.
5. Click **Status of Updates**.
6. In the **Computer group** box, select **All Computers**.
7. Select the **Needed** and **Unknown** check boxes and then click **Apply**. This shows how many computers need updates and how many computers are unknown; meaning that they have not yet reported their update status.
8. Click **Reports**.
9. Click **Status of Computers**.
10. In the **Computer group** box, select **All Computers**.
11. Select the **Needed** and **Unknown** check boxes and click **Apply**.
12. Expand **den-cl1.contoso.msft** to see the status of each update for DEN-CL1.

Note You may have to wait up to 15 minutes for DEN-CL1 to report its status. Once it has reported its status, you will see the number of updates needed for the client.

13. Close Internet Explorer.

▶ **To prepare for the lab**

- Start the DEN-SRV1 virtual machine.

Lab: Maintaining Software by Using Windows Server Update Services

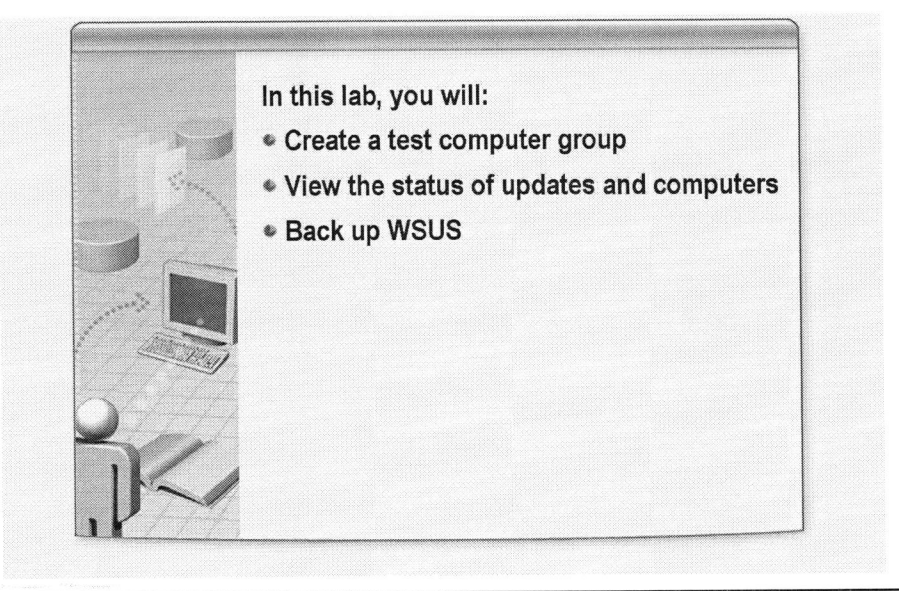

![In this lab, you will: Create a test computer group; View the status of updates and computers; Back up WSUS]

Objectives

After completing this lab, you will be able to:

- Create a test computer group.
- View status of updates and computers.
- Back up WSUS.

Instructions

Ensure that the DEN-DC1, DEN-CL1 and DEN-SRV1 virtual machines are running.

Estimated time to complete this lab: 25 minutes

Exercise 1
Create a Test Computer Group

In this exercise, you will create a test computer group and place DEN-SRV1 in it.

Tasks	Specific instructions
1. Add DEN-SRV1 as a computer in WSUS.	a. Log on DEN-SRV1 as **Administrator**. b. Run **GPupdate /force**. c. Run **wuauclt.exe /detectnow**.
2. Open the WSUS Administration Web site.	a. If necessary, log on to DEN-DC1 as **Administrator**. b. Open the WSUS Administration Web site.
3. Create a Test computer group.	a. Create a computer group named **Test**. b. Add DEN-SRV1 to the Test computer group.
4. Approve an update for the Test group.	▪ Approve the most current update for **Microsoft Windows Installer 3.1** for the **Test** group. Hint: You will need to change the view to all updates which have been synchronized at any time.

Exercise 2
View the Status of Updates and Computers

In this exercise, you will view the status of updates and computers.

Tasks	Specific instructions
1. View update status.	a. If necessary, open the WSUS Administration Web site. b. Click **Reports**. c. View the Status of Updates that are needed or unknown for the computer group **Test**.
2. View computer status.	a. Click **Reports**. b. View the Unknown status of Computers for the computer group Test. c. Notice that DEN-SRV1 reports unknown updates.

Exercise 3
Back up WSUS

In this exercise, you will back up the WSUS database and updates.

Tasks	Specific instructions
1. Stop the database service.	▪ On DEN-DC1, stop the MSSQL$WSUS service.
2. Back up the updates and database.	▪ Use **Backup** in System Tools to: • Back up D:\WSUS\MSSQL$WSUS\Data. • Back up D:\WSUS\WsusContent. • Back up to file D:\WSUS.bkf.
3. Start the database service.	▪ Start the MSSQL$WSUS service.
4. Complete the lab exercise.	a. Close all programs and shut down all computers. Do not save changes. b. To prepare for the next module, start the DEN-DC1 virtual computer.

Module 9: Securing Windows Server 2003

Contents

Overview	1
Lesson: Introduction to Securing Servers	2
Lesson: Implementing Core Server Security	10
Lesson: Hardening Servers	25
Lesson: Microsoft Baseline Security Analyzer	38
Lab: Securing Windows Server 2003	49
Course Evaluation	53

Information in this document, including URL and other Internet Web site references, is subject to change without notice. Unless otherwise noted, the example companies, organizations, products, domain names, e-mail addresses, logos, people, places, and events depicted herein are fictitious, and no association with any real company, organization, product, domain name, e-mail address, logo, person, place or event is intended or should be inferred. Complying with all applicable copyright laws is the responsibility of the user. Without limiting the rights under copyright, no part of this document may be reproduced, stored in or introduced into a retrieval system, or transmitted in any form or by any means (electronic, mechanical, photocopying, recording, or otherwise), or for any purpose, without the express written permission of Microsoft Corporation.

The names of manufacturers, products, or URLs are provided for informational purposes only and Microsoft makes no representations and warranties, either expressed, implied, or statutory, regarding these manufacturers or the use of the products with any Microsoft technologies. The inclusion of a manufacturer or product does not imply endorsement of Microsoft of the manufacturer or product. Links are provided to third party sites. Such sites are not under the control of Microsoft and Microsoft is not responsible for the contents of any linked site or any link contained in a linked site, or any changes or updates to such sites. Microsoft is not responsible for webcasting or any other form of transmission received from any linked site. Microsoft is providing these links to you only as a convenience, and the inclusion of any link does not imply endorsement of Microsoft of the site or the products contained therein.

Microsoft may have patents, patent applications, trademarks, copyrights, or other intellectual property rights covering subject matter in this document. Except as expressly provided in any written license agreement from Microsoft, the furnishing of this document does not give you any license to these patents, trademarks, copyrights, or other intellectual property.

© 2005 Microsoft Corporation. All rights reserved.

Microsoft, Active Directory, ActiveX, Authenticode, BizTalk, IntelliMirror, MSDN, PowerPoint, Windows, Windows Media, Windows NT, and Windows Server are either registered trademarks or trademarks of Microsoft Corporation in the United States and/or other countries.

All other trademarks are property of their respective owners.

Overview

- **Introduction to Securing Servers**
- **Implementing Core Server Security**
- **Hardening Servers**
- **Microsoft Baseline Security Analyzer**

Introduction

Security is no longer the responsibility of a specific person in the Information Technology (IT) department. Every administrator must understand how to secure servers to prevent them and their data from harm. This module introduces you to securing Microsoft® Windows Server™ 2003.

Objectives

After completing this module, you will be able to:

- Describe how servers are secured.
- Explain core server security.
- Harden servers in various roles.
- Use Microsoft Baseline Security Analyzer.

Lesson: Introduction to Securing Servers

- Security Challenges for Small and Medium-Sized Businesses
- Fundamental Security Trade-Offs
- What Is the Defense-in-Depth Model?
- Microsoft Windows Server Security Guidance

Introduction

Organizations now know that effective security is essential to their business operations. The big question is how to implement security. This lesson describes the challenges to implementing security and the trade-offs that must be made.

This lesson also describes the defense in depth model for security analysis and provides some sources of security information from Microsoft.

Lesson objectives

After completing this lesson, you will be able to:

- Describe security challenges for small and medium-sized businesses.
- List fundamental security trade-offs.
- Explain the defense-in-depth model.
- List sources of Microsoft security information.

Security Challenges for Small and Medium-Sized Businesses

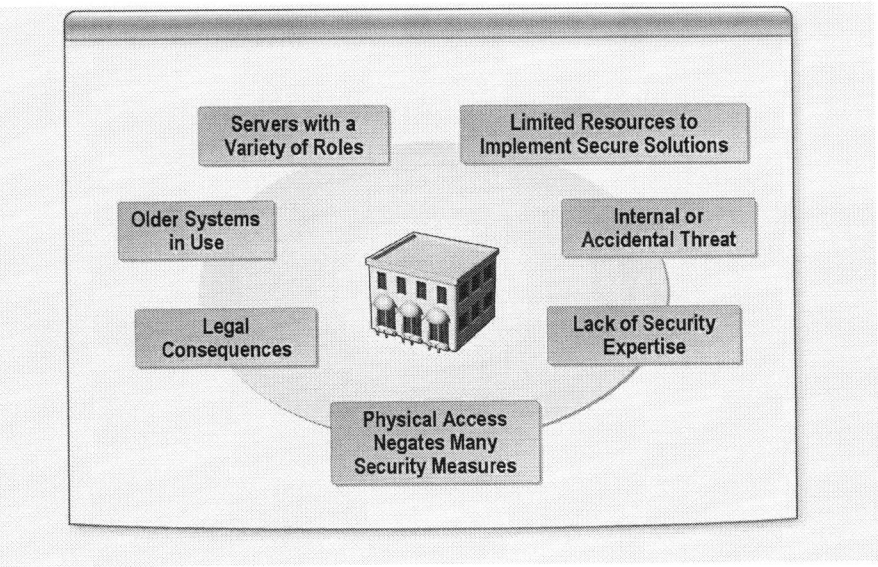

Introduction

The security threats that are encountered by small and medium-sized businesses are unique from the security threats encountered by larger businesses. Smaller organizations typically have fewer formal procedures and fewer resources devoted to security.

Security challenges

Security challenges that are encountered by small and medium-sized businesses include:

- *Servers that have a variety of roles.* In businesses with limited resources, servers can have multiple roles. You can easily apply multiple security templates to a server, but the templates can conflict. When a server performs multiple roles, it is more difficult to protect that server. In addition, a server performing multiple roles presents a larger attack surface. If a security breach occurs, all the roles that are performed by that server can be compromised.

  For example, many small businesses have deployed Microsoft Windows Small Business Server 2003, which operates as a domain controller, Exchange server, file server, database server, remote-access server, and possibly a firewall. Servers that provide a variety of services should be isolated from the Internet, and all unnecessary services and applications disabled or uninstalled.

- *Limited resources to implement secure solutions.* If a business has limited resources, it might not be able to provide components for a secure solution. Implementing multiple firewalls is an example of an expensive solution that might not be financially feasible.

- *Internal or accidental threat.* Internal compromise of systems, either malicious or accidental, accounts for a high percentage of attacks on small business and enterprise networks worldwide. Attackers usually find their attacks easier to perform if they have internal access to the network (either personal access or access by means of an unsuspecting or compromised accomplice).

- *Lack of security expertise.* Smaller IT departments may lack personnel that have appropriate security expertise. Not having the appropriate expertise can lead to overlooked security issues. In this situation, using standard security templates can be beneficial.

- *Physical access negates many security measures.* Physical access to a system can allow an attacker to execute utilities, install malicious programs, change configurations, remove components, and cause physical damage. Always lock servers in a secure room and require visible identification of anyone authorized to be in the server room.

- *Legal consequences.* Security breaches can have legal consequences. Depending on the state or country that has jurisdiction over the organization, a business may face legal liability resulting from a breach of its server security. Examples of such legislation include the Sarbanes-Oxley Act of 2002, which requires full compliance by all public firms in the United States by the second half of 2005, the Health Insurance Portability and Accountability Act of 1996 (HIPAA), the Gramm-Leach-Bliley Act (GLBA), California Senate Bill (SB) 1386, and Directive 95/46/EC of the European Parliament and of the Council of 24 October 1995.

- *Using older systems.* Older systems might not support security configurations without an upgrade. If older systems are not upgraded, the risk of a security breach is greater than it is for newer systems.

Security facts

Security is essential for small organizations and large organizations. Consider the following:

- Many computer users do not properly update their antivirus software definitions.

- Spyware infects many computers, which can cause extremely slow performance, excessive pop-up ads, hijacked home pages, and loss of personal information including account passwords. Often users are unaware that their computers are infected.

- Some organizations do not have an effective strategy for applying security updates. Other organizations do not apply updates due to concerns that they will break applications.

Note For more information about the unique security issues that are encountered by small businesses, see the "Security Guide for Small Business" document under **Additional Reading** on the Student Materials compact disk.

Fundamental Security Trade-Offs

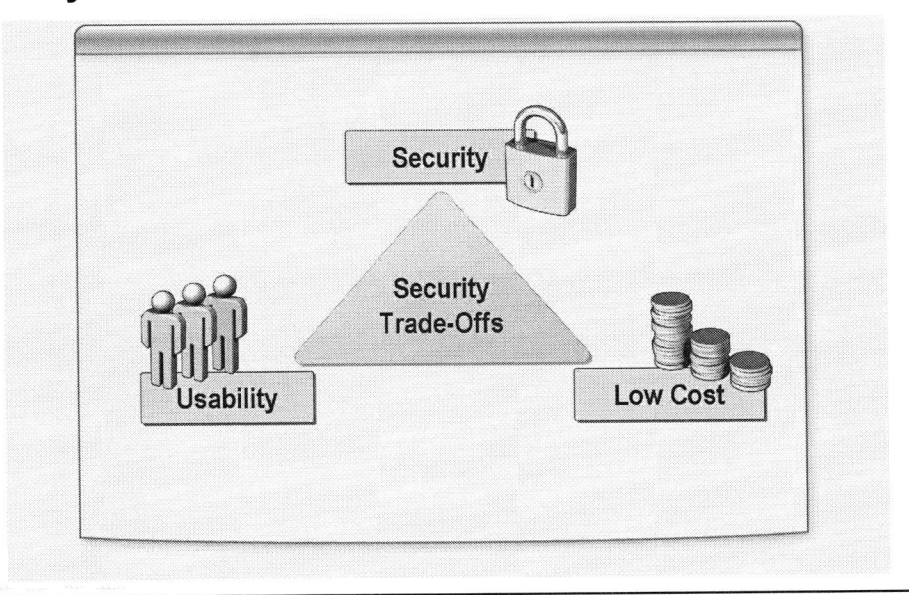

Introduction

When you plan your network security strategy, consider the fundamental security trade-offs that are involved.

Goals

The goals for a computer system or network vary depending on your role in the system. Consider the goals for security administration and network administration:

- The goal of security administration is to safeguard network resources by restricting access to them.
- The goal of network administration is to ensure that users can access all the network applications and programs that they need to do their jobs.

Security vs. usability

The first fundamental security trade-offs that you must consider are security versus usability:

- When you install an application on any operating system, you enable additional functionality, which may make the system less secure because it increases the attack surface of the system. The attack surface of a system is the available opportunities to compromise the system.
- You can make technology more secure but, by doing so, you may make the technology less usable.
- The most secure system is one that is disconnected and locked in a safe. Such a system is secure, but not usable.

Security vs. low cost

The next trade-off to consider is low cost versus security:

- In an ideal world, where resources are unlimited, most companies would choose to make their networks as secure and usable as possible. In the real world, however, cost is often a significant factor that affects the amount of security and usability that can be achieved.

- You may be familiar with the principle of "good, fast, and cheap—you get to choose any two." The principle of fundamental security trade-offs is similar: "secure, usable, and cheap—you get to choose any two." It is possible to have both security and usability, but there is a cost in terms of money, time, and personnel.

Note For more information about fundamental security trade-offs, see the "Security Management—The Fundamental Tradeoffs" article on the Microsoft TechNet Web site.

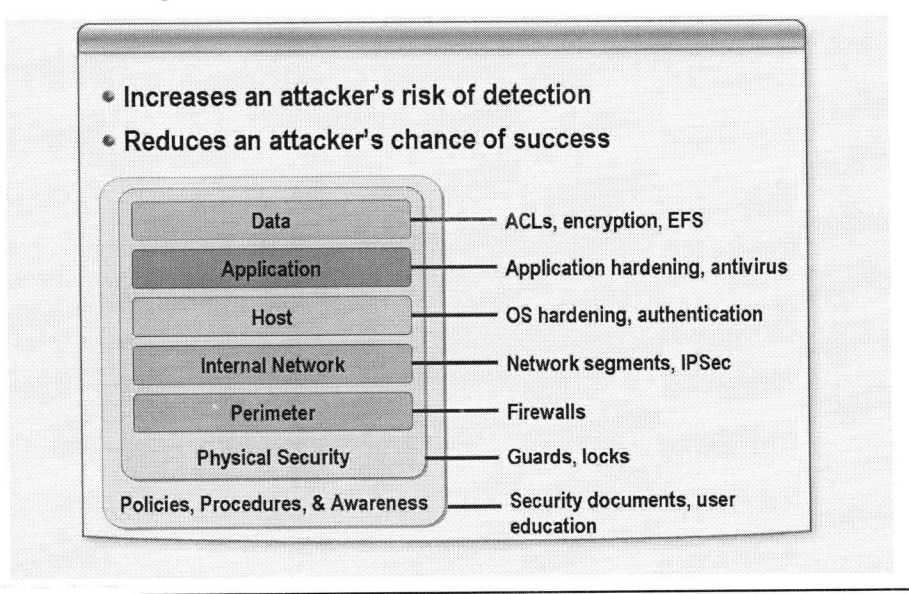

What Is the Defense-in-Depth Model?

- Increases an attacker's risk of detection
- Reduces an attacker's chance of success

Data	ACLs, encryption, EFS
Application	Application hardening, antivirus
Host	OS hardening, authentication
Internal Network	Network segments, IPSec
Perimeter	Firewalls
Physical Security	Guards, locks
Policies, Procedures, & Awareness	Security documents, user education

Introduction

A security strategy for an organization is most effective when data is protected by more than one layer of security. A defense-in-depth security model uses multiple layers of defense so that, if one layer is compromised, it does not necessarily mean that the attacker will be able to access all the resources on your network. A defense-in-depth model increases an attacker's risk of detection and reduces an attacker's chance of success.

Base layers

The defense-in-depth model consists of a series of interconnected layers. The base layers of the defense-in-depth model are:

- *Policies, procedures, and awareness layer.* This foundational layer affects every other defense-in-depth layer. Components in this layer include security policies, security procedures, and security education programs for users.

- *Physical security layer.* This layer wraps around the remaining five core layers. Components in this layer include security guards, locks, and tracking devices.

Core layers

There are many tools, technologies, and best practices you can use to protect each of the five core layers. Examples include:

- *Perimeter layer.* Hardware or software firewalls, or both, and virtual private networks that use quarantine procedures.

- *Internal network layer.* Network segmentation, Internet Protocol security (IPSec), and network intrusion-detection systems (NIDS).

- *Host layer*. Server and client operating system hardening practices, strong authentication methods, update management tools, and host-based intrusion-detection systems (HIDS).
- *Application layer*. Application hardening practices and antivirus and antispyware software.
- *Data layer*. Access control lists (ACLs), encryption, and the Encrypting File System (EFS).

This module focuses on securing your Windows-based servers. Security methods and practices discussed in this module relate primarily to the application, host, and internal-network layers.

Important Remember that server security is only *part* of the overall security strategy of your organization.

Microsoft Windows Server Security Guidance

> - Threats and Countermeasures Guide
> - Windows Server 2003 Security Guide
> - Default Access Control Settings in Windows Server 2003
> - Security Innovations in Windows Server 2003
> - Technical Overview of Windows Server 2003 Security Services

Introduction

One of the best sources of information on securing servers running Windows is Microsoft. Microsoft provides several documents that contain prescriptive guidance on how to secure computers running Windows Server 2003.

Documents

Security documents available from Microsoft include:

- *Threats and Countermeasures Guide.* Provides a reference to many of the security settings that are available in the current versions of the Microsoft Windows operating systems.

- *Windows Server 2003 Security Guide.* Focuses on providing a set of easy to understand guidance, tools, and templates to help secure Windows Server 2003 in many environments. This guide provides background information about risks, methods to mitigate those risks, and information about the impact of those methods beyond mitigating the risk.

- *Default Access Control Settings in Windows Server 2003.* Describes the default security settings for components of the Microsoft Windows Server 2003 operating system. These components include the registry, file system, user rights, and group membership. This white paper also details the implications of these settings for developers and system administrators, and provides answers to frequently asked questions.

- *Security Innovations in Windows Server 2003.* Describes the security feature enhancements in Windows Server 2003 and outlines how they facilitate business scenarios such as building a secure Web application platform, providing secure mobile access, and streamlining identity management across the enterprise.

- *Technical Overview of Windows Server 2003 Security Services.* Discusses the tools and processes that deliver important security benefits to organizations deploying Windows.

Lesson: Implementing Core Server Security

- Core Server Security Practices
- Recommendations for Hardening Servers
- Windows Server 2003 SP1 Security Enhancements
- What Is Windows Firewall?
- Post-Setup Security Updates
- What Is the Security Configuration Wizard?
- Practice: Implementing Core Server Security

Introduction

This topic explores the components of core server security. The security recommendations in this section apply to *all* servers in a Windows 2000– or Windows Server 2003–based network environment. In addition, this section also provides an overview of the security enhancements available in Windows Server 2003 Service Pack 1 (SP1).

Lesson objectives

After completing this lesson, you will be able to:

- Describe core server security practices.
- List recommendations for hardening servers.
- Explain Windows Server 2003 SP1 technologies enhancements.
- Explain what Windows Firewall is and describe its features.
- Describe post-setup security updates.
- Explain what the Security Configuration Wizard is.
- Implement core server security.

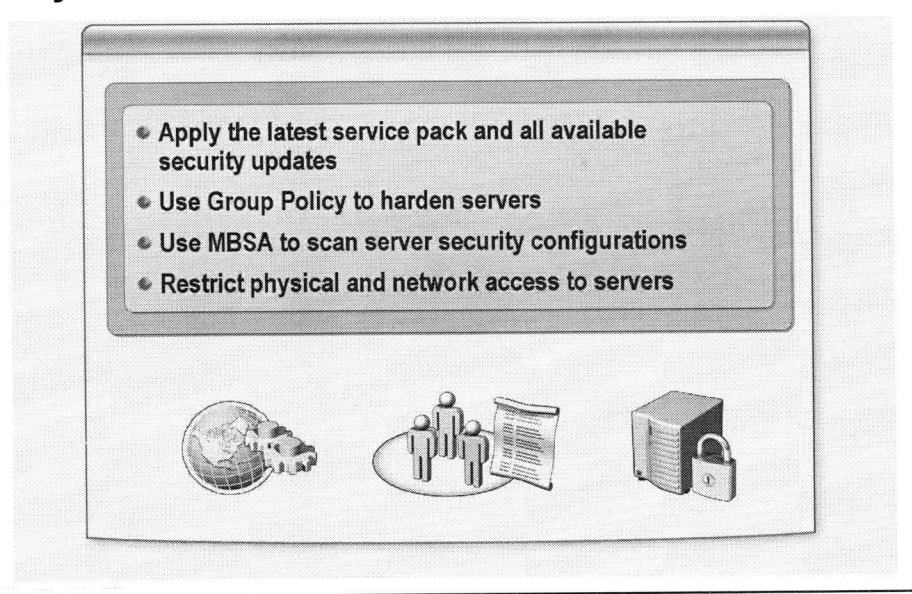

Core Server Security Practices

> - Apply the latest service pack and all available security updates
> - Use Group Policy to harden servers
> - Use MBSA to scan server security configurations
> - Restrict physical and network access to servers

Introduction

There are several core server security practices. The following is not an exhaustive list; however, it contains some of the more common fundamental server security practices. You may already be using many, if not most, of these core security practices on your network servers.

Important The security practices and measures recommended in this lesson apply to *all* servers in a Windows 2000– or Windows Server 2003–based network environment, including member servers, domain controllers, servers that perform specific roles, and stand-alone servers.

Apply updates and service packs

Applying the latest service pack and available security updates is important because:

- Service packs increase operating system security and stability.
- Most attacks against servers exploit vulnerabilities that have been previously reported and fixed in a service pack or in an operating system security update.
- Computers that do not have the latest service pack and security updates installed are vulnerable.

Use Group Policy

Use Group Policy to harden servers. By using Group Policy, you can:

- Disable services that are not required. Any service or application is a potential point of attack. Therefore, disable or remove all unneeded services to reduce the attack surface.
- Implement secure password policies. You can strengthen the password and account lockout policy settings for a domain controller, member server, or stand-alone server by applying the settings in an appropriate security template.

- Disable LAN Manager and NTLMv1 authentication and storage of LAN Manager hashes. LAN Manager and NTLMv1 are authentication methods required by pre-Windows 2000 clients. Implementing this practice may prevent access by pre-Windows 2000 clients, so you must ensure that you can configure these settings without disabling the functionality that you require.

Use MBSA

Use Microsoft Baseline Security Analyzer (MSBA) to scan server security configurations. MSBA can perform local or remote scans of computers running Windows to identify missing security updates and potential configuration issues. MBSA displays the results of the scan in a Web-based report.

Restrict server access

Use the following guidelines to restrict physical and network access to servers:

- Store servers in a locked room. Use card-key locks or cipher locks on the entrance to the locked room.
- Prevent domain controllers from starting to an alternate operating system by disabling floppy drives, universal serial bus (USB) ports, and CD-ROM drives.
- Allow only trusted personnel to have access to servers. Establish security practices for service administrators and data administrators to ensure that only personnel who require access to servers for their job have access.
- Assign only the permissions and user rights that are necessary to each user in your organization.

Build on core practices

Consider the previous core server security practices a baseline to which you can add advanced server security practices. Examples of advanced server security practices include applying customized security templates to servers and manually configuring IPSec port filtering based on server roles.

Note For more information about core server security practices, see the "Windows Server 2003 Security Guide" on the Microsoft TechNet Web site.

Recommendations for Hardening Servers

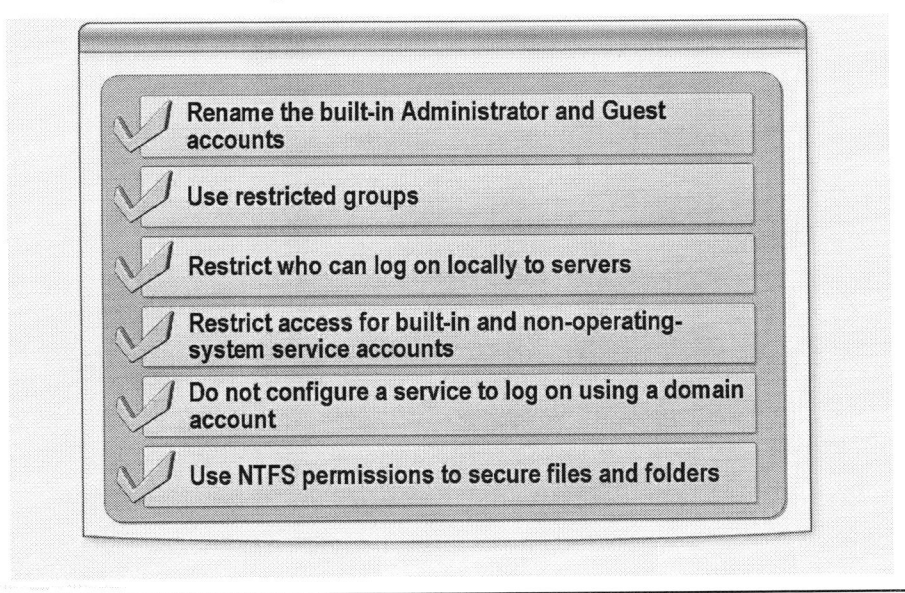

- Rename the built-in Administrator and Guest accounts
- Use restricted groups
- Restrict who can log on locally to servers
- Restrict access for built-in and non-operating-system service accounts
- Do not configure a service to log on using a domain account
- Use NTFS permissions to secure files and folders

Introduction

Consider implementing the following recommendations for hardening all servers on your Windows Server 2003–based network:

Built-in accounts

Recommendations for managing built-in accounts include:

- Renaming the built-in Administrator and Guest accounts, and changing their descriptions. Renaming these accounts to use unique names can make it easier to identify attempted attacks against these accounts. In almost all cases, the Guest account should be disabled.

- Assigning long and complex passwords or passphrases to the built-in Administrator and Guest accounts.

- Using scripts or third-party utilities to periodically verify local passwords on all workstations and servers in the enterprise.

- Using different passwords for the built-in Administrator and Guest accounts on each server so that a compromise of one of these accounts on one server does not enable an attacker to compromise additional servers.

Restricted groups

Use restricted groups to limit the memberships of administrative groups. By using the Restricted Groups option in Active Directory® directory service, you can ensure that administrative groups contain only authorized users.

Log on locally

Restrict the users who can log on locally onto the servers. Use Group Policy to configure user rights so that only authorized administrators can log on locally onto the servers.

Restrict access	Restrict access to the system for built-in and service accounts other than the system service accounts. Configure user rights assignments as follows: - Deny access to this computer from the network for the Built-In Administrator, Support_388945a0 (the account that is used for remote assistance), Guest accounts, and all service accounts other than the system service accounts. - Deny logon as a batch job for the Support_388945a0 and Guest accounts. - Deny logon using Terminal Services for the Built-In Administrator, Support_388945a0, Guest accounts, and service accounts other than the system service accounts.
Services	Do not configure a service to log on by using a domain account. Whenever possible, use a local account for each service. In addition, do not use the same user account name and password for a service on multiple servers.
Use NTFS	Use NTFS permissions to secure files and folders. Convert any FAT or FAT32 volumes to NTFS, and then apply the appropriate permissions to the files and folders on those volumes.

Windows Server 2003 SP1 Security Enhancements

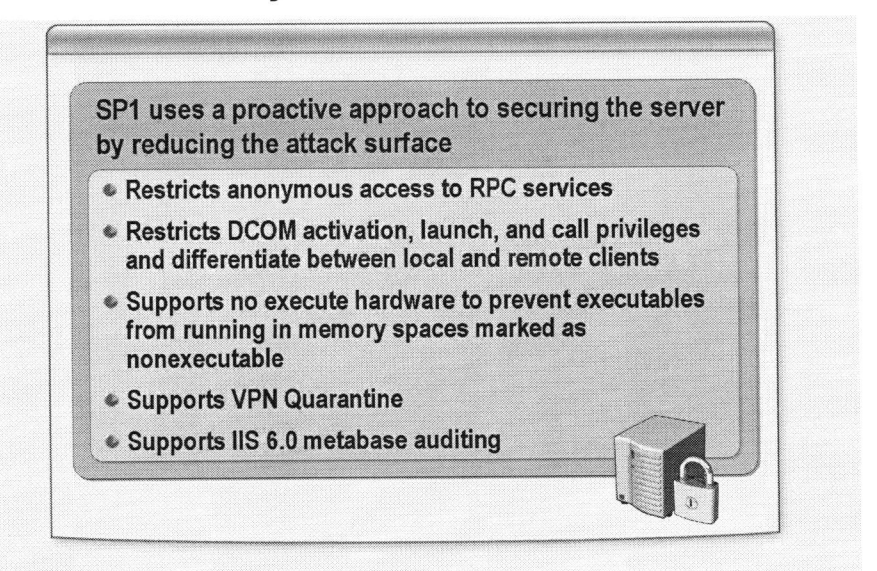

> **SP1 uses a proactive approach to securing the server by reducing the attack surface**
> - Restricts anonymous access to RPC services
> - Restricts DCOM activation, launch, and call privileges and differentiate between local and remote clients
> - Supports no execute hardware to prevent executables from running in memory spaces marked as nonexecutable
> - Supports VPN Quarantine
> - Supports IIS 6.0 metabase auditing

Introduction

The primary objective of Windows Server 2003 SP1 is to increase server security. Instead of focusing on update management to respond to threats after they have been discovered, SP1 takes a more proactive approach of reducing the attack surface on the server.

RPC configuration

Microsoft Windows operating systems rely on remote procedure call (RPC) services to run. Many of these RPC services are accessible to anonymous network users. Service Pack 1 makes RPC interfaces more secure by enabling the **RestrictRemoteClients** and the **EnableAuthEpResolution** registry keys.

The **RestrictRemoteClients** registry key enables you to modify how the computer will accept connections on all RPC interfaces to eliminate remote anonymous access to RPC interfaces on the system. If you restrict access to the RPC services to only authenticated users, then you must configure the **EnableAuthEpResolution** registry key on each client so that it will use NTLM authentication when connecting to the RPC Endpoint Mapper.

> **Important** You can configure both the **RestrictRemoteClients** and the **EnableAuthEpResolution** registry entries by using Group Policy if your servers and clients are members of an Active Directory domain.

> **Note** RPC clients that use the named pipe protocol sequence (**ncacn_np**) are exempt from all restrictions discussed in this section. The named pipe protocol sequence cannot be restricted due to several significant backward-compatibility issues.

DCOM configuration

With DCOM, an anonymous remote client can ask a DCOM server to perform a task that normally requires authentication. Some Component Object Model (COM) servers allow unauthenticated remote access and can be called by anyone, including unauthenticated users. Service Pack 1 addresses this issue by using:

- New computerwide restrictions that apply to DCOM activation, launch, and call privileges that differentiate between local and remote clients. By default, everyone is granted local launch, local activation, and local call permissions, which should enable all local scenarios to continue to work without change. In addition, all authenticated users are granted remote call permissions by default, which allow most common server applications to function properly if the client is not anonymous. The default configuration grants only administrators remote activation and launch permissions.

- More specific COM permissions that allow individual COM servers to restrict the rights that are available to users. There are four new launch permission levels for COM servers: local launch, remote launch, local activate, and remote activate. There are two new access permission levels for COM servers: local calls and remote calls. The default permission levels will work properly for almost all situations.

Note For more information about DCOM configuration enhancements, see Changes to Functionality in Microsoft Windows Server 2003 Service Pack 1 on the Microsoft Web site.

No-execute support

For both 32-bit and 64-bit systems, support for "no execute" hardware eliminates one of the broadest and most exploited methods of information attack. Service Pack 1 allows Windows Server 2003 to use functionality built in to computing hardware from such companies as Intel and Advanced Micro Devices to prevent malicious code from launching attacks that originate from areas of computer memory that should have no code running in it.

VPN quarantine

VPN quarantine automatically provides the means for limiting network access for computers on virtual private networks (VPNs) that do have the most current security updates.

IIS 6.0 metabase auditing

The metabase is the XML-based, hierarchical store of configuration information for Internet Information Services (IIS) 6.0. IIS 6.0 metabase auditing allows network administrators to see which user accessed the metabase in case it becomes corrupted.

What Is Windows Firewall?

- Enabled by default in new installs
- Audit logging to track firewall activity
- Boot-time security
- Global configuration
- Port restrictions based on the client network
- On with no exceptions
- Exceptions list
- Group Policy support

Definition

Windows Firewall is a software-based firewall for Windows XP and Windows Server 2003. Windows Firewall provides protection for computers that are connected to a network by preventing unsolicited inbound connections through Transmission Control Protocol/Internet Protocol (TCP/IP) version 4 (IPv4) and TCP/IP version 6 (IPv6).

Windows Firewall features

Some of the changes to Windows Firewall include:

- *Enabled by default for new installations of Windows Server 2003 SP1.* Provides more network protection by default for Windows Server 2003. Windows Firewall blocks all outside sources from connecting to the computer with the exception of those that are identified on the exception list.

- *Audit logging.* Enables customers to track changes that are made to Windows Firewall settings and to see which applications and services requested a port to be opened. After you enable audit logging, audit events are logged in the security event log. Auditing the activity of Windows Firewall is part of a defense-in-depth strategy that allows customers to react quickly to attacks on their systems.

- *Boot-time security.* In earlier versions of Windows, there was a period of time between when the computer would accept network connections and when Internet Connection Firewall (ICF) started to provide protection on the network. During this brief period of time, the computer was on the network and unprotected by Internet Connection Firewall. With boot-time security, only such basic networking functions as Domain Name System (DNS), Dynamic Host Configuration Protocol (DHCP), and communication with a domain controller are allowed. Other networking functions are disabled until the firewall service starts.

- *Global configuration.* In earlier versions of Windows, Internet Connection Firewall was configured on a per-interface basis. This meant that each network connection had its own firewall policy, making it difficult to synchronize policy between connections. With global configuration, whenever a configuration change occurs, the change applies to all network connections. When you create new connections, the configuration is applied to them also. The global policy makes it easier for users to manage their firewall policy across all network connections. It also makes it easier to configure network applications.

- *Port restrictions based on the client network.* Traditionally, when a service listens on a port it is open to incoming traffic from any network location, such as a local network or the Internet. With Windows Firewall, you can configure the port to receive only network traffic with a source address from the local subnet, from specific IP addresses or from specific subnets, or from both.

- *On with no exceptions operational mode.* You can configure Windows Firewall to allow unsolicited incoming traffic to provide server services. However, if you discover a security issue in one or more of the services or applications that are running on the computer, you can switch into a client-only mode, which is called "On with no exceptions." Switching into this client-only mode configures Windows Firewall to prevent unsolicited inbound traffic without having to reconfigure the firewall. In this mode, all static ports are closed and any existing connections are dropped. Viruses, worms, and attackers look for services to exploit. When in this operational mode, Windows Firewall helps to prevent such types of attacks from succeeding.

- *Windows Firewall exceptions list.* An application that needs to accept connections from the network can be added to the Windows Firewall exceptions list. Only administrators can add an application to the exceptions list. When an application is on the Windows Firewall exceptions list, only the necessary ports are opened, and they are opened only for the duration that the application is accepting connections on those ports.

- *Group Policy Support.* With Windows Server 2003 SP1, you can configure every Windows Firewall configuration option by using Group Policy. Examples of the new configuration options available include:

    - Define program exceptions
    - Allow local program exceptions
    - Allow Internet Control Message Protocol (ICMP) exceptions
    - Prohibit notifications
    - Allow file and printer sharing exception
    - Allow logging
    - You can also use Security Configuration Wizard to configure the Windows Firewall settings

Post-Setup Security Updates

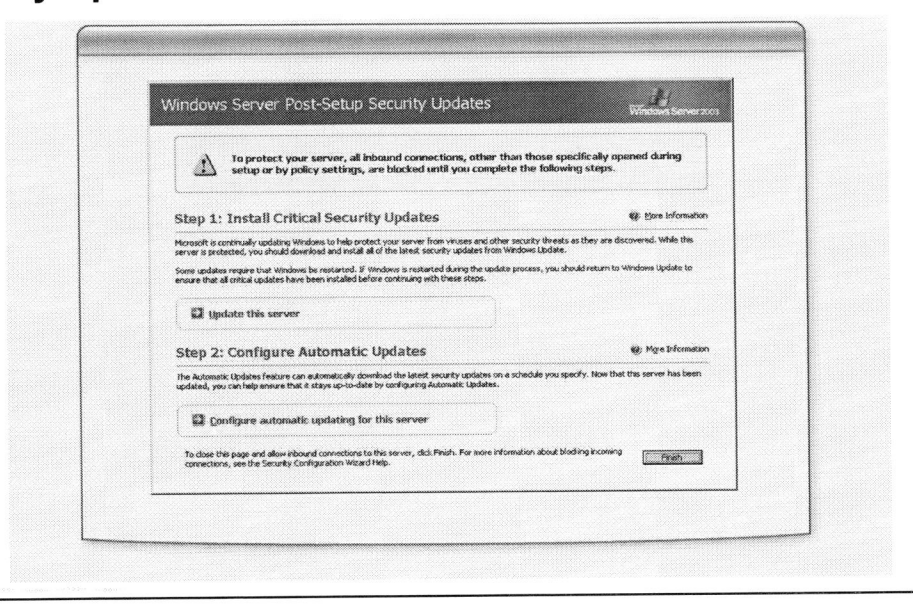

Introduction

Post-Setup Security Updates (PSSU) is designed to protect the server from risk of infection between the time the server is first started and the application of the most recent security updates from Windows Update.

PSSU

To protect the server, Windows Firewall is enabled during a new installation of any version of Windows Server 2003 Service Pack 1. If Windows Firewall is enabled and the administrator did not explicitly enable it by using an unattended-setup script or Group Policy, PSSU opens the first time an administrator logs on. Inbound connections to the server are blocked until the administrator has clicked the **Finish** button on the **PSSU** dialog box; this allows the administrator to download and install updates securely from Windows Update. If the administrator set exceptions to the firewall by using Group Policy or by enabling Remote Desktop during installation, inbound connections assigned to these exceptions remain open.

PSSU:

- Is not available from the **Start** menu.
- Does not appear when the server is being upgraded from the following operating systems:
  - Windows 2000 to Windows Server 2003 with Service Pack 1
  - Windows Server 2003 to Windows Server 2003 with Service Pack 1
- Is displayed when the server is being upgraded from Microsoft Windows NT® 4.0 to Windows Server 2003 with Service Pack 1.
- Does not apply to installations of Windows Server 2003 that use either an unattended setup script or an application of a Group Policy that enables or disables Windows Firewall.

What Is the Security Configuration Wizard?

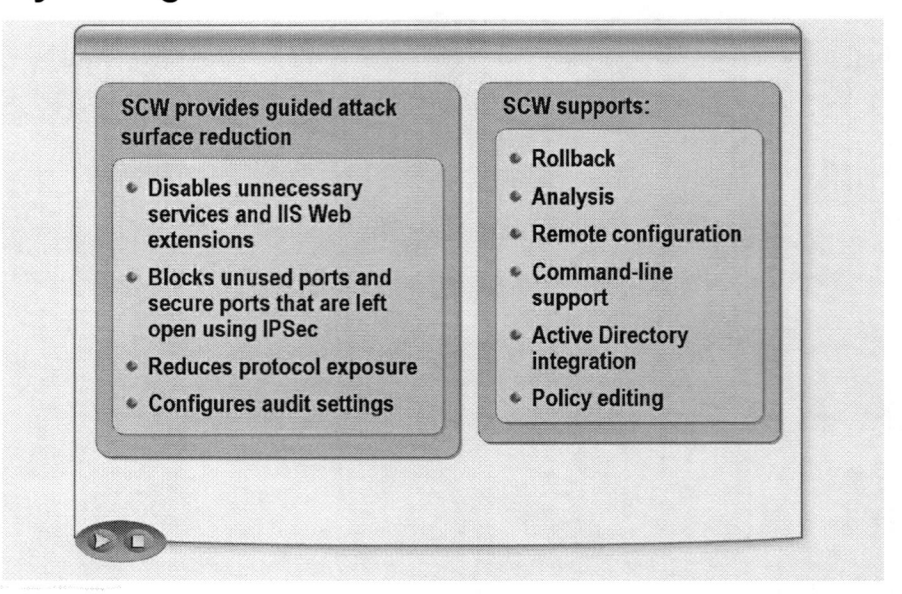

SCW provides guided attack surface reduction
- Disables unnecessary services and IIS Web extensions
- Blocks unused ports and secure ports that are left open using IPSec
- Reduces protocol exposure
- Configures audit settings

SCW supports:
- Rollback
- Analysis
- Remote configuration
- Command-line support
- Active Directory integration
- Policy editing

Definition

The Security Configuration Wizard (SCW) provides guided attack surface reduction for servers running Windows Server 2003 SP1. When you run the wizard, it asks a series of questions to determine the server role or roles, and then uses a roles-based metaphor that is driven by an extensible XML knowledge base that defines the services, ports, and other functional requirements for more than 50 different server roles. Any functionality that is not required by the roles that the server is performing will be disabled.

Reduce attack surface

To reduce attack surface, the wizard allows administrators to:

- Disable unnecessary services.
- Disable unnecessary IIS Web extensions.
- Block unused ports, including support for multihomed scenarios.
- Secure ports that are left open by using IPSec.
- Reduce protocol exposure for Lightweight Directory Access Protocol (LDAP), LAN Manager, and server message block (SMB).
- Configure audit settings with a high signal-to-noise ratio.
- Import Windows security templates for coverage of settings that are not configured by the wizard.

SCW features

In addition to role-based, guided security policy authoring, SCW also supports:

- *Rollback.* Returns the server to the state that it was in before the SCW security policy was applied, which can be useful when applied policies disrupt service expectations.
- *Analysis.* Verifies that servers are in compliance with expected policies.
- *Remote access.* Supports remote access for configuration and analysis operations.
- *Command-line support.* Enables remote configuration and analysis of groups of servers.
- *Active Directory integration.* Supports deploying SCW policies by using Group Policy.
- *Editing.* Enables modification of a security policy that is created by using SCW as necessary, such as when server roles are redefined.

Practice: Implementing Core Server Security

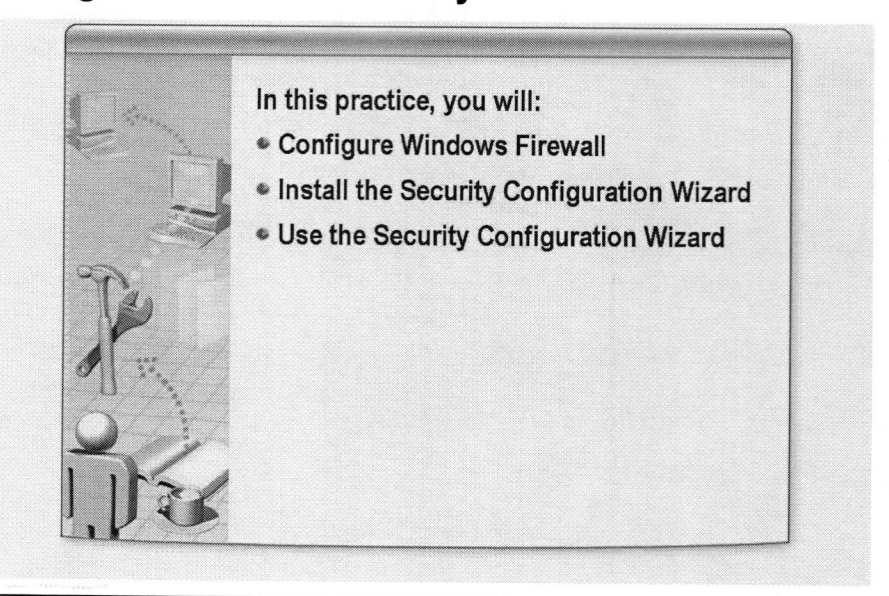

Objective

In this practice, you will:

- Configure Windows Firewall.
- Install the Security Configuration Wizard.
- Use the Security Configuration Wizard.

Instructions

Ensure that the DEN-DC1 virtual machine is running.

Practice

▶ **Configure Windows Firewall**

1. On DEN-DC1, log on as **Administrator** with a password of **Pa$$w0rd**.
2. Click **Start**, point to **Control Panel**, and click **Windows Firewall**.
3. Click **Yes**, to start the Windows Firewall/ICS service.
4. Click **On**.
5. On the **Exceptions** tab, select the **Remote Desktop** check box.
6. Click **Edit**. This shows the ports allowed by the Remote Desktop rule.
7. Click **Change scope**, click **My network (subnet) only** and then click **OK**. This limits communication with Remote Desktop to only computers on the same subnet as the server. Click **OK**.
8. On the **Advanced** tab, in the **Security Logging** area, click **Settings**.
9. Select the **Log dropped packets** check box, and then click **OK**.
10. Click **OK** to close Windows Firewall.

▶ Install the Security Configuration Wizard

1. On DEN-DC1, click **Start**, point to **Control Panel**, and then click **Add or Remove Programs**.
2. Click **Add/Remove Windows Components**.
3. Scroll down in the **Components** box, select the **Security Configuration Wizard** check box., and then click **Next**.
4. If prompted for the location of the Service Pack 1 CD-ROM, use **C:\win2k3\I386**.
5. Click **Finish**.
6. Close **Add or Remove Programs**.

▶ Use the Security Configuration Wizard

1. Click **Start**, point to **Administrative Tools**, and then click **Security Configuration Wizard**.
2. Click **Next** to begin the Security Configuration Wizard.
3. Ensure that **Create a new security policy** is selected, and then click **Next**.
4. Ensure that DEN-DC1 is the server to be used as a baseline for the policy, and then click **Next**.
5. Click **View Configuration Database**.
6. Scroll through and read the list of Server Roles, Client Features, Services, Ports, Applications, and Administration and Other Options.
7. Close **SCW Viewer** and then click **Next** twice.
8. Click **Next** again to accept the installed roles.
9. Click **Next** to accept the installed client features.
10. Click **Next** to accept the installed administration and other options.
11. Click **Next** to accept the additional services.
12. Ensure that **Do not change the startup mode of the service** is selected and then click **Next**.
13. Scroll through the list of changed services and note which ones are being disabled.
14. Click **Next**.
15. Click **Next** again to start configuring network security.
16. Scroll through the list of ports that will be opened and click **Next**.
17. Click **Next** again to accept the list of ports that will be opened.
18. Check the **Skip this section** check box, and then click **Next** to skip configuring registry settings.
19. Check the **Skip this section** check box, and then click **Next** to skip configuring audit policies.
20. Check the **Skip this section** check box, and then click **Next** to skip configuring Internet Information Services.
21. Click **Next** to begin saving the security policy.

22. In the **Security policy file name** box, type **C:\WINDOWS\security\msscw\Policies\NewDC.xml** and then click **Next**.
23. Click **Apply now**, and then click **Next**.
24. When the application of the security policy is complete, click **Next**.
25. Click **Finish**.
26. Restart DEN-DC1.

Important Do not shut down the virtual machines.

Lesson: Hardening Servers

- What Is Server Hardening?
- What Is the Member Server Baseline Security Template?
- Security Threats to Domain Controllers
- Implement Password Security
- Security Templates for Specific Server Roles
- Best Practices for Hardening Servers for Specific Roles
- Practice: Hardening Servers

Introduction

This lesson shows you how to implement server hardening to protect data and services.

Lesson objectives

After completing this lesson, you will be able to:

- Explain server hardening.
- Describe the Member Server Baseline Security template.
- List security threats to domain controllers.
- Explain the importance of password security.
- Describe using security templates for specific server roles.
- Use best practices for hardening servers for specific roles.
- Harden a server.

What Is Server Hardening?

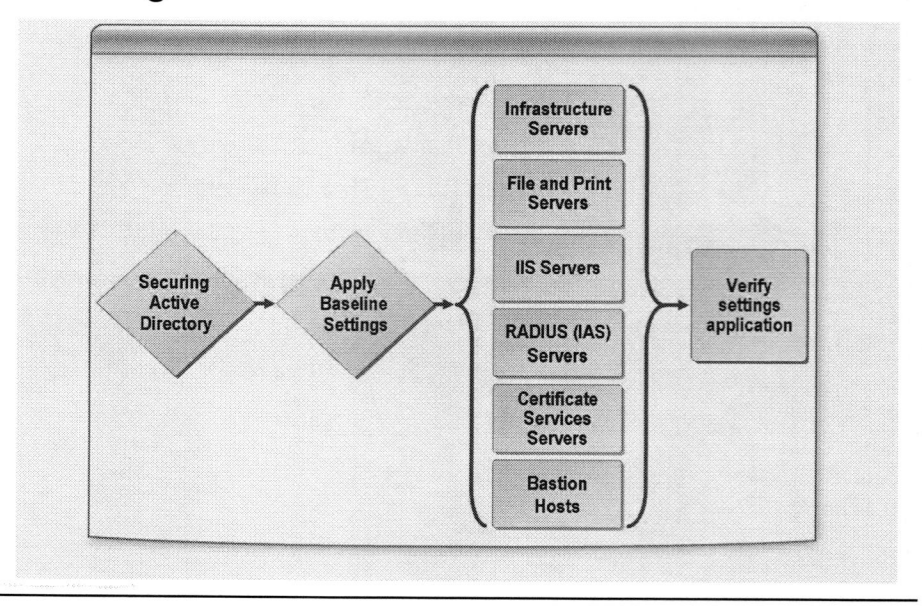

Definition

Server hardening is the process of securing a server by implementing security settings that are specific to the servers' role. For example, you can restrict the right to log on locally to a server to only administrators.

Server hardening process

The server hardening process is as follows:

1. Secure Active Directory. This includes creating an organizational unit (OU) structure that is appropriate for delegating administrative permissions and then delegating permissions. It is also common to create separate OUs for servers that fulfill similar roles. This allows easy implementation of Group Policy to configure server security.

2. Apply a set of baseline security settings to all servers in the domain. For member servers, use the Member Server Baseline security template. For domain controllers, use the Domain Controller security template.

3. After you apply baseline security settings, you can use various security templates and Group Policy to apply additional, incremental security settings to servers that perform specific roles, such as infrastructure servers, file servers, print servers, and IIS servers. These incremental security settings are different for each type of server role.

4. After you apply security settings to servers, you can use GPResult on a computer running Windows Server 2003, or use the Local Security Policy snap-in on a computer running Windows 2000 Server to verify that these settings have been applied correctly.

What Is the Member Server Baseline Security Template?

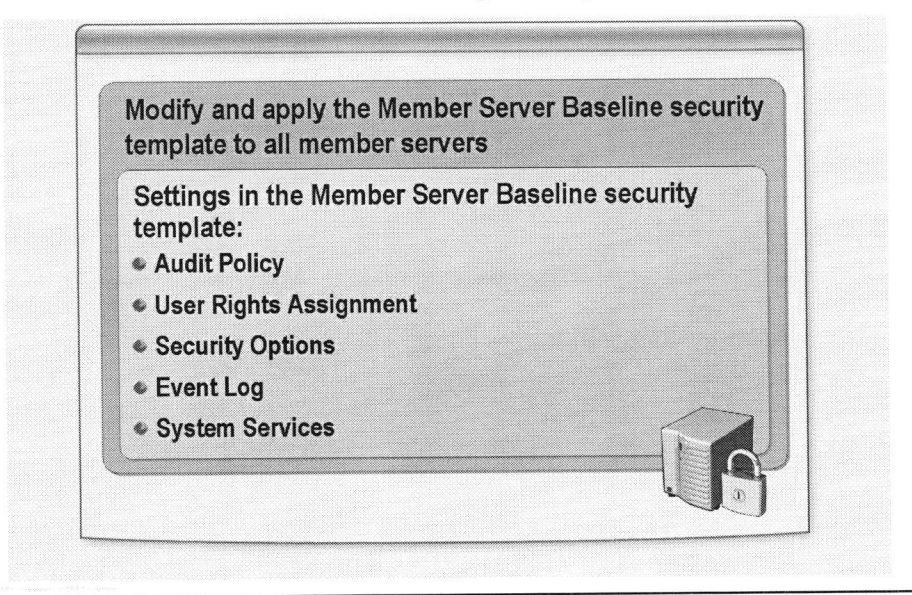

> **Modify and apply the Member Server Baseline security template to all member servers**
>
> Settings in the Member Server Baseline security template:
> - Audit Policy
> - User Rights Assignment
> - Security Options
> - Event Log
> - System Services

Introduction

You can apply baseline security settings to all member servers by using the Member Server Baseline security template that is included with the Windows Server 2003 Security Guide.

After you modify this template to meet the needs of your organization and test the template's security configurations by using your organization's business applications, import this template's settings into a Group Policy object (GPO) and link the GPO to the Member Servers OU.

Note Do not apply the member server template to domain controllers; instead, apply the domain controller template to the Domain Controllers OU.

Member Server Baseline security template security settings

The Member Server Baseline security template contains numerous security settings, including:

- *Audit Policy settings*. Specify the security events that are recorded in the Event Log. You can monitor security-related activity, such as who attempts to access an object when a user logs on to or logs off a computer, or when changes are made to an Audit Policy setting.

- *User Rights Assignment settings*. Specify users or groups that have logon rights or privileges on the member servers in the domain.

- *Security Options settings*. Used to enable or disable security settings for servers, such as digital signing of data, administrator and guest account names, floppy-disk drive and CD-ROM drive access, driver installation behavior, and logon prompts.

- *Event Log settings.* Specify the size of each event log and what actions to take when each event log becomes full. There are several event logs that store logged security events, including the Application log, the Security log, and the System log.
- *System Services settings.* Specify the startup type and permissions for each service on the server.

Note For more information about security templates and to obtain a comprehensive set of security templates, download the *Windows Server 2003 Security Guide* from the Microsoft Download Center Web site.

Security Threats to Domain Controllers

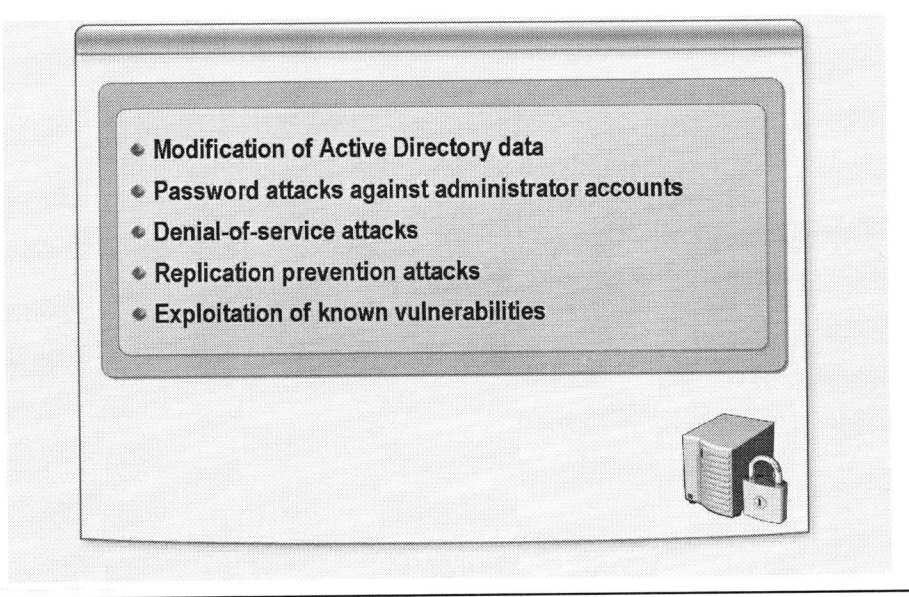

- Modification of Active Directory data
- Password attacks against administrator accounts
- Denial-of-service attacks
- Replication prevention attacks
- Exploitation of known vulnerabilities

Introduction

Domain controllers are central to the security of a Windows Server 2003 network. They hold a copy of the Active Directory database which contains user credentials and other network information. Domain controllers are a tempting target for hackers because of the information that they contain.

Threats

Domain controllers are targets for specific security threats, including:

- *Modification or addition of Active Directory objects.* If attackers can compromise a domain controller, they can make whatever changes that they want to Active Directory. This includes creating a user account for their purposes, and adding that user account to any group in the domain.

- *Password attacks.* If attackers can gain access to a domain controller, they can back up the Active Directory database by performing a System State backup or by copying the Active Directory database and logs to another computer. The attacker can use the backup of the domain controller restore a remote computer and then initiate an offline password attack.

- *Denial-of-service attacks.* Attackers can prevent users from performing authentication by executing denial-of-service (DoS) attacks against domain controllers. Denial-of-service attacks typically take advantage of security vulnerabilities for which updates have not been installed. Denial-of-service attacks can also result when account lockout thresholds are turned off or set too low. DNS servers are logical targets of denial-of-service attacks because when a DNS server is disabled, a potentially large number of clients is prevented from finding a domain controller.

- *Replication prevention attacks.* If attackers are able to disrupt replication between domain controllers, they might be able to prevent the application of GPOs, which secure domain controllers. For example, if you modify the GPO that is applied to all domain controllers and the GPO is not replicated to all domain controllers, some of the domain controllers will not have the new security settings applied. Also, if DNS resource records are modified or deleted, a domain controller might not be able to find its replication partners. Likewise, if wide-area network (WAN) links are blocked, replication traffic might not be able to reach domain controllers at remote sites.

- *Exploitation of known security issues.* Attackers might be able to compromise a domain controller that is not kept up to date with the latest service packs and security updates. For example, if the latest service packs are not applied to a domain controller, attackers might be able to disable the domain controller by performing a buffer-overflow attack. The result of such an attack could be to prevent the domain controller from responding to any network requests. Worse, a buffer overflow might allow attackers to modify configuration and take control of a domain controller.

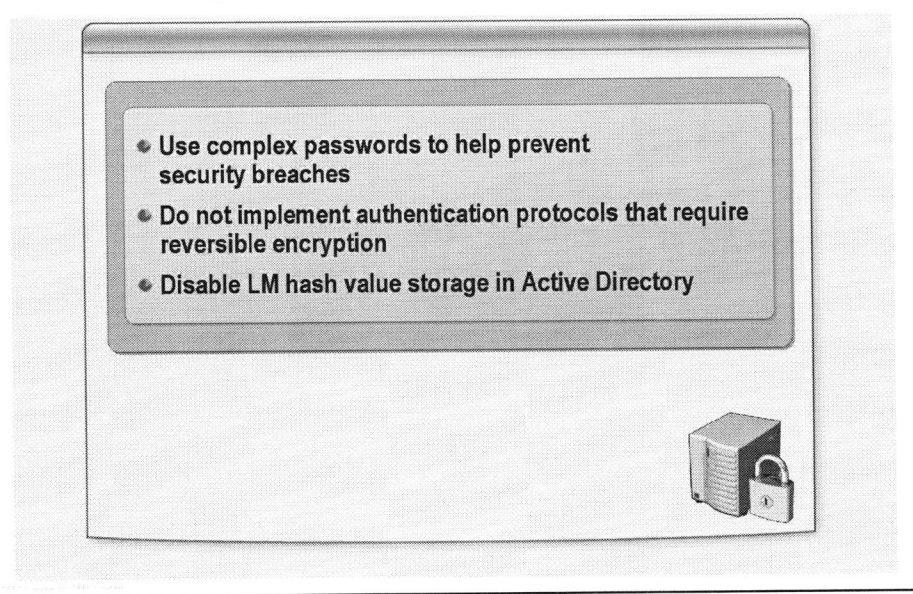

Implement Password Security

> - Use complex passwords to help prevent security breaches
> - Do not implement authentication protocols that require reversible encryption
> - Disable LM hash value storage in Active Directory

Introduction

One important step to increase domain controller and domain security is to implement password security.

Complex passwords

You should require complex passwords for all user accounts. A long, complex password is very difficult to for hackers to discover. To enable complex passwords, enable the Password Must Meet Complexity Requirements setting on a GPO that is assigned to the domain. When this setting is enabled, passwords must be at least six characters in length and consist of at least three of the following four forms:

- English uppercase letters
- English lowercase letters
- Numbers
- Nonalphanumeric characters, such as punctuation marks or symbols

Important Before you require users to use complex passwords, you may need to provide some training on how to remember these passwords. You can teach users to use passphrases (for example, "AnewPa$$word4me!") or use mnemonic tricks to create and remember complex passwords. (For example, "To be or not to be" becomes 2Bee0rkNOT2b?.)

Reversible encryption

Do not implement protocols that require passwords to be stored in a reversibly encrypted format, such as Challenge Handshake Authentication Protocol (CHAP) or digest authentication for Web applications. A password that is stored in this format is more susceptible to password attacks if attackers gain physical access to a domain controller.

LAN Manager hash values

Disable LAN Manager (LM) hash values in the Active Directory database. When you set a password that contains fewer than 15 characters, Windows generates both a LAN Manager hash and a Windows NT LAN Manager (NTLM) hash of the password. A password that is stored in an LM hash value is more susceptible to password attacks. You can disable the storage of passwords in this format by enabling the Network Security: Do Not Store LAN Manager Hash Values On Next Password Change Group Policy setting in Security Options.

Security Templates for Specific Server Roles

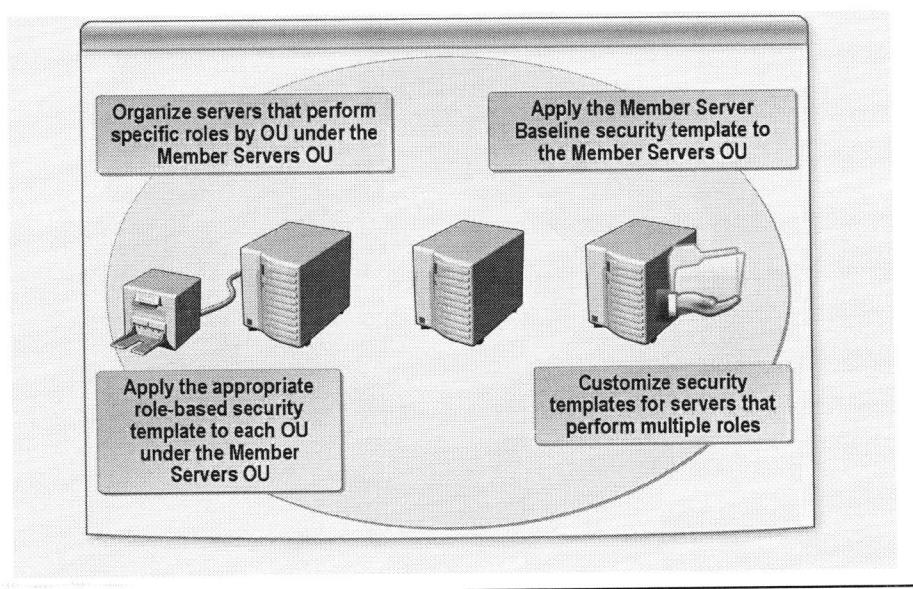

Introduction

In an Active Directory environment, there are member servers that perform specific server roles. You can organize these servers by creating an appropriate child OU for each server role under the Member Servers OU. For example, you might have a File Servers OU and a Print Servers OU under the Member Servers OU in your OU hierarchy.

Applying templates

To harden member servers you can apply the Member Server Baseline security template to all member servers. In addition to this security template, you can apply incremental, role-based security settings to servers that perform specific roles. You accomplish this by modifying the settings in a role-based security template, importing the settings within this template into a GPO, and then linking the GPO to the OU for the specific server role.

The *Windows Server 2003 Security Guide* includes security templates for the following specific server roles:

- Infrastructure server
- File server
- Print server
- Internet Information Services (IIS) server
- Internet Authentication Service (IAS) server
- Certificate services server
- Bastion host

Multiple roles If you need to combine roles for some of the servers in your environment, you can customize security templates so that the appropriate combination of services and security options is configured for the servers that perform multiple roles.

Note The *Windows Server 2003 Security Guide* can be found on the Microsoft TechNet Web site.

Best Practices for Hardening Servers for Specific Roles

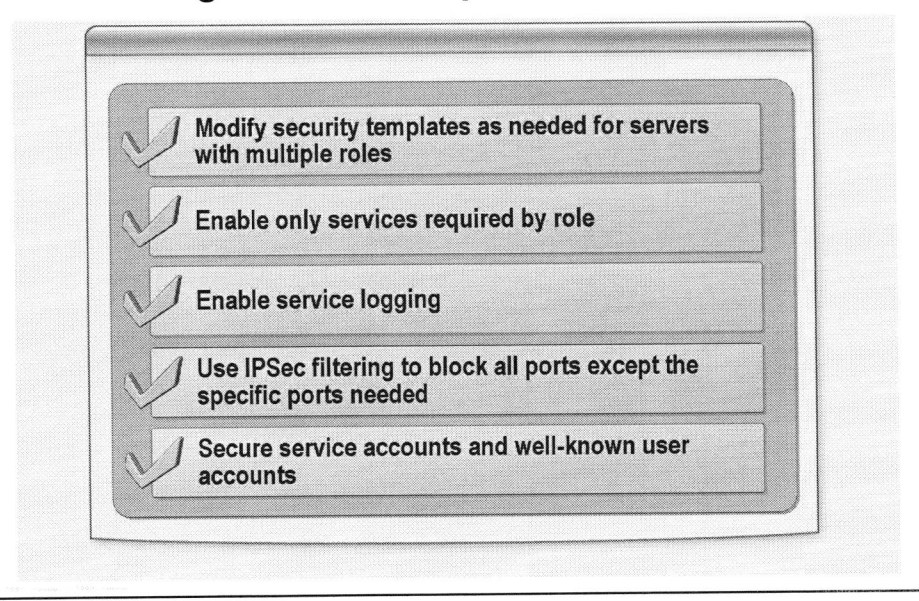

- Modify security templates as needed for servers with multiple roles
- Enable only services required by role
- Enable service logging
- Use IPSec filtering to block all ports except the specific ports needed
- Secure service accounts and well-known user accounts

Introduction

Hardening servers for specific roles includes applying the appropriate security templates and manually configuring server settings for the role. Most of the recommended security settings are applied to role-based servers by using the Member Server Baseline security template and, incrementally, by using a role-based security template.

Best practices

Consider the following best practices when hardening servers for specific roles:

- *Modify templates as needed for servers with multiple roles.* Servers that perform multiple roles require a customized template that specifically configures the server's security settings to enable it to perform multiple roles. You may need to start with the pre-configured template for one of the roles the server performs, and then modify the template so that services and other security settings required by the additional role are correctly configured in the template. Be sure to preserve the original template so you can revert to it if required.

- *Enable only services that are required for the role.* Any that is service not required by the server to fulfill its assigned role should be disabled.

- *Enable service logging to capture relevant information.* Consider enabling logging for critical services that are required by the server role. For example, enable DHCP logging for a DHCP server.

- *Use IPSec filtering to block all ports except the specific ports needed, based on server role.* For more information about the specific ports that should be allowed on a server for a specific role, see the appropriate chapter in the *Windows Server 2003 Security Guide*.

- *Secure service accounts and well-known user accounts.* Do not configure a service to log on by using a domain account unless absolutely necessary. Rename the built-in Administrator and Guest accounts and change their descriptions. In addition, assign long and complex passwords to these built-in accounts. Finally, use different passwords for these accounts on each server so that a compromise of one of these accounts on one server does not enable an attacker to compromise additional servers.

Practice: Hardening Servers

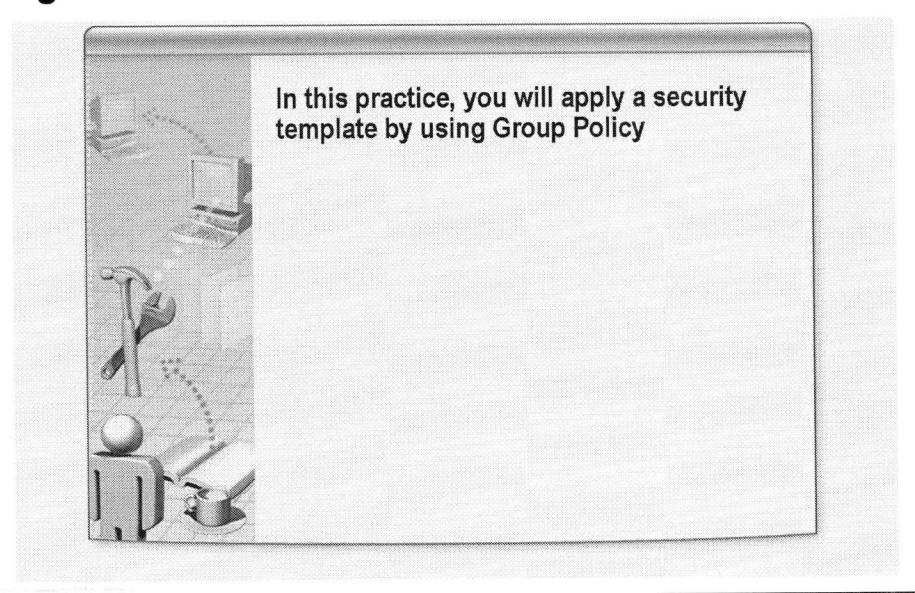

In this practice, you will apply a security template by using Group Policy

Objective

In this practice, you will:

- Apply a security template by using Group Policy.

Instructions

Ensure that the DEN-DC1 virtual machine is running.

Practice

▶ **Apply a security template through Group Policy**

1. On DEN-DC1, log on as **Administrator** with a password of **Pa$$w0rd**.
2. Click **Start**, point to **Administrative Tools**, and then click **Group Policy Management**.
3. Expand **Forest: Contoso.msft**, expand **Domains**, expand **Contoso.msft**, and then expand **Domain Controllers**.
4. Right-click **Domain Controllers**, and click **Create and Link a GPO Here**.
5. In the **Name** box, type **DC Security** and then click **OK**.
6. Click **DC Security** and then click **OK** to clear the dialog box.
7. Right-click **DC Security** and click **Edit**.
8. Under **Computer Configuration**, expand **Windows Settings**, right-click **Security Settings**, and click **Import Policy**.
9. Select **D:\2275\Practices\Mod09\Security Templates\Enterprise Client – Domain Controller.inf**, and then click **Open**.
10. Close the Group Policy Object Editor.
11. Close Group Policy Management.

Important Do not shut down the virtual machines.

Lesson: Microsoft Baseline Security Analyzer

- What Is MBSA?
- MBSA Benefits
- How MBSA Works
- MBSA Scan Options
- Practice: Microsoft Baseline Security Analyzer

Introduction

The Microsoft Baseline Security Analyzer (MBSA) tool is used to identify security weaknesses in Windows networks. It is available from Microsoft at no charge and is an essential tool for security analysis.

Lesson objectives

After completing this lesson, you will be able to:

- Describe MBSA.
- List MBSA considerations.
- Describe how MBSA works.
- Describe MBSA scan options.
- Use Microsoft Baseline Security Analyzer.

What Is MBSA?

> - Scans systems for:
>   - Missing security updates
>   - Potential configuration issues
> - Works with a broad range of Microsoft software
> - Allows an administrator to centrally scan multiple computers simultaneously
>
> MBSA is a free tool, and can be downloaded from the Microsoft TechNet Web site

Definition

The MBSA, which includes a graphical and command-line interface, can perform local or remote scans of computers running Windows to identify missing security updates and potential configuration issues. MBSA displays the results of the scan in a Web-based report.

MBSA features

MBSA runs on computers running Windows XP, Windows 2000, and Windows Server 2003 and will scan for missing security updates and potential configuration issues on a broad range of Microsoft software. MBSA scans for:

- Missing security updates and updates on these products:
    - Microsoft BizTalk® Server 2000, 2002, and 2004
    - Microsoft Commerce Server 2000 and 2002
    - Microsoft Content Management Server 2001 and 2002
    - Microsoft Exchange Server 5.5, Exchange 2000 Server, and Exchange Server 2003
    - Microsoft Host Integration Server 2000 and 2004
    - Microsoft Internet Explorer 5.01 and later versions
    - Internet Information Services (IIS) 4.0, IIS 5.0, IIS 5.1, and IIS 6.0
    - Microsoft Data Access Components (MDAC) 2.5, 2.6, 2.7, and 2.8
    - Microsoft Virtual PC
    - MSXML 2.5, 2.6, 3.0, and 4.0
    - Microsoft Office 2000, Office XP, and Office 2003 (for local scans only)

- Microsoft SNA Server 4.0
- Microsoft SQL Server™ 7.0 and SQL Server 2000 (including Microsoft Data Engine)
- Microsoft Windows Media® Player 6.4 and later versions
  Microsoft Windows NT 4.0, Windows 2000, Windows XP (including SP 2), and Windows Server 2003

- Potential configuration issues on these products:
  - Internet Explorer 5.01 and later versions
  - IIS 4.0, IIS 5.0, and IIS 6.0
  - Office 2000, Office XP, and Office 2003
  - SQL Server 7.0 and 2000
  - Windows NT 4.0, Windows 2000, Windows XP, and Windows Server 2003

MBSA will not run on computers running Windows NT 4.0. However, it can be used to remotely scan a computer running Windows NT 4.0 when run from a supported operating system. Other benefits of MBSA:

- An administrator can use MBSA to centrally scan multiple computers simultaneously.
- MBSA requires minimal configuration.
- MBSA is available as a free download from the Microsoft Web site.
- MBSA version 2 integrates with Windows Server Update Services (WSUS).

MBSA Benefits

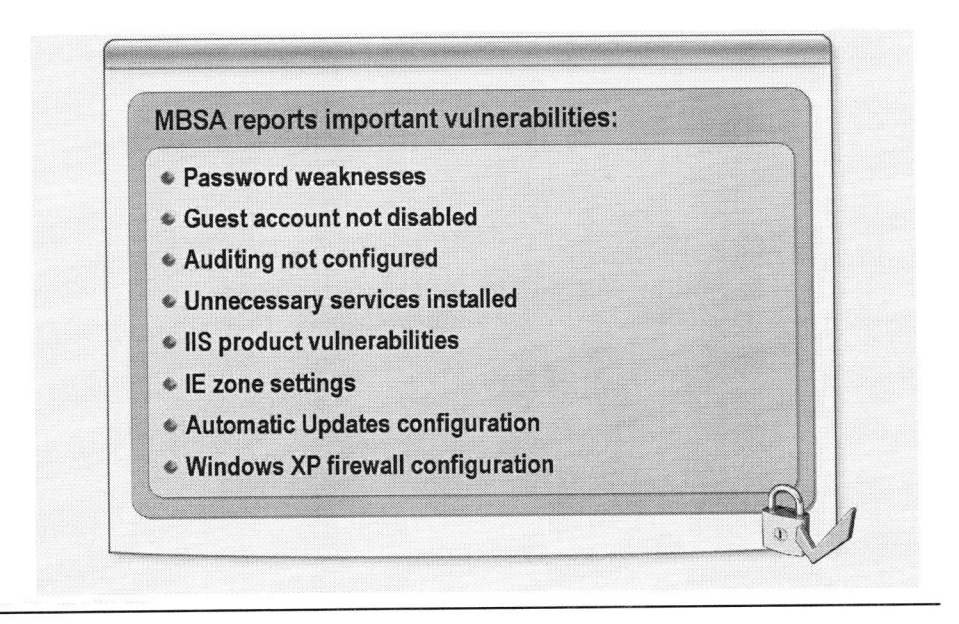

> **MBSA reports important vulnerabilities:**
> - Password weaknesses
> - Guest account not disabled
> - Auditing not configured
> - Unnecessary services installed
> - IIS product vulnerabilities
> - IE zone settings
> - Automatic Updates configuration
> - Windows XP firewall configuration

Introduction

In addition to detecting missing security updates, MBSA scans for numerous security issues and weaknesses. These include weak passwords and common configuration errors.

Weak passwords

MBSA performs a password test on each local user account on the computer. This check is not performed on domain controllers. MBSA identifies common password vulnerabilities, such as:

- Blank passwords
- Passwords that are the same as the corresponding user account names
- Passwords that are the same as the corresponding machines
- Passwords that use the word "password"
- Passwords that use the words "admin" or "administrator"

Important The password scan is resource-intensive; skipping the password scan dramatically increases performance, especially when scanning over the network.

Configuration errors

MBSA checks for other important security issues, such as:

- Whether the Guest account is disabled
- Whether there are any user accounts that have nonexpiring passwords
- Whether auditing is configured
- Whether the computer is properly restricting anonymous access
- Unnecessary services that are installed on the system
- IIS security issues

- Internet Explorer zone settings and Enhanced Security Configuration checks for Windows Server 2003
- Office macro security
- Automatic Updates configuration
- Internet Connection Firewall (ICF) and Windows Firewall configuration

How MBSA Works

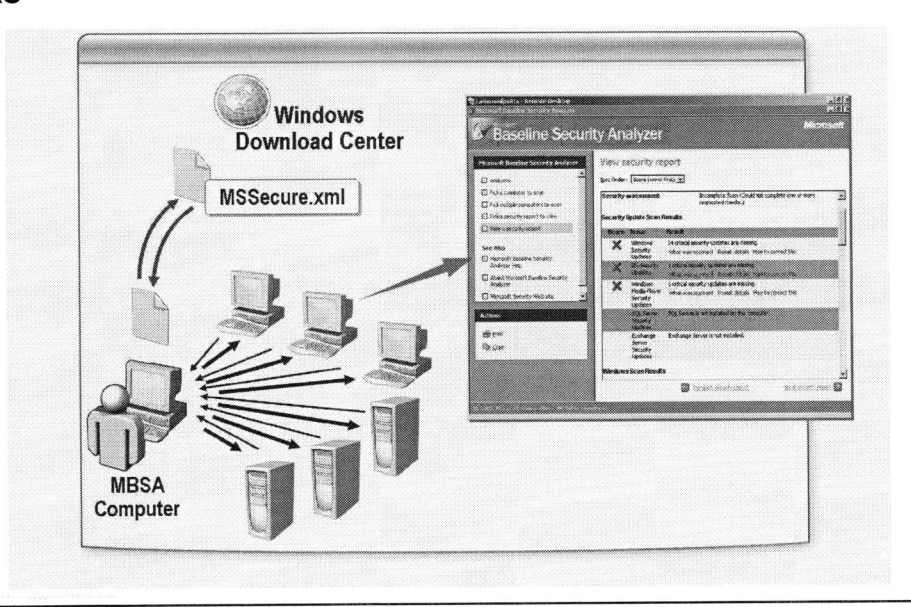

The MSSecure.xml file

The file MSSecure.xml is the list of security weaknesses that is used by MBSA to scan for problems. This file can be obtained automatically by using MBSA or downloaded manually when an Internet connection is not available.

The MSSecure.xml contains:

- Security bulletin names
- Product-specific updates
- Version and checksum information
- Registry keys changes
- Microsoft Knowledge Base article numbers

MBSA process

How MBSA works:

1. Run MBSA and specify the target computers to scan.
2. MBSA downloads the MSSecure.cab file containing MSSecure.xml and verifies its digital signature.

   MBSA attempts to contact the Microsoft Download Center to obtain this file; alternatively, the file can be downloaded and copied to the computer that initiates the scan and then placed in the MBSA installation folder.
3. MBSA scans the target systems for operating systems, operating system components, and applications.
4. MBSA parses the MSSecure.xml file to see if updates are available.
5. MBSA checks the system to see if required updates are missing.
6. MBSA generates a time-stamped report that lists any security updates missing from your system.

Note You can manually download the MSSecure.cab file from the Microsoft Download Web site. MBSA Version 2 uses Wsusscan.cab instead of MSSecure.cab.

MBSA Scan Options

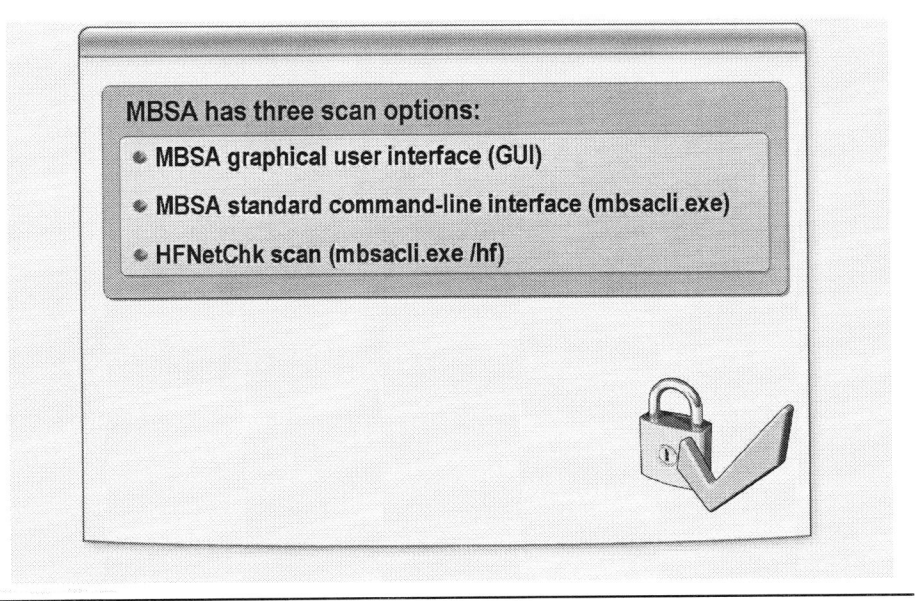

MBSA has three scan options:
- MBSA graphical user interface (GUI)
- MBSA standard command-line interface (mbsacli.exe)
- HFNetChk scan (mbsacli.exe /hf)

Introduction

You can use MBSA through a graphical user interface (GUI) or either of two command-line interfaces: the MBSA standard command-line interface or the HFNetChk scan interface. The GUI is used most often by administrators because it is easy to use.

The MBSA standard command-line interface is used in batch files. The HFNetChk scan interface is used for backwards compatibility with scripts created for HFNetChk.

Graphical user interface

When you use the MBSA graphical user interface, you initiate the scan from a GUI interface and MBSA generates a report that you can view in the same interface.

Standard command-line interface

You can use standard command-line interface to perform the same types of scans as the GUI version of MBSA. You can use the command-line interface to scan for missing security updates as well as for potential configuration issues.

When you run MBSA from the command line, you can specify numerous options, such as a range of IP addresses of the computers to be scanned, the various security issues for which you want MBSA to scan, and the manner in which you want the output from the scan to be displayed. The output from a command-line interface scan is displayed as text in the command-line window.

One of the advantages of using the command-line interface is that MBSA can be run from a script, which enables you to run scans on a schedule or use other tools to automate the use of MBSA in your environment.

To see the full list of available MBSA command-line switches, type **mbsacli /?** at a command prompt.

HFNetChk interface

The HFNetChk scan interface is an MBSA command-line interface parameter that enables MBSA to emulate the HFNetChk tool. This scan option can be used only to scan for missing security updates.

The HFNetChk scan, like the standard MBSA command-line interface, displays scan results as text in the command-line window.

Note By default, the command-line and HFNetChk scans perform checksum checking, which is turned off by default on MBSA GUI scans.

Practice: Microsoft Baseline Security Analyzer

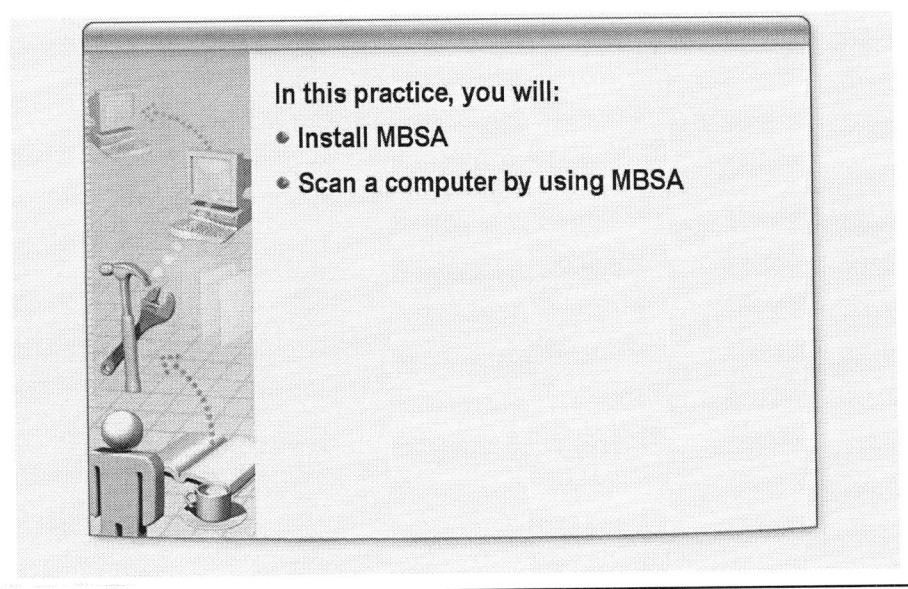

Objective

In this practice, you will:

- Install MBSA.
- Scan a computer by using MBSA.

Instructions

Ensure that the DEN-DC1 virtual machine is running.

Practice

▶ **Install MBSA**

1. If necessary, log on to DEN-DC1 as **Administrator** with a password of **Pa$$w0rd**.
2. Open Windows Explorer.
3. Browse to **D:\2275\Practices\Mod09** and double-click **MBSASetup-EN**.
4. Click **Next** to begin the MBSA setup.
5. Click **I accept the license agreement**, and then click **Next**.
6. Click **Next** again to accept the default installation folder.
7. Click **Install**, and then click **OK**.
8. Copy **MSSecure_1033.cab** from the **D:\2275\Practices\Mod09** folder to the **C:\Program Files\Microsoft Baseline Security Analyzer** folder.
9. Close Windows Explorer.

▶ **Scan a computer using MBSA**

1. On the desktop, double-click **Microsoft Baseline Security Analyzer 1.2.1**.
2. Click **Scan a computer**.
3. In the **Computer name** box, type **CONTOSO\DEN-DC1**.

4. Click **Start scan**.
5. Scroll down to an item with a yellow X beside it and click **Result details**. This shows why the item was marked with a yellow X.
6. Close the window with the result details.
7. Click **How to correct this**, read the contents of the pop-up window, and close the pop-up window.
8. Close Microsoft Baseline Security Analyzer.

▶ **To prepare for the next lab**

1. Start the DEN-SRV1 virtual machine.
2. Start the DEN-CL1 virtual machine.

Important Do not shut down the virtual machines.

Lab: Securing Windows Server 2003

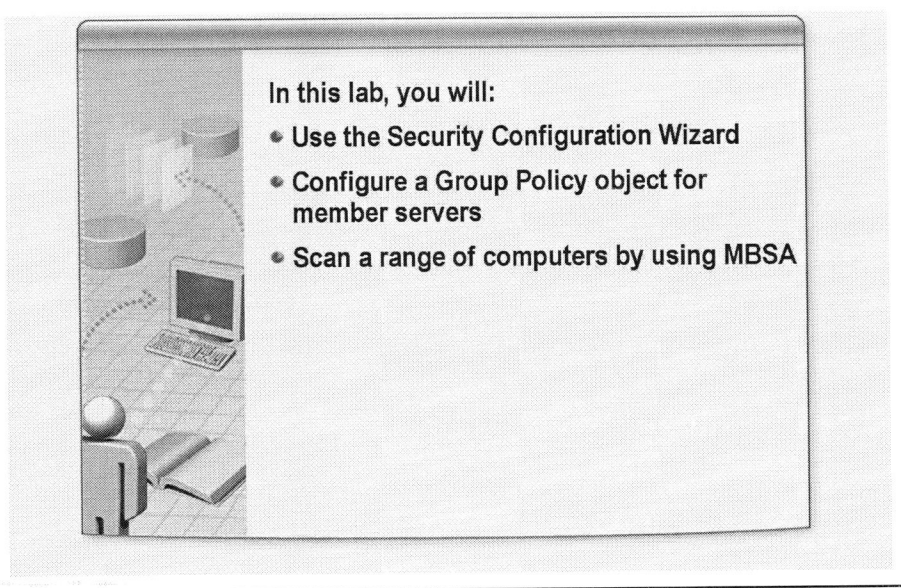

In this lab, you will:
- Use the Security Configuration Wizard
- Configure a Group Policy object for member servers
- Scan a range of computers by using MBSA

Objectives

After completing this lab, you will be able to:

- Use the Security Configuration Wizard.
- Configure a Group Policy object for member servers.
- Scan a range of computers by using MBSA.

Instructions

Ensure that the DEN-DC1, DEN-SRV1, and DEN-CL1 virtual machines are running.

Scenario

As the system administrator for a mid-sized organization you are exploring your options for securing servers and workstations. You are testing the Security Configuration Wizard, Group Policy objects, and MBSA to compare the differences in their capabilities.

Estimated time to complete this lab: 30 minutes

Exercise 1
Using the Security Configuration Wizard

In this exercise, you will install and run the Security Configuration Wizard.

Tasks	Specific instructions
1. Install the Security Configuration Wizard.	a. Log on to DEN-SRV1 as **Administrator** with a password of **Pa$$w0rd**. b. Open **Add or Remove Programs**. c. Open **Add/Remove Windows Components**. d. Select the **Security Configuration Wizard** component. If required, Windows Server 2003 SP1 is located in **C:\win2k3\i386**.
2. Run the Security Configuration Wizard.	a. Open the **Administrative Tools** menu and click **Security Configuration Wizard**. b. Create a new policy and accept the default settings as presented by the wizard. c. Save the setting in the default location called **NewMember.xml**. d. Apply the settings to the server. e. Restart DEN-SRV1.

Exercise 2
Configuring a Group Policy Object for Member Servers

In this exercise, you will configure a group policy object for member servers.

Tasks	Specific instructions
1. Create an OU for member servers.	a. Log on to DEN-DC1 as **Administrator** with a password of **Pa$$w0rd**. b. Open **Active Directory Users and Computers**. c. Create an OU called **MemberServers**. d. Move the **DEN-SRV1** computer object into the **MemberServers** OU.
2. Create a Group Policy object for member servers.	a. Open Group Policy Management. b. Create and link a GPO to **MemberServers** called **Member Security**. c. Edit the **Member Security** GPO.
3. Import a security template into the Group Policy object for member servers.	a. Expand Computer Configuration\Windows Settings, and then click Security Settings. b. Import the **D:\2275\Practices\Mod09\Security Templates\Enterprise Client – Member Server Baseline.inf** template into the newly created GPO. c. Close all open windows.

Exercise 3
Scanning a Range of Computers by Using MBSA

In this exercise, you will scan all computers on a subnet by using MBSA.

Tasks	Specific instructions
1. Scan a range of computers from DEN-DC1.	a. On DEN-DC1 start **MBSA**. b. Click the **Scan more than one computer** link. c. Use an IP range of **10.10.0.1** to **10.10.0.20**.
2. View the reports for all computers.	a. Click Pick a security report to review. b. Click the first report in the list. c. Click Next security report.
3. Complete the lab exercise.	▪ Close all programs and shut down all computers. Do not save changes.

Course Evaluation

Your evaluation of this course will help Microsoft understand the quality of your learning experience.

To complete a course evaluation, go to the Metrics That Matter page of the Knowledge Advisors Web site at http://www.metricsthatmatter.com/MTMStudent/ClassListPage.aspx?&orig=6&VendorAlias=survey.

Microsoft will keep your evaluation strictly confidential and will use your responses to improve your future learning experience.

This page left intentionally blank.

Index

Note: Numbers preceding the hyphens indicate the module in which the entry can be found.

A

Account Operators group, 1-4
Active Directory, backing up, 7-12
Administrators group, 1-3
alerts
   best practices, 3-34
   configuring, 2-32
   functions, 2-25 to 2-26
   limitations, 2-27
   overview, 2-25 to 2-26
   reasons to use, 2-25
   searching for, 2-31
   viewing, 2-32
Application log, Event Viewer, 2-28 to 2-29
archive attribute, 7-16
ASR (Automated System Recovery), 7-22
ASR Backup Wizard, 7-22
asymmetric encryption. *See* public-key encryption
Automated System Recovery (ASR), 7-22
Automatic Updates. *See also* Windows Server Update Services (WSUS)
   client deployment, 8-6
   configuring, 8-15 to 8-16
   defined, 8-5
   Group Policy options, 8-15 to 8-16
   notification, 8-6
   role of digital signatures, 8-6
   update options, 8-5

B

backing up data
   Backup utility, 7-14 to 7-15
   best practices, 7-28 to 7-29
   how often to back up, 7-8
   on networks, 7-9
   ntbackup command-line tool, 7-19 to 7-21, 7-23 to 7-24
   overview, 7-8 to 7-9
   performing backups, 7-23 to 7-24
   permissions and user rights for, 7-10 to 7-11
   restoring backed-up data, 7-32 to 7-36
   sample scenarios, 7-17 to 7-18
   scheduling backup jobs, 7-26, 7-30 to 7-31
   types of backups, 7-16 to 7-18
   what to back up, 7-8
   WSUS and, 8-27
Backup Operators group, 1-3
Backup or Restore Wizard, 7-22
Backup utility, 7-14 to 7-15, 7-23, 7-60
baseline, establishing for performance monitoring, 2-6, 3-34
basic disks. *See* disks
best practices
   backing up data, 7-28 to 7-29
   compressed files and folders, 6-9
   disks, 5-9
   hardening servers, 9-35
   monitoring server performance, 3-33 to 3-35
   remote administration, 1-30 to 1-31
   shadow copies, 7-45 to 7-46

boot files
   backing up, 7-12
   how they work, 7-59
bottlenecks, disk
   counters for, 3-19 to 3-20, 3-32
   identifying, 3-19 to 3-20
   overview, 3-17
   resolving bottlenecks, 3-20
bottlenecks, memory
   counters for, 3-7, 3-31
   identifying, 3-6 to 3-7
   overview, 3-4
   resolving, 3-7
bottlenecks, network
   counters for, 3-26, 3-32
   identifying, 3-26
   overview, 3-24 to 3-25
   resolving, 3-27
bottlenecks, processor
   counters for, 3-11, 3-31
   identifying, 3-12 to 3-13
   overview, 3-11
   resolving, 3-13
built-in domain local groups, 1-3 to 1-4

C

CAs (certification authorities), 6-16
certificates
   backing up Certificate Services, 7-12
   defined, 6-19
   how EFS uses, 6-19
   recovery, 6-27, 6-30 to 6-31
   role in sharing encrypted files and folders, 6-21
certification authorities (CAs), 6-16
Cipher command-line tool, 6-15
COM (Component Object Model), 9-16
command-line tools
   cipher, 6-15
   command, 6-5 to 6-6
   convert, 5-16 to 5-18
   diskpart, 5-4 to 5-5
   mstsc, 1-21
   ntbackup, 7-19 to 7-21, 7-23 to 7-24
   runas, 1-6
   tracerpt, 2-20
Compact command-line tool, 6-5 to 6-6
complex passwords, 9-31
compressed files and folders
   best practices, 6-9
   copying, 6-7 to 6-8, 6-10 to 6-12
   creating, 6-10
   moving, 6-7 to 6-8, 6-10 to 6-12
   overview, 6-3 to 6-4
Compressed (zipped) Folders feature, 6-4
computer groups, 8-23
Computer Management console
   administrative tool categories, 1-7 to 1-8
   defined, 1-7

2   Control Panel

Computer Management console, *continued*
   role in performing remote administration tasks, 1-22
   Services and Applications tools, 1-7, 1-8
   Storage tools, 1-7, 1-8
   System Tools category, 1-7, 1-8
   ways to use, 1-7
Control Panel, configuring remotely, 1-15
Convert command-line tool, 5-16 to 5-17, 5-18
converting
   disks from basic to dynamic, 5-25, 5-29 to 5-30
   FAT and FAT32 file systems to NTFS file system, 5-16 to 5-17, 5-18
Copy backup type, 7-16
copying
   compressed files and folders, 6-7 to 6-8, 6-10 to 6-12
   encrypted files and folders, 6-20, 6-22 to 6-25
counter logs
   configuring and managing, 2-16 to 2-23
   creating, 2-22 to 2-23
   file formats, 2-19 to 2-20
   overview, 2-17
   Performance console data, 2-18
   Performance Logs and Alerts data, 2-18
   reasons to schedule, 2-21
counters
   availability for specific applications, 2-13
   for disk bottlenecks, 3-19 to 3-20, 3-32
   for memory bottlenecks, 3-7, 3-31
   for network usage bottlenecks, 3-26, 3-32
   for processor bottlenecks, 3-11, 3-31
CPU usage. *See* processors

D

Daily backup type, 7-17
data recovery. *See* recovery agents, EFS
defense-in-depth security model, 9-7 to 9-8
device drivers
   configuring properties by using Device Manager, 4-6
   configuring signing options, 4-13 to 4-14
   defined, 4-1, 4-5
   list of properties, 4-7 to 4-8
   overview, 4-5 to 4-6
   role of Device Manager, 4-6
   rolling back, 4-16 to 4-19
   signed, 4-9 to 4-14
   uninstalling, 4-17
   unsigned vs. signed, 4-9
Device Manager
   defined, 1-8
   disabling device drivers, 4-17
   rolling back device drivers, 4-16, 4-18 to 4-19
   uninstalling device drivers, 4-17
   ways to use, 4-6
devices. *See also* device drivers
   disabling vs. uninstalling, 4-17
   examples, 4-3
   non-Plug and Play, 4-4
   overview, 4-3 to 4-4
   Plug and Play, 4-3 to 4-4, 4-17
   types, 4-3 to 4-4
   uninstalling, 4-17
Differential backup type, 7-17
digital signatures
   Automatic Updates and, 8-6
   maintaining for device drivers, 4-10
Directory Services Restore Mode (DSRM), 7-55

disaster recovery
   Automated System Recovery, 7-22
   backing up data, 7-7 to 7-31
   guidelines, 7-5 to 7-6
   Last Known Good Configuration startup option, 7-54
   overview, 7-3 to 7-4
   preparing for, 7-2 to 7-6
   Recovery Console, 7-55 to 7-57
   restoring backed-up data, 7-32 to 7-36
   role of Safe mode, 7-51, 7-52 to 7-53
   role of shadow copies, 7-38 to 7-49
   server failure, 7-50 to 7-64
   summary of methods, 7-60 to 7-61
Disk Defragmenter, 1-8
disk groups, 5-27 to 5-28
Disk Management MMC snap-in
   converting basic disks to dynamic disks, 5-29 to 5-30
   defined, 1-8, 5-3
   vs. DiskPart tool, 5-4
   initializing disks, 5-6
   overview, 5-3
disk quotas
   configuring limits, 6-36 to 6-37
   overview, 6-34 to 6-35
DiskPart command-line tool, 5-4 to 5-5
disks. *See also* dynamic disks; NTFS file system; startup disks; volumes
   basic vs. dynamic, 5-25 to 5-26
   best practices, 5-9
   bottleneck conditions, 3-17
   configuring System Monitor to monitor disk counters, 3-21 to 3-22
   converting from basic to dynamic, 5-25, 5-29 to 5-30
   counters for monitoring, 3-16 to 3-22, 3-32
   creating volumes, 5-36 to 5-37
   documenting properties, 5-18
   drive letters, 5-7, 5-10
   external storage, 5-46 to 5-47
   file system overview, 5-8
   foreign, 5-49 to 5-50
   formatting, 5-7
   identifying and resolving bottlenecks, 3-19 to 3-20
   importing, 5-49 to 5-50
   initializing, 5-6
   managing mounted drives, 5-20 to 5-23
   managing properties, 5-13 to 5-19
   monitoring efficiency, 3-17 to 3-18
   monitoring usage bottlenecks, 3-19 to 3-20
   moving between computers, 5-49 to 5-50
   offline, 5-51
   partitioning, 5-6 to 5-7
   preparing, 5-2 to 5-12
   properties information, 5-14 to 5-15
Distributed COM (DCOM), 9-16
domain controllers
   password security, 9-31 to 9-32
   security threats, 9-29 to 9-30
domain local groups, 1-3 to 1-4
drive letters, 5-7, 5-10
drives, logical, 5-6, 5-10
dynamic disks
   vs. basic disks, 5-25 to 5-26
   benefits, 5-25
   converting basic disks to, 5-29 to 5-30
   creating volumes, 5-31 to 5-48
   fault-tolerant volumes on, 5-38 to 5-48

foreign, 5-49 to 5-50
importing, 5-49 to 5-50
moving between computers, 5-49 to 5-50
reasons to convert from basic disks, 5-25
usage example, 5-26

E

EFS encryption
    configuring recovery agents, 6-26 to 6-31
    decrypting data, 6-15, 6-17
    how it works, 6-17
    moving and copying encrypted files and folders, 6-20
    overview, 6-14 to 6-15
    role of certificates, 6-19 to 6-20
    sharing encrypted files and folders, 6-21
encrypted files and folders. *See also* EFS encryption
    configuring, 6-13 to 6-25
    copying encrypted files and folders, 6-20, 6-24 to 6-25
    creating, 6-22
    moving encrypted files and folders, 6-20, 6-24 to 6-25
    recovering, 6-28 to 6-29
    sharing, 6-21 to 6-25
Encrypting File System. *See* EFS encryption
encryption. *See* EFS encryption; encrypted files and folders
Event Viewer
    Application log, 2-28 to 2-29
    defined, 1-8
    filtering events, 2-29
    log settings, 2-28
    overview, 2-28
    viewing alerts, 2-32
EventCombMT tool
    alerts and, 2-31
    overview, 2-30 to 2-31
    search capabilities, 2-30
    viewing alerts, 2-32
extended partitions, disk, 5-7, 5-10
extended volumes
    creating, 5-36 to 5-37
    limitations, 5-33
    overview, 5-33
    usage examples, 5-33
external disk-based storage, 5-46 to 5-47

F

FAT and FAT32 file systems. *See also* NTFS file system
    compressed files and folders, 6-4
    converting to NTFS file system, 5-16 to 5-17, 5-18
    vs. NTFS file system, 5-8, 6-4, 6-8, 6-20
fault tolerance, 5-39
fault-tolerant volumes
    creating, 5-48
    mirrored, 5-40 to 5-41, 5-48
    overview, 5-39
    RAID-5 type, 5-42 to 5-45
file compression. *See* compressed files and folders
file encryption. *See* EFS encryption; encrypted files and folders
File Signature Verification, 4-11
file systems. *See* NTFS file system
firewalls. *See* Windows Firewall
folders, compressed, 6-3 to 6-4
foreign disks, 5-49 to 5-50
formatting disks, 5-7
formatting volumes, 5-9

G

Group Policy
    applying security templates by using, 9-37
    Automatic Updates options, 8-15 to 8-16
    setting for unsigned device drivers, 4-12

H

hard disks. *See* disks
hardening servers
    applying security templates, 9-33, 9-37
    baseline settings, 9-27 to 9-28
    best practices, 9-35
    overview, 9-26
    password security for, 9-31 to 9-32
    recommendations, 9-13 to 9-14
    security template overview, 9-33
hard-page faults, 3-6
HFNetChk MBSA interface, 9-45 to 9-46

I

importing disks, 5-49 to 5-50
Incremental backup type, 7-17
Indexing Service tool, 1-8
initializing disks, 5-6
Internet Connection Firewall (ICF), 9-17
Internet Information Services (IIS), installing, 8-17

L

LAN Manager, disabling hash values, 9-32
Last Known Good Configuration startup option
    defined, 7-60
    overview, 7-54
    recovering from server failure, 7-62 to 7-63
Local Users and Groups tool, 1-8
logical drives, 5-6, 5-10

M

MBSA. *See* Microsoft Baseline Security Analyzer (MBSA) tool
Member Server Baseline Security template, 9-27, 9-33
memory
    bottleneck conditions, 3-4
    configuring System Monitor to monitor counters, 3-8 to 3-9
    counters for monitoring, 3-7, 3-31
    excessive paging, 3-5
    identifying and resolving bottlenecks, 3-6 to 3-7
    insufficient, 3-4
    leaks, 3-5, 3-7
    monitoring effects on server performance, 3-3 to 3-9
    reasons to monitor, 3-4 to 3-5
Microsoft Baseline Security Analyzer (MBSA) tool
    benefits, 9-41
    command-line interface, 9-45
    features, 9-39 to 9-40
    GUI interface, 9-45
    HFNetChk interface, 9-45 to 9-46
    how it works, 9-43
    installing, 9-47
    overview, 9-39 to 9-40
    scanning options, 9-45 to 9-46
Microsoft Management Console (MMC). *See also* Disk Management MMC snap-in
    creating custom consoles, 1-10 to 1-11
    defined, 1-9
    role in remote administration, 1-9
Microsoft Operations Manager 2005 tool, 3-39

Microsoft Update. *See also* Automatic Updates
  overview, 8-4
  update categories, 8-4
mirrored volumes, 5-40 to 5-41, 5-48
MOM 2005 tool, 3-39
mounted drives, 5-20 to 5-23
moving
  compressed files and folders, 6-7 to 6-8, 6-10 to 6-12
  dynamic disks between computers, 5-49 to 5-50
  encrypted files and folders, 6-20, 6-22 to 6-25
mstsc command-line tool, 1-21

N-O

NAS (network attached storage), 5-46 to 5-47
network attached storage (NAS), 5-46 to 5-47
networks. *See also* servers
  backing up data, 7-9
  bottleneck conditions, 3-24 to 3-25
  configuring System Monitor to monitor usage counters, 3-28 to 3-29
  counters for monitoring usage bottlenecks, 3-26, 3-32
  identifying and resolving bottlenecks, 3-26 to 3-27
  measuring bandwidth, 3-24
  monitoring usage, 3-23 to 3-29
  reasons to monitor usage, 3-24 to 3-25
  usage overview, 3-24 to 3-25
Normal backup type, 7-16
ntbackup command-line tool, 7-19 to 7-21, 7-23 to 7-24
NTFS file system
  compressed files and folders, 6-3
  converting from FAT and FAT32 file systems, 5-16 to 5-18
  effects of copying or moving compressed files and folders, 6-7 to 6-8
  vs. FAT and FAT32 file systems, 5-8, 6-4, 6-8, 6-20
  formatting volumes, 5-9
  managing mounted drives, 5-20 to 5-23
offline disks, 5-51

P

paged RAM, 3-6
partitions, disk
  extended, 5-7, 5-10
  overview, 5-6 to 5-7
passwords
  complex, 9-31
  MBSA test for vulnerabilities, 9-41
  security measures, 9-31 to 9-32
Performance console. *See also* Performance Logs and Alerts tool; System Monitor
  calculating % Processor Time, 3-11
  disk-specific counters, 3-16 to 3-22
  options for monitoring remote servers, 2-13
  Performance Logs and Alerts overview, 2-12
  System Monitor overview, 2-11 to 2-12
  tools overview, 2-11 to 2-12
Performance Logs and Alerts tool
  best practices, 3-33
  configuring alerts, 2-24 to 2-31
  defined, 1-8
  overview, 2-12
  ways to use, 2-12
performance monitoring
  best practices, 3-33 to 3-35
  disk usage, 3-16 to 3-22
  doing in real-time, 2-14 to 2-15
  establishing baseline, 2-6, 3-34
  guidelines for counters and recommended thresholds, 3-31 to 3-32
  logged, 2-8
  memory usage, 3-3 to 3-9
  network usage, 3-23 to 3-29
  processor usage, 3-10 to 3-15
  real-time vs. logged, 2-8
  reasons for doing, 2-3 to 2-4
  reasons for monitoring servers remotely, 2-13
  role of Task Manager, 2-9 to 2-10
  troubleshooting performance, 3-36 to 3-38
permissions
  assigning through domain local groups, 1-3 to 1-4
  for backing up data, 7-10 to 7-11
Plug and Play devices
  disabling, 4-17
  overview, 4-3 to 4-4
  uninstalling, 4-17
Post-Setup Security Updates (PSSU), 9-19
Previous Versions client software, 7-40 to 7-41, 7-48 to 7-49
Print Operators domain local group, 1-4
processors
  configuring System Monitor to monitor counters, 3-14 to 3-15
  counters for monitoring, 3-11, 3-31
  identifying and resolving bottlenecks, 3-12 to 3-13
  monitoring usage, 3-10 to 3-15
  usage, 3-11
PSSU (Post-Setup Security Updates), 9-19
public-key encryption
  key pair characteristics, 6-16
  overview, 6-16
  role in EFS, 6-17

Q-R

quotas. *See* disk quotas
RAID-5 volumes
  cost aspect, 5-43
  vs. mirrored volumes, 5-43
  overview, 5-42
  performance, 5-42 to 5-43
  software vs. hardware, 5-44 to 5-45
random-access memory (RAM), paged vs. unpaged, 3-6
RDP (Remote Desktop Protocol), 1-13
real-time performance monitoring
  defined, 2-8
  vs. logged performance monitoring, 2-8
  performing, 2-14 to 2-15
  role of System Monitor, 2-11
recovery agents, EFS. *See also* disaster recovery
  adding through Group Policy, 6-28
  backing up recovery key, 6-27, 6-29, 6-31
  configuring, 6-30
  defining through Group Policy, 6-28
  exporting recovery certificates, 6-27, 6-30 to 6-31
  overview, 6-27
  recovery key overview, 6-27
Recovery Console
  available commands, 7-56 to 7-57
  defined, 7-55, 7-61
  installing, 7-55, 7-63 to 7-64
  logging in, 7-55
  starting, 7-55
registry, backing up, 7-12
remote administration. *See* Remote Desktop for Administration
Remote Desktop Connection
  configuring client preferences, 1-18 to 1-19
  defined, 1-13

earlier versions of Windows and, 1-15
managing, 1-26 to 1-33
monitoring remote sessions, 1-32 to 1-33
vs. Remote Desktops snap-in, 1-20 to 1-21
timeout settings, 1-27 to 1-28
Remote Desktop for Administration
best practices, 1-30 to 1-31
configuring to administer servers, 1-12 to 1-25
overview, 1-13 to 1-14
reasons to use, 1-15 to 1-16
role in performing remote administration tasks, 1-23
tools for administering remote servers, 1-13 to 1-14
Remote Desktop Protocol (RDP), 1-13
Remote Desktop Service
configuring, 1-17
enabling, 1-17
requirements, 1-14, 1-17
Remote Desktops snap-in
overview, 1-13
vs. Remote Desktop Connection, 1-20 to 1-21
when to use, 1-13, 1-20
remote procedure call (RPC) services, 9-15
Removable Storage tool, 1-8
restoring
backed-up data, 7-32 to 7-36
WSUS database and updates folder, 8-27
reversible encryption, 9-31
rolling back device drivers, 4-16 to 4-19
Run as feature
as command-line tool, 1-6
opening MMC-created custom consoles by using, 1-5
overview, 1-5 to 1-6
ways to use, 1-6

S
Safe mode
defined, 7-51, 7-60
recovering from server, 7-62 to 7-63
troubleshooting options, 7-52 to 7-53
SANs (storage area networks), 5-46
scheduling
backup jobs, 7-26, 7-30 to 7-31
counter log tasks, 2-21
for making shadow copies, 7-42 to 7-43
security
baseline server settings, 9-27 to 9-28
core server practices, 9-11 to 9-12
cost tradeoffs, 9-6
defense-in-depth model, 9-7 to 9-8
domain controller threats, 9-29 to 9-30
hardening servers, 9-13 to 9-14, 9-25 to 9-37
Post-Setup Security Updates, 9-19
role of Security Configuration Wizard, 9-20 to 9-21
small and medium-sized business challenges, 9-3 to 9-4
strategic tradeoffs, 9-5 to 9-6
types of threats, 9-29 to 9-30
usability tradeoffs, 9-5
Windows Firewall, 9-17 to 9-18, 9-22
Windows Server 2003 SP1 enhancements, 9-15 to 9-16
Security Configuration Wizard
creating security policies, 9-22 to 9-24
features, 9-21
installing, 9-22
overview, 9-20 to 9-21
security templates
applying, 9-33, 9-37
list of specific server roles, 9-33

Member Server Baseline Security template, 9-27, 9-33
overview, 9-33
servers. *See also* Windows Server Update Services (WSUS)
administering in Windows Server 2003, 1-1 to 1-33
core security practices, 9-11 to 9-12
hardening, 9-13 to 9-14, 9-25 to 9-37
monitoring disks, 3-16 to 3-22
monitoring memory usage, 3-3 to 3-9
monitoring processor usage, 3-10 to 3-15
performance monitoring, 3-1 to 3-40
recovering from failure, 7-50 to 7-64
role of Security Configuration Wizard, 9-20 to 9-21
security issues, 9-2 to 9-48
security-related documents, 9-9
tools for monitoring, 2-2 to 2-31
and WSUS deployment, 8-12 to 8-14
Services and Applications administrative tools, Computer Management console, 1-7, 1-8
Services tool, 1-8
shadow copies
best practices, 7-45 to 7-46
characteristics, 7-39
configuring, 7-47 to 7-49
creating by using Backup utility, 7-14 to 7-15
overview, 7-38 to 7-39
restoring, 7-44
role of Previous Versions client software, 7-40 to 7-41, 7-48 to 7-49
sample scenarios, 7-38
scheduling, 7-42 to 7-43
storing, 7-39
Shared Folders tool, 1-8
sharing encrypted files and folders, 6-21
signed device drivers
maintaining digital signatures, 4-10
overview, 4-9
reasons to use, 4-9
simple volumes
creating, 5-36
formats, 5-32
overview, 5-32
SMS. *See* Systems Management Server 2003
spanned volumes
creating, 5-36 to 5-37
formats, 5-34
overview, 5-34
performance, 5-34
usage example, 5-34
startup disks
defined, 7-58
how boot files function, 7-59
how to use, 7-58
required files, 7-58
startup options
Last Known Good Configuration startup option, 7-54
Safe mode, 7-51, 7-52 to 7-53
Storage administrative tools, Computer Management console, 1-7, 1-8
storage area networks (SANs), 5-46
striped volumes
creating, 5-36 to 5-37
overview, 5-35
performance, 5-35
RAID-5 type, 5-42 to 5-45
usage examples, 5-35
symmetric-key encryption, 6-17
synchronizing WSUS, 8-22

System File Checker, 4-10
System Monitor
    configuring to monitor disk counters, 3-21 to 3-22
    configuring to monitor memory counters, 3-8 to 3-9
    configuring to monitor network counters, 3-28 to 3-29
    configuring to monitor processor counters, 3-14 to 3-15
    overview, 2-11 to 2-12
    viewing logged counter data, 2-12
    ways to use, 2-11
system state data
    backing up, 7-12 to 7-13
    list of components, 7-12
    overview, 7-12 to 7-13
System Tools category, Computer Management console, 1-7, 1-8
Systems Management Server 2003, 3-40
SYSVOL directory, backing up, 7-12

T

Task Manager
    determining memory bottlenecks, 3-7
    determining processor usage, 3-11
    role in performance monitoring, 2-9 to 2-10
Terminal Services
    allowing multiple Remote Desktop connections, 1-14
    reasons to use for managing Remote Desktop sessions, 1-29
timeout settings, Remote Desktop Connection, 1-27 to 1-28
tracerpt command-line tool, 2-20
troubleshooting performance, 3-36 to 3-38

U

unpaged RAM, 3-6
unsigned device drivers
    Group Policy setting, 4-12
    options for handling, 4-9
user rights, for backing up data, 7-10 to 7-11

V

virtual memory, 3-6
volumes
    creating, 5-36 to 5-37
    creating shadow copies by using Backup utility, 7-14 to 7-15
    enabling disk quotas on, 6-34 to 6-35
    extended, 5-33
    fault-tolerant, 5-38 to 5-48
    RAID-5 type, 5-42 to 5-45
    simple, 5-32
    spanned, 5-34
    status when disks are moved, 5-50
    striped, 5-35, 5-42 to 5-45

W

Windows File Protection, 4-10
Windows Firewall
    configuring, 9-22
    defined, 9-17
    features, 9-17 to 9-18
    PSSU and, 9-19
    Remote Desktop and, 1-14
Windows Installer, 8-13
Windows Server 2003
    administering servers, 1-1 to 1-33
    Backup utility, 7-14 to 7-18
    ntbackup command-line tool, 7-19 to 7-21, 7-23 to 7-24
    restoring backed-up data, 7-32 to 7-36
    security issues, 9-1 to 9-48
    security-related documents, 9-9
    SP1 security enhancements, 9-15 to 9-16
Windows Server 2003 Security Guide, 9-9, 9-27
Windows Server Update Services (WSUS)
    administrative Web site, 8-21
    approving updates, 8-24
    Automatic Updates option, 8-5
    automating approvals, 8-25
    backing up, 8-27
    client-side process for using, 8-9
    declining updates, 8-25
    defined, 8-1, 8-7
    deployment scenarios, 8-12
    guidelines for deploying updates, 8-28 to 8-29
    installing and configuring, 8-11 to 8-19
    managing, 8-20 to 8-30
    overview, 8-2, 8-7 to 8-8
    removing updates, 8-25
    report options, 8-26
    restoring, 8-27
    server requirements, 8-13 to 8-14
    server synchronization process, 8-22
    server-side process for using, 8-9
Windows Storage Server 2003, 5-47
wizards
    ASR Backup Wizard, 7-22
    Backup or Restore Wizard, 7-22
    Security Configuration Wizard, 9-20 to 9-21
WMI Control, 1-8
WSUS. *See* Windows Server Update Services (WSUS)

Notes

Notes

Notes

Notes

Notes

Notes

Notes

Notes

Notes

Notes

MSM2275CCPN/C90-04715